D1038744

INSIDE THE MINSTREL MASK

Inside the Minstrel Mask

Readings in Nineteenth-Century Blackface Minstrelsy

Edited by

Annemarie Bean, James V. Hatch,
and Brooks McNamara

Foreword by

Mel Watkins

Wesleyan University Press
Published by University Press of New England
Hanover and London

Wesleyan University Press
Published by University Press of New England, Hanover, NH 03755
© 1996 by Wesleyan University Press
All rights reserved
Printed in the United States of America 5 4 3 2 1
CIP *data appear at the end of the book*

Some of the material in this volume has been previously published:

"Blackface and Blackness: The Minstrel Show in American Culture." From *Love and Theft: Blackface Minstrelsy and the American Working Class* by Eric Lott. Copyright © 1993 by Eric Lott. Reprinted by permission of Oxford University Press, Inc.

"The Performance of the Virginia Minstrels." From *Dan Emmett and the Rise of Early Negro Minstrelsy* by Hans Nathan. Copyright © 1962 by the University of Oklahoma Press.

"Black Musicians and Early Ethiopian Minstrelsy" by Eileen Southern. Originally published in the *Black Perspective in Music*, vol. 3, no. 1 (1975), ed. Eileen Southern. Reprinted by permission of the author.

"Blackface Minstrelsy." From *The Rise and Fall of the White Republic* by Alexander Saxton. Copyright © 1990 by Alexander Saxton. Reprinted by permission of Alexander Saxton and Verso.

"Social Commentary in Late-Nineteenth-Century White Minstrelsy." From *Blacking Up: The Minstrel Show in Nineteenth-Century America* by Robert C. Toll. Copyright © 1974 by Oxford University Press, Inc. Reprinted by permission.

"Early Minstrel Show Music, 1843–1852" by Robert B. Winans. Originally published in *Musical Theatre in America: Papers and Proceedings of the Conference on the Musical Theatre in America*, ed. Glenn Loney. Copyright © 1984 by Greenwood Publishing Group, Inc. Reprinted with permission of Greenwood Publishing Group, Inc., Westport, Conn.

"The Georgia Minstrels: The Early Years" by Eileen Southern. Originally published in the *Inter-American Music Review*, vol. 10, issue 2 (1989), ed. Robert Stevenson.

"Ethiopian Skits and Sketches: Contents and Contexts of Blackface Minstrelsy, 1840–1890" by William J. Mahar. Originally published in *Prospects*, vol. 16 (1991). Copyright © by Cambridge University Press. Reprinted with the permission of Cambridge University Press.

"Juba and American Minstrelsy" by Marian Hannah Winter. Originally published in *Dance Index* 6 (1947), and subsequently reprinted by Arno Press.

We dedicate this book to John Graziano

CONTENTS

MUSIC

HUMOR

DANCE

IMAGES OF GENDER AND CLASS

CONTINUUM

FOREWORD

Mel Watkins

For more than half of the nineteenth century, minstrelsy was America's preeminent form of entertainment. Blackface performers dominated the popular stage, many becoming nationally recognized celebrities, and the music, dance, and humor that was created by and for those performers dominated America's popular culture. Until recently, however, the true historical significance of the minstrel phenomenon (its origins; its role in shaping our national identity; and its impact on society's perception of African Americans and women, as well as on political and policymaking decisions molded by those perceptions) has been generally ignored or minimized by the facile assumption that blackface performance was merely innocuous entertainment.

In fact, as I discovered while researching a recent study of African-American humor, minstrelsy was a critical and complex phenomenon that revealed more about our national character and concerns than we would like to admit or have heretofore adequately assessed.

This avoidance is in part attributable to our lingering unease with openly confronting and examining the shadowy and ineluctably ambivalent issues comprised by the paradigm of race. Much has been made of the divisive effects of the distorted images of black cultural expression and negative stereotypes established and perpetuated by blackface depictions of African Americans, for instance, but far less has been written about the potentially salutary aspect of the apparent fascination and attraction that has impelled white mimicry of blacks from the nineteenth century to the present.

Similarly, on the performance level, while many bemoan the historical limitations placed on black performers by nineteenth-century minstrels' creation of a fraudulent "stage Negro," few readily affirm that it was partially through opposition to that distortion of black cultural forms

Mel Watkins is the author of *On the Real Side* (1994), a history and examination of African-American humor from slavery to Richard Pryor.

that authentic African-American arts evolved and flourished as perhaps the most influential cultural expression of the twentieth century. The irony is that, as Langston Hughes pointed out, "the joke is on you but hits the other fellow first—because it boomerangs . . . what makes it funny [is] the fact that you don't know you are laughing at yourself." The minstrel stage established the platform on which the authentic African American would evolve within America's oppressive racial environment, and nearly all early twentieth-century black performers cut their teeth in that venue. As implausible as it may seem, the emergence of such innovative artists as Charlie Parker, Alvin Ailey, and Richard Pryor was ultimately facilitated, perhaps even assured, by the creation of Jim Dandy, Zip Coon, and Sambo.

The scholarly essays and primary materials included in this collection not only provide essential writings that characterize and examine what the editors call the "performance genealogies" of nineteenth-century minstrelsy but also demonstrate how minstrel forms have been perpetuated in America's popular culture throughout the latter half of the twentieth century. It is a long overdue compendium that succinctly adumbrates a critical period of America's entertainment history that continues to influence the nation's race, gender, and class distinctions.

New York, 1995

EDITORS' PREFACE

Blackface minstrelsy is now recognized as America's first original contribution to world theatre—a dubious honor, certainly. But, more important for us today, minstrelsy was America's first popular mass entertainment. In February 1843, four white men in blackface, wearing ill-fitting, ragtag clothing, took the stage in New York City to perform, for the first time, an entire evening of the "oddities, peculiarities, eccentricities, and comicalities of that Sable Genus of Humanity." Minstrelsy dominated nineteenth-century entertainment for sixty years. By the time of its decline at the turn of the century, the dances, dialects, costume, jokes, music, and form of minstrelsy had changed and changed again, evolving into a national pastime. While its roots begin before the American Revolution, minstrelsy's great, great, not-so-great grandchildren still make jokes, still sing and dance today; as recently as 1993 at the Friar's Club in New York, we saw Ted Danson don blackface and engage in a ritual insult of an African-American woman, Whoopi Goldberg. Scholarship has been slow to examine minstrelsy because of its racist character. In the last twenty years, however, scholars such as Robert Toll in his book *Blacking Up* (1974) have discovered that minstrelsy is a gigantic mirror, reflecting America's struggle and policies on issues of race, class, and gender. By studying minstrelsy, we discover who we were and how we got to be who we are.

The initial idea behind this anthology lies with a joint seminar in American minstrelsy given for students in the Ph.D. Program in Theatre at the Graduate Center of the City University of New York and the Department of Performance Studies at the Tisch School of the Arts, New York University. During the course two important issues about the field became clear. First, we found that materials were widely scattered and often could be obtained only with difficulty. Some articles had appeared in several dozen different periodicals; primary materials such as showbills and minstrel guides often were inaccessible; and, of the two major modern books on minstrelsy, one was out of print and the other primarily useful only to students and scholars. We hope that this anthology will bring together, for the first time, primary material written by and for minstrels, and critical scholarship on blackface minstrelsy in America, providing key documents for everyone interested in exploring the performance history of the form.

Second, and perhaps most important, we found that minstrelsy was far more significant a force in nineteenth-century American life than we had ever imagined. Theatre historians and scholars in American music history have long realized that minstrelsy was an interesting musical form and a major force in popular entertainment. But the course taught all of us—both students and faculty—how truly significant minstrelsy has been in shaping American ideas about race, class, and gender. At some level, of course, this fact is painfully obvious; at another level, it is clear that we have only scratched the surface in our investigation of the social and political significance of the form.

Several years ago Joseph Roach wrote about what he called "performance genealogies"—which he defined as "the historical transmission and dissemination of cultural practice and attitudes through collective representation." In a sense, the "performance genealogies" of blackface minstrelsy became a major part of our course. Most people today are aware in a general way that minstrelsy was a significant feature of American entertainment life—and, indeed, American culture—from the 1840s through the Civil War. And most people know that the stereotypes of African Americans developed in minstrelsy before the Civil War helped shape our attitudes in important ways. And, finally, most people are aware that from that time onward many of those attitudes continued as a significant thread in American life. But a central question of the course became: *Specifically, what happened?* In short, what were the performance genealogies of blackface minstrelsy and how did they affect American thought?

In this book, we have assembled scholarship and primary materials drawn from the body of performance scholarship on minstrelsy conducted thus far. The contributions to scholarship begin with Eric Lott, who deftly outlines the social relations of "racial" production at the beginning of blackface minstrelsy (1820–1840), highlighting the elevation of "blackness" as an American cultural commodity. Because blackface minstrelsy was the first prolonged, featured appearance of black culture on the American stage, Lott emphasizes that minstrelization was an "affair of copies and originals, theft and love."

The remainder of the book is centered on the areas of significance discovered during our course on minstrelsy. We learned, for instance, that—as the chief American popular entertainment of the nineteenth century—blackface minstrelsy exploded out of traditions in blackface clowning and burlesque. Journalistic accounts (Southern) speak of the positive audience response to early minstrelsy, and how the general popularity of such groups as the Virginia Minstrels (Nathan) caused the near-instant assimilation of their humor, songs, and dances into an American culture in the Jacksonian age, a time ripe for transmission on a national stage of social, political, and sexual commentary (Bean, Lewis, and Saxton). The "authentically black" music was actually a blend of Irish folksongs accented by African-influenced Southern plantation culture (Winans). The frenetic dances (Winter) and low-brow humor (Mahar) were mimicry of dubious authenticity as well, yet their lasting legacy can be seen in contemporary black and white comedy. In the later nineteenth century, minstrelsy, closely tied to circuses, variety theatres, and burlesque, led to comic social commentary about many cultures, including Native American, Chinese, Irish, German, and Jewish (Toll). Blacks in blackface entered the American popular performance arena after the Civil War, by way of one of the few theatrical forms open to them—minstrel houses. Black minstrels, however, managed to project some of their own variations on the now-stock stereotypical images (Southern and Lewis). By the end of the nineteenth century blackface minstrelsy had—ironically and painfully—become, in the words of Mel Watkins, a "proving ground" for such African-American performers of stature as W. C. Handy, Bessie Smith, Josephine Baker, and many others. Ralph Ellison summarizes the tradition of minstrelsy—and America's historical intertwining of race and rebellion—in his landmark essay, "Change the Joke and Slip the Yoke." In the final essay of the book, Lhamon looks at the cyclical nature of minstrelsy's tropes, connecting early black humor on the plantation to hip-hop culture.

In addition to scholarship, both old and new, we have included a section of primary material: minstrelsy guides, jokes, sketches, and sheet music. We feel that this material should be considered along with critical and historical work, because it is to traditional minstrel words, sounds, and images that we should refer in order to reacquaint ourselves with the origins of minstrel stereotypes. We also hope to encourage scholars to formulate their own opinions and critiques of minstrelsy, and we feel that the inclusion of primary material will encourage this.

We have designed the book to address two points demonstrated in our own minstrelsy course: First, that the stereotypes begun in antebellum minstrelsy continued to flourish down through the nineteenth and twentieth centuries. And second, that among the major carriers of these stereotyped images were later forms of popular entertainment—both live and recorded—that borrowed elements from the evolving blackface minstrel show, among them vaudeville, burlesque, the revue, and later, film, radio, and television. Popular entertainments have great power. They tell us what is on the minds of ordinary people at any given moment—their concerns and biases and anxieties—and, in turn, refine them and restate them in a palatable, easily understood way. So it was with minstrelsy. White performers in blackface were in control of the stereotype; as a result, some African-American performers in the post-Civil War period found it necessary to employ the blackface image in their own work. Even before the Civil War, issues other than race, including gender and class, were dramatized and commodified by the white minstrel men, all of the time utilizing the blackface convention and stereotypes of minstrelsy.

Does it come as any surprise, then, that the stereotypes first brought together and codified in blackface minstrelsy before the Civil War have remained with us? If one explores the "performance genealogies" of this powerful entertainment form—if one traces its descendants in other entertainments—the answer should become increasingly apparent. We hope that this anthology will help readers understand the origins of those genealogies of blackface minstrelsy in the nineteenth century.

The editors would like to gratefully acknowledge the support, encouragement, and insightful contributions of the following individuals: Camille Billops, Rosemary L. Cullen of the John Hay Library at Brown University, Jan Heissinger, Eric Lott, Bill Mahar, Eileen Southern, the Spring 1994 and Spring 1995 Minstrelsy I and II classes, Suzanna Tamminen of Wesleyan University Press, Michele Wallace, Sylvia Wang, Mel Watkins, and especially John Graziano.

A.B.
J.V.H.
B.McN.

INTRODUCTION

Blackface and Blackness: The Minstrel Show in American Culture

Eric Lott

In the theatrical world, as in the aesthetic world more generally, ideology is always in essence the site of a competition and a struggle in which the sound and fury of humanity's political and social struggles are faintly or sharply echoed. —LOUIS ALTHUSSER

The current consensus on blackface minstrelsy is probably best summed up by Frederick Douglass's righteous response in the *North Star.* Blackface imitators, he said, were "the filthy scum of white society, who have stolen from us a complexion denied to them by nature, in which to make money, and pander to the corrupt taste of their white fellow citizens," a denunciation that nicely captures minstrelsy's further commodification of an already enslaved, noncitizen people (October 27, 1848). From our vantage point, the minstrel show indeed seems a transparently racist curiosity, a form of leisure that, in inventing and ridiculing the slow-witted but irrepressible "plantation darky" and the foppish "northern dandy negro," conveniently rationalized racial oppression. The culture that embraced it, we assume, was either wholly enchanted by racial travesty or so benighted, like Melville's Captain Delano, that it took such distortions as authentic. I want to suggest, however, that the audiences involved in early minstrelsy were not universally derisive of African Americans or their culture, and that there was a range of responses to the minstrel show which points to an instability or contradiction in the form itself. My project is to examine that instability for what it may tell us about the racial politics of culture in the years before the Civil War.

Writing in Horace Greeley's antislavery *New York Tribune* in 1855, an anonymous advocate of blackface minstrel songs celebrated the "earliest votaries of the colored opera":

Why may not the banjoism of a Congo, an Ethiopian or a George Christy [one of the most famous blackface performers of the 1840s and 1850s], aspire to an

> equality with the musical and poetical delineators of all nationalities? . . . Absurd as may seem negro minstrelsy to the refined musician, it is nevertheless beyond doubt that it expresses the peculiar characteristics of the negro as truly as the great masters of Italy represent their more spiritual and profound nationality. . . . [And] has there been no change in the feelings of the true originators of this music—the negroes themselves? . . . Plaintive and slow, the sad soul of the slave throws into his music all that gushing anguish of spirit which he dare not otherwise express. ("The Black Opera" 107)

Surprising lines, these, from a writer sympathetic to the idea of African-American art. We tend not to associate an approving view of minstrelsy with a determination to take slave culture seriously, let alone a determination to take minstrelsy *as* slave culture. Moreover, the writer's egalitarian rhetoric links one of the strongest antebellum cases on behalf of minstrel songs with a sympathetic (if typically condescending) attitude toward black people. The motivating idea here is a Herderian notion of the folk, articulated in the year of *Leaves of Grass* for much the same reason: to celebrate the popular sources of a national culture. It is possible, of course, to take such lines as evidence of the incomprehension that greeted minstrelsy, a position that is certainly defensible. But it does not fully account for the frequency of responses such as the one just quoted—the ready imputation of folk authenticity to patently "impure" songs such as "Ole Dan Tucker," "Jump Jim Crow," and "Zip Coon." Nor does it explain the desire to put moderate racial attitudes and minstrel shows together.

Indeed, Margaret Fuller spoke in a similar vein about this cultural form. In "Entertainments of the Past Winter," published in the *Dial* in 1842, she claimed that Americans were "beggars" when it came to the arts of music and dancing:

> Our only national melody, Yankee Doodle, is shrewdly suspected to be a scion from British art. All symptoms of invention are confined to the African race, who, like the German literati, are relieved by their position from the cares of government. "Jump Jim Crow," is a dance native to this country, and one which we plead guilty to seeing with pleasure, not on the stage, where we have not seen it, but as danced by children of an ebon hue in the street. Such of the African melodies as we have heard are beautiful. But the Caucasian race have yet their rail-roads to make. (52)

We will have occasion to return to the juxtaposition of American blacks with the idea of governance, particularly in the notion of slaves as poet-legislators. Interesting here, in addition, is the assumption that the only music and dance which are *not* false coin are those found in blackface minstrelsy, which represents, Fuller hints, something like the folk culture of an American peasantry. These comments begin to suggest that when, in the decades before the Civil War, northern white men "blacked up" and imitated what they supposed was black dialect, music, and dance, some people, without derision, heard Negroes singing.

Blackface minstrelsy as an African-American people's culture: this may seem an odd view. But it is one perception of the minstrel show that has been understandably repressed in antiracist accounts of it. Most scholars have yet to appreciate W. E. B. Du Bois's belief that Stephen Foster compositions such as "Old Black Joe" and "Old Folks at Home" were based on African-American themes; Du Bois included them in his assertion that black music was the "only real American music" ("Negro" 231; *Souls* 382). In *Black Manhattan*, James Weldon Johnson similarly remarked that minstrelsy originated on the plantation, and constituted the "only completely original contribution" of America to the theater (87). These judgments appear terribly misguided now, given that blackface minstrelsy's century-long commercial regulation of black cultural practices stalled the development of African-American public arts and generated an enduring narrative of racist ideology, a historical process by which an entire people has been made the bearer of another people's "folk" culture. We ought nonetheless to know how such positive assessments of the minstrel show were possible as well as wrong. Without a fuller understanding of blackface performance, one that includes the intensely conflicted set of responses it called forth, we miss the part it played in the racial politics of its time—the extent to which, for that matter, it *was* the racial politics of its time—from its northern emergence as an entr'acte in about 1830 to the various New York stage versions of *Uncle Tom's Cabin* in the mid-1850s.

In the pages that follow I return the minstrel show to a northeastern political context that was extremely volatile, one whose range can be seen in the antinomy of responses I have identified, themselves anticipatory of twentieth-century debates about the nature of the "popular." On one side there is a disdain for "mass"-cultural domination, the incorporation of black culture fashioned to racist uses; on the other a celebration of an authentic people's culture, the dissemination of black arts with potentially liberating results.[1] Let me suggest that one finds elements of both in early minstrelsy: there is as much evidence to locate in it the public emergence of slave culture (as Constance Rourke argued in *American Humor*) or pointed political protest (as David Grimsted and William Stowe have written) as there is to finger its racism, this last needing little demonstration. Ultimately, however, this stubborn dualism is an impoverished, not to say obsolete, way of thinking about one of America's first culture industries. Our simplistic (and almost completely ahistorical) understanding of minstrel shows comes partly as a result of swinging between one position and the other—or at least of the notion that these are our only choices.

Recent research into popular culture has allowed us to see the popular instead as a sphere characterized by cultural forms of social and political conflict, neither, in Gareth Stedman Jones's terms, entirely the "social control" of the ruling classes nor the "class expression" of the dominated. Because the popular is always *produced*, capitalized, it is hardly some unfettered time-out from political pressures, a space of mere "leisure"—a clear enough distinction in the case of minstrelsy—nor does it arise in some immediate way from collective popular desires. But, as Stuart Hall has insisted, neither does it passively mirror political domination taking place in other parts of the social formation, as though it were only epiphenomenal—a form of dominant-cultural "reinforcement," as commentators on the minstrel show have often said—or, in the Frankfurt School scenario, wholly administered and determined. Since the popular emerges at the intersection of received symbolic forms, audiences' experiences of authority and subordination in workplace, home, and social ritual, and new articulations by various producers of symbolic forms—local teachers and labor organizers, storytellers and journalists, theater managers and actors—it is itself a crucial place of contestation, with moments of resistance to the dominant culture as well as moments of supersession. Talking about the minstrel show this way reveals the most popular American entertainment form in the antebellum decades as a principal site of struggle in and over the culture of black people.[2] This struggle took place largely among antebellum whites, of course, and it finally divested black people of control over elements of their culture and over their own cultural representation generally. But it was based on a profound white investment in black culture which, for a time, had less certain consequences. My study documents in early blackface minstrelsy the dialectical flickering of racial insult and racial envy, moments of domination and moments of liberation, counterfeit and currency, a pattern at times amounting to no more than the two faces of racism, at others gesturing toward a specific kind of political or sexual danger, and all constituting a peculiarly American structure of racial feeling.

So far are we from any idea of what the vagaries of this structure of feeling might have been—the relationship of blackface to "blackness"—that it is useful to generate some sense of the contradictions and ambiguities in blackface representation and its place in American culture. Let me, for instance, elaborate what I mean in calling minstrelsy a popular form by returning briefly to the symptomatic moments of the debate I have sketched. Each position has its partial force, and taken together they define the range of possible forms and effects that could be produced in the minstrel show. To be sure, minstrelsy was an arena in which the efficient expropriation of the cultural commodity "blackness" occurred, demonstrated in what this *Atlantic Monthly* writer (writing in 1867) supposes is a hilarious account of "originator" T. D. Rice's first blackface performance in Pittsburgh around 1830:

> Rice prepared to take advantage of his opportunity. There was a negro in attendance at Griffith's Hotel, on Wood Street, named Cuff,—an exquisite specimen of his sort,—who won a precarious subsistence by letting his open mouth as a mark for boys to pitch pennies into, at three paces, and by carrying the trunks of passengers from the steamboats to the hotels. Cuff was precisely the subject for Rice's purpose. Slight persuasion induced him to accompany the actor to the theatre, where he was led through the private entrance, and quietly ensconced behind the scenes. . . . Rice, having shaded his own countenance to the "contraband" hue, ordered Cuff to disrobe, and proceeded to invest himself in the cast-off apparel. . . . [Onstage] the extraordinary apparition produced an instant effect. . . . The effect was electric. . . .
>
> Now it happened that Cuff, who meanwhile was crouching in dishabille under concealment of a projected *flat* behind the performer, by some means received intelligence, at this point, of the near approach of a steamer to the Monongahela Wharf. Between himself and others of his color in the same line of business, and especially as regarded a certain formidable competitor called Ginger, there existed an active rivalry in the baggage-carrying business. For Cuff to allow Ginger the advantage of an undisputed descent upon the luggage of the approaching vessel would be not only to forget all "considerations" from the passengers, but, by proving him a laggard in his calling, to cast a damaging blemish upon his reputation. Liberally as he might lend himself to a friend, it could not be done at that sacrifice. After a minute or two of fidgety waiting for [Rice's] song to end, Cuff's patience could endure no longer, and, cautiously hazarding a glimpse of his profile beyond the edge of the flat, he called in a hurried whisper: "Massa Rice, Massa Rice, must have my clo'se! Massa Griffif wants me,—steamboat's comin'!"
>
> The appeal was fruitless. Massa Rice did not hear it, for a happy hit at an unpopular city functionary had set the audience in a roar in which all other sounds were lost. . . . [Another appeal went unheeded, when,] driven to desperation, and forgetful in the emergency of every sense of propriety, Cuff, in ludicrous undress as he was, started from his place, rushed upon the stage, and, laying his hand upon the performer's shoulder, called out excitedly: "Massa Rice, Massa Rice, gi' me nigga's hat,—nigga's coat,—nigga's shoes,—gi' me nigga's t'ings! Massa Griffif wants 'im,—STEAMBOAT'S COMIN'!!"
>
> The incident was the touch, in the mirthful experience of that night, that passed endurance. (Nevin 609–10)

This passage, in all its woozy syntax and headlong rush, is probably the least trustworthy and most accurate account of American minstrelsy's appropriation of black cultural practices. Indeed, this eulogy to the minstrel composer Stephen Foster reads something like a master text of the racial economy encoded in blackface performance. For one thing, it calls on minstrel devices (ventriloquized dialect, racial burlesque) to narrate the origins of minstrelsy, as if this particular narratable event generated or secreted "naturally" the formal means appropriate to it; its multiple frames (minstrelsy within minstrelsy) amount to so many techniques of black subordination. True to form, a diminished, not to say "blackfaced" Cuff has replaced Rice as this account's center of attention. And its talk of opportunity and investment, lending and ownership, subsistence and competition is more preoccupied with cultural value than we might have expected. Its social unconscious, we might say, reveals a great deal of anxiety about the "primitive accumulation" it ostensibly celebrates.[3] Perhaps this is also why the passage is fully a third longer than what I have just quoted. The fascination with Cuff's nakedness, moreover, highlights the affair as one of male bodies, in which racial conflict and cultural exchange are negotiated between men. Cuff's stripping, a theft that silences and embarrasses him onstage but which nevertheless entails both his bodily presence in the show and the titillating threat that he may return to demand his stolen capital, is a neat allegory for the most prominent commercial collision of black and white cultures in the nineteenth century. Cultural expropriation is the minstrel show's central fact, and we should not lose sight of it.[4] But it is also a fact that needs explaining, for in itself it establishes little about the cultural commerce suggested by one performer's enthusiasm as he gathered material for his blackface act: "I shall be rich in black fun."[5]

Even in expropriation there was a strong white attraction to the material which surfaced in less malign ways. White people believed the counterfeit, often sympathetically, as I have begun to suggest; the blackface hieroglyph so fully unpacked in the *Atlantic Monthly* account went largely unread. There were, it is true, nudges and winks folded into claims like that of the Apollo Minstrels to be the "only original Negroes travelling," or in the *New York Herald*'s coy references to Christy's Minstrels as "the very pinks of negro singers."[6] But often, in the minds of many, blackface singers and dancers became, simply, "negroes." How else explain the tireless references to "these amusing darkies" (*New York Herald*, January 21, 1848), as if the originals had somehow gotten lost? Early audiences so often suspected that they were being entertained by actual Negroes that minstrel sheet music began the proto-Brechtian practice of picturing blackface performers out of costume as well as in, and there are several existing accounts of white theatergoers mistaking blackface performers for blacks.[7] Even Mark Twain's mother, at her first (and presumably only) minstrel show, believed she was watching black performers. Like Margaret Fuller (and, as we shall see, Walt Whitman), Mark Twain was himself intrigued by what he called the "happy and accurate" representations of the minstrel show.[8]

Of course, belief in the authenticity of blackface hardly ruled out racial ridicule; the oscillation between currency and counterfeit in the minstrel show was related to but often discrete from the oscillation between sympathy and ridicule toward its representations. Indeed, the wayward valuations attached both to irony toward the fakes and belief in them make the task of gauging audience response a dizzying one. What was the precise mix of irony, false consciousness, interest, and interracial recognition in a white Union soldier's perception that two blacks in his barracks "look[ed] exactly like our minstrels" (Howe 91)? We are back where we began, but with a difference: although minstrelsy was indeed in the business of staging or producing "race," that very enterprise also involved it in a carnivalizing of race, as the range of critical response has begun to suggest, such that the minstrel show's ideological production became more contradictory, its consumption more indeterminate, its political effects more plural than many have assumed. It is worth asking what those effects could possibly have amounted to. Ultimately I would like to make some sense of the dialectical relationship noted in Constance Rourke's observation that "little Jim Crow appeared at almost the precise moment when *The Liberator* was founded" (*American* 98). What was the brief shared history of blackface minstrelsy and racial ideologies of liberation? And was their relationship a story of racist compensation, or were there unsuspected similarities?

A Genealogy of Jim Crow

I begin with a brief genealogy of Jim Crow.[9] This will offer a glimpse of blackface's ambiguous modes of authority based on certain of its earlier, as well as its minstrel-show, manifestations. The virtue of the genealogy, as Fredric Jameson suggests, is that it defamiliarizes the cultural object, revealing from a diachronic perspective, as in an X ray, functional elements in forms such as minstrelsy that probably seem transparent enough (*Political* 139). Although it will be necessary to trace the formal contradictions noted here in the various appearances of blackface through to the American cultural contradictions they figure, this genealogy begins to suggest the range of purposes the black minstrel mask could serve, both onstage and in public. It thus constitutes a certain groundwork for that dialectic of white responses to "blackness" which I believe traversed not only the early minstrel show but antebellum racial feeling as well.[10]

It would certainly be a mistake to see the minstrel types that began to emerge in the late 1820s as continuous outgrowths of slave tales à la Constance Rourke, though there exist certain similarities. They should rather be placed at the intersection of slave culture and earlier blackface stage characters such as the harlequin of the commedia dell'arte, the clown of English pantomime and the clown of the American circus, the burlesque tramp, perhaps the "blackman" of English folk drama. This intersection establishes the political and emotional range within which minstrel songs characteristically worked. The twin infusion of these antecedents in minstrel representations lends a highly uncertain status to an already ambiguous stage tradition.[11] Clowns and harlequins are as often lovable butts of humor as devious producers of it; slave-tale tricksters are frequently (though not always) champions, heroes, backdoor victors for the weak over the strong. Early minstrel figures overlapped with each tradition, tending more or less toward self-mockery on the one hand and subversion on the other. The overlap was registered, first, in British productions such as *Cowardy, Cowardy, Custard; or Harlequin Jim Crow and the Magic Mustard Pot* (1836), which marked a trend beginning in the 1830s of appending the name Jim Crow to all sorts of British clowns and Punch-and-Judy figures;[12] and, second, in the animal tales early blackface performers set to music, not to mention the alleged black derivation of the "Jim Crow" tune itself.

This contradictory lineage, the stage trickster overdetermined by the slave trickster, highlights some hint of danger in the earliest blackface types which few have been willing to grant them. Consider T. D. Rice's mid-1830s version of "Clar de Kitchen":

A jay bird sot on a hickory limb,
He wink'd at me and I wink'd at him;
I pick'd up a stone and I hit his shin,
Says he you better not do dat agin.

A Bull frog dress'd sogers close,
Went in de field to shoot some crows;
De crows smell powder and fly away,
De Bull frog mighty mad dat day.[13]

Such small victories were won continually in early minstrelsy. Small and undoubtedly self-diminishing though they were, the coded triumphs of black men over sinister jaybirds and black crows over patrolling bullfrogs were triumphs all the same, reminiscent indeed of certain slave tales. It might even be said that part of the triumph lay precisely in their recalling slave lore, in which foxes flee roosters, goats terrorize lions, and Brer Rabbit gleefully taunts Wolf.

Other early minstrel characters veered much more toward an intentionally ridiculous blustering, inherited less from the slaves or conventional stage figures than from the Mike Finks and Davy Crocketts of southwestern humor. Whether plantation rustics (Jim Crow) or urban dandies (Zip Coon), these figures of exaggerated strength and overwhelming power, as Lawrence Levine has suggested, have little in common with the slave tricksters' underhanded manipulations and deceits (*Black* 104). There was thus a third tradition infusing the most common characters of antebellum minstrelsy, who, Nathan Huggins argues, were often little more than blackfaced versions of heroes from southwestern humor.[14] Characters based on those heroes, however, sometimes took on "black" lineaments as well (Toll 42); and there was in any case an inherited power that came with the bluster, however culturally fraudulent that bluster may have been. Selected verses from the first song sheet edition of "Jim Crow" (published by E. Riley in the early 1830s) capture this ambiguity:

Come listen all you galls and boys
I'se jist from Tuckyhoe,
I'm goin to sing a little song,
My name's Jim Crow.

Weel about and turn about
And do jis so,
Eb'ry time I weel about
And jump Jim Crow.

Oh I'm a roarer on de fiddle,
And down in old Virginny,
They say I play de skyentific
Like Massa Pagannini.

• • •

I'm a full blooded niggar,
Ob de real ole stock,
And wid my head and shoulder
I can split a horse block.

• • •

De great Nullification,
And fuss in de South,
Is now before Congress,
To be tried by word ob mouth.

Dey hab had no blows yet,
And I hope dey nebber will,
For its berry cruel in bredren,
One anoders blood to spill.

• • •

Should dey get to fighting,
Perhaps de blacks will rise,
For deir wish for freedom,
Is shining in deir eyes.

An if de blacks should get free,
I guess dey'll fee some bigger,
An I shall consider it,
A bold stroke for de nigger.

• • •

An I caution all white dandies,
Not to come in my way,
For if dey insult me,
Dey'll in de gutter lay.
(Dennison 51–57)

This is hardly the stuff of which revolutions are made; it was easy enough to patronize such happy-go-lucky bravado. Still, references to sectional conflict (Andrew Jackson's 1832–1833 nullification fight with John C. Calhoun over states' rights) and to a black desire for freedom (only a couple of years after the Nat Turner insurrection), all in a context of general insolence, were certainly nothing to be laughed off. Like most of the potentially subversive moments of early minstrelsy, they are qualified by "darky" dialect (in the theater) and orthographic derision (on the page); but in the mouth of the very figure who had begun to make the question of national unity an issue, such lyrics could be dangerous, even if it was understood that the singer need not be taken seriously. One ought not immediately assent to the anthropological truism that social formations are always buttressed by the permission of certain experiences not normally permitted. With regard to antebellum minstrelsy so much remains to be seen. As Barbara Babcock-Abrahams notes, "Any form of symbolic inversion has an implicitly radical dimension" (183). We should in any case avoid the essentialist notion that such representations are *inherently* anything, for given the right context, Peter Stallybrass and Allon White imply, they may indeed take on a transformative capacity (14).

These ambiguities were owing in part to the iconography such figures employed—that of blackface and male transvestism—features also commonly found together in public uses of blackface. Quite strikingly, many minstrel performers began their careers in the circus, perhaps even developing American blackface out of clowning (whose present mask in any case is clearly indebted to blackface), and continually found under the big top a vital arena of minstrel performance. Clowning is an uncanny kind of activity, scariest when it is most cheerful, unsettling to an audience even as it unmasks the pretentious ringmaster. Blackface performers, often inspiring a certain terror as well as great affection, relied precisely on this doubleness. Ralph Ellison locates their specifically American resonance:

When the white man steps behind the mask of the [blackface] trickster his freedom is circumscribed by the fear that he is not simply miming a personification of his disorder and chaos but that he will become in fact that which he intends only to symbolize; that he will be trapped somewhere in the mystery of hell . . . and thus lose that freedom which, in the fluid, "traditionless," "classless" and rapidly changing society, he would recognize as the white man's alone. ("Change" 53)

The black mask offered a way to play with collective fears of a degraded and threatening—and male—Other while at the same time maintaining some symbolic control over them. Yet the intensified American fears of succumbing to a racialized image of Otherness were everywhere operative in minstrelsy, continually exceeding the controls and accounting, paradoxically, for the minstrel show's power, insofar as its "blackness" was unceasingly fascinating to performers and audiences alike. This combined fear of and fascination with the black male cast a strange dread of miscegenation over the minstrel show, but evidently did not preclude a continual return to minstrel miming.

Far from simple indulgence, however, the returns began to take on the aura of attempted mastery, of a culture trying to contain what Ellison calls "disorder and chaos" but which could more historically be called intermixture and insurrection.[15] The effete but potent black "dandy" figure incarnated these threats, as in "Long Tail Blue" (1827):

As I was going up Fulton Street
  I hollerd arter Sue,
The watchman came and took me up,
  And spoilte my long tail blue.

• • •

If you want to win the Ladies hearts,
  I'll tell you what to do;
Go to a tip top Tailor's shop,
  And buy a long tail blue.[16]

"Raw, undomesticated bodily and collective power," as Victor Turner would have it, the blackface trickster, "long tail blue" or not, suggests white men's obsession with a rampageous black penis ("Myth" 580). As Ellison puts it, "The mask was the thing (the 'thing' in more ways than one)" ("Change" 49). Bold swagger, irrepressible desire, sheer bodily display: in a real sense the minstrel man *was* the penis, that organ returning in a variety of contexts, at times ludicrous, at others rather less so.[17] Such contexts were contradictory in any case, invoking the power of "blackness" while deriding it, in an effort of cultural control, through the very convention that produced its power—the greasepaint and burnt cork of blackface.

Transvestism, of course, is subject to similar instabilities, though, as Marjorie Garber has powerfully argued, male cross-dressing can resist the stasis of ambiguity and thoroughly undermine traditional gender categories.[18] Garber herself admits, however, that women often become the target of such humorous disguises. This is certainly the case with minstrelsy's many "wench" characters (played by men at a time when women regularly appeared on the legitimate stage), which offer one of the most revealing discourses on male sexuality in America at midcentury.[19]

Gal from the South

Ole massa bought a colored gal,
He bought her at the south;
Her hair it curled so very tight
She could not shut her mouth.
Her eyes they were so bery small,
They both ran into one,
And when a fly light in her eye,
Like a June bug in de sun.

Her nose it was so berry long,
It turned up like a squash,
And when she got her dander up
She made me laugh, by gosh;
Old massa had no hooks or nails,
Or nothin' else like that,
So on this darkie's nose he used
To hang his coat and hat.

One morning massa goin' away,
He went to git his coat,
But neither hat nor coat was there,
For she had swallowed both;
He took her to a tailor shop,
To have her mouth made small,
The lady took in one long breath,
And swallowed tailor and all.[20]

This portrait is fairly typical of the representation of black women on the minstrel stage, whether simply narrated or fully acted out; the two modes occurred simultaneously as often as not, the narrative detailing the jokey blazon, the oblivious "wench" ridiculed in person on another part of the stage. The anxieties aroused by such figures are also typical: the empowering insistence of the two "boughts" attempts to cancel the threatening open mouth (later to be "made small"), while the phallic nose and the engulfing, vaginal throat finally wreak revenge on the master.

White men's fear of female power was dramatized with a suspiciously draconian punitiveness in early minstrelsy, usually in the grotesque transmutations of its female figures. It is as if that fear were so fundamental that only a major effort of surveillance—like a dream, revealing its anxieties even as it devises its censors—would do. The widespread prostitution in the theater's notorious third tier, the literal analogue of the song's wish to buy women, comes to seem an ugly kind of compensatory space given the unruliness of these stage figures, if the figures did not themselves contain the female threat.[21] These "female" bodies, it is true, were "also" male, and minstrel performers did not hesitate to flirt with the homosexual content of blackface transvestism (the master's hat on the black "woman's" nose), which no doubt created an atmosphere of polymorphous license that could blur conventional gender outlines (for men). But a flight from such "compromising" subtexts may in fact have produced the reassertion of masculinity in misogynist representations, which usually constituted the reactionary face of a perhaps more "undecidable" racial masquerade.

When we turn from these dramatic roles to the public display of the blackface convention, we find as long a history. Victor Turner defends such displays—in parades, protests, carnivals, processions—as a mode of "public reflexivity," during which societies think in sometimes displaced and condensed ways about their forms and functions. He links them to "times of radical social change," when they can form part of the "repertoire of prophetic leaders who mobilize the people against invaders or overlords threatening their deep culture" ("Frame" 36). For this reason Barbara Babcock-Abrahams has likened stage tricksters to E. J. Hobsbawm's "primitive rebels," those backward, marginal antinomians who demonstrate quite literally that "oppression can be turned upside down" and who inspire myths and legends about their lives (Hobsbawm 24). Natalie Davis has more dialectically described these public performances as both harmless communal "safety valves" that deflect attention from social reality and proposals of new social paradigms or models; they "can on the one hand perpetuate certain values of the community (even guarantee its survival), and on the other hand criticize political order" (97). In conjunction with transvestism, the blackface mask has indeed been worn as an equivocal emblem of popular resistance, on behalf, variously—even simultaneously—of tradition and innovation. (The Boston Tea Party, with its howling "Indians" and "blacks," is only the most famous American occasion.) In her essay "Women on Top," Davis describes several instances of "ritual and festive inversion." In the Beaujolais of the 1770s, for example, "male peasants blackened their faces and dressed as women and then attacked surveyors measuring their lands for a new landlord" (147). The "Whiteboys" of Ireland, for about a decade (the 1760s), dressed in long white frocks and blackened their faces, setting themselves up as an "armed popular force to provide justice for the poor, 'to restore the ancient commons and redress other grievances'" (149); they tore down enclosures, punished greedy landowners, and forced masters to release unwilling apprentices. They referred to themselves as "fairies," and signed themselves "Ghostly Sally"—prototypes, says Davis, of the Molly Maguires and Ribbon Societies of the nineteenth century (149).

In each of these instances the "unruly" resonances of blackness and femaleness emerged from the dramatic frame into public, where they were put to new uses by men in a political realm that obviously excluded both blacks and women. Davis observes:

> On the one hand, the disguise freed men from the full responsibility for their deeds and perhaps, too, from fear of outrageous revenge upon their manhood. After all, it was mere women [or mere blacks, or indeed black women] who were acting in this disorderly way. On the other hand, the males drew upon the sexual power and energy of the unruly woman and on her license (which they had long assumed at carnival and games)—to promote fertility, to defend the community's interests and standards, and to tell the truth about unjust rule. (149)

There was no immediate internal racial context for blackface in these examples, but the European slave trade provided the broadest conditions of possibility; and the assumed inferiority, sexuality, license, and perhaps even sense of injustice associated with women were clearly ascribed to black people as well. Davis does not mention whether blackface was seen as representational rather than abstract or "metaphysical" (recall the diabolical associations with blackness that Winthrop Jordan extensively documented in *White over Black*), but there is no question that by the late eighteenth century blackface had taken on representational force, as the many sentimentally "noble" black characters on the British stage illustrate. The dynamic of the processional mask in these instances thus preserves the ascription of certain detested qualities to "blackness" while momentarily paying tribute to their power, a power that even in peasants' or workers' movements is compromised by such ascription. Herein lay the meaning of blackface in the American context of rioting and revelry, though it is perhaps not surprising that in such a conflictual racial scene the mask was increasingly used for reactionary purposes.

Susan Davis has demonstrated that in militia burlesques and Christmas street festivities, public "masking"—the assumption through disguise of a new or inverted identity—became common in northern American cities after the 1820s, precisely contemporary with the rise of minstrelsy (and over against similar traditions of black pageantry).[22] During carnivalesque Christmas Eve celebrations, for instances, roving young working-class men parodied the militia, marched to the rough music of kitchen-utensil instruments, and brawled on street corners. On one occasion in Philadelphia in 1834, one hundred men in intentionally makeshift uniforms conducted elaborate sham maneuvers, accompanied, one newspaper said, by a masked band of "Indians, hunters, Falstaffs, Jim Crows and nondescripts." Women and blacks, as usual, were the most frequent sources of disguise. While only public transvestism, not blackface, brought a stiff fine—a fact that underscores both the permissiveness of the popular theater and the possible radicalism of men in drag during this period—blackface cross-dressing, as in its extended European history, was a popular favorite. Such disguises appear to have served similarly duplicitous purposes as those of Natalie Davis's peasants, but the American context added an even more troubling dimension. Gang attacks on blacks, mobbings on black churches, and battles between black and white gangs were commonplace holiday occurrences.[23] Other racially motivated mobs repeated the pattern: during the 1834 Philadelphia race riot in the Moyamensing district, some of the antiabolitionist rioters who attacked the homes of well-to-do blacks, burned black churches, and destroyed racially integrated places of leisure wore black masks and shabby coats (Runcie 209).

This "blackface-on-Black violence," as David Roediger has called it, would seem to indicate a fairly direct correspondence between racial hostility, public masking, and the minstrel show (*Wages* 106). In many instances we find this to be the case, but such a notion generally underrates the complexity of both antebellum racial politics and minstrelsy itself. Susan Davis suggests of the Christmas celebrations, for instance, that "masking made an ambiguous statement about race despite its violent mocking tone, for blackface found use as a way to play with racial identity, important in a city where black inferiority was taken for granted yet segregation was incomplete" ("Making" 193). Stage blackface was to be called on to negotiate just such contradictions in the culture of the antebellum American popular classes—between "white egalitarianism" and interracial urban practices,[24] or between antislavery and antiabolitionism—called on so frequently, in fact, that its primary purpose appears to have been to provide "imaginary" resolutions to intractable social conflicts. Moreover, if minstrelsy was a theatrical celebration of how deeply American racism is "embedded into a sense of racial and class affection and even envy" (Grimsted and Stowe 95), this contradictory structure occasionally witnessed unexpected returns of the indentificatory desire.[25] At the very least, symbolic crossings of racial boundaries—through dialect, gesture, and so on—paradoxically engage and absorb the culture being mocked or mimicked (Szwed 27–28). Acting black: a whole social world of irony, violence, negotiation, and learning is contained in that phrase.[26]

Minstrel representations, then, were not continuous with either earlier dramatic blackface figures or the deployment of blackface in rioting and revelry; although in certain cases there clearly were borrowings and affinities, these were scarcely all structurally "the same." Such traditions do, however, highlight a feature of American blackface masking that critics have been slow to recognize: an unstable or indeed contradictory power, linked to social and political conflicts, that issues from the weak, the uncanny, the outside. Above all, the slippery political valences of the traditions I have outlined are instructive. For it was with precisely this slipperiness that the minstrel mask resonated: a derisive celebration of the power of blackness; blacks, for a moment, ambiguously, on top.

People's Culture or Cultural Domination?

To put it another way, the early minstrel show was a Janus-faced figure for the cultural relationship of white to black in America, a relationship that even in its dominative character was far from self-explanatory. The duplicity of this cultural form is suggested not only by my genealogy, minstrelsy's formal makeup, but also by its role in American racial discourses. In many kinds of racially fraught cultural production—novels, cultural histories, and minstrel commentaries no less than antebellum blackface performance—minstrelsy has been a ground of American racial negotiation and contradiction, based on the antebellum collision course of competing modes of production and the various historical transformations in its aftermath. From this perspective certain representative critical engagements with the minstrel tradition turn out to be little less than furtive serial positions in a debate on American racial politics. The critical problem announced in this section's title—people's culture versus cultural domination—is thus an ideological problem of the broadest import, and it bears so much on the minstrel show's place in American culture that we ought to do what we can to unpack it before we attempt to supersede it. The fact is that these two positions both have their paradigmatic nineteenth-century instances: Mark Twain's vexed relationship to the minstrel tradition and Frederick Douglass's various writings on it in the *North Star*. In their nineteenth-century guises, however, these perspectives are actually more ambivalences than positions, betraying slippages, coming off conflicted. Like the traditions they exemplify, they are worth examining for what they tell us about minstrelsy's role in the racial politics of American culture.

As I have said, the position favoring minstrelsy as a people's culture typically celebrates the minstrel show's folk authenticity, its elevation of black types and black culture through blackface to a place in the national mythology.[27] The rather revealing problem inherent in this position, however, is that it regularly slips into an indulgence of racist typing. Mark Twain's avowed love of minstrelsy—"if I could have the nigger show back again in its pristine purity and perfection I should have but little further use for opera" (*Autobiography* 59)—is contradictory in just this way. Twain first saw rural minstrel productions in early-1840s Hannibal, where they burst on the unwitting town as a "glad and stunning surprise":

> The minstrels appeared with coal-black hands and faces and their clothing was a loud and extravagant burlesque of the clothing worn by the plantation slave of the time; not that the rags of the poor slave were burlesqued, for that would not have been possible; burlesque could have added nothing in the way of extravagance to the sorrowful accumulation of rags and patches which constituted his costume; it was the form and color of his dress that was burlesqued. (*Autobiography* 59)

This perception is far from incautious. Twain even observes that minstrels had "buttons as big as a blacking box," collapsing blackface masquerade, the means of its artifice and an echo of one of its literal sources—Negro bootblacks—in a single self-conscious figure. His involvement here, however, soon outstrips all moderation:

> The minstrel used a very broad negro dialect; he used it competently and with easy facility and it was funny—delightfully and satisfyingly funny. . . . [Minstrels'] lips were thickened and lengthened with bright red paint to such a degree that their mouths resembled slices cut in a ripe watermelon. . . . The minstrel troupes had good voices and both their solos and their choruses were a delight to me as long as the negro show continued in existence. (*Autobiography* 59–61)

Twain's response marks a real (and perhaps typical) attraction to and celebration of black culture. Indeed, in *Following the Equator* (1897) he notes his love of beautiful black bodies and his disgust for white ones. But when such observations do not fall into derision, they are clearly the patronizing obverse of it, and at the very least signify an unexamined investment in exoticism. Ralph Ellison's remark to the effect that *Huckleberry Finn*'s Jim rarely emerges from behind the minstrel mask is to the point here.[28]

Huckleberry Finn (1884), as more than one critic has observed, was not only written but situated in minstrelsy's boom period. Anthony Berret has argued that this fact accounts for the odd indebtedness of the novel's language, rhetorical strategies, and structure to blackface minstrelsy: the preponderance of comic dialogues between Jim and Huck (much of the comedy at Jim's expense); the burlesques of both elite and popular literature; and the tripartite comic dialogue-olio-burlesque structure.[29] In the spring of 1882 Twain visited George Washington Cable and Joel Chandler Harris in New Orleans, and suggested that they do a lecture tour (which he called a circus or menagerie) to include William Dean Howells and Thomas Bailey Aldrich. As Berret points out, this authorial circus was, in conception at least, little more than the variety acts of a minstrel show; and the reading tour that finally materialized, with Cable's straight man countering Twain's comic, found both authors reading the roles of black characters onstage, Cable even singing songs (Berret 38). It was during this tour that American audiences first heard parts of *Huckleberry Finn*, notably the "King Sollermun" and "How come a Frenchman doan' talk like a man?" passages, scenes whose fit with the minstrel tradition is rather close. These passages may even have been expressly written, after the novel's completion, for readings in just such a context (Woodard and MacCann 5). The ideological complexity of this affair is compounded by the fact that Cable rather remarkably wrote a stinging rebuke of southern racism, "The Freedman's Case in Equity," which appeared during the tour in the same issue of *Century Magazine* that printed an excerpt from *Huck Finn*. But this perhaps collective commitment did not prevent blackface tones from creeping into the readings, or Twain from naming one of his offerings "Can't Learn a Nigger to Argue," a title he changed only at Cable's behest.[30] These events no doubt put a highly ambiguous spin on America's greatest nineteenth-century political novel, but they indicate as well that the contradiction between the book's overt politics and its indebtedness to the minstrel show was much less cumbrous in the nineteenth century. Many antiracist arguments, that is, were unfortunately not so far from the exoticism and hierarchical assumptions of the minstrel tradition. The ideological cement of such a seemingly outrageous yoking was of course nineteenth-century sentimentalism—"romantic racialism," as George Fredrickson has termed it—which underwrote the widespread and arguably radical attraction of an African-American people's culture even as it postulated innate differences between the "Anglo-Saxon" and "African" races.

Regrettably, the recent major histories of sentimental or women's culture find no place for racial categories. Neither Ann Douglas's *Feminization of American Culture* nor Mary Kelley's *Private Woman, Public Stage*, for example, pauses over the centrality of the passive, sentimentalized, often male slave in the mid-nineteenth-century culture of feeling;

even Jane Tompkins's soteriological reading of *Uncle Tom's Cabin* deemphasizes the racial component of that novel's power. In fact, Tompkins's reading is compelling because the sentimentalist strategies for representing white women and blacks were often identical, each image lending the other emotional and political force. "Blackness" was indeed a primary site of the religious appreciation of the emotions that came with the decline of Calvinism. In the 1830s, Fredrickson observes, theories of Negro personality were in a state of relative flux; the debate was largely one between "environmentalist defenders of a single human nature and proponents of deep-seated racial differences" (*Black* 101). With the emergence of the "American school of ethnology" in the 1840s and 1850s, however, which argued the case for "polygenesis," or the separate creation of the races as distinct species (there were biblical versions of this argument as well), both sides of the dialogue increasingly assumed the fundamental difference of the races. A new kind of theoretical fluidity now entered the picture. On the polygenetic view, blacks were intellectually inferior because in thrall to the emotions. But since this notion was closer to a racial relativism of the Herderian variety—that the various races make contributions of their special "gifts" to humanity—than to a hierarchical racism, both evangelical religion and literary romanticism could virtually recuperate such a belief into an ideology of black superiority. As William Ellery Channing put it in 1840: "We are holding in bondage one of the best races of the human family. The negro is among the mildest and gentlest of men" (50). Like women, blacks were considered creatures of feeling at a time when feeling was paramount in the culture; what fund of emotion the "go-ahead-ative," aggressive Anglo-Saxon lacked, blacks would surely supply. Thus, stereotypes and arguments of this kind already in place in the plantation school of fiction tended to be taken over, but *revalued*: slavery was evil, for example, because it destroyed the great good nature, the blithe innocence, and above all the family structure of, in Methodist Bishop Gilbert Haven's words, "the choice blood of America." Blacks, it came to be argued, were not only exemplars of virtue but natural Christians.[31]

Nor was the antislavery movement exempt from such condescension. Awkward attempts to rewrite what were believed to be natural differences into special racial capacities resulted in notions of racial "variety without inferiority," as Lydia Maria Child, editor of the *National Anti-Slavery Standard*, put it: "Flutes on different keys . . . will harmonize the better."[32] Although the idea was to move "feminine" values to the cultural center, such arguments relied on the black inferiority they sought to displace. Karen Sánchez-Eppler has suggested that this tendency derived in part from the final asymmetry of white women and blacks in such rhetoric. Child's story "Mary French and Susan Easton" (1834), for example, urges the sentimental ideal of equality-in-difference, but can imagine even this outcome only by obliterating the racial lineaments of the good Negro figure, as though blackness, even when feminized, were inferior by definition (Sánchez-Eppler 39). Black leaders themselves, it should be said, did little to contest such unwittingly hierarchical thinking. Martin Delany, perhaps the most vehement of midcentury black nationalists, spoke of his race on several occasions as a repository of natural aestheticism and morality; thus it flourished in music and oratory, while whites "probably excel in mathematics, . . . commerce and internal improvements." Frederick Douglass attributed his implicitly feminized "love of letters" to the Negro ancestry of his mother rather than to his Anglo-Saxon paternity.[33] Such widespread attitudes, Wilson Moses argues, may have been responsible for the emphasis of black leaders from Douglass to Booker T. Washington on specifically industrial training (46).

The key text of explicitly antislavery romantic racialism is of course Harriet Beecher Stowe's *Uncle Tom's Cabin* (1852). With the character of Uncle Tom we are already on our way to the gentle, childlike, self-sacrificing, essentially *aesthetic* slave Mark Twain created in Jim and thought he recognized on the minstrel stage; and it is instructive to remind ourselves that *Uncle Tom's Cabin* and *Huck Finn* were among the most powerful antislavery or antiracist novels of the nineteenth century. All the more remarkable, then, that Tom bears so much resemblance to the many sentimental slaves of Stephen Foster's complacent "Plantation Melodies": Old Uncle Ned, Old Black Joe, and so on. Very little distinguishes the types in such minstrel songs from those in Stowe or Twain. Loosed from Stowe's rhetoric into stage tableaux, they are quite continuous with the minstrel tradition; T. D. Rice, who began his career in the 1830s playing Jim Crow, ended it in the 1850s playing Uncle Tom on the stage. And *Huckleberry Finn*, as Anthony Berret observes, seems nowhere closer to the sentimental ethos of Foster's songs than during Huck's many fictional tales of disunited families, or his returns to the raft and an emotional Jim (42–43). If Foster's "Old Folks at Home" or "Oh! Susanna"—somewhat better versions of staple minstrel themes in the 1840s—depend for their effect on the pathos culled from black families forced to split up or attempting to reunite, Twain's novel relies on similar "familial" reunions whose resonance derives from the stereotyped emotionality of the black slave.

Notwithstanding the desperate ambiguity contained in the sentimental make-over of these black types, in their culture they were capable of wielding enormous power. As William Taylor has written, "To attribute to someone the simplicity of a child, . . . especially in the middle of the nineteenth century, was a compliment of the first order, and dangerous, too, if the child were to be mistreated and sympathy was not the response sought for" (305). Hence the somewhat backhanded power of *Uncle Tom's Cabin* and, in a more vestigial way, *Huckleberry Finn.* And yet, obviously, such a racial philosophy very quickly fell into one of white supremacy. Romantic racialist thinking, George Fredrickson notes, "was one aspect of the retreat from environmentalism and the Enlightenment view of a common human nature" (*Black* 125). At this point the minstrel show rears its ungainly head; but precisely because it reveled in the contradictions I have outlined, unmistakably present in the work of Mark Twain, among others, we must attend to the rather gnarled effects of blackface performance in the context of nineteenth century racial ideologies.

To be sure, the ambiguity easily empties out of this perspective, and its later nineteenth century instances represent little more than the ritual, reactionary celebration of an ideologically rigidified minstrelsy meant to counter American antislavery practice.[34] (In intention at least *Huckleberry Finn* is something of an "immanent critique" of this tradition.) In the guise of what has come to be called "scientific racism"—a set of post-Darwinian explanations for the arrested development of blacks—this period's anthropology straitjacketed the relative fluctuations of earlier racial ideologies. Thus legitimized, white historians and memoirists in the nostalgic mood frequently recounted stories of the minstrel show's origins, tales of famous performers, even formal histories of the representation of blacks on stage, assuming (when they thought about it at all) that minstrelsy's scurrilous representations of black people were scrupulously authentic. "Their gibes, their gambols, their songs, their flashes of merriment," wrote one such historian, "still linger in our eyes and in our ears; and before many readers scores of quaint figures with blackened faces will no doubt dance to half-forgotten tunes all over these pages" (Hutton 144). The nostalgia of this view is ultimately for a simpler, pre-emancipation America: "That such [distinguished men] should have appeared at a leading theatre, between the acts, in plantation dress and blackened face, shows perhaps better than anything else the respectable position held by the negro minstrel half a century ago" (Hutton 140). By 1915 Brander Matthews of Columbia University was sadly detailing minstrelsy's decline, which he attributed to the fact that blackface performers were less and less true to life, increasingly "content to be comic without any effort to catch the special comicality of the darky" (758). This emphasis—deriving just as much as Twain's from the idea of blackface as a people's culture—is racist either by default or design, and it has infected its share of modern theater historians. The important point about this tendency is not only that it deserves censure but that it, no less than others, stands for the historical existence of a certain kind of audience response.

It was thus critical that a revisionist corrective, denouncing minstrelsy's patent inauthenticity, its northern white origins, its self-evidently dominative character, should have come to displace the more complacent views.[35] This critique, inaugurated by Frederick Douglass, later sustained treatments of the minstrel stage in novels such as Paul Laurence Dunbar's *Sport of the Gods* (1901) and Wallace Thurman's *The Blacker the Berry* (1929); both fictionalize black stage performances derived from the minstrel tradition to represent some version of racial false consciousness—in Dunbar the facile, corrupted world of northern urban Negroes, in Thurman an indulgence by color-conscious blacks of racial caricature. In certain ways, however, this position is least satisfactory as historical and cultural analysis when it works best as antiracist politics. This is not to urge a position that, somehow avoiding politics, might get the emphases right for once. On the contrary, the minstrel tradition is still too present for us to take antiracist critiques of it for granted. Rather, we must better historicize the minstrel show, for in fact we remain ignorant of exactly what its antebellum political range happened to be. It strikes me as tautological to catalogue racist stereotypes from a time when slavery existed in fifteen states. In their indispensable focus on minstrelsy's oppressive dimension, revisionist accounts leave perfectly intact the cultural dualism—wholly authentic or wholly hegemonic?—that I want to complicate. Outmoded antiracist strategies of reversal and inversion, of simply turning the polarities of racist discourse around, must give way to a wider recognition of the complexities of white subject formation and subjectivity, and of the multiple determinations that make race such a complex lived social reality.[36]

Among these determinations number primarily social class and the sex/gender system. One might return briefly here to *Huckleberry Finn.* Pap's notorious rant about a "free nigger . . . from Ohio" who, in his wealth, his knowledge of languages, and his right to vote, threatens the status of Pap's own working-class whiteness instances one way in which class overdetermines if not overrules race in my account.[37] Conversely, Twain's sly construction of this scene so that Pap, covered with mud after a drunken night in the gutter, is actually blacker than the hated "mulatter" free man suggests the underlying "racial" equations between black and working-class white men that occasionally called forth in the minstrel show interracial recognitions and identifications no less than the imperative to disavow them. And the fact that Twain's fantasy of racial harmony, of Jim and the adolescent Huck, could occur only by excluding conventional manhood altogether reminds us here of the gender dynamic through which the intersections of race and class, in the minstrel show as elsewhere, were lived. When one notes as well that those who "blacked up" and those who witnessed minstrel shows were often working-class *Irish* men, the complex picture of the blackface institution and its audiences is complete. Minstrelsy's role as a mediator of northern class, racial, and ethnic conflict—all largely grounded in a problematic of masculinity—has much to do with the equivocal character of blackface representations. This conflict can be seen to underlie the minstrel show's most politically productive and politically regressive moments. That moments of each kind occurred has not yet been adequately accounted for.

Certain nineteenth-century revisionists were, however, aware of this complexity. James Monroe Trotter, for example, though cognizant of what he called the "often malicious caricaturing" of the race to which he belonged, posed the "fine *musical* achievements" of the black Georgia Minstrels against "severe and somewhat sweeping" denunciations by other critics.[38] This, too, at the most virulently racist moment (the late nineteenth century) in the history of black representation. The most careful assessment of this kind, however, was also the earliest. As I began with one of Frederick Douglass's disdainful comments from the *North Star*, so I will end with his 1849 article on a short-lived black minstrel troupe, Gavitt's Original Ethiopian Serenaders. I believe he has the clearest sense of any contemporary as to what was at stake in early minstrelsy—its limitations, possibilities, and ultimate importance—and has therefore guided my own interpretations. Douglass begins:

> Partly from a love of music, and partly from curiosity to see persons of color exaggerating the peculiarities of their race, we were induced last evening to hear these Serenaders [in Rochester, New York]. The Company is said to be composed entirely of colored people; and it may be so. We observed, however, that they, too had recourse to the burnt cork and lamp black, the better to express their characters, and to produce uniformity of complexion. (141)

Conscious or not, there is a doubleness in that word "characters" (inner self? dramatic role?) which begins to capture Douglass's insight into blackface performance: that "blackness" is a matter of display or theater, as Melville would dramatize in "Benito Cereno" (1855).[39] It is reiterated in his charge that the Gavitts' singing was "not even a tolerable representation of the character of colored people"; indeed, Douglass signifies, "their attempts at it showed them to possess a plentiful lack of it" (141). "Blackness," then, is not innate but produced, a cultural construction. Douglass inverts the racist logic of minstrelsy and locates its actual function of staging racial categories, boundaries, and types even when these possessed little that a black man could recognize as "authentic." That is to say, Douglass also clarifies the way the blackface convention *disguised* "blackness," marking this black troupe's race first as hearsay ("said to be"), and then as latent possibility ("it may be").[40] But this disguise did not close down the political play of blackface; in a culture where "blackness" was construct and exhibition, blackface kept it on display and up for grabs, politically speaking. Although Douglass does not extend his argument to white performers, he does concede that the production of "blackness" remains a potential source of political advantage:

> We are not sure that our readers will approve of our mention of those persons, so strong must be their dislike of everything that seems to feed the flame of American prejudice against colored people; and in this they might be right; but we think otherwise. It is something gained, when the colored man in any form can appear before a white audience; and we think that even this company, with industry, application, and a proper cultivation of their taste, may yet be instrumental in removing the prejudice against our race. (142)

Douglass defined blackface minstrelsy, a few months before the 1850 Compromise debates, as a site of political struggle for representation, debased and suspect though it may have been. "Blackness" in the minstrel show indeed generated a conflictual intensity, occasionally unsettling the notion to its roots—as the complexities in the foregoing traditions of response suggest. We might have expected nothing less than conflicted messages from such a cultural mediator, despite the fact that minstrelsy attempted precisely to mute conflict. The story that follows is one of dissension as much as domination, although we will need to specify its outlines, uncover the codes that clashed.

Writing on minstrelsy has failed to move very much beyond the debate over people's culture versus cultural domination. But as my genealogy and close examinations of Mark Twain and Frederick Douglass reveal, this dualism, like that of class expression versus social control, may be a fabrication. Already encoded in these antinomies are the political conflicts and cultural contradictions early minstrelsy was devised to repress. Modern writing on the minstrel show turns out to have been an unwitting accomplice in this repression. By foregrounding the minstrel show's position as one new working-class entertainment industry in the embattled formation of northeastern American capitalist culture, a racially loaded form situated in the most politically explosive moment of the nineteenth century, I hope to show the shifting contours of this racial counterfeit, as well as its currency.

Notes

1. Each of these positions is of course underwritten by an intellectual tradition as old as "mass" culture itself. The view of capitalist popular culture as a "culture industry" that systematically cretinizes and depoliticizes an ever more passive populace is best articulated in the writings of the Frankfurt School; its classic expression is Theodor Adorno and Max Horkheimer, "The Culture Industry." The populist view of mass culture as a less mediated phenomenon of "the people" is perhaps most forcefully argued by Leslie Fiedler in *What Was Literature?*

2. My theoretical framework is indebted to Stuart Hall, "Notes on Deconstructing 'the Popular'"; Michael Denning, *Mechanic Accents*; and T. J. Clark, *The Painting of Modern Life* 205–39. More generally these formulations, and many that follow, are drawn from work on culture industry phenomena by scholars associated with the Birmingham Centre for Contemporary Cultural Studies, including Richard Hoggart, *The Uses of Literacy*; Stuart Hall et al., *Policing the Crisis*; Richard Johnson, "What is Cultural Studies Anyway?"; Paul Gilroy, "*There Ain't No Black in the Union Jack*"; and Dick Hebdige, *Hiding in the Light.* Like-minded work in the United States includes Fredric Jameson, "Reification and Utopia in Mass Culture"; Jean Franco, "What's in a Name?"; Tania Modleski, *Feminism Without Women;* and Hazel Carby, *Reconstructing Womanhood.* The pervasive influence of the work of Steven Marcus should also be acknowledged here, especially his pioneering effort in *The Other Victorians* to make cultural sense of dubious text.

3. As does this minstrel conundrum: "Why are minstrel companies like midnight robbers? Because they live by their deeds of darkness" (*White's New Book* 31).

4. "Cuff"—a kind of common-denominator figure of nineteenth-century white fantasy about black people—shows up again in Harriet Beecher Stowe's "Parson's Horse Race" (1878), in which cultural appropriation is revealed to be a one-way street: "Cuff was the doctor's nigger man, and he was nat'lly a drefful proud critter! The way he would swell and strut and brag about the doctor and his folks and his things! The doctor used to give Cuff his cast-off clothes, and Cuff would prance round in 'em and seem to think he was a doctor of divinity himself, and had the charge of all natur" (472). Obviously this scene is insufficiently ironized—precisely *because* cultural appropriation is a one-way street; black borrowings from the dominant culture, according to whites, result by definition in absurdity. The scene affords a rather bleak, though probably unconscious, commentary on Reconstruction from the author of *Uncle Tom's Cabin.*

5. Mrs. Anne Mathews, *A Continuation of the Memoirs of Charles Mathews, Comedian* 1:239.

6. Carl Wittke, *Tambo and Bones* 75; *New York Herald* January 1, 1848.

7. Among these are Al Field, *Watch Yourself Go By* 113, and "Reminiscences" (I am indebted to Robert Toll, *Blacking Up* 38, for these references). See also P. T. Barnum's *Struggles and Triumphs* (1869), in which a backstage alterca-

tion arises because the young Barnum in blackface is mistaken for an impudent black man (90).

8. Mark Twain, *Autobiography* 62, 60.

9. On the purposes and value of the genealogy, see Michel Foucault, "Nietzsche, Genealogy, History." Concerted attempts to narrate a minstrel-show "ancestry" include Olive Logan, "The Ancestry of Brudder Bones"; Brander Matthews, "Rise and Fall of Negro Minstrelsy"; and George Rehin, "Harlequin Jim Crow." These attempts are mistaken because, while illuminating—I have called on them to produce my genealogy—they finally make no room for historical discontinuity in the wearing of blackface, positing a kind of linear development; and they tend to underplay the central racial dimension—even, in the case of Rehin, to argue its only secondary importance.

10. There is a second, subsidiary purpose to this genealogy, which Cornel West has clarified in a position paper regarding the study of race in Marxist cultural studies. That is briefly to elucidate some specific American resonances of the various western white-supremacist discursive logics: Judeo-Christian (blackness as divine curse), scientific (blackness as anthropological object), and psychosexual (blackness as vengeful father, carefree child, dirt, excrement). See West, "Marxist Theory and the Specificity of Afro-American Oppression" 22–24; see also, in this regard, Joel Kovel, *White Racism.*

In my genealogy I have purposely tried not to privilege literary representations of black people, to respect the relative autonomy of broadly "theatrical" ones. Literary representations, in any case, largely reiterate the contradictions and problems I note in this discussion. For analyses of such literary representations, see Francis Gaines, *The Southern Plantation*; Sterling Brown, *The Negro in American Fiction*; Jean Fagan Yellin, *The Intricate Knot*; William Van Deburg, *Slavery and Race in American Popular Culture* 31–39; and, more generally, William Taylor, *Cavalier and Yankee.* As for artistic representations, see Albert Boime, *The Art of Exclusion*, and Sue Bridwell Beckham, "By 'N' By Hard Times."

11. Harlequin, for instance, was a rustic with a strong dialect, whose role, according to Marmontel, was "that of a patient servant, loyal, credulous, greedy, always amorous, always getting his master or himself into a scrape" (quoted in Nicoll 73–74): a description very close to those of some minstrel types. Indeed, in certain late eighteenth-century theatrical productions a slave is turned into a harlequin by a wizard, and after marrying his master's daughter lives happily ever after (Gates, *Figures* 52). Both the outrage and the amusement of such activities were to be found in the minstrel show. (Pantomime and minstrelsy, Harlequin and Jim Crow, were literally conjoined at New York's Kemp's Lyceum in 1848. George Odell, *Annals of the New York Stage* 5:494).

For slave tricksters, see Lawrence Levine, *Black Culture and Black Consciousness* 102–33. For earlier blackface figures on the stage, see Charles Baskervill, *The Elizabethan Jig* 286–88; Pierre Duchartre, *The Italian Comedy* 124, 135; David Mayer, *Harlequin in His Element* 44; Allardyce Nicoll, *The World of Harlequin* 73–74; Henry Louis Gates, *Figures in Black* 51–53; and George Rehin, "Harlequin Jim Crow."

12. George Rehin, "Harlequin Jim Crow" 687. In *Figures in Black* Henry Louis Gates argues that in minstrel representations the black and white mask of the Harlequin is split into the black "Tambo" and the white "Bones" (52). While some interesting observations follow from this idea, it strikes me as mostly

fanciful. It is even unclear whether the interlocutor of the early minstrel show appeared in whiteface; and I know of no accounts of the endmen which indicate that one was white and the other black.

13. S. Foster Damon, *Series of Old American Songs* no. 16.

14. Huggins suggestively but rather too hastily assimilates all early minstrel figures to those of Mike Fink, Davy Crockett, and (their northern counterpart) Yankee Doodle (*Harlem Renaissance* 249). That there was significant overlap is uncontroversial, as John Blair makes clear in "Blackface Minstrels in Cross-Cultural Perspective" 55. But this overlap neither accounts for the varied cultural effects such figures could produce nor for the songs that do not feature such types. Robert Cantwell somewhat overingeniously argues that minstrel performers who called on such types were involved in a multilayered act of *self*-parody—that minstrel types resembled Fink and Crockett because they parodied black styles that originated in parody of white men (*Bluegrass Breakdown* 261).

15. In *Black Literature in White America* Berndt Ostendorf talks about the minstrel show as a kind of compromise formation between the poles of "intermixture and insurrection" (69).

Nathan Huggins and Sylvia Wynter have produced psychosexual arguments that extend Ellison's critique in interesting ways. Huggins reads minstrel figures as projections of all that the dominant culture deemed undesirable (albeit fascinating) (244–301); Wynter gives them a Lacanian gloss, seeing in the qualities attributed to the (b)lack the inverse of what the dominant culture considered human ("Sambos and Minstrels"). For this line of thinking in regard to the long *durée* of western colonialism and slavery, see Frantz Fanon, *Black Skin, White Masks* 141–209, and George Rawick, *From Sundown to Sunup* 128–33.

16. Damon, *Series of Old American Songs* no. 14.

17. In "Mirror Stages" Barbara Johnson remarks that if the (Lacanian) phallus is almost by definition white, the penis must be black—which accounts for its unruly and threatening potential. I am grateful to Michael Rogin for a similar point in regard to my project. In *Black Skin, White Masks*, Frantz Fanon remarks that in the white imagination, "the Negro . . . *is* a penis" (170; emphasis in original).

18. In *Vested Interests* Garber pursues this thesis rather singlemindedly; see also Natalie Zemon Davis, *Society and Culture in Early Modern France* 132.

19. As Carroll Smith-Rosenberg has demonstrated in "Davy Crockett as Trickster," another would surely be the various 1830s and 1840s Crockett almanacs, revealing compendiums of misogynist and male homosexual fantasy. "Wench" characters were cut from the same cloth.

20. *Christy and Wood's New Song Book* 85–86.

21. See Claudia Johnson, "That Guilty Third Tier" for a discussion of antebellum theater prostitution; see also Patricia Cline Cohen, "Unregulated Youth."

22. Susan Davis, "'Making Night Hideous'" 187–92 and *Parades and Power* 77–111, esp. 106. I have also learned much from Dale Cockrell, "The Early Blackface Minstrel and His World."

23. Davis, "'Making Night Hideous'" 192; see also Paul Gilje, *The Road to Mobocracy* 258–60.

24. Alexander Saxton introduces the useful phrase "white egalitarianism" to describe the adherence of the popular classes in this period to both white supremacy and democratic (class) ideals. See *The Rise and Fall of the White Republic* 221. This is Saxton's version of what Pierre van der Berghe has termed

"herrenvolk democracy." On van der Berghe, see George Fredrickson, *The Black Image in the White Mind* 65, 84, 90–94.

25. For an argument about race in which this is an ever-present possibility, see Stuart Hall, "New Ethnicities" 28–29.

26. This song on the Kensington nativist riot of 1844 *might* be considered a tenuous vindication of minstrelsy in regard to Jacksonian rioting:

> Oh, in Philadelphia folks say how,
> Dat Darkies kick up all de rows,
> But de *riot* up in *Skensin'ton*
> Beats all de darkies twelve to one.
>
> An' I guess it wasn't de niggas dis time.
> I guess it wasn't de niggas dis time,
> I guess it wasn't de niggas dis time, Mr. Mayor,
> I guess it wasn't de niggas dis time.
>
> ("Philadelphia Riots," Dennison 134)

In any case, this song is ambiguous in precisely the ways I have been outlining.

27. This tradition includes Margaret Fuller, "Entertainments of the Past Winter"; "Letter from a Teacher at the South"; "The Black Opera"; "Negro Minstrelsy—Ancient and Modern"; "Songs of the Blacks"; W. E. B. Du Bois, "The Negro in Literature and Art"; Francis Gaines, *The Southern Plantation* 95–111; James Weldon Johnson, *Black Manhattan* 87; Constance Rourke, *American Humor* 77–104; S. Foster Damon, "The Negro in Early American Songsters"; Stanley Edgar Hyman, "American Negro Literature and Folk Tradition"; Hans Nathan, *Dan Emmett*; George Rehin, "The Darker Image"; Orrin Clayton Suthern, "Minstrelsy and Popular Culture"; William Austin, *"Susanna," "Jeanie," and "The Old Folks at Home"*; David Grimsted and William Stowe, "White-Black Humor"; Robert Winans, "The Folk, the Stage, and the Five-String Banjo"; Berndt Ostendorf, *Black Literature in White America* 65–94; Robert Cantwell, *Bluegrass Breakdown* 249–74; William Mahar, "Black English in Early Blackface Minstrelsy" and "'Backside Albany' and Early Blackface Minstrelsy"; W. T. Lhamon, "Constance Rourke's Secret Reserve"; and Carl Bryan Holmberg and Gilbert Schneider, "Daniel Decatur Emmett's Stump Sermons."

28. Ralph Ellison, "Change the Joke" 50. In "Twain's 'Nigger' Jim" Bernard Bell marshalls much evidence of Mark Twain's "socialization in the ethics of Jim Crow": his love of minstrelsy, his brief enlistment in a Confederate militia, the racism of some early (private and published) letters, his apprenticeship in the racism of southwestern humor, and internal evidence from *Huck Finn* itself, obviously the underside of Clemens's complex investment in black culture.

29. See also Fredrick Woodard and Donnarae MacCann's "*Huckleberry Finn* and the Traditions of Blackface Minstrelsy." As they point out, the unfinished "Tom Sawyer's Conspiracy" includes a scene in which Tom goes to his aunt's garret to find "our old nigger-show things" and plan a "nigger" disguise (11–13, n.4). Mark Twain's imaginative encounters with race seem to have been unavoidably bound up with blackface minstrelsy. Soon after leaving Hannibal for New York in 1853, Twain wrote his mother about free blacks in the North: "I reckon I had better black my face, for in these Eastern States niggers are considerably better than white people" (quoted in Bell 11).

30. Guy Cardwell, *Twins of Genius* 105. I have benefited from Steven Mail-

loux's discussion of this issue in *Rhetorical Power* 57–99 and from Forrest Robinson, *In Bad Faith* 111–211.

31. Quoted in Fredrickson, *The Black Image in the White Mind* 102. This is the contradictory "other half" of the image of the potent and frightening black male. These two images, as John Blassingame observes, existed together in a kind of dialectical relationship, the one assuaging fears that the other raised. Both images certainly haunted the minstrel show. See *The Slave Community* 223–38, and, more generally, Fredrickson, *Black Image* 43–129.

32. Quoted in Fredrickson, *Black Image* 107.

33. Delany quoted in Wilson Moses, *The Golden Age of Black Nationalism* 46; Douglass quoted in Waldo Martin, *The Mind of Frederick Douglass* 235–36.

34. This tradition includes R. P. Nevin, "Stephen C. Foster and Negro Minstrelsy"; T. A. Brown, "The Origin of Negro Minstrelsy"; H. D. Stone, *Personal Recollections of the Drama* 240–41; Olive Logan, "The Ancestry of Brudder Bones"; N. M. Ludlow, *Dramatic Life as I Found It* 392–93; H. P. Phelps, *Players of a Century* 165–67; Brander Matthews, "The Rise and Fall of Negro Minstrelsy"; J. G. Burtnett, "National Elements in Stephen Foster's Art"; Dailey Paskman and Sigmund Spaeth, "*Gentlemen, Be Seated!*"; and Carl Wittke, *Tambo and Bones.*

35. This revived tradition includes M. H. Winter, "Juba and American Minstrelsy"; Bernard Wolfe, "Uncle Remus and the Malevolent Rabbit"; Frank Davidson, "The Rise, Development, Decline, and Influence of the American Minstrel Show"; Ralph Ellison, "Change the Joke and Slip the Yoke"; Kenneth Lynn, *Mark Twain and Southwestern Humor* 100–111; Cecil Patterson, "A Different Drum"; LeRoi Jones, *Blues People* 82–86; James Dorman, "The Strange Career of Jim Crow Rice" and "Shaping the Popular Image of Post-Reconstruction American Blacks"; Alan Green, "'Jim Crow,' 'Zip Coon'"; Russell Nye, *The Unembarrassed Muse* 162–69, 308–15; Nathan Huggins, *Harlem Renaissance* 244–301; Robert Toll, *Blacking Up;* Alexander Saxton, "Blackface Minstrelsy and Jacksonian Ideology"; Charles Hamm, *Yesterdays* 109–40; Sylvia Wynter, "Sambos and Minstrels"; Sam Dennison, *Scandalize My Name* 27–186; Jean Baker, *Affairs of Party* 213–43; William Van Deburg, *Slavery and Race in American Popular Culture* 17–24, 39–49; Joseph Boskin, *Sambo* 65–94; Robert Dawidoff, "Some of Those Days"; Houston Baker, *Modernism and the Harlem Renaissance* 17–24; David Roediger, *The Wages of Whiteness* 95–131; Jan Pieterse, *White On Black* 132–56; and Roger Abrahams, *Singing the Master* 131–53.

36. Stuart Hall, "New Ethnicities" 28–29.

37. Mark Twain, *Huckleberry Finn* 26. Indeed, in *Chants Democratic* Sean Wilentz argues that "the real object of scorn in these shows was less Jim Crow than the arriviste, would-be aristo—either the white interlocutor or the dandified black, both parodies of unmerited self-satisfied condescension" (259). Wilentz names the right targets, but I would insist with David Roediger that class meanings were always imbricated with working-class racial feeling ("Labor" 294; *Wages* 123)—though not, to be sure, in simple or politically guaranteed ways, as I argue throughout.

38. James Monroe Trotter, *Music and Some Highly Musical People* 271, 274. For more on the Georgia Minstrels, see Richard Waterhouse, *From Minstrel Shows to Vaudeville* 47–80.

39. Douglass was acutely aware of this problem. On tour in England in 1846, he found himself relentlessly exoticized—minstrelized. As he wrote to an abolitionist friend: "It is quite an advantage to be a nigger here. I find I am hardly black enough for British taste, but by keeping my hair as wooly as possible I make out to pass for at least half Negro at any rate" (quoted in Martin 116). Douglass's wicked irony depends on the fact that he was, precisely, "half Negro"—born of a black mother and a white father.

40. In *Incidents in the Life of a Slave Girl* Harriet Jacobs's escape to the shed where she would spend seven years is made in a blackface disguise; even "the father of [her] children" does not recognize her (437).

EARLY MINSTRELSY

The Performance of the Virginia Minstrels

Hans Nathan

The four Virginia Minstrels sat on the stage in a semicircle, partly turned to the audience, partly to each other to ensure rhythmic coordination. In the center were Emmett with his fiddle and Whitlock with his banjo, flanked by Pelham pounding his tambourine and Brower who furiously rattled the bones.

Their ill-assorted garments, their oddly shaped hats, and their gaudy pants and shirts were in the traditional style of the stage plantation Negro. But the effect of their costuming was heightened by almost frightening countenances which were distinguished by wide-open mouths, bulging lips, and eyes that shone like full moons. When the minstrels addressed themselves on their playbill "To the most sensitive and fastidious beholder" with the promise to be "chaste and elegant," they may have been sincere in their intentions, but they modestly understated their case. For in their efforts to be both laughable and characteristically Negrolike, they went much further than other minstrels before them. Composure indeed was not a part of their temperament; they were boisterous to the point of grotesqueness. When they could force themselves to remain seated, they would stretch out their legs toward their audience in rowdy fashion and bend their feet and their toes at the sharpest possible angles.[1] They would bob up and down and sway to and fro, sputtering uncouth sayings, shouts, and hoarse laughter. The endmen, Pelham on the left and Brower on the right, were the most unruly of the lot, while the banjoist and fiddler indulged in as many contortions as the handling of their instruments allowed. Pelham exhibited "looks and movements comic beyond conception. He seemed animated by a savage energy; and [the handling of his instrument] . . . nearly wrung him off his

From *Dan Emmett and the Rise of Early Negro Minstrelsy,* by Hans Nathan. Copyright ©1962 by the University of Oklahoma Press.

seat. His white eyes rolled in a curious frenzy . . . and his hiccupping chuckles were unsurpassable."[2] When Brower "trucked" around a bit, the clicks of his bones would mingle with the heavy thud of his boots. He and Pelham sometimes burst into breakdowns, usually without ceasing to keep their instruments in motion.

Emmett performed like a real country fiddler; he held his instrument in front of his chest and drew his bow across the strings as if it were an unwieldy pole. Like a hot bass player of our time, Whitlock played his banjo with complete abandon, roughly striking the strings with the nail of his forefinger.[3] His banjo was of the type customary in the thirties and early forties; it had an extremely long thin neck and only four strings (though a fifth appears to have been soon added).[4] Pelham not only jingled his tambourine but pounced on it vehemently as if it were a drum. The bones, which may have measured ten inches or more, were shaken with a loose wrist and, for greater virtuosity, the entire arm.

In order to give the impression of genuine plantation music, the minstrels asserted on their playbills that their "instruments were manufactured by themselves,"[5] which as far as the bones were concerned was undoubtedly true. Moreover, they lent their instruments such picturesque names as "Tuckahoe Violin," "Congo Banjo," and "Cohea Tambourine." "Tuckahoe" and "Cohea" (or rather "Cohee") do not have a direct connection with the Negro; they were, in the early nineteenth century, rural nicknames of the inhabitants of Virginia, the first of those living east of the Blue Ridge, the second of those living west of it. However, if "Tucka" is identical with "Tuckey," it was a Negro name in Jamaica.[6] The word "Congo" was part of a name of a white frontier dance of 1800—a "Congo minuet," which was also observed, as early as the 1780s, at balls given on Haitian plantations.[7]

Although the style of the Virginia Minstrels has not been preserved by tradition, one nevertheless can venture a few guesses concerning its actual sound. The bones produced single clicks as well as "trills" or shakes of short or long duration. Their crispness was varied by dynamic shadings ranging from pianissimo to fortissimo. It was the precision of the clicks which lent articulation to the ensemble.[8] In the main, the bone player followed the meter, but like the banjoist and fiddler, he may have occasionally disturbed it by entering on ordinarily unaccented beats. The tambourine part was similar except that its sound was less clearly defined because of the jingles which prolonged each thump. There were no chords in the ensemble because the banjoist played only a melody; this is evident from banjo methods of the fifties which also described an older practice.[9] They show in addition that the banjoist liked to vary the main melody by inserting into it the open tones of his two highest strings. This insertion was frequent after the fifth, the "thumb-string," had been added to the banjo around the middle of the forties, but it may have also occurred earlier. Motion was intensified by omitting tones on accented beats, creating a type of syncopation which existed in print already in the early forties. In some early ensembles other than the Virginia Minstrels, the banjoist, too, tapped out the regular beats of the music with his foot; differing from his solo acts, he used his sole instead of his heel.[10] The fiddler may have played the tune straighter than the banjoist, though with occasional variants including dotted notes and syncopations, and with open strings as drones, as is still the custom in the backwoods.[11] All four minstrels of course played by ear.

The volume of the minstrel band was quite lean, yet anything but delicate. The tones of the banjo died away quickly and therefore could not serve as a solid foundation in the ensemble. On top was the squeaky, carelessly tuned fiddle. Add the dry "ra, raka, taka, tak" of the bones[12] and the tambourine's dull thumps and ceaseless jingling to the twang of the banjo and the flat tone of the fiddle, and the sound of the band is approximated: it was scratchy, tinkling, cackling, and humorously incongruous.

The Virginians often sang and played at the same time. A soloist took the first part of the song while the others joined him in the second, the refrain, singing in one voice, which was considerably closer to the plantation manner than the four-part glee style of other minstrel bands.[13] Occasionally, fewer than four musicians accompanied the songs. For example, in Emmett's "I'm Gwine Ober De Mountains," only the bones and the banjo were heard in the interludes.

It is likely that the intonation of minstrels was not the conventional one. In imitating the Negro's manner and speech, they must have also imitated his way of singing which was characterized not only by a specific timbre but, as it still is, by pitches outside our tonal system, "slides from one note to another, and turns and cadences not in articulated notes."[14] Features like these hardly ever appeared in printed editions of minstrel songs. Emmett's "Dar He Goes! Dats Him!" is an exception: the ambiguous pitch of two tones of its melody is here implied (following the example of printed banjo pieces) by the use of two adjacent tones, the first "sliding" from below into the second.

Fully aware of the uniqueness of their musical acts, the Virginia Minstrels always called attention on their playbills to their "concert" or "exclusively musical entertainment," "Ethiopian" or "African."

When they presented a minstrel show, performing all by themselves as they did a few times in Boston, they divided the evening into two parts. The first opened with an instrumental piece and often concluded with a stump speech. In both parts, songs with instrumental background alternated with banjo solo songs. All of their scenes were interspersed and linked with droll conversation in Negro dialect, remarks, shouts, acting, and dancing. There was no fixed "interlocutor" yet, and the repartee was not restricted to him and the "end men," as was customary in later minstrel shows. All four minstrels did the talking spontaneously, "asking and answering quaint questions and conundrums in turn," though it seems that Brower and Pelham were more boisterous and active than the others.[15]

In the tradition of the English stage, the songs themselves were interrupted by dialogue, usually before the refrain. No such dialogue of the Virginia Minstrels is preserved, but we can gain an idea of its style from a scene which Emmett and Brower performed about 1846. Its text, if taken literally, amounts to no more than foolish babbling in the manner of circus clowns, but it was a mere outline for improvisation on the spot. Also its dialect must have been more genuine, for it is known that Negro minstrels "made a study of Negro dialect a specialty. . . . As a result, no two adopted the same type of darkey for a study. . . . The Kentuckian differed as much from [the] Virginian, as the South Carolinian did from the Alabamian, or the 'field hand' from the genteel house servant."[16] The song around which Emmett and Brower built their scene was "Lucy Long," which had been a favorite of their Boston audiences.[17] Here is a part of the scene; after the odd beauty of Miss Lucy Long had been commented on, Emmett reported his amorous adventures while singing:

> Pray turkey buzzard lend to me your wing
> Till I fly over de river to see Miss Sally King.
> When I got over de river, Miss Sally she was gone.
> If I had known she'd sarved me so, I stop wid Lucy Long.

[Dialogue.]
FRANK She had a ticklar gagement to go to camp me[e]tin wid dis child.
DAN hah! You went down to de fish Market to daunce arter eels. mity cureous kind ob camp meetin dat!
FRANK I[t] wasnt eels, it was a big cat fish.
DAN What chune did you dance?

Chorus [both singing].

> Take your time Miss Lucy
> Take your time Miss Lucy Long
> Rock de cradle Lucy
> Take your time my dear.

[Dialogue.]
FRANK I trade her off for bean soup.
DAN Well, you is hungryest nigger eber I saw. You'r neber satisfied widout your tinken bout bean soup all de time.

Chorus [both singing].[18]

In Boston "Lucy Long" had been enacted with a different text which appeared in a sheet music edition and in a slender booklet, *Songs of the Virginia Minstrels,* both published by C. H. Keith (Boston, 1843), under the heading "Miss Lucy Long and Her Answer." The song consisted of four stanzas for Lucy's bridegroom and four for herself in which she denied to know "de gemman Dat wrote dat little song, Who dare to make so public De name ob Lucy Long" and expressed her preference for "De 'stinguished Jimmy Crow." Here was what was called a "wench performance"—an impersonation of a colored lady by a male minstrel—although it seems to have been done by the Virginians without the appropriate costume. The earliest impersonators of Lucy Long, doubtless in skirts and pantalettes, are supposed to have been George Christy and Dan Gardner.[19] In another lively scene, the "Boatman's Dance," the minstrels impersonated "the negro boatmen on the Ohio River."[20] Assuming that their representation of the crude voices and insolent manner of these boatmen was totally realistic, they must have gone to the limit of what was permissible on a public stage. An observer in the twenties and thirties remembered having heard Ohio boatmen sing:

> Dance, boatmen, dance
> Dance, dance away
> Dance all night till broad day light
> And go home with the gals in the morning.[21]

These words are almost identical with the refrain of the sheet music edition of the song which Emmett published in 1843; the tune was possibly similar in both cases.

"Virginia Breakdowns," mainly performed by the endmen Pelham and Brower, were not only accompanied by music but spiced with brief, pungent interjections. Among these "sayings"—preserved in Emmett's handwriting, though neither signed nor dated—the following may have been used:

Dats de heel what neber told a lie.

Dars musick in dem ole heels.

Dat deaph to creepin insects.

Dem ole legs is hung on a swibbel.

Wade in Moses.

De nigger gins to sweat to perfection.

O gosh, I kick like an ole warginny hoss wid four shoes on one foot.[22]

Not the least attractive part of the minstrels' performance were comical stump speeches in Negro dialect. Brower's "Definition of the Bankrupt Laws" was a burlesque of a timely financial topic, whereas Pelham's "A brief Battering at the Blues" may have been nothing but a nonsensical, merrymaking speech. Whitlock's "Locomotive Lecture" was probably full of pseudoscientific explanations of the steam engine, the wonder of the age. It was customary in this kind of oratory to ridicule, by means of highfalutin expressions and malapropisms, the attempts of the Negro to imitate the language of their educated white masters.

Conundrums, no doubt identical with what the Virginians called "explanations," were delivered with infectious comicality, though alone they were nothing but trite puns. Evidently this type of humor came from the circus; it was far removed from the humor of the real Negro and the backwoodsman.[23]

Dan Emmett played a prominent part in the ensemble of the Virginia Minstrels. He, in fact, was called their "leader."[24] He wrote many of their lyrics, composed some of their tunes, and even appeared as a solo singer accompanying himself on the banjo. Since Whitlock was a virtuoso on this instrument, Emmett must have been very skillful to hold his own. One of his favorite songs was "The Fine Old Colored Gentleman," originally an English tune to which he had adapted his own text. It was the story of the Tennessee Negro Sambo—in type a backwoodsman—who was distinguished by his enormous height ("'leven feet"), by his banjo playing, by his singing ("He sung so long and sung so loud, he scared the pigs and goats"), by his jumping, racing, and hopping, and finally by his swallowing of "two small railroads wid a spoonful of ice cream . . . and a locomotive bulgine while dey blowin off de steam." When he died in the end, it was "for want of breath."

The Virginia Minstrels became famous overnight. In fact, their name became a symbol of high standards in minstrelsy. Without compunction it was borrowed not only by other minstrel bands but by publishers as well, who realized that their song sheets would recommend themselves to the public with the remark on their cover: "sung by the Virginia Minstrels."

Notes

1. How realistic the appearance of the Virginia Minstrels was can be seen by comparing them to a Negro banjoist as "drawn from life" in *Sketches and Eccentricities*, 38: "He was seated in a corner upon a stool, holding his instrument. . . . His forehead was low and narrow; his eyes red and sunken; his nose . . . protuberant at the sides; his lips as if in scorn at each other. His teeth were . . .

set in at an obtuse angle, which caused them to jut out; and his lower jaw seemed to have a great antipathy to the upper, and when idle, always kept as far off as possible. . . . His leg was placed so nearly in the middle of his foot that, with toes at each end, no one could have tracked him; and the hollow of his feet projected so far outward that it gave them somewhat the appearance of rockers to a chair."

2. An English review in a pamphlet on the Ethiopian Serenaders (1846; Harvard Theatre Collection). Although the quotation refers to the peculiarities of Pelham's performance as a bone player, it may not be amiss to apply it to his tambourine playing as well.

3. That this was the genuine Negro style becomes clear from a description of a colored banjoist in Kemble, *Journal,* 97: "[he] seemed . . . to thump his instrument with every part of his body at once. . . ." The technical details are explained in Thomas F. Briggs, *Briggs' Banjo Instructor* (Boston, 1855), and in *Buckley's Guide for the Banjo* (Boston, 1868).

4. On the cover of sheet editions of minstrel music up to about 1844, the banjo is drawn with four strings. See "De Ole Jaw Bone" (Boston, 1840), and "Lucy Neal" (Boston, 1844). However, the instrument already has five strings on the covers of Emmett's London song series (*c.* 1844). "Good Bye Sally Dear" (Boston, *Songs of the Ethiopian Serenaders*, 1849), shows five strings, Gumbo Chaff (Elias Howe), *The Complete Preceptor for the Banjo* (Boston, 1851), gives the tuning as follows: F-e′-e′-g′-e″ (sounding an octave lower).

5. Playbills of the Olympic Circus (New York, February 24, 1843, and Worcester, March 20–21, 1843).

6. In *A Dictionary of American English*: see "cohee" and "tuckahoe." "Tuckey" is the name of a slave on a sugar plantation in Jamaica in the English opera *Obi*, or *Three-Fingered Jack*. Names of such realistic characters were usually not invented.

7. Cheney, *Travels of John Davis*, 149–50, and Lillian Moore, "Moreau de Saint-Mery and 'Danse,'" *Dance Index* (October, 1946). In Haiti this dance was called "Minuet Congo."

8. The pamphlet on the Ethiopian Serenaders: "He can put as many notes as you like into a bar, and indicate every variety of emphasis between the entremest point of piano and forte, without losing the crispness and distinctness of the click. . . ."

9. *Rice's Correct Method.*

10. See the cover of *Songs of the Virginia Serenaders* (Boston, 1844) and the cover of *Songs of the Nightingale Serenaders* (Philadelphia, 1846).

11. Samuel P. Bayard, "Introduction," *Hill Country Tunes* (Philadelphia, 1944), p. xv. John A. and Alan Lomax, *Our Singing Country* (New York, 1941), 55–57. Cecil J. Sharp, *English Folk Songs from the Southern Appalachians*, I, p. xxvii, wrote of two fiddlers: "Wherever possible they used the open strings as drones. . . ."

12. Onomatopoetic description of the sound of the bones in "De Rattle of de Bones," *The Ethiopian Gleebook.*

13. A newspaper clipping (Chicago, January 24, 1880), as quoted in Moreau, *Negro Minstrelsy,* II, states that the Virginia Minstrels "all sang in one voice." Kemble, *Journal*, 127, remembered that the plantation Negroes "all sing in unison, having never, it appears, attempted or heard anything like part-singing."

14. Allen, *Slave Songs*, pp. vi, xx.

15. Moreau, *Negro Minstrelsy*: "They were then all 'end men,' and all were

'interlocutors'. . . ." On playbills Brower and Pelham were mainly mentioned as offering conundrums.

16. H. B. White, "The Origin of Ethiopian Minstrelsy" (Harvard Theatre Collection, newspaper clipping of the early twentieth century).

17. Whitlock, unduly proud of a nondescript tune, asserted in his autobiography: "I composed . . . 'Miss Lucy Long' (the words by T. G. Booth) in 1838." An 1842 edition of the song without designation of author or composer appears in Damon, *Old American Songs.*

18. This scene, in Emmett's handwriting, was found among his manuscripts. It is not dated, but since it refers to "Santa Anna" and thus to the Mexican War, it was probably written about 1846.

19. *The New York Clipper* (December 8, 1866): "George [Christy] was the first to do the wench business; he was the original Lucy Long. . . ." However, the newspaper clipping "Negro Minstrels and their Dances" maintained that the "'Lucy Long' act was first presented by Dan Gardner and afterward had many and able exponents. . . . George Christy was the second one of those who tried it. . . ."

20. Playbill of the Masonic Temple (Boston, March 11, 1843).

21. W. P. Strickland, *The Pioneers of the West* (New York, 1856), 198; the author lived in Ohio in the twenties and thirties.

22. These "sayings" were no doubt used by other minstrels also. See, for example, the song "Who's Dat Nigga Dar A Peepin" (Boston, 1844): ". . . persipitating dat foot ob hers up so high dat when it dropt it was death to all creeping insects. . . ."

23. "Negro Minstrelsy—Ancient and Modern": "The negro is humorous rather than witty, and his comic songs consist of ludicrous images instead of witty conceits. I do not remember in the whole course of my investigations, to have met with anything like a pun in a genuine plantation melody." The backwoodsman David Crockett in *Col. Crockett's Tour*, 32, thought it ridiculous that Philadelphians were "eternally cutting up jokes on words." The Virginia Minstrels held a conundrum competition at the Tremont Theatre (Boston); the *Evening Transcript* (March 30, 1843) published the conundrum that received a prize. Among Emmett's manuscripts are the conundrums "submitted to the Committee for the Minstrels, Tremont Theatre."

24. See notes on playbills (March 7, 8, and 11, 1843), and on Emmett's edition of "De Boatman's Dance."

Black Musicians and Early Ethiopian Minstrelsy

Edited by Eileen Southern

Ethiopian minstrelsy as a form of theatrical entertainment in the United States began to emerge during the 1820s and reached its zenith during the years 1840s–80s. The first half of the period was dominated by whites, who blackened their faces with burnt cork and took to the stage to impersonate the rural slave and his free urban counterpart. In 1867 the first permanent all-black minstrel troupe was organized, and from that time on black minstrels became as common as white minstrels had been in the earlier part of the century. The black troupes maintained the same traditions as the whites, blackface and all. The roots of Ethiopian Minstrelsy lay in the eighteenth century, in the so-called Negro Songs that were performed between the acts of plays on the stages of England and the United States. By the 1830s these appearances had developed into lengthy performances involving several participants, typically called "Negro" singers, dancers, and instrumentalists. The purpose of this report is to document the story of the black man's involvement in Ethiopian Minstrelsy during its early period—which generally is considered to have been white.[1] [Editor]

New Orleans

It is common knowledge that the white entertainers obtained their materials from blacks by listening to the songs and impersonating them. Two such early "sources" in New Orleans were John "Picayune" Butler (d. 1864) and a street singer known only as "Old Corn Meal" (d. 1842). Butler, a noted banjoist, is said to have emigrated to New Orleans from one of the French islands of the West Indies some time during the 1820s. His fame is celebrated in a popular minstrel song of the fifties, "Picayune

Butler's Come to Town" (in Phil Rice, *Correct Method for the Banjo*, 1858). Old Corn Meal, who began his career as a singing street vendor, was the first black entertainer to appear on a stage in New Orleans.[2] The following excerpt is from Charles H. Day, *Fun in Black; or, Sketches of Minstrel Life, with the Origin of Minstrelsy, by Colonel T. Allston Brown* . . . (New York: Robert M. DeWitt, 1874), pp. 5–7.

The Origin of Negro Minstrelsy

Colonel T. Allston Brown

Much has been said and written of this popular branch of amusement—as to where it had its origin, who were its originators, etc.

Pot Pie Herbert, an actor of the West, sang a song entitled "Back Side of Albany Stands Lake Champlain," many years before Daddy Rice's day. Rice accumulated quite a fortune in the United States and England singing the song of "Jim Crow." He was a man of all work, attached to Ludlow and Smith's Theatre in the South and West. He officiated as property man, lamp lighter, stage carpenter, etc. He first jumped Jim Crow in Louisville, Ky., about the year 1829, and made a great hit. George Nichols, the clown, attached many years to Purdy Brown's Theatre and Circus of the South and West, claims being the first on the list of the burnt cork gentry. Nichols was a man of no education, yet he was the author of many anecdotes, stories, verses, etc. He was an original. He would compose the verses for his comic songs within ten minutes of the time of his appearance before the audience. His "flights of fancy" and "flashes of wit" were truly astonishing and highly amusing. Nichols first sang "Jim Crow" as clown, afterwards as a negro. He first conceived the idea from a French darkie, a banjo player, known from New Orleans to Cincinnati as Picayune Butler—a copper colored gentleman, who gathered many a picayune by singing "Picayune Butler is Going Away," accompanying himself on his four stringed banjo. An old darkie of New Orleans, known as "Old Corn Meal," furnished Nichols with many airs, which he turned to account. This old negro sold Indian meal for a living; he might be seen from morning till night with his cart and horse; he frequently stopped before Bishop's celebrated hotel and sang a number of negro melodies. He possessed a fine falsetto and baritone voice. Corn Meal picked up many bits and pics for his singing. A burlesque was produced at the old Camp Street Theatre, New Orleans, many years ago. It being a local affair, Old

Corn Meal with his horse and cart was introduced in the piece, and in crossing a platform the horse fell and was killed. Bob Farrell, an actor, sang "Zip Coon," composed by Geo. Nichols. Lewis Hyel, of Brown's company, sang "Roley Boley," by Nichols. Hyel died in his native city, Philadelphia. Nichols first sang "Clare de Kitchen." This song he arranged from hearing it sung by the negro firemen on the Mississippi River. The tune of "Zip Coon" was taken from a rough jig dance, called "Natchez Under the Hill," where the boatmen, river pirates, gamblers and courtesans congregated for the enjoyment of a regular hoe-down, in the old time. Sam Tatnall, the equestrian, sang "Back Side of Albany," five years before Rice's time. John and Frank Whittaker sang "Coal Black Rose" in 1830. Bill Keller, an excellent low comedian, a tobacconist by trade, of Philadelphia, was the original "Coal Black Rose." John Clements, leader of the orchestra for Duffy and Forrest, composed the music. I think it was written by one Jamison, of Philadelphia. George Washington Dixon created some *furore* by singing this song.

Barney Burns was known in those days, from Quebec to New Orleans, as a job actor. He was connected with the circus and was also low comedian. His first sang "The Long Tail Blue," and "Sich a Getting Up Stairs," written and composed by Joe Blackburn. Most of these (then) popular negro songs were taken from hearing the darkies of the South singing after the labor of the day was over on the plantation. The verses and airs were altered, written and arranged as I have described. For instance, the original verses of Jim Crow ran in this manner, without rhyme, as sung by the negroes of Kentucky:

> I went down to creek, I went down a fishing,
> I axed the old miller to gimmy chaw tobacker
> To treat old Aunt Hanner.
> *Chorus.*—Fist on the heel tap, den on de toe,
> Ebery time I wheel about I jump Jim Crow.
>
> I goes down to de branch to pester old miller,
> I wants a little light wood;
> I belongs to Capt. Hawkins, and don't care a d——n.
> *Chorus.*—First on de heel tap, etc., etc.

Old Daddy Rice copied his walk and dress from an old negro in Louisville, Ky.

Most of the negro songs of that day seem to have been about the same style as "Jim Crow."

A young man by the name of Lester first composed and sang a song called "Sitting on a Rail"; also another he called "Gumbo Chaff"; this was about the year 1836. Barnum travelled with this show.

Fun in Black

Charles Day

For twenty-five years negro minstrelsy has been one of our public amusements. Ever since 1842 it has been steadily improving, and now it is one of the most popular amusements of the day. As early as 1799 a Mr. Grawpner blacked up and appeared at the old Federal Street Theatre, Boston, and sang a song of a negro, in character. This was on the 30th of December of that year. The first idea of negro minstrelsy, in its present shape, was carried out by a party consisting of Dan. Emmett, Frank Brower, Billy Whitlock and Dick Pelham, who organized in the spring of 1841. They organized for one night only, for the purpose of playing for a benefit to Pelham, who was then dancing, between the pieces, at the Chatham Theatre. Meeting with success, they resolved to continue the business. After a number of rehearsals they called themselves the "Virginia Serenaders." They appeared at the Chatham with great success, and were then engaged by Messrs. Welch and Rockwell for the Park Theatre, where they performed to crowded houses for two weeks. John Diamond, the jig dancer, was in the company. They then proceeded to Boston, where they performed with equal success for six weeks. Returning to New York, they performed three nights for Simpson, at the Park Theatre. Having been so successful here, they determined to visit England. With G. B. Wooldridge (afterwards known as "Tom Quick," of the N.Y. *Leader*) as business manager they appeared in Liverpool and gave two performances. They then visited London, and for six weeks performed at the Adelphi Theatre in conjunction with Prof. J. H. Anderson, the wizard. In a short time Pelham left the company, when Joe Sweeney joined them, and they travelled through Scotland and Ireland for six months. The company consisted of W. Whitlock, T. G. Booth, Barney Williams and Cool White. The Ring and Parker party were next in order. In 1843 Cool White organized the "Virginia Serenaders," composed of Cool White, Jim Sanford, J. R. Myers and Robert Edwards. After performing several engagements in Philadelphia, New York and Boston, a split took place in the party, and Cool reorganized the "Virginia Serenaders" with Eph. Horn, Dave Bowers, Dan. Kelly, J. Moran and Cool White. They then disbanded, and, with the exception of Pelham, returned to this country.

Philadelphia

To my knowledge there were no prominent black minstrels in Philadelphia (a hotbed of minstrelsy for whites), but the evidence suggests that the celebrated Frank Johnson (1792–1844)—composer, bandmaster, orchestra leader, violinist, Kent bugler, and performer on numerous other instruments—had at least one brush with the tradition. Some time during 1843–44 he made an arrangement of the popular "Dandy Jim," obviously for performance by his band. I was at a loss to account for Johnson's involvement with minstrelsy, for his musical activities were on quite a different level, until I came across an advertisement in Philadelphia's *Public Ledger*, dated 2 April 1844, that threw light upon the subject. The Roscoe Association advertised its intent to sponsor a "Grand Concert of Vocal and Instrumental Music" with "eminent talent, including Mr. Creely, the celebrated Negro Melodist." (The word Negro always refers to whites in blackface during this period.) On the same program would appear "Frank Johnson's celebrated Brass and Stringed [sic] Band in several new Pieces." Undoubtedly Johnson intended to use his arrangement of the minstrel tune, as one of the "several new Pieces," as a tribute to Mr. Creely. Johnson may well have had direct contact with the Virginia Minstrels, as the title page of the arrangement suggests.

A street musician associated with minstrelsy was Richard Milburn, singer and whistler. His melody, "Listen to the Mocking Bird," became one of the most popular songs of the century.

It appears that some blacks may have organized minstrel groups primarily for performance in the black theater in Philadelphia. I found no reference to the subjects of the following item in any of the white newspapers of Philadelphia, but obviously this group was active in the 1840s. The quotation is from a list of copyrights entered in December 1844:

> Entered according to the Act of Congress in the Year 1844 by Turner and Fisher [publishers] in the Clerk's Office of the District Court of the Eastern District of Pennsylvania: Charles White's Black Apollo Songster, Being a Collection of Negro Melodies not to be found in any other work, as Sung by Charles White, the Black Apollo and other Colored Savoyards.

New York

The best-known black minstrel of the time was Master Juba (William Henry Lane, ca. 1825–1852). Very little is known of his origin.[3] It is probable that he began his career in one of the "dance houses" of the notorious Five Points district of New York.[4] Just how he moved from there to a New York stage must remain a conjecture. It may be that Phineas T. Barnum, the famed showman, was responsible, as suggested by the following excerpt from Thomas L. Nichols, *Forty Years of American Life* (London: Longmans, Green & Co., 1864), pp. 369–70:

In New York, some years ago, Mr. P. T. Barnum had a clever boy who brought him lots of money as a dancer of negro break-downs; made up, of course, as a negro minstrel, with his face well blackened, and a woolly wig. One day Master Diamond, thinking he might better himself, danced away into the infinite distance.

Barnum, full of expedients, explored the dance-houses of the Five Points and found a boy who could dance a better break-down than Master Diamond. It was easy to hire him; but he was a genuine negro; and there was not an audience in America that would not have resented, in a very energetic fashion, the insult of being asked to look at the dancing of a real negro.

To any man but the originator of Joyce Heth, the veneable negro nurse of Washington, and the manufacturer of the Fiji Mermaid, this would have been an insuperable obstacle. Barnum was equal to the occasion. Son of the State of white oak cheeses and wooden nutmegs, he did not disgrace his lineage. He greased the little "nigger's" face and rubbed it over with a new blacking of burnt cork, painted his thick lips with vermilion, put on a woolly wig over his tight curled lacks, and brought him out as the "champion nigger-dancer of the world." Had it been suspected that the seeming counterfeit was the genuine article, the New York Vauxhall would have blazed with indignation.

Since Master Diamond left Barnum in March 1841, Juba would have had his first introduction to the public during that Spring, if indeed he was the young black dancer hired to replace Diamond.[5] In 1842 Juba was again dancing in Five Points and was observed there by Charles Dickens, who called him "the greatest dancer known." Obviously Juba had won enough of a reputation by that time to be recognized by the visiting novelist from England. The following excerpt is from Dickens's book, *American Notes for General Circulation* (London: Chapman & Hall, 1842), pp. 36–37:

Our leader has his hand upon the latch of Almack's, and calls to us from the bottom of the steps; for the Assembly Room of the Five Points fashionables is approached by a descent. Shall we go in? It is but a moment.

. . . The corpulent black fiddler, and his friend who plays the tambourine, stamp upon the boarding of the small raised orchestra in which they set, and play a lively measure. Five or six couple [sic] come upon the floor, marshalled by a lively young negro, who is the wit of the assembly and the greatest dancer known.

But the dance commences. Every gentleman sets as long as he likes to the opposite lady, and the opposite lady to him, and all are so long about it that the sport begins to languish, when suddenly the lively hero dashes to the rescue. Instantly the fiddler grins, and goes at it tooth and nail; there is new energy in the tambourine; new laughter in the dancers; new smiles in the landlady; new confidence in the landlord; new brightness in the very candles. Single shuffle, double shuffle, cut and crosscut: snapping his fingers, rolling his eyes, turning in his knees, presenting the backs of his legs in front, spinning about on his toes and heels like nothing but the man's fingers on the tambourine; dancing with two left legs, two right legs, two wooden legs, two wire legs, two spring legs—all sorts of legs and no legs—what is this to him? And in what walk of life, or dance of life, does man ever get such stimulating applause as thunders about him, when, having danced his partner off her feet, and himself too, he finishes by leaping gloriously on the barcounter, and calling for something to drink, with the chuckle of a million of counterfeit Jim Crows, in one inimitable sound?

In 1844 Diamond and Juba engaged in a series of dance contests, from which Juba emerged as the "King of all Dancers." Diamond had joined the Ethiopian Serenaders after leaving Barnum. Apparently Juba was not a member of a group at the time the following advertisement appeared in the *New York Herald*, 8 July 1844:

GREAT PUBLIC CONTEST

BETWEEN the two most renowned dancers in the world, the Original JOHN DIAMOND and the Colored Boy JUBA, for a Wager of $200, on MONDAY EVENING July 8th at the BOWERY AMPHITHEATRE, which building has been expressly hired from the Proprietor, Mr. Smith, for this night only, as its accommodations will afford all a fair view of each step of these wonderful Dancers. The fame of these Two Celebrated Breakdown Dancers has already spread over the Union, and the numerous friends of each claim the Championship for their favorite, and who have anxiously wished for a Public Trial between them and thus know which is to bear the Title of the Champion Dancer of the World. The time to decide that has come, as the friends of Juba have challenged the world to produce his superior in the art for $100. That Challenge has been accepted by the friends of Diamond, and on Monday Evening they meet and Dance three Jigs, Two Reels, and the Camptown Hornpipe. Five Judges have been selected for their ability and knowledge of the Art, so that a fair decision will be made.

Rule—Each Dancer will select his own Violin and the victory will be decided by the best time and the greatest number of steps.

On this occasion—Boxes, 25 cents; Pit, 12-1/2 cents. Tickets for sale at the Concert Saloon, 74 Chambers street, and at the Theatre during Monday.

By 1846 Juba had joined White's Serenaders as the tambourine player and dancer. About 1848 he went to England, where he performed with Pell's Serenaders. He remained in England, an idol of the public, until his death in 1852. The critics as well as the public praised Juba's talent, as the following notice from the *Illustrated London News* (5 August 1848) indicates:

JUBA AT VAUXHALL

The only national dance that we really believe in, as a fact, is that of the Niggers. We mistrust the "Cachucha"—that is to say, whenever we have seen it performed by a real Spanish *danseuse*, we have always pronounced it far inferior to Duvernay's in the "Diable Bolteux." We should never expect to see the "Redowa" danced in its own country as Cerito and St. Leon represent it at Her Majesty's Theatre; and we have some doubt as to whether Carlotta Grisi's delicious "Truandaise" was ever known in the Cour des Miracles of old Paris. Hornpipes are entirely confined to nautical dramas and pantomimes, or the square bit of board or patch of carpet of the street dancer; and anything so physically painful, not to say almost impossible, as those peculiar *pas* of the Chinese that we chance to have witnessed in Europe, convince us that at all events the execution must be exceedingly limited.

But the Nigger Dance is a reality. The "Virginny Breakdown," or the "Alabama Kick-up," the "Tennessee Double-shuffle," or the "Louisiana Toe-and-Heel," we know to exist. If they did not, how could Juba enter into their wonderful complications so naturally? How could he tie his legs into such knots, and fling them about so recklessly, or make his feet twinkle until you lose sight of them altogether in his energy. The great Boz immortalised him; and he deserved the glory thus conferred. If our readers doubt this, let them go the very next Monday or other evening that arrives, and see him at Vauxhall Gardens.

But Juba is a musician, as well as a dancer. To him the intricate management of the nigger tambourine is confined, and from it he produces marvellous harmonies. We almost question whether, upon a great emergency, he could not play a fugue upon it.

Certainly the present company of Ethiopians, at the Gardens, are the best we have seen. They have with them Pell, the original "Bones" of Mr. Mitchell's theatre; and he is better than ever.

At least one other widely known black figure of the period should be mentioned in this discussion of early minstrelsy, and that is the actor Ira Aldridge. While it was as an actor that Aldridge won his secure reputation, he was not averse to singing Negro songs on occasion. There is evidence that he sang on the stage of the African Grove Theater in New York during the 1820s as well as acted; in Europe he also sang songs between or after the plays of the evening, and the critics discussed his singing in the same glowing terms that they used for his acting.

The final document offered here is an essay by J. Kennard, a citizen of Portsmouth, New Hampshire, and a regular contributor to the *Knickerbocker Magazine* (New York). His witty comments reveal much about the relationship between blacks and whites in the development of Ethiopian Minstrelsy and give proper credit to the original sources of minstrel materials—the songs and dances of the slaves.

*Who Are Our National Poets?**

By Our "Salt-Fish Dinner" Correspondent [James K. Kennard, Jr.]

Who says we have no American Poetry? No American Songs? The charge is often made against us, but (as will be hereinafter proved) without the slightest foundation of truth. Foreigners read BRYANT, and HALLECK, and

**Knickerbocker Magazine* (1845), pp. 331–341.

LONGFELLOW, and hearing these called our best poets, and perceiving nothing in their poems which might not just as well have been written in England, or by Englishmen, they infer that as the productions of those who stand highest among our poets have nothing about them which savors *peculiarly* of America, therefore America has no national poetry; a broad conclusion from narrow premises.

What are the prerequisites of national poetry? What is necessary to make the poet national?—this being, in the opinion of these foreign critics, the highest merit he can possess. Certainly, liberal education and foreign travel cannot assist him in attaining this desirable end; these denationalize a man; they render any but the narrowest soul cosmopolitan. By these means the poet acquires a higher standard than the national. By a kind of eclecticism, he appropriates forms and thoughts, images and modes of expression, from all countries and languages; by comparing the specific, the transient, and the idiosyncratic, he arrives at the general and the permanent; and when he has written in his own language a poem in accordance with his new ideal standard, he may have produced a noble work, but it can hardly be a *national* poem. He has striven to avoid the faults peculiar to his own countrymen, faults which he might have deemed beauties had he finished his education in his village school, and never ventured out of his native valley. He has become enamoured of the excellencies of the poets of other nations, the very knowledge of which prevents him from being national himself. He has become acquainted with the rules of universal poetry, as the linguist learns, in the study of foreign tongues, the principles of universal grammar. His standard is universal, not national.

From what has been said, it follows that if it be so desirable, as some people think, that poetry should smack strongly of the locality in which it is written, then in order to obtain that end we must keep our poets at home, give them a narrow education, and allow them no spare money by which they might purchase books, or make excursions into other ranks of society than their own. If we could only pick out the born poets when they were a fortnight old, and subject them to this regimen, the nation would be able to boast of original poets in plenty, during the next generation. This is the way in which BURNS became Scotland's greatest national poet. If he had been born a lord, had been educated at Cambridge, and had made the grand tour of the world, does any one suppose he would have been a better poet? or half so good? At best, he could not have been so original nor so Scottish; and he might have proved to be only a tasteful HAYNES BAYLEY, or BARRY CORNWALL; or perhaps a miserable, moody, misanthropic Lord BYRON. Where would have been the glory of England, the immortal SHAKESPEARE, had the boy WILLIAM received an education like that given in the nineteenth century to lads of genius who have rich fathers?

Applying this rule to America; in which class of our population must we look for our truly original and American poets? What class is most secluded from foreign influences, receives the narrowest education, travels the shortest distance from home, has the least amount of spare cash, and mixes least with any class above itself? Our negro slaves, to be sure! *That* is the class in which we must expect to find our original poets, and there we *do* find them. From that class come the Jim Crows, the Zip Coons, and the Dandy Jims, who have electrified the world. From them proceed our ONLY TRULY NATIONAL POETS.

When Burns was *discovered*, he was immediately taken away from the plough, carried to Edinburgh, and feted and lionized to the "fulness of satiety." James Crow and Scipio Coon never were discovered, personally; and if they had been, their owners would not have spared them from work. Alas! that poets should be ranked with horses, and provided with owners accordingly! In this, however, our negro poets are not peculiarly unfortunate. Are not some of their white brethren owned and kept by certain publishing houses, newspapers, and magazines? Are not the latter class, like the former, provided with just sufficient clothing and food to keep them in good working condition, and with no more? And do not the masters, in both cases, appropriate all the profits?

Messrs. Crow and Coon could not be spared from the hoe, but they might be introduced to the great world by proxy! And so thought Mr. THOMAS RICE, a "buckra gemman" of great imitative powers, who accordingly learned their poetry, music and dancing, blacked his face, and made his fortune by giving to the world his counterfeit presentment of the American national opera; counterfeit, because none but the negroes themselves *could* give it in its original perfection. And thus it came to pass, that while James Crow and Scipio Coon were quietly at work on their master's plantations, all unconscious of their fame, the whole civilized world was resounding with their names. From the nobility and gentry, down to the lowest chimney-sweep in Great Britain, and from the member of Congress, down to the youngest apprentice or school-boy in America, it was all:

> Turn about and wheel about, and do just so,
> And every time I turn about I jump Jim Crow.

Even the fair sex did not escape the contagion: the tunes were set to music for the piano-forte, and nearly every young lady in the Union, and the United Kingdom, played and sang, if she did not *jump*, "Jim Crow." "Zip Coon" became a fashionable song; "Lubly Rosa, Sambo come," the favorite serenade, and "Dandy Jim of Caroline" the established quadrille-music. White bards imitated the negro melodies; and the familiar song:

> As I was gwine down Shinbone Alley,
> Long time ago;

appeared, in the following shape:

> O'er the lake where dropped the willow,
> Long time ago!

What greater proofs of genius have ever been exhibited, than by these our National Poets? They themselves were not permitted to appear in the theatres, and the houses of the fashionable, but their songs are in the mouths and ears of all; white men have blacked their faces to represent them, made their fortune by the speculation, and have been caressed and flattered on both sides of the Atlantic.

Humorous and burlesque songs are generally chosen for theatrical exhibition, and this fact may have led many to believe that the negroes composed no others. But they deal in the pathetic as well as the comical. Listen to the following, and imagine the hoe of Sambo digging into the ground with additional vigor at every emphasized syllable:

> Massa an Misse promised me
> When they died they'd set me free;
> Massa an Misse dead an' gone,
> Here's old Sambo hillin'-up corn!'

Poor fellow! it seems a hard case. His "massa and misse" are freed from *their* bonds, but Sambo still wears his. He might here very properly stop and water the corn with his tears. But no; Sambo is too much of a philosopher for *that.* Having uttered his plaint, he instantly consoles himself with the thought that he has many blessings yet to be thankful for. He thinks of his wife, and the good dinner which she is preparing for him, and from the depths of a grateful and joyous heart he calls out, at the top of his voice:

> "Jenny get your hoe-cake done, my darling,
> Jenny get your hoe-cake done, my dear!"

and Jenny, in her distant log hut, which is embowered in Catalpa and Pride-of-India trees, gives the hommony another stir, looks at the hoe-cake, and giving the young ones a light cuff or two on the side of the head, to make them "hush," answers her beloved Sambo in the same strain:

> "De hoe-cake is almost done, my darling,
> De hoe-cake is almost done, my dear."

Now if that field of corn belonged to Sambo, and the hut and its inmates were his own, and he belonged to himself, that would be a delightful specimen of humble rural felicity. But perhaps his young master may be so unfortunate as to lose the ten thousand dollars which he has bet upon the race that is to take place to-morrow; and poor Sambo and his family may be sold, separated, and sent just where their new masters may please; possibly to labor on a sugar plantation—the hell of the blacks.

The greater portion of our national poetry originates in Virginia, or among involuntary Virginian emigrants. Slaves are worked very lightly in that state, comparatively speaking. They are raised chiefly for exportation. Every year thousands are sent to the far south and southwest for sale. The Virginian type of negro character therefore has come to prevail throughout the slave states, with the exception of some portions of Louisiana and Florida. Thus every where you may hear much the same songs and tunes, and see the same dances, with little variety, and no radical difference. Taken together, they form a system perfectly *unique.* Without any teaching, the negroes have contrived a rude kind of opera, combining the poetry of motion, of music, and of language! "Jim Crow" is an opera; all the negro songs were intended to be *performed,* as well as sung and played. And, considering the world-wide renown to which they have attained, who can doubt the genius of the composers? Was not the top of Mount Washington, once upon a time, the stage on which "Jim Crow" was performed, with New Hampshire and Maine for audience and spectators? So saith one of the albums at the foot of the mountain. And doth not William Howitt tell us that the summit of the Hartz mountains was the scene of a similar exhibition?

These operas are full of negro life: there is hardly any thing which might not be learned of negro character, from a complete collection of these original works. A tour through the south, and a year or two of plantation life, would not fail to reward the diligent collector; and his future fame would be as certain as Homer's. Let him put his own name, as compiler, on the title-page, and (the real author's being unknown) after a lapse of a few centuries the contents of the book will be ascribed to him, as "the great American Poet," the object of adoration to the poetical public of the fiftieth century! What was Homer but a diligent collector? Some learned people *say* he was nothing more, at any rate. Thou who pantest for glory, go and do likewise!

While writing this, your city papers advertise: "Concert this evening, by the African Melodists." *African* melodists! As well might the Hutchinson's call themselves *English* melodists, because their ancestors, some six or eight generations back, came from England. Whether these performers are blacks, or whites with blacked faces does not appear; but they are doubtless meant to represent the native colored population of "Old Varginny," and as such should be judged. They are *American* melodists, *par excellence.*

It is a true test of genius in a writer, that he should be able to put his sayings into the mouths of all, so that they may become household words, quoted by every one, and nine times in ten without knowledge of the author of them. How often do we find in Shakspeare [sic], Sterne, and other celebrated old writers, the very expressions we have been accustomed to hear from childhood, without thought of their origin! They meet us every where in the old standard works, like familiar faces. And how often, when uttering one of these beautiful quotations, if questioned as to its origin, we feel at loss whether to refer the querist to Milton, Sterne, or the Bible! Proverbs are said to be "the wisdom of nations," yet who knows the author of a single proverb? How many, of the millions who weekly join their voices to that glorious tune Old Hundred, ever heard the name of the composer? How transcendent, then, must be the genius of the authors of our negro operas! Are not snatches of their songs in everybody's mouth, from John O'Groat's to Land's End, and from Labrador to Mexico? Three hundred and fifty times a day (we took the pains to count, once) we have been amused and instructed with "Zip Coon," "Jim Crow," and the tale of a "Fat Raccoon, a-sittin on a rail." Let Webster tell of the tap of Britain's drum, that encircles the world! Compared with the time occupied by Great Britain in bringing this to pass, "Jim Crow" has put a girdle round about the earth in forty minutes. At no time does the atmosphere of our planet cease to vibrate harmoniously to the immortal songs of the negroes of America. At this present moment, a certain ubiquitous person seems to be in the way of the whole people of these United States simultaneously (a mere pretender, doubtless, dressed up in some cast-off negro clothing), and any one may hear him told, a hundred times a day, to "Get out ob de way, old Dan Tucker!" But if he gets out of any body's way, it is only that of "Dandy Jim, of Caroline." Oh, that he *would* obey the command altogether! but depend upon it, he will do no such thing, so long as the young ladies speak to him in such fascinating tones, and accompany their sweet voices with the only less sweet music of the piano. Dan takes it as an invitation to stay; and doubtless many a lover would like to receive a similar rejection from his lady-love; a fashion, by the way, like that in which the country lass reproved her lover for kissing her: "Be done, Nat!" said she, "and (*soto voce*) begin again!"

Who is the man of genius? He who utters clearly that which is dimly felt by all. He who most vividly represents the sentiment, intellect and taste of the public to which he addresses himself. He to whom all hearts and heads respond. Take our "national poets," for example, who being unknown individually, we may personify collectively as the American SAMBO. Is not Sambo a genius? All tastes are delighted, all intellects are astonished, all hearts respond to his utterances; at any rate, all piano-fortes do, and a hundred thousand of the sweetest voices in christendom. What more convincing proof of genius was ever presented to the world? Is not Sambo the incarnation of the taste, intellect and heart of America, the ladies being the judges? Do not shrink from the answer, most beautiful, accomplished, delicate and refined lady-reader! You cannot hold yourself above him, for you imitate him; you spend days and weeks in learning his tunes; you trill his melodies with your rich voice; you are delighted with his humor, his pathos, his irresistible fun. Say truly, incomparable damsel! is not Sambo the realization of your poetic ideal?

But our national melodists have many imitators. Half of the songs published as theirs are, as far as the words are concerned, the productions of "mean whites"; but base counterfeits as they are, they pass current with most people as genuine negro songs. Thus is it ever with true excellence! It is always imitated, but no one counterfeits that which is acknowledged by all to be worthless. The Spanish dollar is recognised as good throughout the world, and it is more frequently counterfeited than any other coin. The hypocrite assumes the garb of virtue and religion; but who ever thought of feigning vice and infidelity, unless upon the stage? Every imitator acknowledges the superior excellence of his model. The greater the number of imitators, the stronger is the evidence of that superiority; the warmer their reception by the public, the more firmly becomes established the genius of the original.

But the music and the dancing are all Sambo's own. No one attempts to introduce any thing new *there*. In truth they, with the chorus, constitute all that is essentially permanent in the negro song. The blacks themselves leave out old stanzas, and introduce new ones at pleasure. Travelling through the South, you may, in passing from Virginia to Louisiana, hear the same tune a hundred times, but seldom the same words accompanying it. This necessarily results from the fact that the songs are unwritten, and also from the habit of extemporizing, in which the performers indulge on festive occasions. Let us picture one of these scenes, which often occur on the estates of kind masters, seldom on those of the cruel. So true is this, that the frequent sound of the violin, banjo, or jaw-bone lute, is as sure an indication of the former, as its general absence is of the latter.

Like the wits of the white race, the negro singer is fond of appearing to extemporize, when in fact he has everything "cut and dried" beforehand.

Sambo has heard that his "massa" is going to be put up as candidate for congress; that his "misse" has that day bought a new gold watch and chain; that Miss Lucy favors one of her lovers above the rest; that "massa and misse" have given their consent; and in fact, that Violet, the chamber-maid, saw Miss Lucy looking lovingly on a miniature which she had that morning received in a disguised package. Sambo has learned all this, and he has been engaged the whole day, while hoeing corn, in putting these facts, and his thoughts thereon, into verse, to his favorite tune, "Zip Coon." He never did such a day's work in his life. He hoed so fast, that his fellow-laborers looked at him in astonishment, and said Sambo had "got de debbil in him; dumb debbil, too; no get a word out ob him all day." Sambo finished his hoeing task by three o'clock, but not his rhyming. He could not sit still, so he went to work in his little garden-patch; and just at sun-down, having completed his verses to his satisfaction, and hummed them over till confident that he could sing them through without hesitation, he threw down his hoe, and shouted and capered for joy, like a madman.

Soon after tea, Violet enters the parlor: "Sambo sends compliments to Massa and Misse, and de young gemmen and ladies, and say he gwine to gib musical entertainment to company dis evening in de kitchen and be happy to hab a full house." Sambo is a favorite servant, and so, with an air of kindness and dignity, the master replies: "Give our compliments to Sambo, and say that we will attend with pleasure"; and soon the whole family go out to the kitchen, which at the South is always a building by itself. The master's family occupy one end of the room, standing; the doors and windows are filled with black faces, grinning ivory, and rolling eyes. Sambo emerges from behind a rug, hung across the corner of the kitchen; and the orchestra, consisting of one fiddle, played by old Jupe, strikes up: "Clar de kitchen, old folks, young folks, old Varginny neber tire." This is a feint, skilfully planned by Sambo, just as if he intended nothing more than to sing over the well-known words of one or two old songs. He goes through this performance, and through two or three more, with the usual applause: at last old Jupe strikes up "Zip Coon," and Sambo sings two or three familiar stanzas of this well-known song; but suddenly, as if a new thought struck him, he makes an extraordinary flourish; looks at his master, and sings:

Oh, my ole massa gwine to Washing*ton*,
Oh, my ole massa gwine to Washing*ton*,
Oh, my ole massa gwine to Washing*ton*,
All'e niggers cry when massa gone.

I know what I wish massa do,
I know what I wish massa do,

I know what I wish massa do,
Take me on to Washington to black him boot an' shoe.
   Zip e duden duen, duden duden da.

Misse got a gold chain round her neck,
Misse got a gold chain round her neck,
Misse got a gold chain round her neck:
Da watch on toder end tick tick tick,
Da watch on toder end tick tick tick,
Jus de same as Sambo when he cut up stick:
   Zip e duden duden, duden duden da.

Miss Lucy she hab a gold chain too,
Miss Lucy she hab a gold chain too,
Miss Lucy she hab a gold chain too;
No watch on de toder end ob *dat*, I know,
No watch on de toder end ob dat, I know,
No watch on de toder end ob dat, I know,
I reckon it's a picture ob her handsome beau:
   Zip e duden duden, duden duden da.

Great tittering and grinning among the blacks; hearty laughter among the whites; blushes and a playfully-threatening shake of the finger at Sambo, from Miss Lucy. Sambo meanwhile "does" an extra quantity of jumping at an extra height. His elation at the sensation he has produced really inspires him, and he prolongs his saltations until he has concocted a genuine impromptu stanza:

Who dat nigger in e door I spy?
Who dat nigger in e door I spy?
Who dat nigger in e door I spy?
Dat old Scip, by de white ob him eye:
   Zip e duden duden, duden duden da.

By de white ob him eye an he tick out lip,
By de white ob him eye an he tick out lip,
By de white ob him eye an he tick out lip,
Sambo know dat old black Scip:
   Zip e duden duen, duen duden da.

Exit Sambo, behind the rug. Great applause; and white folks *exeunt*. The evening winds up with a treat of whiskey, all round, furnished by "massa" on the occasion, and in due time all disperse to their several log huts, and retire to rest, after one of the most joyous evenings they ever passed in their lives. All sleep soundly but Sambo; he lies awake half the night, so excited is he by the honors he has acquired, so full of *poetical thoughts,* seeking to shape themselves into words. Slumber at last falls on him; but his wife declares, next morning, that Sambo talked all night in his sleep like a crazy man. Thousands at the South would recognize the foregoing as a faithful sketch of a not infrequent scene:

> The man who has no music in his soul,
> Nor is not moved by concord of sweet sounds,
> Is fit for treasons, stratagems and spoils;
> Let no such man be trusted.

Shakspeare [sic] never uttered a more undeniable truth; and if he were living at the present day, and needed evidence to back his opinions, a short experience as a cotton planter would furnish him with the requisite proof. This thing is well understood at the South. A laughing, singing, fiddling, dancing negro is almost invariably a faithful servant. Possibly he may be lazy and idle, but "treasons, stratagems and spoils" form not the subject of *his* meditations. He is a thoughtless, merry fellow, who sings "to drive dull care away"; sings at his work, sings at his play, and generally accomplishes more at his labor than the sulky negro who says nothing, but looks volumes. These last words have struck "the electric chain" of memory, and forthwith starts up a picture of by-gone days. "The time is long past, and the scene is afar," yet the mental daguerreotype is as fresh as if taken yesterday.

One day during the early part of the Indian war in Florida, we stepped into a friend's boat at Jacksonville, and with a dozen stout negro rowers, pushed off, bound up the St. Johns with a load of muskets, to be distributed among the distressed inhabitants, who were every where flying from the frontier before the victorious Seminoles. As we shot ahead, over the lake-like expanse of the noble river, the negroes struck up a song to which they kept time with their oars; and our speed increased as they went on, and become warmed with their singing. The words were rude enough, the music better, and both were well-adapted to the scene. A line was sung by a leader, then all joined in a short chorus; then came another solo line, and another short chorus, followed by a longer chorus, during the singing of which the boat foamed through the water with redoubled velocity. There seemed to be a certain number of lines ready-manufactured, but after this stock was exhausted, lines relating to surrounding objects were extemporized. Some of these were full of rude wit, and a lucky hit always drew a thundering chorus from the rowers, and an encouraging laugh from the occupants of the sternseats. Sometimes several minutes elapsed in silence; then one of the negroes burst out with a line or two which he had been excogitating. Little regard was paid to rhyme, and hardly any to the number of syllables in a line: they condensed four or five into one foot, or stretched out one to occupy the space that should have been filled with four or five; yet they never spoiled the tune. This elasticity of form is peculiar to the negro song. But among these negroes there was one who rowed in silence, and no smile lighted up his countenance at the mirthful sallies of his sable companions. When the others seemed merriest, he was unmoved, or only showed, by a transient expression of contempt, the bitterness which dwelt in his heart. In physiognomy he differed entirely from his companions. His nose was straight, and finely cut, his lips thin, and the general cast of his countenance strikingly handsome. He was very dark, and in a *tableau vivant* might have figured with credit as a bronze statue of a Grecian hero. He seemed misplaced, and looked as if he felt so. The countenance of that man, as he carelessly plied his oar, in silent contempt of the merry, thoughtless set around him, made an impression on my mind which will never be effaced. He spoke not, but "looked unutterable things." He had no "music in his soul"; he was not "moved by concord of sweet sounds"; but his thoughts were on "treasons, stratagems and spoils"; he was thinking of the muskets and ammunition which the boat contained, and of the excellent use that might be made of them, in the way of helping the Indians instead of repelling them. "Let no such man be trusted!" would have been a proper precaution in this case. A few weeks after this he ran away and joined the Seminoles, and was suspected to have acted as a guide to the party that subsequently laid waste his master's plantation.

Comparatively speaking, however, there are few negroes at the South who have "no music" in their souls. The love of music and song is characteristic of the race. They have songs on all subjects; witty, humorous, boisterous and sad. Most frequently, however, specimens of all these classes are mingled together in the same song, in grotesque confusion. Variety is the spice of the negro melodies. Take the following as a fair specimen of negro humor and pathos:

Come all you jolly niggers, to you de truf I tell-ah;
Never lib wid white folks, dey never use you well-ahh:
Cold frosty mornin', nigger bery good-ah,
Wid he axe on he shoulder, he go to cut de wood-ah;
  Dingee I otten dotten, balli' otten dotten,
  Dingee I otten, *who dar*?

Come home to breakfast, get somethin' to eat-ha;
And dey set down before him a little nasty meat-ah;
Den at noon poor nigger, he come home to dine-ah,
And dey take him in de corn-field, and gib him thirty-nine-ah!
  Dingee I otten dotten, balli' otten dotten,
  Dingee I otten, *who dar*?

Den de night come on, and he come home to supper-ah,
And dey knock down, and break down, and jump ober Juber-ah!
Den a little cold pancake, and a little hog-fat-ah,

And dey grumble like de debbil, if you eat too much ob dat-ah!
Dingee I otten dotten, balli' otten dotten,
Dingee I otten, *who dar*?

Den oh! poor nigger, I sorry for your color-ah;
Hit you on de back-bone, you sound like a dollar-ah!
Cold frosty mornin', nigger bery good-ah;
Wid de axe on he shoulder, he go to cut de wood-ah!
Dingee I otten dotten, balli' otten dotten,
Dingee I otten, *who dar*?

The intelligent reader, conversant with Howitt's "Student Life in Germany," cannot have failed to note the close similarity of style between the foregoing and some of the student-songs, translations of which are therein given. The question arises, Who was the imitator? Surely not the negro: he knows not that there is in existence such a being as a German student. But the students know the whole history of the negroes, and doubtless are acquainted with their world-renowned songs. The inference is irresistible: the student is the imitator of the negro, just in the same way that he is the imitator of Homer, and Anacreon, and Sappho. The student is a man of discernment, able to recognize true genius, and not ashamed to emulate it, however lowly the circumstances in which it may be found. He remembers that Homer was a blind, wandering beggar, and knowing that simplicity and adversity are favorable to the growth of true poetry, he is not surprised to find it flourishing in perfection among the American negroes. Or, say that the student is *not* an imitator of the negro: then we have a case which goes to establish still more firmly the well-known truth that, human nature being the same every where, men of genius, living thousands of miles apart, and holding no communication with each other, often arrive at the same results!

Proofs of the genius of our American poets crowd upon us in tumultuous array from all quarters. A few of them only are before the reader, but enough, it is hoped, to establish their claim beyond a doubt. Now let justice be done! Render to Caesar, and Pompey, and Scipio, and Sambo, the just honor which has been so long unjustly withheld; and render to America the meed of praise which has been so pertinaciously denied to her. Sambo claims honor for the fact that he *is* a true poet: America asks praise for bringing him up, with infinite pains, in the only way in which a true poet should go; which fact was demonstrated in the beginning of this article. Acknowledge, then, ye British critics! your sins of mission and commission; eat your own slanderous words, and proclaim the now undeniable truth, or else be branded as false prophets, and "for ever after hold your peace!"

A wise man has said, "Let me have the making of the songs of a people, and I care not who makes their laws." The popular song maker sways the souls of men; the legislator rules only their bodies. The song-maker reigns through love and spiritual affinity; the legislator by brute force. Apply this principle to the American people. Who are our true rulers? The negro poets, to be sure! Do they not set the fashion, and give laws to the public taste? Let one of them, in the swamps of Carolina, compose a new song, and it no sooner reaches the ear of a white *amateur*, than it is written down, amended, (that is, almost spoilt), printed, and then put upon a course of rapid dissemination, to cease only with the utmost bounds of Anglo-Saxondom, perhaps of the world. Meanwhile, the poor author digs away with his hoe, utterly ignorant of his greatness! "Blessed are they who do good, and are forgotten!" says dear Miss Bremer. Then blessed indeed are our national melodists! "True greatness is always modest," says some one else. How great then are our retiring Samboes! How shrinkingly they remain secluded, and allow sooty-faced white men to gather all the honors and emoluments! The works of great men are always imitated. Even those miserable counterfeits, "Lucy Long," and "Old Dan Tucker," have secured a large share of favor, on the supposition that they were genuine negro songs. With the music, no great fault can be found; that may be pure negro, though some people declare it to be Italian. Be that as it may; the words are far beneath the genius of our American poets; this any student, well-versed in negro lore, can perceive at a glance.

BRYANT, LONGFELLOW, HALLECK, WHITTIER, do you ardently desire fame? Give heed to foreign reviewers; doubt no longer that nationality is the highest merit that poetry can possess; uneducate yourselves; consult the taste of your fair countrywomen; write no more English poems; write negro songs, and Yankee songs in negro style; take lessons in dancing of the celebrated Thomas Rice; appear upon the stage and perform your own operas; do this, and not only will fortune and fame be yours, but you will thus vindicate yourselves and your country from the foul imputation under which both now rest! With *your* names on the list with CROW and COON, who *then* will dare to say that America has no National Poets?

Notes

1. The definitive source of information about early blackface minstrelsy is Hans Nathan, *Dan Emmett and the Rise of Early Negro Minstrelsy* (Norman, Okla.: University of Oklahoma Press, 1962). Its bibliography lists many of the important primary sources as well as significant secondary sources that were consulted for this study.

2. See Henry A. Kmen, *Music in New Orleans: The Formative Years 1791–1841* (Baton Rouge: Louisiana State University Press, 1966), and Ann Charters, *The Ragtime Songbook* (New York: Oak Publications, 1965, c.1955).

3. In addition to those sources cited in the text and contemporary newspapers, see also Marian Hannah Winter, "Juba and American Minstrelsy" in *Chronicles of the American Dance*, ed. Paul Magriel (New York, 1948), pp. 39–63.

4. See George Foster, *New York by Gas Light with Here and There a Streak of Sunshine* (New York, 1850). A chapter from the book, "The Dance House," is reprinted in Eileen Southern, ed., *Readings in Black American Music* (New York: W. W. Norton, 1971), pp. 128–131.

5. See further about Barnum and Ethiopian minstrelsy in *The Life of Barnum, the World Renowned Showman. Written by Himself* (New York, 1855). The role of Barnum in promoting the careers of black entertainers of the nineteenth century calls for further investigation.

POLITICAL CLIMATE

Blackface Minstrelsy

Alexander Saxton

For half a century minstrel shows provided a nationwide medium of mass entertainment, and at the end, far from fading away, they merged into vaudeville and the beginnings of cinema.[1] Blackface minstrelsy epitomized and concentrated the thrust of white racism. In this respect it was always political, but during its early years, from the mid-1840s through the 1860s, overt partisanship linked it to the Democratic party. The exclusiveness of its Jacksonian orientation surpassed that of the penny press, which, although initially Democratic, contained no internal barriers against Whig infiltration.

For minstrelsy, by contrast, whiggish politics were precluded because the mass urban culture from which minstrelsy derived was itself an attack on the moral and economic premises of whiggery; and because, through its stylized form, it propagandized metaphorically the alliance of urban working people with the planter interest in the South. Not till after the war and well into Reconstruction could a nonpartisan or Republican minstrel company have commanded credibility. And such a combination even then would have reflected not so much any basic change in minstrelsy as the gradual success of the Republican coalition in capturing segments of the Democracy.

"If I could have the nigger show back again in its pristine purity," Mark Twain wrote in his autobiography, ". . . I should have but little further use for opera. . . . I remember the first Negro musical show I ever saw. It must have been in the early forties. It was a new institution. In our village of Hannibal . . . it burst upon us as a glad and stunning surprise."[2] Twain's comparison to grand opera suggests that he perceived the minstrel show as a uniquely national expression. So did many of his contemporaries. Thus the preface to one of E. P. Christy's countless "plantation songsters" recounted the origins of the "new institution" in the following terms:

> After our countrymen had, by force of native genius in the arts, arms, science, philosophy and poetry, &c, &c, confuted the stale cant of our European detrac-

tors that nothing original could emanate from Americans—the next cry was, that we have no NATIVE MUSIC; . . . until our countrymen found a triumphant vindicating APOLLO in the genius of E. P. Christy, who . . . was the first to catch our *native airs* as they floated wildly, or hummed in the balmy breezes of the sunny south.

The verbs *floated* and *hummed* served partially to obscure the fact that "our native airs" had been appropriated from the music and dance of African slaves by white professional entertainers, including (among many others) E. P. Christy. Later in the same preface a more realistic account of the actual relationship described the minstrels as having possessed "science and practical skill in music to enable them to harmonize and SCORE systematically the original NEGRO SOLOS." Their labors had resulted in filling "the air of our broad, blest land . . . with the thousand native melodies."[3]

This explanation, with which Twain would probably have concurred, stressed the rural, southern origins of minstrelsy; yet it seems evident that the spread of blackface minstrelsy was closely linked to the rise of the mass circulation press and the nationalization of theater. Hannibal, Missouri, for example, which in Twain's childhood was a rural slaveholding community, could hardly have found fragments of African music and caricatures of black slaves particularly surprising. What made the first minstrel show a "glad" surprise was that it provided a window into the complex culture developing in the new cities.[4] Through that window appeared cultural identifications and hostilities, ethnic satire, and social and political commentary of a wide-ranging, sometimes radical character. In addition, the shows often transmitted sexual messages. Taken as a whole, they provided a kind of underground theater in which the blackface convention rendered permissible topics that were difficult to handle explicitly on the Victorian stage or in print. Spontaneity and ad-libbing, built into minstrelsy from its inception, favored a flexible approach to different audiences and regions, changing moods and times. This combination of adaptiveness and liberty of subject explains in part the popularity and staying power of minstrelsy as mass entertainment. Finally, the convention of blackface was by no means separate from, or neutral with regard to, social content; on the contrary, the blackface convention saturated that content. For a study of the ideology of minstrel shows, the interpenetration of form and content is at the crux of the matter.

The content of minstrelsy was shaped in part by the social experience of its founders and purveyors. Three men, Thomas Rice, Dan Emmett, and E. P. Christy, are generally recognized as founders of blackface minstrelsy. To these should be added the name of Stephen Foster, the major *white* innovator of minstrel music. Where did these men come from and how did they happen to launch a new mode of mass entertainment? Rice, oldest of the four, was born in New York in 1808. He tried unsuccessfully to break into New York theater, then drifted west, working as stagehand and bit player throughout the Mississippi Valley. In 1831, imitating a shuffle he had seen performed by a black man on the Cincinnati levee, Rice for the first time "jumped Jim Crow"—and Jim Crow made Rice's fortune. Adapting his act to various issues—eventually including a minstrel burlesque of Uncle Tom—Rice was applauded in London and became a perennial favorite at New York's famous Bowery Theatre. The second founder of minstrelsy, Dan Emmett, son of a village blacksmith in Mt. Vernon, Ohio, was born in 1815. He ran away to become a drummer in the army and served briefly at posts in Kentucky and Missouri. Dismissed for being underage, Emmett followed circuses and sideshows, occasionally singing comic songs in blackface. Early in 1843 he organized the first blackface quartet as a one-night fill-in at New York's Chatham Theatre. Emmett devoted the rest of his long career to minstrelsy.[5]

Edwin P. Christy, also born in 1815, was the son of "respectable" Philadelphia parents who sought to launch him on a commercial career by arranging to place him in a New Orleans counting house. Christy rebelled and took to the road with traveling circuses. In 1843, he and several other young men were providing musical entertainment at a theater-saloon on the Buffalo waterfront. Apparently having heard of Emmett's success in New York, the Buffalo entertainers called themselves Christy's Plantation Minstrels; later, moving down to New York City, they became a permanent fixture at Mechanic's Hall on lower Broadway. It was through Christy's Minstrels that many of Stephen Foster's early songs reached the public. Foster, eleven years younger than Christy or Emmett, was born in Pittsburgh in 1826. Like Christy, he came of parents with intimations of upward mobility who tried to provide him with a proper education, then sent him off to work as a bookkeeper for an older brother in Cincinnati. Foster was meanwhile writing songs for minstrel shows for which he received ten or fifteen dollars apiece. His "Old Folks at Home," according to the publisher, sold 130,000 copies in three years.[6]

The careers of these four men show several similarities. All were northerners and all except Emmett of urban origin. At least three came of old stock American families and were clearly of middle-class background. They all rejected the straight ways of the Protestant ethic and sought escape into the bohemianism of the entertainment world. Three had direct contact through their wanderings in the lower Mississippi Valley with the music and dance of black slaves, and we know from their own accounts that they consciously exploited this resource. None had achieved success in the theater or in any other pursuit prior to the venture into blackface minstrelsy; and in each case that venture brought spectacular success.[7] The pattern suggested by these summaries probably approximates the experiences of many professionals active during the first three decades of minstrelsy. A sample of forty-three men born before 1838 who achieved prominence as blackface performers in large northern cities or San Francisco yields the following information: five were born south of the Mason-Dixon line (including Baltimore); most of the rest (thirty-one) were born in the North, but of these only five were New Englanders. With respect to urban background, New York, Brooklyn, Rochester, Utica, Troy, Philadelphia, Baltimore, Providence, New Haven, and Salem (Mass.) accounted for twenty-four of the forty-three (with London and Paris probably claiming three or four more). Regionally, upstate New York matched New York City and Brooklyn with nine each; Philadelphia came next with six.[8]

Typical purveyors of minstrelsy, then, were northern and urban; they were neither New Englanders nor Southerners (although their parents may have been); and if of rural or small town origin, were most likely to have come from upper New York State. Eager to break into the exclusive and inhospitable precincts of big city theater, they needed new and exciting materials. These they found during their forced marches through the Mississippi Valley South in the music and dance of slaves and in the half-horse, half-alligator braggadocio of the river and the frontier. The two separate lines had merged to some extent before the minstrels took them over:

> My mammy was a wolf, my daddy was a tiger,
> And I'm what you call de old virginia nigger;
> Half fire, half smoke, a little touch of thunder,
> I'm what dey call de eighth wonder.[9]

Ambivalent especially toward the black component of their borrowings, the minstrels coveted the power and newness of the music, yet failed to recognize its Africanness, or to perceive in it segments of an idiom distinct and separate from the European idiom. They ascribed the impact of slave music to its being close to nature. It "floated wildly" or "hummed . . . in the breezes," to repeat the metaphor of E. P. Christy's preface, and its wildness could be taken simply as part of the general crudity of frontier style. In any case the work of white entertainers with such materials was to "turn them to shape," to Europeanize them sufficiently so that they would not offend refined ears. The dual task of exploiting and suppressing African elements thus began from the first moments of minstrelsy. But these elements possessed great vitality. It was suggested earlier that a major factor in the popularity and staying power of minstrel entertainment was its freedom of subject matter; certainly another—perhaps *the* other—major factor was the persistence of African borrowings (especially in dance movements and sense of rhythm) throughout the entire half-century of blackface minstrelsy.[10]

Partial acceptance of these African musical elements was facilitated by the fact that they fitted logically into a portrayal of the old South that took on a symbolic and powerful, although derivative, meaning for many white Americans during the nineteenth century. But before examining that somewhat removed aspect of minstrel content, it is necessary to turn to a set of meanings that were direct and immediate. For the minstrels, as for the new mass audience upon which they depended, the city was the focal experience of life. The city offered (or seemed to offer) new sorts of work, money, movement, excitement. It offered access to liquor and sex, to education, culture, progress. All this was ignored in the high culture of the established upper classes; Walt Whitman, almost alone among nineteenth-century American poets, celebrated the city. The purveyors of minstrelsy shared in this celebration; but in order to do so, they had to impose some startling transformations upon materials the primary reference of which was to frontier and plantation. Here is one of the early mutations:

> I'm de sole delight of yaller galls,
>   De envy ob de men,
> Observe this nigger when he turns,
>   And talk of dandies then.[11]

The Broadway dandy was in one respect a transplant of the swaggering southwest frontier hero, already widely rendered in blackface. But the dandy also caricatured a new social type in the United States—the urban free black.

Possible uses of this stereotype, which expressed an enthusiasm for city life uncloyed by nostalgia or regret, were limitless.[12] Early in 1852, one of New York's permanent minstrel companies began performing a number titled, "Wake Up, Mose." The hero appeared in the first verse as the already familiar urban free black. "He used to run de railroad—he was de bulgine tender"; and it was clear from the context that "bulgine tender" meant a railroad fireman. The chorus then made an abrupt switch, followed up in subsequent verses, to a fireman of a different sort, and presumably of different race:

> . . . Round de corner de smoke am curling.
> Wake up, Mose! the engine's coming;
> Take de rope and keep a running![13]

The original Mose, as noted earlier, was a characterization of New York's Bowery Boy. Butcher's helper, apprentice carpenter or stonecutter, Mose the Bowery Boy was a gallant volunteer fireman, wheelhorse of city politics and invincible pugilist. As an urban culture hero he derived from, yet stood against, older rural heroes like the New England Yankee or the half-horse, half-alligator of the Mississippi Valley. Mose cared nothing for Yankees or alligators either; he breathed the fire of burning buildings; and when it came to warfare, he could tell even an old frontier fighter like Zachary Taylor how to run his campaigns. Mose transcended regionalism, however, and stood for the new urban mass culture as against the "high" culture of the old elite.[14]

But Mose in blackface was something else. There was of course a historical logic in rendering the Broadway dandy as Mose in blackface, since both had reached the city by different routes from a common ancestry in frontier folklore. But this hardly explains *why* it was done. The value of such a characterization was that it extended minstrel show content to include class satire. As minstrelsy became more formalized, it moved from separate song-and-dance numbers to routines including spoken repartée, and finally to elaborate composites of song, dance and drama. The original foursome of undifferentiated musicians expanded into a line in which customary position corresponded roughly to class identification. The end-men, who always played tambourine and bones, were lower class. By costume and vernacular they were "plantation nigger," or "Broadway dandy," often one of each. The middleman, or *interlocutor*, served as bogus mouthpiece for the high culture.[15] His dress and speech were upper class, sometimes straight, more often burlesqued; and the plot was usually the putting down of the interlocutor by the end-men. Even after the ad-lib repartee of the original line had evolved into more formal presentations, the class character and plot remained substantially the same. Blackface could thus serve to enhance the ridicule directed against upper-class pretensions.[16] More important, it had the effect of preserving the comic mood, since otherwise social satire tended toward serious drama. The careers of real "Bowery boys"—John Morrissey, the prize fighter, for example, or the proletarian congressman Michael Walsh, and especially of David Broderick—acted out mortal conflicts between the new urban culture and the cultures of older elites.[17] This was too serious to be fun. Blackface defused such meanings without denying them. It did so by placing social content in the background of a conventional proscenium that permitted instantaneous escape through shifts of scene and mood and that constantly intervened to discredit serious implications.

Part of the entertainment lay in skating on thin ice. Temperance, a topic taken very seriously by many mid-nineteenth-century Americans, was nearly always an object of ridicule in minstrel songs:

> Nigger, put down dat jug,
> Touch not a single drop, . . .

Parodying the sentimental ballad, "Woodman Spare that Tree," this song, published about 1850, went on to hint at more than the simple pleasures of alcohol:

> I kiss him two three time
> And den I suck him dry
> Dat jug, he's none but mine
> So dar you luff him lie.[18]

Minstrelsy had become mass entertainment in the decade of war against Mexico and the California gold rush. Shows were generally performed by males before largely male audiences. Both in the East and West, the male population was concentrated in factories, boardinghouses, and in construction and mining camps. Frontier settlements had few women, and contemporary accounts tell of men dancing in saloons and hotel dining rooms dressed as women. Given this context, the song quoted above appears as a permissive reference to homosexuality and masturbation, veiled but not negated by the blackface convention. The point here is not the prevalence of homosexuality, but the tolerance of sexuality in general, the realism and the flexibility of standards that flourished behind the false facade of blackface presentation. A more typical sort of minstrel pornography, doubtless derived from Restoration comedy, would be a duet titled "Cuffee's Do-it," in which Cuffee was typed as a Broadway dandy:

> He. O Miss Fanny let me in
> for de way I lub you is a sin
> She. (spoken) O no I cannot let you in . . .
> He. Oh, when I set up an oyster cellar
> You shall wait upon de feller,
> Sell hot corn and ginger pop,
> You be de lady ob de shop.
> She. Oh, Sam, if dat's de trufe you tell . . .
> Oh, Sam Slufheel, you may come in.
> He. Oh, Miss Fanny, I'se a comin' in . . .[19]

Moral permissiveness was not accidental or idiosyncratic: it was an aspect of life-style. The life-style expressed in minstrelsy could appropriately be called *urbanity* since it had developed in middle Atlantic cities, moved west with the Erie Canal and urbanization of the Mississippi Valley and its tributaries, and west again with the acquisition of California. It was both urban and frontier. During the last two major frontier decades, the 1850s and 1860s, even the frontier had become urbanized: its new cities were the garrison towns and mining camps that sprang into existence before much in the way of a rural hinterland had developed around them. When Charles DeLong made the following entry in his diary for Christmas Eve, 1859,

> Spent the day in the office hunting up authorities . . . in the evening went to the gymnasium, and the sparring school, and then called on Elida . . . saw the Christmas tree and then went in and celebrated Christmas with Lide. Came downtown went to Nigger Festival [a minstrel show] and got supper and then went to the Catholic Church to high mass, and then down and got a little burden and went to bed late, raining some . . . .

he might have been describing a day in the life of a moderately successful Bowery politician. Actually DeLong was working out of Marysville, some fifty miles northeast of Sacramento. A political henchman of Stephen Douglas, DeLong earned his living at the time by collecting the California foreign miners' tax from Chinese laborers. "Started with Dick Wade and Bob Moulthrop collecting," he wrote for 23 October 1855, ". . . supper at Hesse's Crossing went down the river in the night collected all the way had a great time, Chinamen tails cut off."[20] DeLong attended performances of many of the same minstrel troupes he would have seen had he lived in New York, because minstrelsy was invading the towns and camps of the Pacific slope. So prominent was San Francisco as a minstrel city that for several years one of New York's leading companies styled itself the "San Francisco Minstrels."[21]

The dual relationship of city and frontier profoundly affected the social content of minstrelsy. Blackface singers (again like Walt Whitman) were protagonists of Manifest Destiny:

> Mose he went to Mexico, and dar he saw Santa Anna;
> He sent a message to de camp, telling Zack [Zachary Taylor] not to surrender.
> Says Santa Anna, "Who are you—you seem to be so witty?"
> Says Mose, "Go 'long—I'm one of de boys—I'm from de Empire City."[2]

Always the West and the westward movement were focal:

> Den I step on board de Oregon
> For de gemman say who bought her
> Dat she for sure's de fastest crab
> What lives upon de water.[23]

Stephen Foster's "Oh! Susanna" (of which the verse above was a topical variation) was first performed in the year of Scott's conquest of Mexico City and reached the height of its popularity during the California Gold Rush. A later cliché, perpetuated by Hollywood and television, has associated the song with westering pioneers from rural regions such as

Kansas and Missouri. Kansas wagonmasters may certainly have sung "Oh! Susanna"; but its origin was Pittsburgh, and it was first popularized in New York's minstrel halls.[24]

Underlying the sociological congruency between city and frontier was a psychological similarity between traveling to the city and traveling west. Each was a difficult journey involving a traumatic break with a previous life. In minstrelsy's complex matrix of social content, the *journey* became the central theme. It stood in contrast to the celebration of urban opportunity and permissiveness as a lament for what had been left behind and lost. This theme, I believe, entered minstrelsy in its beginnings, not in any sense as a reflection of journeys made by black slaves, but as a projection by the white performers of their own experience. The projection was then magnified because it also expressed the psychic experience of urban audiences. The notion of a symbolic journey suggests minstrelsy's powerful impact upon white viewers. At the same time it helps to place in perspective one of the most puzzling aspects of minstrel repertory: the endless evocation of the old South.

Early minstrels (as represented by the samples above) had understood slave music not as African but as close to nature. Correspondingly, they perceived slaves as *part* of nature—part of the nature of the South; and from this curiously ahistorical viewpoint undertook to "delineate" the plantation culture of the South. City dwellers by birth or adoption, they were strangers and interlopers in plantation society. While they might observe and borrow from slave music, their social contacts were with whites, and it is scarcely surprising that their depiction of the South overlapped and duplicated the plantation myth that white southerners were then bringing to perfection as part of their defense of slavery. That myth was also ahistorical because its inspiration was to fix the black slave as an everlasting part of nature rather than as a figure in history.

When the wandering minstrels carried their fragments of African-American music back to northern and western cities, they took them encased in a mythology of the South as a region fascinatingly different, closely wedded to nature, and above all, timeless. The word *timeless* defines the relationship that would develop between the image of the South and the *anomie* experienced by men and women of rural, eastern background who lived in cities or who moved out west. The South became symbolically their old home: the place where simplicity, happiness, all the things we have left behind, exist outside of time.

> Down by the river our log hut stands
> Where father and mother once dwelt
> And the old door latch that was worn by
> our hands . . .[25]

What has been left behind collectively may be a rural past, but individually it is childhood. New cities and new frontiers, attractive to conspiring and perspiring adults, have little room for children; and the South, in the legend of blackface minstrelsy, became the antithesis to both.[26]

Minstrelsy's social content keyed into its politics. When E. P. Christy organized his first entertainments in Buffalo in 1842, he brought in a younger man, George Harrington, who adopted the name Christy and eventually became more famous than his mentor. The senior Christy retired in the mid-1850s; George Christy went into partnership with a New York theatrical promoter, Henry Wood. Under their joint direction, Christy and Wood's became a metropolitan establishment and one of the best-known companies of the pre-war era. Henry Wood belonged to a remarkable family. His brother Benjamin served three terms as a Democratic congressman from the city and one term as state senator; for almost half a century he presided over the aggressively Democratic New York *Daily News*. A second brother was Fernando Wood, copperheadish mayor of New York, fighter for control of Tammany Hall, several times congressman.[27]

George Christy went to San Francisco in 1857. There he performed under the sponsorship of Tom Maguire, West Coast tycoon of minstrelsy, opera and varied theatricals. Maguire had spent his younger days on New York's Bowery as a saloon keeper, hack driver, fight promoter, volunteer fireman and Tammany stalwart. When David Broderick, a New York stonecutter from a similar background, abandoned the Bowery for the Golden Gate in 1849, he lived for several years as a boarder at Maguire's house and apparently helped Maguire to escape bankruptcy by arranging the sale of his Jenny Lind Theatre for $200,000 to an obliging (Democratic) city administration of San Francisco. Maguire was soon back in business with other theaters.[28]

After launching the nation's first minstrel quartet on the New York stage, Dan Emmett toured England with middling success, then returned to White's Minstrel Melodeon on lower Broadway. By the late 1850s, Emmett had worked out a lasting connection with Bryants' Minstrels of New York, next to Christy's the most enduring of the pre-war troupes. Composer of dozens of songs and musical farces, Emmett was especially noted for his walkarounds or group finales. One of these, which took its title from its New York premiere, "Dixie's Land," became popular in the South, where it was appropriated by itinerant minstrels and emerged during the war as "Dixie," the de facto Confederate national anthem. In post-war years, the Bryants, following the trend of theater and fashion, moved uptown to East Fourteenth Street. Emmett by this time had drifted back to the Midwest, but the Bryants commissioned a special walkaround in honor of their uptown location, and Emmett obliged with a piece called "The Wigwam." In May 1868, "The Wigwam" climaxed the Bryants' opening in their new theater at Tammany Hall's recently constructed Fourteenth Street headquarters.[29]

Stephen Foster, drinking himself to death in New York during the Civil War, sometimes peddled his handwritten songs along Broadway, and at least one of the buyers was Henry Wood of Wood's Minstrels. In happier days, Foster had helped to organize the Allegheny City Buchanan-for-President Club. All ardent Democrats, the Fosters were related by marriage to President Buchanan's brother, an Episcopalian minister. In 1856 Stephen Foster contributed two songs to the Buchanan Glee Club. One was a lampoon of Abolitionism; the other was a paean to the unifying spirit of the South:

> We'll not outlaw the land that holds
> The bones of Washington,
> Where Jackson fought and Marion bled
> And the battles of the brave were won.[30]

From such fragments of evidence, several "founding" minstrels as well as two or three of the nation's best-known minstrel companies can be placed in a scattered but consistent pattern of pro-Southern expression and intimate contact with Democratic party leaders in New York and San Francisco.[31] The pattern points to a more general typicality when considered against the background of minstrelsy's political orientation, which has already been defined—in a negative sense—by its social content. Temperance, hostility to recent European immigration, and lack of enthusiasm for, or direct opposition to, territorial expansion were frequently (not always) characteristic of the Whig, Liberty, Free Soil, Native American and Republican parties. Regardless of mutual antagonisms, these parties always opposed the Democratic party, which, in turn, was nearly always hostile to temperance, receptive to recent European immigration, and strenuously in favor of territorial expansion. The positions of the Democratic party on these issues were congruent to the outlook expressed by blackface minstrelsy; the positions of anti-Democratic parties generally were not. Minstrelsy, then, appears to have been oriented toward the Democratic party. Since minstrels were usually northern, as was most of their mass audience, it would seem reasonable to pursue an inquiry into the politics of minstrelsy by investigating its responses to major problems confronting the northern wing of the Democratic party.

[I have previously] defined the Jacksonian legitimizing construct as comprising three basic components: egalitarianism (anti-monopoly), nationalism (territorial expansion), and white supremacy. I argued that northern party leaders could be expected, both for their own career ambitions and through commitment to Democratic principle, to seek to perpetuate, or regain, control of the federal government. In the period of Democratic dominance before the Civil War it was largely a matter of perpetuating Democratic control; and at any particular moment continued control over the federal apparatus depended on unity among the party's regional branches. The price of unity, as set by southern Democrats, was defense of the institution of slavery by the national party. Consequently, a major task of northern leaders was to resist criticisms of slavery from outside the party and to prevent anti-slavery sentiment from infiltrating party ranks. This became no easy task as views hostile to slavery gained widening acceptance in the North and West.[32]

For blackface minstrelsy, slavery was an inescapable topic and its political stance was a defense of slavery. That this should seem a statement of the obvious is in itself a revealing commentary. In a broader frame of reference, artistic endeavors aimed at "delineating" the cultural traditions of oppressed or enslaved peoples would more commonly be associated, I think, with ideologies of liberation than of oppression. Minstrelsy, however, faithfully reproduced the white slaveowners' viewpoint.

Old Massa to us darkies am good
Tra la la, tra la la
For he gibs us our clothes
and he gibs us our food . . .[33]

Slaves loved the master. They dreaded freedom because, presumably, they were incapable of *self*-possession. When forced to leave the plantation they longed only to return. These themes in minstrelsy worked at several levels. On the one hand, propagating the plantation myth, they portrayed slavery as benign and desirable. On the other hand, they reinforced the image of the South as symbol of the collective rural past and of individual childhood, thus appropriating an emotional impact that was logically unrelated to their content. At the same time, the docility attributed to slaves, commendable as this might seem to a southern planter, was certain to strike northern audiences imbued with Jacksonian principles of upward mobility as ridiculous and contemptible.

Was minstrelsy monolithic in its justification of slavery? Almost, but not quite. There appeared a scattering of anti-slavery expressions that entered the genre in two different ways. First, the early borrowings of African-American music and dance carried anti-slavery connotations that sometimes persisted subliminally in traditional verses like this from "The Raccoon Hunt":

My ole massa dead and gone,
A dose of poison help him on
De debil say he funeral song.[34]

Subversive sentiments might be negated in chorus or verses, perhaps added later. This seems to have been the case with the ballad "De Nigga Gineral," which referred to Nat Turner's rebellion, although parts of the song were apparently of older origin. Here the anti-slavery thesis represented by a black general, "chief of the insurgents," is carefully set at rest by antithetical verses telling of his defeat, repudiation by his own followers, and execution.

O, Johnson Ben he drove de waggon
  Ho, boys yere most done . . .
And dey hung him and dey swung him
  Ho, boys, yere most done.[35]

A second and later means of entry for anti-slavery content was through the essentially white identity of romantic and nostalgic songs, European in tradition and style, which quickly became a staple of minstrel repertory. Performed in blackface, yet dealing seriously with themes of parted lovers, lost children, and so forth, these songs both invited identification with the situation of the slave and suggested that slavery might have been the cause of separation or loss. But to admit such a possibility was to contradict the myth of the benign plantation and yield ground to anti-slavery propagandists. Thus, even when rendered in "darkey" vernacular, sentimental minstrel songs seldom made direct mention of slavery. Occasional references did nonetheless break through. They were then usually softened or disguised by shifting specific griefs to the generalized sorrows of time and distance, or by emphasizing the troubles blacks were likely to encounter in the North.[36]

The two sorts of expressions described above represented the only penetration into minstrelsy of anti-slavery views. By contrast, a major trend through the 1850s and into the war years consisted of attacks against Abolitionists, who were portrayed as stupid, hypocritical, cowardly, subservient to England, and practitioners of miscegenation. Minstrelsy not only conveyed explicit pro-slavery and anti-Abolitionist propaganda; it was, in and of itself, a defense of slavery because its main content stemmed from the myth of the benign plantation. Critics of slavery were well aware that the incompatibility between that myth and romantic concepts of love and family were a weak point in slavery's defense, and against this point was directed one of their main attacks—that slavery prevented marriage and broke up families. This was the central message of *Uncle Tom's Cabin*; and anti-slavery singers (never minstrels) like the Hutchinson Family of New Hampshire had been developing similar criticisms long before Stowe's novel appeared. The counter to this attack—in which minstrelsy led the field—took the form of ridiculing the very notion of love, or any other human or humane emotion, among blacks. Within a few months after the appearance of *Uncle Tom's Cabin*, minstrels had coopted the title and main characters, while reversing the message.[37] The famous T. D. Rice "jumped Jim Crow" in the role of Uncle Tom. Indeed, all that was needed to render a serious theme ludicrous in blackface minstrelsy was to permit its dehumanizing form to overbalance the content. In an age of romantic sentiment, minstrels sang love songs like this one:

My Susy she is handsome
  My Susy she is young . . .
My Susy looms it bery tall
  Wid udder like a cow
She'd give nine quarts easy
  But white gals don't know how.[38]

By 1860 the infiltration of anti-slavery sentiments into northern party ranks, combined with the mounting anxiety and aggressiveness of southern Democrats, had made further compromise impossible. The party split; Lincoln was elected; secession and civil war followed. Although virtually impotent at the national level, the Democracy remained locally powerful in many regions of the North. The task now facing its activists was to hold together their potentially large constituency through protestations of loyal Unionism while at the same time seeking to discredit Republican leadership. Once again slavery was at the heart of the matter. The South, Democrats argued, would fight to the bitter end, convinced that the Republicans intended to destroy slavery. But the war could be settled and the Union preserved, if—through ouster of the Republicans from control of the federal apparatus—the slavery issue were fully set at rest. This line was vigorously pushed in mass media accessible to Democratic leaders; and these were primarily newspapers and blackface minstrelsy.

Minstrels readapted the plantation myth to wartime purposes, their message being that a struggle against slavery was neither necessary to save the Union, nor desirable. Traditional blackface caricatures were politicized. The "plantation nigger" now lamented the inexplicable "white folks" war that was causing everyone so much trouble, while up North the "Broadway dandy" thrived like the green bay tree. He conspired with Republican leaders, rejoiced in the war but dodged the draft; paraded in fancy uniform, but took to his heels at the first whiff of gunpowder:

> Niggers dey can pick de cotton—dey'll do it very freely
> But when dey smell de bullets, how dey'll run for Horace Greeley![39]

To their basic paradox of lauding the plantation system in the midst of a war against the plantation South, the minstrels added a satirical and sometimes brilliant critique of Republican war policy. They questioned the competence of particular leaders (including Lincoln). They attacked political generals, profiteers, and shoddy contractors. Songs like Dan Emmett's "How Are You, Greenbacks?" provided a framework for variations upon the class and ethnic sequences worked out during the 1850s.

> We're coming Father Abram, one hundred thousand more
> Five hundred presses printing us from morn til night is o're . . .
> To line the fat contractor's purse, or purchase transport craft
> Whose rotten hulks shall sink before the winds begin to waft.

The bearers of true patriotism, according to minstrel repertory, were honest workingmen who battled to save the Union. Outstanding among these were regiments raised from New York's volunteer fire companies ("For I belong to the Fire Zouaves that started from New York . . ."); and the Irish ("Meagher is leading the Irish Brigade"); and—while nearly always treated comically—the lager-drinking Germans ("I'm Going to Fight Mit Sigel"). General McClellan became a symbol of the straightforward Union-loving soldier as opposed to the profiteering, Abolition-tainted Republican politician. Minstrelsy in 1864 mounted an extensive campaign for McClellan, whose platform as Democratic presidential candidate called for peace on any terms of reunion acceptable to the South.

> We're willing, Father Abram, ten hundred thousand more
> Should help our Uncle Samuel to prosecute the war;
> But then we want a chieftain true, one who can lead the van,
> George B. McClellan you all know he is the very man . . .[40]

Thus while loyal workers and soldiers defended the nation, their efforts were sabotaged by profiteers and politicians, and worst of all, their lives needlessly expended for the benefit of the "niggers":

> Abram Linkum said to me
> Send de sojers down!
> He's gwine to make de niggers free
> Send de sojers down!

At this level the entire spectrum of minstrelsy from the plantation myth through its urban repertory of ethnic humor and class satire was permeated by the blackface form:

> I wish I was a blinkin' [Abe Lincoln], a blinkin', a blinkin'
> I wish I was a blinkin'

I'll tell you what I'd do . . .
Oh, if I was much bigger—some bigger—great bigger,
 Oh, if I was some bigger I tell you what I'd do:
I'd buy up all de niggers—de niggers—de colored African American citizens,
I'd buy up all de niggers, and—sell 'em, wouldn't you?[41]

This "comic-banjo" piece, as it was described, appeared in a songster published in New York in 1863. Geographically and emotionally, it was only a block or two from a song such as this to the lynching of blacks on the sidewalks of New York during the draft riots of the same year.[42]

National historians have traditionally attached major importance to the Jacksonian era. The effects of that era have been interpreted variously in terms of nationalism, politics, social status, population movement, and technological and economic growth. Each of these interpretations assumes the diffusion of new ideas and attitudes through a population, which, during the period under consideration, was moving from the Mississippi Valley to the Pacific Coast and increasing from 17 million to 50 million. Doubtless diffusion of ideas and attitudes occurred in such traditional ways as by word of mouth and written correspondence; but it occurred also through steam-powered presses and popular entertainment that brought mass audiences into the tents, town halls, and theaters of new population centers.

Thus gathered together, they could rejoice in what Mark Twain had described as a "glad and stunning surprise." At other times a vitriolic critic of American society, Twain's uncritical approval of minstrelsy is testimony to the pervasiveness of its influence. Minstrel songs, Twain wrote, "were a delight to me as long as the Negro show continued in existence. In the beginning the songs were rudely comic . . . but a little later sentimental songs were introduced such as 'The Blue Juniata,' 'Sweet Ellen Bayne,' 'Nelly Bly,' 'A Life on the Ocean Wave,' 'The Larboard Watch,' etc."[43] Two of the five songs mentioned were Stephen Foster's. What probably had gladdened Twain on his first encounter with minstrelsy was its portrait of the new urban culture. What he remembered, writing his autobiography long afterward, was the white voice of the sentimental ballads. For Twain, as for many of his contemporaries, these songs touched a central chord of white American consciousness—the place left behind, the endless outward journey: "O! Susannah, don't you cry for me, I'm bound for Californie. . . ." This self-pityingly heroic image, cameoed in a conventional form that negated non-white humanity, epitomized the Jacksonian imagination. Here is the Free Soil hero on his passage to India, strumming blackface minstrel songs.

Notes

1. T. Allston Brown, "The Origins of Minstrelsy," in Charles H. Day, *Fun in Black or Sketches of Minstrel Life* (New York, 1874), pp. 5–10.

2. Mark Twain, *The Autobiography of Mark Twain* (New York, 1961), p. 64.

3. Edwin P. Christy, *Christy's Plantation Melodies No. 4* (Philadelphia and New York, 1854), pp. v–vii.

4. Hans Nathan, *Dan Emmett and the Rise of Early Minstrelsy* (Norman, Okla., 1962); Nathan Huggins, *Harlem Renaissance* (New York, 1971), pp. 244–301; Robert C. Toll, *Blacking Up: The Minstrel Show in Nineteenth-Century America* (New York, 1974). Toll's study provides a nearly definitive survey. Two older but still useful works are Carl Wittke, *Tambo and Bones: A History of the American Minstrel Stage* (Durham, N.C., 1930), and Dailey Paskman and Sigmund Spaeth, *"Gentlemen Be Seated!" A Parade of the Old-Time Minstrels* (Garden City, N.Y., 1928). An earlier version of this chapter appeared under the title "Blackface Minstrelsy and Jacksonian Ideology," *American Quarterly*, 27 March 1975, pp. 3–28.

5. Nathan, *Dan Emmett*, pp. 98–120; Edward LeRoy Rice, *Monarchs of Minstrelsy from "Daddy" Rice to Date* (New York, 1911), pp. 7–8.

6. *Christy's No. 4*, pp. v–vii; John Tasker Howard, *Stephen Foster, America's Troubadour* (New York, 1934), pp. 65–201, 372–77.

7. Brown, *Origins of Minstrelsy*, pp. 5–10; *Christy's No. 4*, p. vii; Nathan, *Dan Emmett*, pp. 70–71, 116–22; Howard, *Stephen Foster*, pp. 202–14.

8. The biographical data comes from Rice, *Monarchs of Minstrelsy*. See also *Bryant's Essence of Old Virginny* (New York, 1857), pp. vii–viii, and *Buckley's Melodies* (New York, 1853), pp. v–vii.

9. Charley White, *White's New Illustrated Melodeon Song Book* (New York, 1848), pp. 51–52; *Christy's Ram's Horn Nigga Songster* (New York, n.d.), pp. 99–100; "'Twill Nebber Do to Gib It Up So," *Old Dan Emmit's Original Banjo Melodies* (Boston, 1843), sheet music in "Dan Emmett" folder, Theater Collection, Harvard Library. See also Nathan, *Dan Emmett*, pp. 50–56, and Constance Rourke, *American Humor: A Study of the National Character* (New York, 1931), pp. 77–103.

10. *Christy's No. 4*, p. v; Nathan, *Dan Emmett*, pp. 70–97; Toll, *Blacking Up*, pp. 11–20, 25–57; Jean and Marshall Stearns, *Jazz Dance* (New York, 1968), pp. 11–60; Marshall Stearns, *The Story of Jazz* (New York, 1956), pp. 3–33, 109–22; LeRoi Jones, *Blues People* (New York, 1963), pp. 1–59, 82–86.

11. "The Dandy Broadway Swell," *Wood's New Plantation Melodies* (New York, n.d.), pp. 50–51.

12. *Christy's Panorama Songster* (New York, n.d. [1850?]), p. 93, for an example of ethnic satire in blackface.

13. M. Campbell, *Wood's Minstrels' Songs* (New York, 1852), p. 25.

14. *Christy's Plantation Melodies No. 1* (Philadelphia and New York, 1851), pp. 45–46. Playbills, Theater Collection, Harvard Library: Chatham Theatre

(New York, 1848); Jenny Lind (San Francisco, 1851); St. Charles (New Orleans, 1857). Walter J. Meserve, *Heralds of Promise: The Drama of the American People in the Age of Jackson, 1828–1849* (Westport, Conn., 1986), pp. 120–22. See also David Grimsted, *Melodrama Unveiled: American Theater and Culture, 1800–1850* (Chicago, 1968), pp. 65–75; and Alvin F. Harlow, *Old Bowery Days: Chronicles of a Famous Street* (New York, 1931), p. 264.

15. Twain, *Autobiography*, pp. 65–66.

16. "Mose he went to college, he said he was a poet . . ." in *Wood's Minstrels*, p. 25. Minstrel burlesques of tragedy and grand opera exemplified this usage. See Harlow, *Old Bowery Days*, p. 265, for an account of T. D. Rice in a burlesque of *Othello*.

17. "Michael Walsh," *Dictionary of American Biography* (New York, 1936), 19:390–91; Jack Kofoed, *Brandy for Heroes: A Biography of the Honorable John Morrissey, Champion Heavyweight of America and State Senator* (New York, 1938); David A. Williams, *David C. Broderick: A Political Portrait* (San Marino, Calif., 1969).

18. *Christy's Ram's Horn*, 76–77.

19. Ibid., 109–10. Many male performers built reputations playing "wench parts," Rice, *Monarchs of Minstrelsy*, pp. 71, 86–87. And see Frank C. Davidson, "The Rise, Development, Decline and Influence of the American Minstrel Show," Diss. New York Univ., 1951, pp. 130–31.

20. Carl I. Wheat, ed., "'California's Bantam Cock': The Journals of Charles F. DeLong," *California Historical Society Quarterly*, 8:346 and 10:185.

21. Rice, *Monarchs of Minstrelsy*, pp. 27, 68–70.

22. *Wood's Minstrels*, p. 25.

23. *George Christy and Wood's Melodies* (Philadelphia, 1854), pp. 39–40.

24. Howard, *Stephen Foster*, pp. 119, 136–39, 144–45.

25. *Christy's Plantation Melodies No. 2* (Philadelphia, 1853), p. 35.

26. Twain repeatedly makes these connections; see Twain, *Autobiography*, pp. 5–6.

27. Rice, p. 20; Samuel A. Pleasants, *Fernando Wood of New York* (New York, 1948); Leonard Chalmers, "Fernando Wood and Tammany Hall: The First Phase," *New York Historical Society Quarterly*, 52 (October 1968): 379–402. On Henry Wood, see Paskman and Spaeth, pp. 155–56.

28. Rice, 20; "DeLong Journals," *California Historical Society Quarterly*, 9:385; "Continuation of the Annals of San Francisco," *California Historical Society Quarterly*, 15 (June 1936): 178–80, 184; *New York Clipper*, 23 May 1868; Kofoed, *Brandy for Heroes*, pp. 69–86; Williams, *Broderick*, pp. 29–31.

29. *Clipper*, 25 April and 30 May 1868; Nathan, *Dan Emmett*, pp. 135–42, 214–75.

30. Howard, *Stephen Foster*, pp. 27–28, 43–45, 256–64.

31. I know of no comparable linkage between any individual minstrel or minstrel group and any party opposed to the Democracy. Song books issued by such parties seem generally to have excluded songs of identifiable minstrel origin.

32. Eric Foner, *Free Soil, Free Labor, Free Men: The Ideology of the Republican Party Before the Civil War* (New York, 1970), pp. 149–55; Foner, *Politics and Ideology in the Age of the Civil War* (New York, 1980), pp. 57–76; Jean H. Baker, *Affairs of Party: The Political Culture of Northern Democrats in the Mid-Nineteenth Century* (Ithaca, N.Y., 1983), pp. 212–58.

33. *Christy's Panorama Songster*, p. 79. See also Toll, *Blacking Up*, pp. 72–97. I think Toll here somewhat overemphasizes the expression of anti-slavery sentiment in minstrelsy.

34. *Christy's Ram's Horn*, p. 102.

35. Ibid., p. 200; *Christy's No. 2*, pp. 44–45.

36. Twain, *Autobiography*, p. 66; Howard, *Stephen Foster*, pp. 210–11, 246; *White's Serenaders' Song Book: No. 4* (Philadelphia, 1851), p. 40.

37. *Christy's Panorama Songster*, p. 85; *Christy's Plantation Melodies No. 3* (Philadelphia and New York, 1853), pp. 10–11, 40–41; *Hooley's Opera House Songster* (New York, 1864), p. 5; "Joshua" [Hutchinson], *A Brief Narrative of the Hutchinson Family: Sixteen Sons and Daughters of the "Tribe of Jesse"* (Boston, n.d.); A. B. Hutchinson, *The Granite Songster* (Boston, 1847); George W. Clark, *The Liberty Minstrel* (New York, 1845). On the permutations of *Uncle Tom's Cabin*, see Harry Birdoff, *The World's Greatest Hit* (New York, 1912), p. 6, and Toll, *Blacking Up*, pp. 93–97.

38. *Christy's Ram's Horn*, pp. 46–47.

39. Frank Converse, *"Old Cremona" Songster* (New York, 1863), pp. 9–10.

40. Dan Bryant, *How Are You Greenbacks* (New York, 1863), sheet music, "Bryant's Minstrels" folder, Theater Collection, Harvard Library. *Hooley's Opera House*, pp. 16–17; *The Little Mac Songster* (New York, 1863), pp. 11–13, 29, 42–43, 53.

41. Converse, "Old Cremona," pp. 44–45, 47–48.

42. James B. Fry, *New York and the Conscription Act of 1863: A Chapter in the History of the Civil War* (New York, 1885); A Volunteer Special [William Osborn Stoddard], *The Volcano Under the City* (New York, 1887).

43. Twain, *Autobiography*, p. 66.

Social Commentary in Late-Nineteenth-Century White Minstrelsy

Robert C. Toll

After the Civil War, the content of minstrelsy changed as pervasively and fundamentally as its form did. Faced with basic changes in American society as well as with increased entertainment competition that included large numbers of black minstrels who made the plantation their specialty, white minstrels devoted much less attention to Southern Negroes and much more to national developments. Minstrels had begun to look more critically at life in the Northern states during the sectional crisis of the late 1850s. But more than anything else it was the Civil War experience—the jarring contrasts between war profiteering and corruption and national idealism and sacrifice—that made white minstrels strikingly expand the range and depth of their social commentary. This became the primary concern of white minstrelsy in the late nineteenth century when immigration, urbanization, and modernization forced the American public to undergo fundamental institutional, social, and moral changes.

In their own informal, perhaps unconscious way, minstrels tried to help their audiences cope with their deepest concerns, anxieties, and needs. But since minstrels, like most other people, did not really understand the complex forces that were transforming their lives, they focused their criticism and explanations on only the most superficial features and the most striking evidence of these changes. In the short run, this oversimplification allowed minstrel audiences to feel that they understood what was happening to them and to their country. Minstrelsy's simplified ethnic caricatures made the nation's diverse immigrants seem comprehensible to native white Americans. Similarly, its attacks on cities as the causes, not the evidence, of social and moral decay gave audiences convenient, though inappropriate, targets for public dissatisfaction and anxiety. In the long run, minstrelsy implanted these stereotypes in American popular thought. As decades passed and conditions grew steadily worse and more uncontrollable, minstrels intensified their criticisms. They also became increasingly frustrated with their inability to offer any solutions. Ultimately, they took refuge in sentimental nostalgia.

When minstrels shifted away from Negro topics, they did not, however, automatically discard their blackface. From the beginning of minstrelsy, one of the functions of the blackface had been to give the minstrel a position similar to the classical fool. Set apart from the society, believed to be mentally inferior and immature, black characters could express serious criticism without compelling the listener to take them seriously. Through the antics and opinions of these characters, audiences could laugh at some of their own difficulties and anxieties while being assured that someone was more ignorant and worse off than they.[1] The blackface that was originally such an eye-catching novelty became, after the war, little more in most cases than a familiar stage convention. The use of Negro dialect was what indicated to the audience that minstrels were portraying Negroes, usually the ludicrous low-comedy types that peopled minstrel farces and provided both the targets and the vehicles for minstrelsy's social criticism. The absence of dialect, on the other hand, permitted blackface characters to sing of their blue-eyed, blond-haired lovers without provoking any protests or to use Irish and German dialects to portray immigrant groups.

Before the Civil War, minstrels ranged widely in their social commentary. They lampooned other entertainment, from Barnum to Jennie "Leather-lungs" Lind, and joked about the telegraphic cable to England, the world's fair in London, and country rubes falling in love with Hiram Powers' nude sculpture "The Greek Slave." Through their ignorant black characters, they "explained" natural phenomena like gravity and electricity. They sympathetically conveyed both the high hopes and the bitter disappointments produced by the California gold rush; and they made light of some of the cults and fads of the day—Millerites, spirit-rapping, "free-knowledgey" (Phrenology), and the Shakers.[2]

Aside from slavery and the abolitionists, however, the only serious subject they extensively treated before the war was the women's rights movement, which they consistently ridiculed and condemned. Some performers, like Eph Horn, specialized in parodying women's rights, and the "Women's Rights Lecture" became one of the standard stump speeches. Besides the typical malaprops, non sequiturs, and convoluted verbiage, these stump speakers hammered at the same point:

When woman's rights is stirred a bit
De first reform she bitches on
Is how she can wid least delay
Just draw a pair ob britches on.

The alleged desire of women to wear pants, and thereby symbolically reject their traditional subservient role, was the minstrels' greatest concern. Predictably, they ridiculed bloomers and any suggestion of equality for women. Mocking women's demand to participate in politics and to "direct the ship of state," minstrels often punned about women loving "parties" and being "vessels."

Jim, I tink de ladies oughter vote.

No. Mr. Johnson, ladies am supposed to care berry
little about polytick, and yet de majority ob em am
strongly tached to parties.

If women had equal rights, minstrels argued, they would be "lowered" from their exalted moral position until they would lose their femininity and act like rowdy men.

I'll run and fight and gouge and bite and
tumble in de mud
Till all de ground for miles around am
kivered wid my blood.

Women, like Negroes, provided one of the few stable "inferiors" that assured white men of their status. Since women's rights seemed to be challenging that, minstrels lashed out against the movement almost as strongly as they attacked Negroes who threatened white male superiority. After the war, when minstrels increasingly turned to social and moral problems, women's challenge to men's traditional role became part of a broader critique of the general decay of social values.[3] Before the war it was a deeply disturbing topical issue, closely linked to the Negro's threat to proper social order. But throughout the nineteenth century, minstrels never varied from their complete condemnation of women's rights.

In the 1850s minstrels began to take note of America's human diversity, a subject that became a major post-Civil War theme. Besides making extensive use of the frontier lore and characters, they occasionally portrayed other native white American folk types: "Sam Simple" the Yankee, "Sam Patch the Jumpin' Man," and "Mose the B'howery B'hoy." But only Mose got more than slight coverage and that only in the mid-1850s.[4] After the mid-1850s the grave questions about slavery and blacks that seriously threatened the nation dampened the buoyant optimism expressed in these white folk types. Furthermore, based as they were on regional folklore, they could not serve as unifying symbols that transcended sectionalism. Thus, they virtually disappeared from the popular stage before the Civil War.

But the most exotic native American, the Indian, who also first came to minstrels' attention in the antebellum years, interested them until about 1880. Over these decades, minstrelsy's portrayals of Indians sharply changed, revealing the public's fluctuating attitudes toward them. Traditionally, white attitudes toward Indians have been characterized by ambivalence. As natural products of America, Indians were viewed as a noble, honorable, fiercely independent people—traits white Americans liked to believe all native Americans had.[5] But as occupants of the land "destined" for white Americans, they were viewed as barbaric pagans, blocking the fulfillment of the American mission. Vacillation between these views typified white attitudes during the nineteenth century.

Although minstrels treated Indians only sporadically before the Civil War, they consistently followed in the idealized footsteps of James Fenimore Cooper's Red Noblemen of Nature and the heroic Sagamore in the popular play *Metamora*. Despite a few negative comments, such as "it was great fun when Tecumseh was shot,"[6] minstrels usually presented Indians as innocents in any idyllic American setting that white men had destroyed. The "Indian Hunter," for example, portrayed an Indian pleading with the white man to let him return to his Western home, to his valiant chieftain father, who had resisted the "insolent conquerors," and to his dark-eyed maid whose "fawn's heart was as pure as snow." Again, minstrels invoked the familiar themes of the idealized home and family threatened by "progress." Why had the white man come to take the Indian's land, the hunter asked, when he had abundant riches of his own? "Why should he come to harm one who never harmed him?" Minstrels completed their tragic images by describing gallant warriors giving their lives to defend their wigwams and their way of life.[7]

Caught up in the turbulence of modernization, antebellum white Americans grasped for symbols of an idealized, romantic past. Since Indians were not at that time a threat or an obstacle to whites, while plantation blacks (not yet fully romanticized) were, in fact, threatening the existence of the Union, the minstrels cast Indians as representatives of a more innocent time and place that had been destroyed by modernization. In mourning for them, the audiences could mourn for their own lost simplicity and for a heroic American past.

In 1865 Bryant's Minstrels enjoyed great success with a long run of "The Live Injin," a typical minstrel farce, except that it centered on an Indian. In the skit, a young lover hired a black servant, Pete, to smuggle notes past his girl friend's interfering father. But when Pete tried it disguised as a woman, his skirt was pulled off and the father chased him away. Deciding that he needed a completely different approach, he masqueraded as an "injin." After several comic Indian songs and dances, he was possessed by his role, went on a rampage, and scalped all the other cast members. This "innocent," heavily slapstick farce signaled a striking change in minstrelsy's portrayals of Indians. Even in lighthearted comedies like this one, the central minstrel image of the Indian shifted from the noble red man to the vicious scalper. Thus, in 1870, when Duprez and Benedict's Minstrels featured an account of their transcontinental railroad trip, they concluded with a railroad explosion after which the "festive red man" rushed in and scalped his "pale(?) faced brother."[8]

After the Civil War, Indians again stood in the way of American expansion. Throughout the 1870s Indian wars raged mercilessly as white Americans, again invoking their "manifest destiny," moved Westward, literally destroying the red man in the process. In this decade, minstrels devoted a good deal of attention to Indians by regularly portraying them in farces, the featured spot in the show. Performed around the nation by many troupes, these skits were consistently, even violently, anti-Indian. In 1872–1873 "Life on the Indian Frontier, or The Comanches" had successful runs performed by different troupes in at least San Francisco, Philadelphia, and Chicago. Set in a frontier town, the skit opened with Indians and whites eating and drinking together. But as the Indians drank more and more, they became increasingly belligerent and threatening, and the villagers retreated. Only the help of the army averted "the attempted Wholesale Murder" of the townspeople by the Indians. The skit concluded with the "downfall of the Savages," underscoring the message that whites should not mix with or trust Indians.[9]

That same year, Schoolcraft and Coes, in a vicious skit, "The Three Chiefs," attacked Indian treaties as too lenient and generous. The minstrels' treaty with Chief Black Foot provided that the government supply every male Indian with rifles, revolvers, and 1,000 rounds of ammunition on the condition he agreed to kill no more than three white people a year or steal no more than two horses every six months. The whole tribe was to get roast beef, plum pudding, custard pie, and ice cream if they committed no more than one massacre and burned down no more than one town a week. Despite this generosity, Black Foot became a renegade, and a $3,000 reward was put on his head. When a Negro deputy, disguising himself as Black Foot, attempted to turn himself in to collect the reward, he was recognized, and the skit ended with people yelling "kill the nigger" and firing guns in a general chase scene.[10]

"WARPATH, SCALPING KNIVES, TOMAHAWKS, Or Adventures in the Black Hills," the San Francisco Minstrels titled their skit about General "Muster." The minstrels evidently portrayed all of the soldiers being killed, because the minstrel playing Muster later appeared as "Crawling Lizzard," and other military men later played other roles. The synopsis, too, indicated that Muster and his men went to the Black Hills and unsuccessfully met the Sioux Nation. "Get your scalps insured," it warned. The Sioux were "a strange tribe. No mercy. Retreat cut off." The scene then shifted to a battle between Ned Buntline, a noted Indian slayer, and Crawling Lizzard. With the woods burning and all seemingly lost, Pond Lilly, a lovely Indian maiden played by Ricardo the prima donna, emerged out of nowhere to lead the backwoodsman out of danger. Except for the happy ending, this was an unusually morose way for the San Francisco Minstrels to close a show. But once they had decided to do a skit about Custer, they really had no choice. In this period, nationalistic white Americans simply could not laugh about or romanticize Indians, who were the enemies in a bloody war. But they could still accept the convention of the Indian girl who aided and loved a white man.[11]

At least two other farces in this period attacked the notion that Indians were anything other than terrifying. In one, Mr. Bones, wearing war-paint, feathers, and a ring in his nose, was adopted into a tribe, which he persuaded to give up fighting in favor of show business. The Indians hired members of the Nebraska legislature and the governor to appear with them in "Wild Bullalum ob de Wilderness," the governor acting as one chief and Bones as the other. They may not have made money, the skit reported, but they did get "lots of scalps worth $100 a piece on the reservation."[12] "Noble Savage," first performed by Duprez and Benedict in 1874 in Providence, Rhode Island, lampooned a tenderfoot writer's romanticized image of Indians. In the skit, a suitor had to bring a real Indian to his prospective father-in-law in order to win his daughter's hand. Rather than actually go West, the suitor hired a black man to impersonate an Indian. When the bogus Indian appeared before the father-in-law, who had been writing romantic novels about the Indian as a noble savage, the father-in-law took one look at him, was terrified, and fled in panic, screaming for someone to "shoot the savage." Like Dan Bryant's "Injin," this black imitator got carried away with the role and went on a scalping binge.[13] This skit explicitly stated minstrelsy's message about Indians in the 1870s: only from the secure armchair did the Indian seem to be a nobleman of nature; in the real world, he was a frightening, vicious enemy.

Minstrels had come full circle from their views of only twenty years before. By the 1870s, caricatures of darkies, in their idyllic plantation homes, served minstrels as romantic symbols of stability, simplicity, and order. Furthermore, minstrel darkies were contented subordinates. Even on stage, minstrels could not portray Indians as content to be the white man's subordinates, either because they in fact violently resisted subordination or because white Americans wanted to believe their country produced only brave, independent people who would rather die than become anyone's subordinates. To fulfill their roles, Indians had to die, either as cruel enemies or as tragic victims—there was literally no "place" for them within white American society.

In 1877, Bret Harte and Mark Twain wrote a play based on Harte's poem about the "heathen chinee." On opening night in New York, Twain explained their purpose to the audience. "The Chinaman is getting to be a pretty frequent figure in the United States," Twain observed, "and is going to be a great political problem and we thought it well for you to see him on the stage before you had to deal with that problem."[14] Although he was wrong about the scope of the "Chinese problem," Twain explicitly stated one of the most important functions of minstrelsy's presentations of ethnic characters. Although on the surface they just sang songs and told jokes about peculiar people, minstrels actually provided their audiences with one of the only bases that many of them had for understanding America's increasing ethnic diversity.[15]

Minstrels delighted in the strange-looking and -sounding immigrants who arrived in America in the mid-nineteenth century and provided unusual material for their shows. As entertainers, minstrels tried to create vivid stage characters, recognizable and amusing types. To do this, they used the technique of the caricaturing cartoonist. That is, they selected highly visible traits unique to a group and then constructed their characterization, really caricatures, around them.[16] Asians had odd-sounding languages, bizarre diets, and wore pigtails; Germans spoke "Dutch," drank lager beer, and ate sauerkraut and sausage; and Irishmen had brogues, drank whisky, partied, and fought. Exaggerating these ethnic "peculiarities" and minimizing or ignoring their commonplace features, minstrels and their vaudeville successors molded distinct ethnic caricatures, each of which sharply contrasted to all the others. Furthermore, since minstrels presented them as if they were adequate representations of these groups, these caricatures made America's human heterogeneity and complexity seem comprehensible and psychologically manageable to members of the audience. Although the minstrels only intended to entertain their public and to increase their own popularity, what they did in the process was to embed ethnic stereotypes in their audiences' minds.

Minstrelsy's most exotic foreigners were the Asians. Although they were rarely seen in most of the country in the mid-nineteenth century, the California gold rush brought white Americans, including minstrels, in contact with the Chinese. Different from Americans in race, language, and culture, the Chinese quickly became a part of the minstrels' array of minor curiosities. Although they referred to the Chinese only occasionally, minstrels consistently presented them as totally alien. They concentrated on the strange sound of their language, their odd clothing, and their reported preference for exotic foods: "Ching ring, chow wow, ricken chicken, a chew/Chinaman loves big bow wow and little puppies too."[17] They did "Burlesque Chinese Dances," mocked the sounds of the language with their "Ching, chang, chung," and were obsessed with the notion that Chinese ate cats and "Bow-wow soup, roasted bow-wow, and bow-wow pie." In the 1870s, Bret Harte's popular poem "The Heathen Chinee" and Dennis Kearny's vehemently anti-Chinese political campaigns in California produced a mild revival of minstrel interest. But except for the ethnic slur, probably inspired by Kearny, "He's no more suited to it [the job] than a chinaman for the Presidency," minstrelsy's portrayals remained unchanged.[18] Even though minstrels never devoted much attention to the Chinese, the way they caricatured them reveals how this process worked at its simplest level. As a new and different group caught the public's eye, minstrels selected a few of their most visible and distinctive features for inclusion in the shows, and when interest in them did not develop further, minstrelsy's treatment remained superficial and laughable.

The dramatic news of Commodore Perry opening up Japan to the United States, coupled with the establishment of a Japanese Embassy in America in 1860, made the Japanese greater public sensations in the Northeast, where minstrelsy was concentrated, than the Chinese ever were. In fact, minstrelsy figured in the initial contacts between the United States and Japan. After the Japanese had entertained Perry and his crew with a Kabuki performance, members of the American crew staged a minstrel show for their Japanese hosts. If this was the end of Japanese interest in minstrelsy, it was just the beginning of minstrelsy's involvement with the Japanese.

"Everybody expects to make a pile by the advent of the 'outside barbarians,'" the editor of the New York *Clipper* observed after the arrival of the Japanese diplomats in June 1860. By that time, George Christy already had incorporated the "Japanese Treaty" into his show with a skit featuring characters like "Simnobudgenokamia," "More Hoecakeawake Moonshee," and "Princess Ko-ket." As a further enticement for audiences, Christy boasted that several members of the Japanese

Embassy would attend the "Grand Japanese Matinee" to be held every Saturday afternoon "for the accommodation of ladies and children."[19] Following their familiar pattern, minstrels capitalized on an eye-catching group, treated them humorously, and even offered them as curiosities for the audience to gawk at.

Minstrel portrayals of the "jap-oh-knees" peaked between 1865 and 1867 when a troupe of Imperial Japanese Acrobats toured in America. Billing themselves as "The Flying Black Japs," at least eight major minstrel companies performed take-offs on this new sensation.[20]

> BALANCING, JUGGLING, TOP SPINNING, AND ENCHANTED LADDERS, HAM-SAND-WICH-CELLAR-KITCHEN and his beautiful son ALL WRONG . . .

"will appear assisted by eleven or eight other 'japs'," Carncross and Dixey boasted in typical fashion in 1865.[21] Although they did not use real Japanese in their shows, minstrels actually attempted spectacular acrobatics. Several, in fact, injured themselves when they fell over thirty feet while performing these gyrations. Yet, the principal attractions remained racial, not gymnastic. Kelly and Leon's large advertisement in the *Clipper* simply announced:

[22]

The original burst of interest in these exotics of the Orient subsided until Gilbert and Sullivan's *Mikado* again brought the Japanese into public attention. In the mid-1880s J. H. Haverly presented a "Colossal Japanese Show" including jugglers, tumblers, necromancers, from "the court theatre of his Imperial Majesty the Mikado of Japan." Haverly evidently had hired an actual Japanese troupe. The playbills and posters advertised what appeared to be authentic Japanese names and showed pictures of Oriental acrobats.[23] Other than this extravaganza, minstrelsy limited its treatments of the Japanese in the 1880s to their extremely popular burlesques of the *Mikado*. In 1885, for example, Thatcher, Primrose, and West advertised the 138th consecutive performance of the *Black Mikado*, which ran well in 1886. The political commentary at the heart of some of these burlesques was revealed by the cast that Carncross's Minstrels used: "Alvin Blackberry," a "smart Coon, chairman of the Ward Committee"; "Whatdoyousay," a Japanese "Black and Tan"; "Grover Tycoon Cleveland," the big "Fly Coon from Washington"; a Japanese "no account"; and "as a special curiosity," a few honest New

York Aldermen. Another company added "Boodle Taker," a Japanese alderman, to the same political cast.[24]

By the 1880s minstrels were not really interested in the Japanese themselves. They were just burlesquing a popular musical and condemning political corruption in America. As they had with the Chinese, minstrels presented the Japanese only as a curiosity and only when some unusual event focused public attention on them. Minstrels never pretended to portray Asians' feelings, attitudes, or motives. For minstrels, Asians were just strange, passing fancies, like Barnum's curiosities. Contrary to Twain's prediction, nineteenth-century white Americans did not have to come to grips with the nature of Asians and their place in America.

Since both the Irish and the Germans made a permanent place for themselves in America, they earned a similar position in the minstrel show. Minstrelsy' treatment of the Germans, which became frequent only after 1860, was consistently more favorable than that it accorded any other group. Although minstrels created comic characterizations of them, they portrayed Germans as practical, hard-working people. Usually played for good-natured comedy, robust German women and burly men, speaking "Dutch" dialects, indulged their immense appetites for sauerkraut, sausage, cheese, pretzels, and beer. Although men frequented lager beer saloons, sometimes drank too much, or ran up tabs they could not pay, they were never rowdy or obnoxious as the minstrel Irish often were. German women were usually built like the "Radish Girl," who was "butty as a shack horse," but, despite their tendency to overeat, they were good, solid, practical women. Minstrels joked about German courtship only because of the characters' hefty physiques and even heftier appetites:

> Vonce dere lifed a dailor's darter
> Und a vellar vot loofed her very much;
> Dat vellar used to take her up to Shon's Woods
> Und dreat her do everding fine,
> Lager bier, und pretzels, blenty of Limburger Cheese,
> Good bologny sausage and Rhine Wine.

Except for the abundance of odd foods, minstrels presented German courting as very proper, indeed almost a model. Unlike many of the frivolous fashion butterflies whom minstrels condemned, German women did not waste their money on senseless fads or flirt their lives away. They always demanded that suitors ask their fathers for permission to court and to marry them; they did not make expensive demands on their wooers; they got married after a proper, if somewhat comical, courtship; and they were efficient homemakers. Even when poor and living in a shanty, a German would always "give you shelter mit something to eat,/Un not from his door turn you into de street."[25]

Minstrels also testified that Germans had earned themselves a place in America by valiantly fighting for the Union. One such character, a shoemaker, enlisted with German "Sigel's" forces to "schlauch dem tam Secession volks," even though he did not want to give up his sauerkraut, "switzer kase," and beer for army salt pork. And, minstrels asserted, Germans also paid the brutal costs of the war along with the native Americans. Many died, and others like "Shonny" had his legs blown off. But despite such sacrifices and the good lives they led, Germans still suffered discrimination. Know-Nothings who attacked Germans, Frank Converse charged in 1863, did not even know the difference between good and bad people. And thirteen years later, Sam Devere, a German minstrel who, like Luke Schoolcraft and other Germans, performed a good deal of German material, had one of his characters say he hated to complain about America, but he had been harassed wherever he went and whatever he did by "loafers" who should "be dead for making fun of the Dutchman."[26]

Reflecting their bias in favor of the industrious Germans, minstrels contrasted German successes in America to Irish failures. One song, for example, compared a German to an Irish woman. Although Biddy, who had been in America for five years, was still a complete failure, Hans, who had come to America without a cent only two years before, already owned his own home, a sausage and bakery shop, and was worth $2,000. Hard work and a keen business sense had paid off for him. But Biddy, with her lackadaisical manner, did not realize that she could not succeed selling flat beer and stale food. After he purchased her business, Hans quickly converted Biddy's failure into another of his successes.[27] To minstrels, as to many other Americans, all Germans were like Hans. Because they fit so well into white American values and world-view, Germans seemed model immigrants. Thus, from the beginning, minstrels portrayed them as positively as they could any group while still playing for laughs and emphasizing group peculiarities.

If Germans were the favorite immigrants in the minstrel show, the Irish were the most numerous. In the 1840s prejudice and discrimination against the Irish in America were rampant, principally because the Irish were a rapidly growing cheap labor force that drove wages down, but also because they were Catholics, who natives feared were Papal agents sent to corrupt the American democratic experiment. Although the earliest minstrel portrayals of the Irish were less vitriolic than most of the anti-Irish rhetoric, they reflected some of these feelings. As early as 1843, minstrels attacked "Paddy" as "de biggest fool dat eber walk" because he did not know how to do anything right. When he got political rights, minstrels charged, he just sold his vote to the highest bidder. In 1848, they condemned the Irish for rioting in Philadelphia and killing both blacks and "natives" in violent raids supposedly led by priests. Minstrels also complained that the city officials offered a reward to find the people who had burned a Catholic church: "But to cotch dem [Irishmen] dat killed freedom's sons,/De state couldn't find no law nor funds."[28] In the 1840s minstrels also began to describe the Irish as heavy-drinking, free-swinging brawlers. But minstrelsy's tone in much of this was light, not sinister or threatening. Even the fights were brotherly brawls gleefully enjoyed by all, much like the last dance at a party—a happy, if violent, closing formula.[29] This light tone made these songs the antithesis of the somber temperance songs on the same theme and of the menacing "razor-toting nigger" songs of later years. But they still presented unfavorable, stereotyped images of Irish men and of nagging and/or brawling Irish women.

But in subsequent years, the large number of Irishmen who became minstrel stars, including Dan Bryant, George Christy, Matt Campbell, Billy Emerson, and a host of others, broadened and softened these negative images of the Irish. Beginning in the 1850s, when minstrelsy was still concentrated in the Eastern cities where the heavy proportions of Irish population must have comprised part of the minstrel audience, minstrels began to portray more favorable images of the Irish. A collection of the Sable Harmonists' songs published in about 1850, for example, contained six Irish songs by John Collins. Except that he used Irish names like "Molly Malone" and "Katy O'Conner" and referred to St. Patrick's birthday, his songs were indistinguishable from typical romantic and sentimental ballads of the period. Later in the decade, Collins sang of the beauties of Ireland and his sorrow at leaving it, concluding with a prayer that Erin become a free nation. The Irish, Collins asserted in song, differed only in name; they too were romantic lovers and freedom-loving patriots. In 1859, Matt Peel, also an Irish minstrel, added another favorable dimension by singing that although Paddy was poor and had only a small shabby house, "no king in his palace" was prouder than he was when at home with the family he loved "more than gold."[30]

Complexity and humanity in portraying the Irish became common only in the 1870s, when an Irishman, Edward Harrigan, left minstrelsy for the variety theater and traded his blackface for his more natural Irish brogue. Called both the "American Dickens" and the "American Gilbert and Sullivan," Harrigan and his partner, Tony Hart, began with a short Irish skit in 1873. Within five years they had developed a series of full-length plays portraying ethnic life in New York City. Concentrating on common people and on the vitality of their cultures, the team won unprecedented success by weaving an intricate web of ethnic life and conflict with the Irish at the center and blacks, Germans, and Italians intertwined around them.[31]

Although his German and black characters were important, Harrigan's greatest achievement was his presentation of the Irish point of view. Through his major character Dan Mulligan, who came to America in 1848, fought in the Civil War, bought a grocery store, and became a successful local politician, Harrigan portrayed the complexity of the Irish—and their humanity. His Irishmen were laughed at, but they were also laughed with; they were drinkers and brawlers, but they were also hard workers; they engaged in political graft, but at the same time worked for their people. Harrigan also praised the strong Irish sense of group identity and their flourishing social organizations; he applauded their bravery during the Civil War, lamented the human anthills they had to live in, and denounced the discrimination they had to endure. In short, he presented a full panorama of Irish life.

Although greatly influenced by Harrigan and Hart's portrayal of the Irish, minstrels could never present characters with the complexity, depth, and humanity that Harrigan achieved. The forms they worked in differed too greatly. Harrigan and Hart had a resident theatrical company in New York that presented full-length plays to a heavily ethnic, working-class audience. Although not strictly speaking an exclusively ethnic theater, like Yiddish theater that was meaningless to people who did not understand Yiddish, Harrigan and Hart's shows were in-group experiences. Because of this and because full-length plays allowed, almost required, depth of characterization, they presented relatively complex, multifaceted characters and plots that unfolded throughout the series of plays. Since minstrels, on the other hand, traveled extensively to the heartland of white America, they did not usually have an ethnic audience and could not build up a consistent clientele with whom they could develop continuities. Furthermore, minstrelsy as a form had its roots in caricature, not characterization, and it required diversity: short, self-contained acts, lavish production numbers, and slapstick farces. None of these allowed the in-depth characterization or the presentation of different perspectives on the same subject that were necessary to capture humanity. Minstrels could easily *diversify* their portrayals of groups but could not easily capture human complexity. Consequently, when they borrowed from Harrigan and Hart, they took individual pieces, not the complex networks of interrelated characters and events.

Although some minstrels did not acknowledge their debt to him, Harrigan's presence overshadowed minstrelsy's portrayals of the Irish after the mid-1870s. While continuing to sing of Irishmen drinking and fighting, as Harrigan himself did, minstrels greatly diversified their images of the Irish. Drawing both on Harrigan's description of Irish problems and on the vogue for temperance songs, several minstrels sang of Irish parents lamenting the ill effects of drinking and city life on their children. "Since Terry First Joined the Gang" and "Since Dennis Took to Drink," Irish parents complained, they both used slang, had no jobs, got into trouble, talked back to their parents, and even ended up in jail.[32] Like so many other parents, minstrels pointed out, the Irish too worried about their children facing the city's many temptations and vices. Such concerns were never expressed by minstrelsy's Northern Negro characters, who were living embodiments of vice and folly at their most absurd. In great contrast to their diverse portrayals of both the Germans and the Irish, minstrels presented blacks in only a few stereotyped roles: as contented subordinates on the plantation, as ignorant low-comedy fools, and as ludicrous, pretentious incompetents. Whites needed these fixed images of blacks to reassure them about their own positions. Since they did not use the Irish in this way, minstrels had much greater flexibility in portraying them.

Again following Harrigan, minstrels praised Irish social clubs, policemen, and politicians as representatives of their community. The politicians threw parties for the people, held office in their name, and gave everyone a "fair shake." When there were no jobs, they properly "made them up." Minstrel characters also rejoiced in the dignity all Irishmen gained when John L. Sullivan became heavyweight boxing champion. Irishmen of all sorts worshipped him, minstrels sang, and even lined up to shake the "hand that shook the hand of Sullivan."[33] Minstrels also protested the discrimination the Irish suffered despite their commitment to America. "No Irish Need Apply," minstrels complained, was what honest Irishmen heard when they looked for work. But when America wanted soldiers, it "never said no Irish need apply." The Irish, moreover, had contributed generals, soldiers, statesman, and poets to America. Although minstrel Irish expressed the hope that Ireland would be free, they did not reject America. They merely longed for their homeland to be free from British tyranny, a desire Americans fully understood.[34]

By the 1880s, minstrelsy's images of the Irish had become quite varied and diverse. Unlike the Germans, who had gotten favorable treatment from the beginning, the minstrel Irish went from simple, negative caricatures to a more diversified treatment than that given any other group, even the Germans. Since this so sharply contrasted to their treatment of blacks, it is important to understand why it happened. Certainly Harrigan's great success, which caused minstrels to incorporate some of his features, was a major factor. But this is an insufficient explanation. Minstrels, after all, could have borrowed selectively and maintained their simple negative images. To be sure, the substantial numbers of Irishmen who became minstrels played an important part in humanizing minstrel portrayals. But when blacks became minstrels, they could make only minor changes in minstrel stereotypes of Negroes. The critical point was that native, white Americans had no deep-seated need to keep the Irish in "their place" or to justify the place they were kept in as they did with blacks. Furthermore, a great many Americans probably had no preconceived image of the Irish, which meant that Harrigan and the Irish minstrels' diverse, humane ideas about the Irish could have great impact. Probably most important of all, the Irish and the Germans were fellow white men, whom white Americans could much more easily accept than they could native-born blacks.

Besides ethnic diversity, minstrels were deeply concerned about the social and moral decay that they saw taking place. To them, cities, where these developments were most obvious, seemed the problem. Although some minstrel songs neutrally described cities, minstrels, like most Americans were overwhelmingly negative toward cities from the time they first noticed them.[35] The only substantial changes in their treatment over time were in the breadth of charges they leveled and in the growing importance urban topics assumed in the shows. As their audience changed, so did their emphasis. In the 1850s, while still based in cities, minstrels limited themselves to attacking the dire living conditions and to lambasting the unproductive and often immoral lives of urban dilettantes; in the 1860s, as they traveled more, they added warnings about "city slickers" preying on new arrivals; and in the financially rocky 1870s and 1880s they also attacked inequities in wealth, which they associated with cities.

Beginning in the 1850s minstrels, speaking to urban audiences, protested a wide range of urban problems: stage coaches that drove too fast and knocked women and babies down, filthy streets that were never cleaned, policemen who demanded bribes, people selling votes and buying wives, manipulating politicians, high taxes, and continual robberies. They frequently complained about the atrociously high rents people had to pay, but what they got for these high prices was even worse—or at least funnier. When moving into a new place, Charlie Fox complained, he and an old lady were asked by the cigar-smoking landlord whether smoke bothered them. Both said it did not, paid their money, and then were told that it was a good thing smoke did not disturb them because the fireplaces smoked so badly that they would be smoked beef in less than two weeks. Fox also said he was changing boardinghouses because the food, which consisted of stewed cat, raw crocodile, monkey's feet, broiled flunkies, and arsenical soups, had hair in it. But at least, he concluded, there was not a single bug in the house. All of them were married and had children.[36]

Minstrels were very seriously disturbed by what seemed a shocking deterioration of moral values in the city. But they attacked only symptoms, not causes. People no longer attended churches, they lamented.

Pompey, does you eber attend church?

Why yes, I go a good deal—considerable—almost ebery Sunday—occasionally—once in a while—a little—not much if any.

And, when the city dwellers did go, minstrels complained, "churches built for prayer are where people show off their fashions."[37] Everywhere they looked they saw conventional morality being ignored and families disintegrating. Men put ads in newspapers to meet pretty girls and, what was worse, got answers. Divorce and infidelity seemed to be sharply increasing. One minstrel character's wife "fell to temptation" and deserted him to "live in luxury with her lover." Many husbands became drunkards and adulterers. One drunken man even tried to pick up his own wife on the street, while a number of others boasted of their nightly sexual exploits.[38]

To minstrels, the city's most pernicious effect was its corruption of the young. In Central Park, minstrels complained, there were many wayward young people, often mere boys, who:

> Instead of being home with their mamas
> Are running round smoking penny cigars
> And girls scarcely sixteen years old
> Laughing and chatting with them so bold
> And doing the thing that is not right
> On Central Park on a Sunday night.

Many of the younger generation even showed complete disregard for their aging parents. One old minstrel character, for example, who had loved and cared for his children, found them sending him off to the poorhouse to die alone. "God knows how their father loved them," he lamented, "but they've driven him out into the street."[39]

Perhaps worst of all, young people were obsessed with frivolous and self-indulgent dilettantism like the decadent European aristocrats whom Americans so often condemned.

> Our dandies now have lots of brass, But very little brains,
> Their pants are made to fit so tight, Their legs are like a crane's.
> Our ladies too are like the men, They've got to wearing boots,
> With dresses made of costly silk, Spread out with barrel hoops.

Calculated dishonesty, expensive clothing, lives spent in trivial flirtations, a complete rejection of useful work, a tendency to "obey society not himself": all the best American traits inverted. The very heart of the egalitarian experiment seemed lost. Minstrels continually hammered at these changes by ridiculing the "dandies" and "swells" who epitomized them. Again, ludicrous black characters carried these trends to ridiculous extremes, providing audiences with models of this social inversion at its worst. But minstrels had long presented ludicrous blacks "out of their places." Now they added nondialect characters—their own children. Senseless young women wore hoop skirts, hair pieces, bustles, extravagant silks and satins, and "palpitators to swell their bosoms"; they showed their legs, painted their faces, and shamelessly flirted with strangers; they shirked all work, but read every new romance and sonnet and flocked to lavish balls and parties; and, fancying themselves better than poor people, they forced their parents deeply into debt to maintain their position in the "better set."[40] Minstrels also satirized male dandies, but more often, they portrayed men, even dandies, as victims of demanding females who forced them to live beyond their means. One such "Modern Fast Young Gentleman" gave lavish parties, had fast horses, several yachts, and many servants to turn poor people away from his gates. Finally, his creditors caught up with him and sent him to prison.[41] Although minstrels attacked both male and female dilettantes, they placed much more blame on the women, who minstrels felt should have forced men to settle down and raise families.

Beginning in the 1860s, as minstrels traveled more widely, they warned their new audiences about the hazards awaiting urban visitors. Again, they commonly blamed women and pictured men as victims. Although they occasionally ridiculed the visitors as "gawks" or "countrymen green as peas"[42] who foolishly squandered their money on women, fashions, drinking, and gambling, they usually pictured them as naïve prey for professional thieves and extortionists. One young farm boy from New Jersey learned of the hardships of the city while he was still on the train. After a young widow asked him to hold her baby and then disappeared, he discovered a note from her telling him that the baby was dead and that she could not afford to bury it.[43] Others were bilked on the train, but most fell victim when they went looking for recreation in the cities. Women picked men up, got them drunk, drugged their wine, and robbed them; some even had male accomplices who "rolled" the victims. One woman, for example, allowed herself to be picked up and then started screaming that she was being molested. After her "date" was arrested, she wrote him a note saying that if he paid her, she would drop the charges and her friends at the police station would release him. Women, too, fell victim to city slickers, especially "old maids" all too willing to trade money for companionship.

Rural visitors, minstrels asserted, simply did not know how to cope with the new urban morality, which stressed that the only way to survive was "to be stronger than everybody else—lie, cheat, and steal if necessary." And lest these examples were not enough, minstrels preached directly to their audiences: "Whoever you meet," George Christy warned, "look for their little game."[44]

Besides condemning the living conditions, the social and moral changes, and the hazards of city life, minstrels also associated it with extreme inequities of wealth. During the economically disastrous 1870s and 1880s some minstrels became overtly "antirich man." The wealthy complained of hard times, minstrels claimed, only because they could not get even more money than they already had. "De poor man and his family do all de sufferin," a minstrel charged, "and de rich all de jawin." The rich, another minstrel alleged, "own all the railroads and all of the land, and tell all the people to go and be d——." Employers callously disregarded the welfare of their workers as long as they stayed on the job. Although coal miners labored hard at their dangerous jobs, the "great ones," secure in the warmth of their homes, cared nothing about the danger of the mines even though:

> The very fires their mansions boast
> To cheer themselves and wives
> Mayhap were kindled at the cost
> Of jovial colliers lives.

In 1884, a minstrel complained that businessmen, taking advantage of the economic difficulties, lowered wages and left the workingman's children crying for bread. Another referred to "blood-sucking, thieving employers," while arguing for fair wages. Minstrels also strikingly contrasted the luxurious lives of the rich and the dire fate of orphan children freezing to death in the street while begging for pennies. These songs and speeches constituted a strong indictment of the insensitivity and social irresponsibility of the wealthy.[45]

But like many other Americans in the late nineteenth century, minstrelsy's only remedies were traditional platitudes.[46] In the face of open violence between unions and employers, Bobby Newcomb of the San Francisco Minstrels typically urged: "Let capital shake hands with labor/Let the poor have the bread they earn." After naïvely pleading for this gentlemanly agreement, he concluded by preaching to his audience:

> Remember the poor love their children,
> So give them a smile not a frown.
> Live and let live, be your motto,
> Oh, don't put the poor working man down.[47]

Consistently sympathetic to the poor, who probably sat in their audiences, minstrels still thought only in terms of conventional morality. They reminded their audiences that even thieves and "nymphs of the pave" could mend their ways and urged everyone to "offer a helping hand" to the less fortunate. They incessantly intoned familiar aphorisms extolling nineteenth-century American values: "Always Be Ready When Your Chance Comes," "Pull Hard Against The Stream," "Slow and Steady Wins The Race," "Where There's A Will There's a Way," and many others. They also offered lessons in interpersonal relations and personal morals: "Forgive and Forget, But If You Can't Do Both, At Least Forgive," "Never Hit a Man When He's Down, Boys," "Always Do to Others As You'd Wish to Be Done By," "Put the Brake on When You're Going Down the Hill."[48]

Confronted with what they saw as fundamental decay of their world, minstrels were unable to offer any solution. They made the nation's growing ethnic diversity seem comprehensible by adding more caricatures to the show. They lashed out at the effects of urbanization and industrialism, but they had only moralisms for remedies. Consequently, they became increasingly escapist, wallowing in sentimentalism and nostalgia. Longing for a simple, secure time when there were no problems, they looked back to an idealized past. In grandfather's day, one minstrel recalled, men were judged by merit, not money; styles were sensible; young men did not ogle girls; married men were faithful; politicians were honest; and there was no war. One hundred years ago, another intoned, farmers did not cut their legs off with mowing machines; there were few divorces; lamps did not explode and kill people; there were no "Turkish harems at Salt Lake"; young women did not lose status if they did a little work; everyone made his own clothes; and everybody was honest.[49]

Even the plantation was not immune from the destructive forces of "progress." After the Civil War, white minstrels concentrated their portrayals of Southern Negroes, a minor but significant portion of the show, on the nostalgic Old Darky. Whether these characters had gone North and then returned or had never left, they found their old plantation gone, destroyed by the war. Aged, weak, and alone, they recalled the happy, carefree prewar days, which further underscored the tragedy of the destruction of the plantation. Since it was gone, however, audiences did not have to hear protests against the more unfortunate aspects of the plantation—like slavery. Yet they could still bask in its warmth through the memories of the Old Darky. They could envy his carefree life of perpetual childhood—singing, dancing, and frolicking. They could even momentarily share his simple world, free of the worries, insecurities, and responsibilities that they had to face. At the same time, they could feel comfortably superior to him and certain that, whatever else changed in their lives, he would always be their subordinate. Through him they could also mourn for lost simplicity, order, and control. Although he certainly did not offer an antidote for their problems, the Old Darky provided a temporary diversion, a reassuring certainty that whites desperately needed and clung to.

Notes

1. For a discussion of the minstrel as fool, see Constance Rourke, *American Humor* (New York, 1931, Anchor ed.), pp. 84–85; and Charles Haywood, "Negro Minstrelsy and Shakespearean Burlesque," Bruce Jackson, ed., *Folklore and Society: Essays in Honor of B. A. Botkin* (Hatboro, Pa., 1966), pp. 77–92.

2. "Listen to the Darky Band," *De Susannah and Thick Lip Melodist* (New York, 1850), pp. 18–19; "The Minstrel Band," *Sable Songster* (Philadelphia, 1859), pp. 70–71; Charles White, "Atlantic Steamship," *White's Serenaders Song Book* (New York, 1851), pp. 77; E. P. Christy, "Julius' Trip to the World's Fair," *Plantation Melodies #2* (New York, 1851), pp. 18–19, and *Old Uncle Ned Songster* (Philadelphia, 185–?), pp. 97–98; "Jordan is a Hard Road to Travel," *Wood's New Plantation Melodies* (New York, 1855), pp. 5–6; *Charley White's Ethiopian Joke Book* (New York, 1855), pp. 27, 36, 60; "Billy Barlow," *Bryant's Songs from Dixie Land* (New York, 1861), pp. 15–17; "I'm Off to California," *White's Serenader*, pp. 30–31; *White's Joke Book*, pp. 29, 45; "California Emigrant," *New Negro Band Songster* (Philadelphia, n.d. [185–?]), pp. 241–42; "Going Around the Horn," *Bryant's Dixie*, pp. 32–33; "Around the Horn," *Bob Hart's Plantation Songster* (New York, 1862), p. 6; *White's Serenader*, p. 57; Ordway Aeolians, "The Returned Californian," Boston, 1852, sheet music, HTC [Harvard Theater Collection]; "Joe Bowers," *Bryant's Dixie*, pp. 25–27.

3. "Phoebe Anna White," *Songs of Kunkel's Nightingale Opera Troupe* (Baltimore, 1854), pp. 18–19; for Eph Horn's use of women's rights, see programs of Wood's Minstrels, Morris Brothers, Pell and Trowbridge Minstrels, and Buckley's Serenaders, HTC; T. Allston Brown, *History of the American Stage* (New York, 1870); Christy and Wood's Minstrels, "The Bloomer Paraders," May 1857, G. D. Odell, *Annals of the New York Stage*, 15 vols. (New York, 1927–49), Vol. VI, p. 584; Fellows Opera House, New York, July 2, 1851, Odell, Vol. VI, p. 76; *White's Joke Book*, pp. 40–41, 53. For discussions of woman's role as the keeper of morals and the great anxiety about changes in that role, see Ruth Elson, *Guardians of Tradition* (Lincoln, Neb., 1964), pp. 301–12; William R. Taylor, *Cavalier and Yankee* (New York, 1961, Anchor ed.), pp. 141–43; James C. Hart, *The Popular Book* (Berkeley, 1961, paperback ed.), p. 86; Barbara Welter, "The Cult of True Womanhood," *American Quarterly*, XVIII (1966), 151–75.

4. Charles White, *Sam's Courtship* (New York, 1874 [first performed in 1852]); *White's Joke Book*, p. 46; for more information of Sam Patch, see Richard M. Dorson, "Sam Patch Jumping Hero," *New York Folklore Quarterly*, LXIV (1947), 741–47; For Mose in minstrelsy, see Odell, *Annals of the New York Stage*, Vol. VI, p. 76; Matt Campbell, *Wood's Minstrel Songs* (New York, 1855), p. 25; *White's Serenaders*, pp. 9–10; E. P. Christy, *Plantation Melodies #1; Ned Songster,* pp. 67–68.

5. Winthrop Jordan, *White over Black* (Chapel Hill, N.C., 1968), pp. 90–91.

6. "Double Back Action Spring," *Negro Forget Me Not Songster* (Philadelphia, n.d.[1848]), pp. 38–40.

7. "Indian Hunter," *New Negro Forget Me Not Songster* (Cincinnati, 1848), pp. 128–29, and *Harry Pell's Ebony Songster* (New York, 1864), p. 61; Harmoneons, "Indian Warrior's Grave," Boston, 1850, sheet music, HTC.

8. Dan Bryant, *The Live Injin* (Chicago, 1874); see Bryant's Minstrels, New York, 1865, programs, HTC; New York *Clipper*, Nov. 5, 1870.

9. *Clipper*, Sept. 14, 1872, Sept. 21, 1872, Oct. 4, 1873; Simmons, Slocum, and Sweatnam's Minstrels, Philadelphia, 1873, playbill, HTC.

10. J. C. Stewart, *The Three Chiefs* (New York, 1876).

11. San Francisco Minstrels, New York City, n.d., program, HTC.

12. *Minstrels Gags and End Men's Hand-Book* (New York, 1875), pp. 35–36.

13. Frank Dumont, *Noble Savage* (New York, 1880), first performed Aug. 21, 1874.

14. Quoted in Arthur H. Quinn, *A History of the American Drama Since the Civil War* (New York, 1943), pp. 110–11.

15. Robert Merton, *Social Theory and Social Structure* (Glencoe, Ill., 1957), pp. 19–84, clearly distinguishes between manifest and latent functions, basically the difference between stated purposes and practical or objective results.

16. Milton Gordon, *Assimilation in American Life* (New York, 1964, paperback ed.), pp. 79–81, argues that highly visible (extrinsic) traits are often more important in perpetuating stereotypes than internal (intrinsic) traits. Minstrelsy certainly supports this view.

17. "A Chinaman's Tail," *Buckleys' Ethiopian Melodies #4* (New York, 1857), p. 66.

18. Thomas Carey, *Brudder Gardner's Stump Speeches and Comic Lectures* (New York, 1884), pp. 37–40; New York *Clipper*, Oct. 5, 1878; Campbell's Minstrels, New York, n.d. (1850s), playbill, NYLC [New York Public Library Collection]; *White's Jokebook*, p. 45; "Heathen Chinee," Luke Schoolcraft, *Shine On Songster* (New York, 1873), "Hong Kong Gong," *Bobby Newcomb's San Francisco Minstrels' Songster* (New York, 1868), pp. 22–23; "Big Long John," *Charles H. Duprez's Famous Songster* (New York, 1880), p. 25.

19. *Clipper*, June 16, 1860; advertisement for George Christy's Minstrels, n.p., June 21, 1860, clipping, NYLC.

20. Carncross and Dixey's Minstrels, Campbell's Minstrels, Hooley's Minstrels, Kelly and Leon's Minstrels, Arlington Minstrels, San Francisco Minstrels, George Christy's Minstrels, and La Rue's Minstrels, programs and playbills, HTC, NYLC.

21. Carncross and Dixey's Minstrels, Philadelphia, 1865, playbill, HTC.

22. *Clipper*, July 20, 1867, Nov. 17, 1867; Odell, *Annals of the New York Stage*, Vol. VIII, p. 220.

23. Haverly's American European Original Mastodons, n.p., n.d. [1883?], poster and playbills, NYLC.

24. Done frequently by Haverly's, McIntyre and Heath's, Carncross', Thatcher, Primrose, and West's Minstrels in 1886, see programs and playbills in HTC and NYLC; Biemiller's Opera House, Sandusky, Ohio, Feb. 4, 1887, program, HTC.

25. "Der Slate," *Shoofly Don't Bodder Me Songster* (New York, 1871), pp. 78–79; Dan Bryant, "New York City," *Bryant's Essence of Old Virginia*

(New York, 1857), p. 12; "The Radish Girl," *Bob Hart's Plantation Songster*, pp. 46–47; "She Shook the Tailor," and "The Schoos Maker's Daughter," *Corporal Jim Songster* (n.p., n.d.[1870s]), pp. 58, 61; "Wake Out Serenade," *The Dockstaders' T'shovel Songster* (New York, 1880), p. 25; "The Dutchman's Shanty," *Bob Hart's*, p. 55.

26. "I'm Going to Fight Mit Siegal," *Pell's Ebony*, pp. 14–15; "Cruelty to Shonny," *Bob Hart's*, p. 22, and *Bryant's Shoo Fly*, p. 29; "The Difference," *Frank Converse's Old Cremona Songster* (New York, 1863), p. 35; "Look at De Dutchman," *Sam Devere's Combination Songster* (New York, 1876), n.p. This songster had fifteen songs in German dialect, an unusually large number but typical of Devere and Luke Schoolcraft, both Germans. See also *Sam Devere's Burnt Cork* (New York, 1877), Schoolcraft, *Shine On*.

27. "Ireland versus Germany," *Cool Burgess' Oh Don't Get Weary Children Songster* (New York, 1877), pp. 16–17.

28. For anti-Irish prejudice see Oscar Handlin, *Boston's Immigrants* (Cambridge, Mass., 1941); "Old Paddy Whack," *Deacon Snowball's Negro Melodies* (New York, 1843), pp. 18–19; "Philadelphia Riots" and "De Southwork Rebellion," *Negro Forget Me Not Songster*, pp. 98–101, 101–106.

29. "Lannigan's Ball," *People's New Songster* (New York, 1864), pp. 27–28; "Away Goes Dufee" and "Mr. McLauglin's Party," *Dan Bryant's New Songster* (New York, 1864), pp. 65–66; "Paddy Connor's Wake," *Ned Turner's Bones and Tambourine Songster* (New York, 1869), pp. 59–60.

30. "Molly Malone," "The Bowld Soger Roy," "The Birth of St. Patrick," "Widow Machree," "Katy O'Conner," "Croos-Keen Lawn," *De Sable Harmonist* (Philadelphia, n.d.[1850]), pp. 19–27; Charles Fox, "Irish Patriot's Farewell," *Sable Songster* (Philadelphia, 1859), p. 79; Matt Peel, "The Irishman's Shanty," New York, 1859, sheet music, HTC.

31. E. J. Kahn, Jr., *The Merry Partners: The Age and Stage of Harrigan and Hart* (New York, 1955); chapters 3–6 discuss the content of their shows in some detail.

32. *Johnson and Bruno's Mania Monia Nigs Songster* (New York, 1875), pp. 34, 36; William Delehanty, *I Hope I Don't Intrude* (New York, 1877), n.p.

33. "Alderman Flynn"; "Casey's Social Club," and "Are You There Moriarity?," *Haverly's United Mastodon Minstrels Song Book* (Chicago, 1880), pp. 9, 56–57; "Muldoon the Solid Man" [by Harrigan], *Bobby Newcomb's Love Letters and Packet of Poems Songster* (New York, 1880), p. 32; "Moriarity the Dandy M.P.," *Jay Rial's Ideal Uncle Tom's Cabin Song Book* (San Francisco, 1883), p. 8; "Mulligan's Promises" [by Harrigan], *Cool Burgess' I'll Be Gay Songster* (New York, 1880); "Pat Delaney," *Sam Devere's Burnt Cork*, p. 99; Al G. Field, "Let Me Shake the Hand that Shook the Hand of Sullivan," *Field and Co.'s Minstrel Songster* (New York, 1890), pp. 14–15.

34. "No Irish Need Apply," *People's*, pp. 13–14, and *Gems of Minstrelsy* (New York, 1867), pp. 44–45; "Bad Luck to Ould Jefferson Davis," *Pell's Ebony*, pp. 18–19; "Tom Maguffin," *Queen and West's Popular Songster* (New York, 1878), p. 10; "Tim Flaherty," *Dockstaders'*, n.p.; "Flag of Green," *Gems*, p. 37; "Bold Jack Donahue," *Joe Lang's Old Aunt Jemima Songster* (New York, 1873), pp. 24–25.

35. For a sampling of negative American reactions to cities, see Glen Blayney, "City Life in American Drama 1825–1860," A. Doyle Wallace, ed., *Studies in Honor of John Wilcox* (Detroit, 1958), pp. 88–129; Elson, *Guardians of Tradi-*

tion, pp. 25–35; Richard Hofstader, *Age of Reform* (New York, 1955, Vintage ed.), pp. 23–60; Morton and Lucia White, eds., *The Intellectual Versus the City* (New York, 1964, Mentor ed.). For a sampling of minstrels' neutral descriptions of city life, see "Broadway Song," *Buckley's Song Book for the Parlor* (New York, 1855), n.p.; "Chestnut Street Panorama," *Popular Ethiopian Melodies* (Philadelphia, 1856), pp. 15–16; "Fulton Market Saturday Night," *Ned Turner's Bones*, pp. 46–47; "The Brooklyn Ferry," *Devere's Burnt Cork*, pp. 30–31; "Coney Island," *Haverly's Mastodon Minstrel Songster* (Chicago, n.d. [1880?]), p. 30; "Riding on the Elevated Railroad," *Haverly's United*, p. 11.

36. "That's So," *World of New Negro Songs* (Philadelphia, 1856), pp. 60–61; "The Broadway Stages," *Frank Converse's Old Cremona Songster*, pp. 27–28; Christy, "Streets of New York," *Kentucky*, pp. 22–23; Bryant, "Odder Side ob Jordan," "New York Times," *Virginia*, pp. 13–14, 41; Charles Fox, *Fox's Ethiopian Comicalities* (New York, 1859), pp. 28–30; Fox, *Sable*, pp. 39–44.

37. *White's Joke Book*, p. 48; "The Days When This Old Nigger Was Young," *World of Negro Songs*, pp. 74–76; Fox, *Sable*, pp. 37, 39–44.

38. "Personal in the Herald," *Devere's Burnt Cork*, p. 32; "Divorce," Kelly and Leon's Minstrels, *Clipper*, May 4, 1872; "We Never Speak as We Pass By," *Gorton's Original New Orleans Minstrel Songster* (New York, n.d. [1883]), p. 13; "I Do Feel Awfully Loose," *Devere's Burnt Cork*, p. 50; "The Husband's Boot," *Bobby Newcomb's San Francisco Minstrel Songster*, pp. 50–52; "I've Only Been Down to the Club," *Delehanty and Hengler's Song and Dance Book* (New York, 1874), n.p.; "Bobby and His Dear," *Billy Emerson's Nancy Fat Songster* (Washington, D.C., 1880), p. 16.

39. "Central Park on a Sunday Night," *Christy's Bones*, pp. 44–46; "Out in the Street," *Delehanty and Hengler's*, p. 31; "Poor Old Dad," *Barlow Bros. and Frost's Minstrel Songster* (New York, n.d. [1887]), pp. 22–23.

40. "There's Nothing Like It," *Buckley's Ethiopian #4*, pp. 53–55. After 1860, almost every minstrel troupe featured so much material on styles that fashions could be traced through minstrelsy. For examples: "The Style of the Thing," *Gems*, p. 33; "The Shop Gals," *Billy Birch's Ethiopian Melodist* (New York, 1862), pp. 37–38; "Nobody Knows As I Know," *Madame Rentz's Female Minstrel Songster* (New York, 1874), p. 3; "Fearfully and Wonderfully Made," and "Patent Rubber Bustle," *Devere's Burnt Cork*, p. 48; "Nothing to Wear," *Hooley's Opera House Songster* (New York, 1863), pp. 6–7; "A Modern Belle," *World of Negro Song*, pp. 80–81; "The Young Girl of the Period," and "I Wish I'd Been Born a Girl," *Shoofly*, pp. 90–91, 15–17; the latter also in *Thatcher, Primrose, and West's Latest Songster* (New York, n.d. [1885?]), n.p., and *McIntyre and Heath's Scenes in Mississippi Songster* (New York, n.d. [1885]), pp. 32–33.

41. "I Wish I Had been Born a Boy," "I Love to be a Swell," *Shoofly*, pp. 18–20, 45; "Curiosity," *Haverly's United*, pp. 35–36; "The Swell at Saratoga," *Devere's Combination*, pp. 46–47; "Captain Jinks of the Horse Marines," *Bryant's Shoofly*, n.p.; "Matinee Brigade," "Sweet Scented Handsome Young Man," *Devere's Burnt Cork*, pp. 15, 34; "Charlie's Curly Hair," *Joe Lang's Old Aunt Jemima Songster*, pp. 35–36; "Modern Fast Young Gentleman," E. P. Christy, *Christy's New Songster and Black Joker* (New York, 1863), pp. 8–9.

42. "Water Cresses," "How the Money Goes," *Christy's Bones*, pp. 53, 63–65; "That's the Kind of Gawk I Am," *Delehanty and Hengler's*, p. 159.

43. "Charming Young Widow I Met On the Train," *Bryant's Shoofly*, n.p.; *Christy's Bones*, pp. 66–67.

44. "I Really Couldn't Help It," "Jemima Brown," *Billy Emerson's*, pp. 28–30, 37–39; "Old Hats and Rags," "Waiting for the Train," "Under the Gaslight," *Newcomb's San Francisco*, pp. 14–16, 28–29, 61–63; "Soap Fat Man," *Billy Birch's Ethiopian Melodist*, pp. 14–15; "Johnny Stole the Tater Cake," *Ned Turner's*, p. 57; "I Spy Your Little Game," *Christy's Banjo*, pp. 68–69; S. S. Purdy, "The Countryman's Visit," *Paul Pry Songster and Black Joker* (New York, 1865), pp. 11–12.

45. Carey, *Brudder Gardner's*, p. 97; "A Dream," *Devere's Combination*, pp. 34–36; "Perished in the Snow," *Haverly's Mastodons*, p. 12; "Down in a Coal Mine," *Joe Lang's*, pp. 66–68; "Little Barefoot," *Ned Turner's*, pp. 13–14; *Bryant's Shoofly*, p. 42.

46. For an analysis of the ways diverse Americans attempted to use traditional terms and concepts to cope with the qualitative changes in their lives, see Robert Wiebe, *The Search For Order* (New York, 1967).

47. "Oh, Don't Put the Poor Workingman Down," *Newcomb's Love Letters*, pp. 48–49.

48. "Never Too Late to Mend," ibid., p. 59; Delehanty, "Dorkin's Night," *Intrude*, n.p.; "Poor but a Gentleman Still," *Devere's Burnt Cork*, p. 130; "Never Push a Man When He Is Going Down Hill," *Shoofly*, p. 47; "Happy Little Man," *Billy Morris's Songs* (Boston, 1864), pp. 20–22; "It's Not the Miles We Travel," "Pulling Hard Against the Stream," "Where There's a Way," *Shoofly*, pp. 37–38, 54–55, 112; "A Wonderful Wife," *Haverly's Mastodon*, pp. 24–25; "Watermill," *Jay Rial's*, p. 7; "Forget and Forgive," *Gems*, p. 64; "Jonah in de Whale," *Cool Burgess' I'll Be Gay Songster* (New York, n.d. [1880]), p. 50; "The Ballet Girl," *Newcomb's Love Letters*, p. 26; "That's When You Will Know Who's Your Friend," M. H. Foley and C. H. Sheffer, *Big Pound Cake Songster* (New York, 1878), p. 28.

49. "My Grandfather," *McIntyre and Heath's*, pp. 30–31; "Grandfather's Cane," *Thatcher, Primrose and West's Latest*, n.p.; "Our Grandfather's Days," *Carncross and Dixey's Minstrel Melodies* (Philadelphia, 1865), 35–36; "One Hundred Years Ago," Bobby Newcomb, *Tambo: His Jokes and Funny Sayings* (New York, n.d. [1882?]), pp. 17–18.

THE SHOW

Selection of Minstrelsy Memorabilia

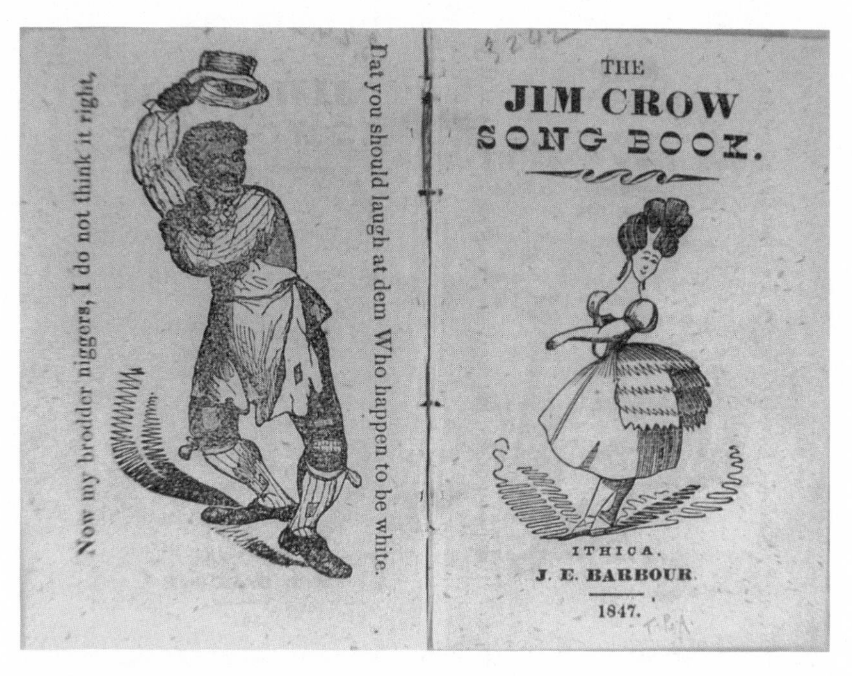

1. Frontispiece and title page of "The Jim Crow Song Book." Published by J. E. Barbour, 1847 (Ithica [sic]). Courtesy of Brown University Library.

2. Front cover of "Willie E. Lyle's Great Georgia Minstrels Song Book." Published by R. M. De Witt, 1878 (New York). Courtesy of Brown University Library.

3. Title page of "Sam Lucas' Careful Man Songster." Published by White, Smith & Co. (Chicago). Courtesy of Brown University Library.

4. "The Coal Black Rose." Written by White Snyder (?), 1827. Courtesy of Brown University Library.

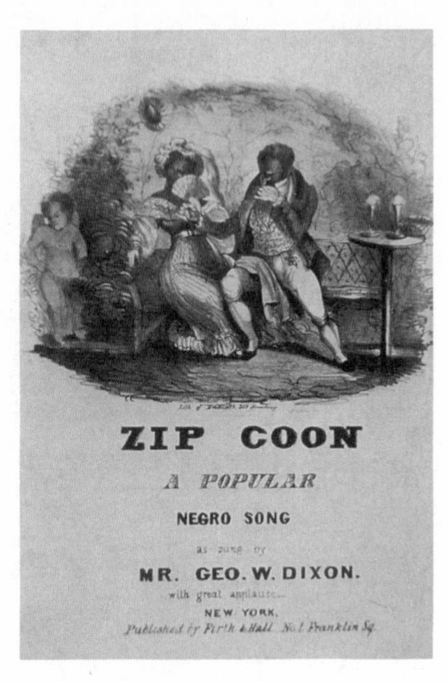

5. "Zip Coon." As sung by George W. Dixon. Published by Firth & Hall, c. 1840. Courtesy of Brown University Library.

6. "Jim Crow." Published by Firth & Hall, c. 1834. Courtesy of Brown University Library.

7. "Dandy Jim, from Carolina." Published by Firth and Hall, 1843 (New York). Courtesy of Brown University Library.

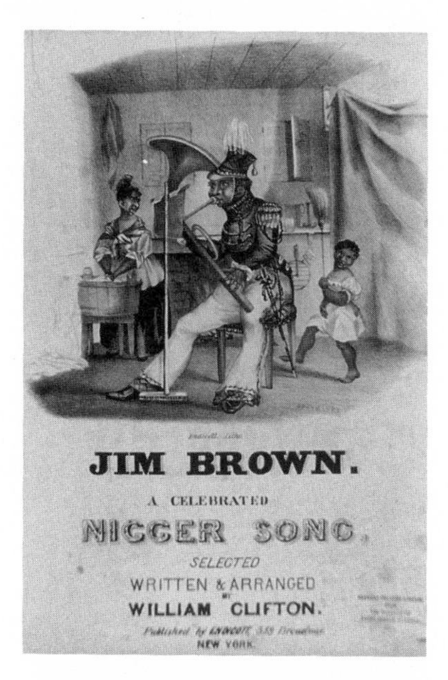

8. "Jim Brown." Arranged by William Clifton, published by Endicott, c. 1836 (New York). Courtesy of Brown University Library.

9. "Old Dan Emmit's [sic] Original Banjo Melodies." Published by Keith's Music Publishing House, 1844 (Boston). Courtesy of Brown University Library.

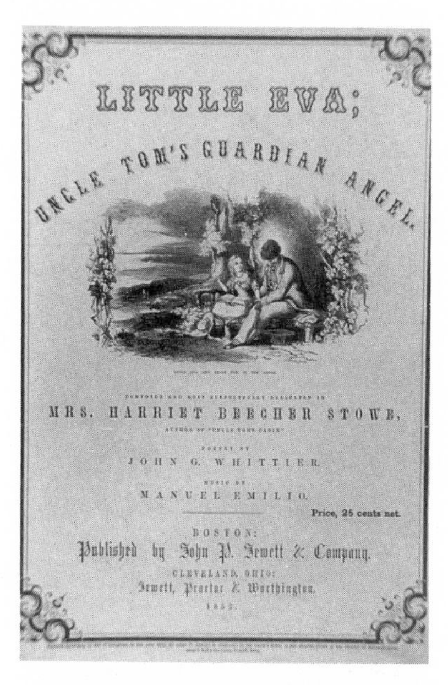

10. "Little Eva, Uncle Tom's Guardian Angel." Poetry by John G. Whittier, music by Manuel Emilio. Published by John P. Jewett & Co., 1852 (Boston). Courtesy of Brown University Library.

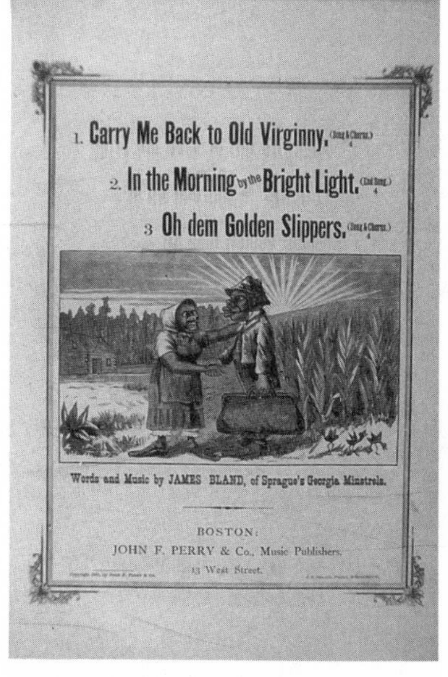

11. "Carry Me Back to Old Virginny." Words and music by James A. Bland. Published by John F. Perry & Co., c. 1870 (Boston). Courtesy of Brown University Library.

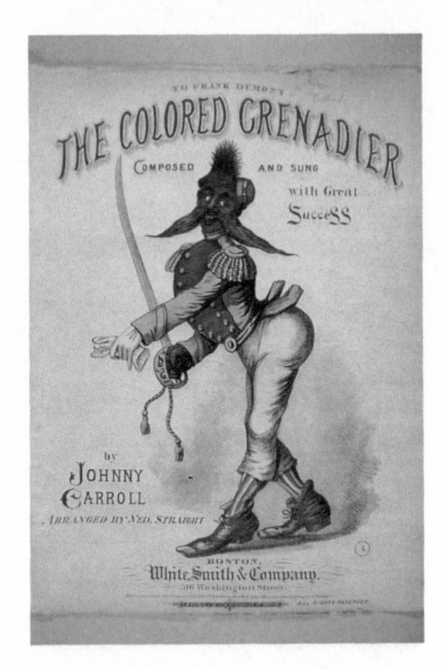

12. "The Colored Grenadier." Words and music by Johnny Carroll, arranged by Ned Straight. Published by White, Smith & Company, 1879 (Boston). Courtesy of Brown University Library.

13. "The Old Contraband." Words by John I. Zieber, music by Rudolph Wittig. Published by W. R. Smith, 1865 (Philadelphia). Courtesy of Brown University Library.

14. "Good Bye Old Cabin Home." Written by C. A. White, as sung by Miss Emma Hyers and Sam Lucas. Published by White, Smith & Co., 1877 (Boston). Courtesy of Brown University Library.

15. "Great Ethiopian Songs." Written by James A. Bland. Published by Hitchcock's Music Store, 1880 (New York). Courtesy of Brown University Library.

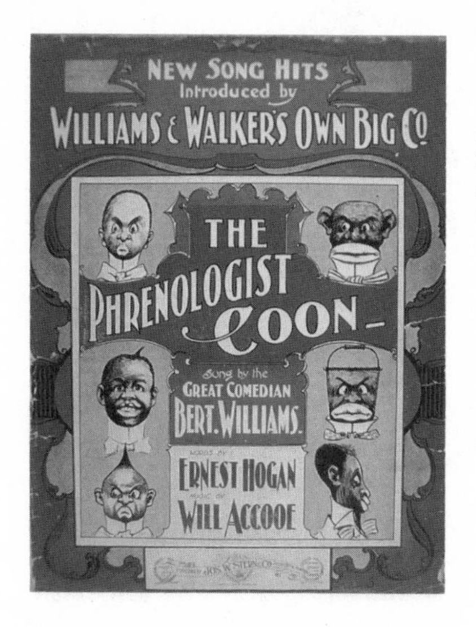

16. "The Phrenologist Coon." Words by Ernest Hogan, music by Will Accooe. Published by Joseph W. Stern & Co., c. 1901 (New York). Courtesy of Brown University Library.

17. "The Wedding of the Chinee and the Coon." Words by Billy Johnson, music by Bob Cole. Published by Howley, Haviland & Co., c. 1907 (New York). Courtesy of Brown University Library.

18. "Come Right in and Sit Right Down, Make Yourself at Home." Written by Bob White, Alfred Anderson, and Bill H. Dixon. Published by Modern Music Publishers, c. 1909 (Chicago). Courtesy of Brown University Library.

19. "The Bird of Freedom and the Black Bird." Cartoon. *Harper's Weekly,* 10, 514:1 (November 3, 1856). Courtesy of Hatch-Billops Collection.

NOW READY, C. BERNARD'S POPULAR SONGS, "THE SAILOR'S WIFE," "EARLY FAITH,"

The Queen's Minstrels
ARE
COMING!

QUEEN'S MINSTRELS
LATE ROYAL & ORIGINAL CHRISTY'S MINSTRELS.
Sole Proprietors, - - - - Messrs. BERNARD & VESTRIS.

THE ACCOMPLISHED VOCALISTS, DANCERS, COMEDIANS, & HUMOURISTS,
Who appeared by SPECIAL COMMAND before
THE QUEEN & COURT,
H.R.H. the Prince of Wales, H.R.H. the Duke of Edinburgh, and the Nobility, Gentry, and the Clergy of nearly every denomination.

HER MAJESTY'S SERVANTS
Will appear in a Musical Melange, Sparkling, Elegant, and Refined.
CHARMING TYROLEAN MELODIES, BALLADS, GLEES, MADRIGALS
BEAUTIFULLY HARMONISED QUARTETTES & CHORUSES.
SCREAMING COMIC ACTS,
GROTESQUE & ECCENTRIC DANCES,
AND
COMIC SONGS AND SAYINGS.

THE GEMS OF MINSTRELSY!
By the Greatest Combination of Minstrel Talent in the United Kingdom.
TWENTY FIVE POPULAR PUBLIC FAVOURITES
IN A MONSTRE PROGRAMME OF
HUMOUROUS, ELEGANT, AND SPARKLING VARIETIES.
An Entertainment Unparalleled in the History of the World's Amusements.

The following distinguished Artistes are permanently attached to this Company, and will appear at every Performance :—

MR. C. BERNARD,
The Queen's Favourite Baritone, who received a special mark of Her Majesty's favour, for his popular Song,
"JUST BEFORE THE BATTLE MOTHER,"
Sung by Special request and command of the Queen.

MR. W. VESTRIS,
(THE ONLY VESTRIS), the Greatest Burlesque Prima Donna, and the first Negro Prima Danseuse in the world.

MR. G. J. WILSOM,
The popular and time-honoured Tenor of the Queen's Minstrels, who first introduced to public notice those charming Ballads—"Beautiful Star," "Willie, we have missed you," "Beautiful Isle of the Sea," "Lovely Alice May," Waiting for the May," &c.

THE FIVE UNAPPROACHABLE COMEDIANS,

MR. E. HALL, The King of Mirth, Wit, and Humour.	MR. JOHNNY JOHNSON, The Celebrated African Comedian, the Funny Little Nigger.

TINY TIM,
The Smallest Comedian in the world, the queerest, most comical, and diminutive specimen of humanity in existence.

MR. FRANK BELL, The Versatile and popular "What is it."	MR. HARRY LESLIE, Prince of the Grinning Tribe.
MR. C. GARLAND, The Favourite Tenor Ligero.	MR. W. WILLIAMS, The New Operatic Tenor Robusto.

MR. C. WARDE AND MR. SINCLARE,
The Royal Christy's Peerless Altos.

MR. SEDMAN. Basso.	MR. JOHNSON, Baritone.
MR. C. BISHOP, Basso.	MR. B. ROWLAND, Solo Flautist.

MR. J. A. CANDY,
Leader and Solo Violin.

MR. A. WAITE, Solo Violoncello.	MR. G. WEBB, Solo Cornet.
MR. W. ROWLAND, Double Bass.	MR. A. ROWLAND, Second Cornet.
MR. JAMES ROWLAND, First Violin.	MR. JOSEPH ROWLAND, Second Violin.

The whole forming the best and most accomplished Troupe in the United Kingdom.
The only Band recognised by the Queen and Court, the Public and the Press, as the Original and Legitimate Christy's Minstrels.

Director, C. BERNARD.

"NEVER SAY DIE," and "NOW THE WAR IS OVER," JEFFREY'S, BERNERS STREET, OXFORD STREET, LONDON, W.

20. "The Queen's Minstrels are Coming!" Broadside. Courtesy of Hatch-Billops Collection.

21. Cover from *The Witmark Amateur Minstrel Guide* by Frank Dumont. New York: M. Witmark & Sons, 1899. Courtesy of Brooks McNamara.

23. "The Only Leon as Sarah Bernhardt." Left half of a poster that has Leon as creole Rose Michon on the right side. Courtesy of Harvard Theatre Collection, The Houghton Library.

22. Cover from *The Boys of New York End Men's Joke Book*. New York: Frank Tousey, 1902. Courtesy of Brooks McNamara.

24. "Harrigan and Hart in 'The Little Fraud.'" Courtesy of Harvard Theatre Collection, The Houghton Library.

25. "Kelly and Leon's Minstrels, 1878." Courtesy of Harvard Theatre Collection, The Houghton Library.

Negro Minstrels

Charles Townsend

People like to laugh. Anything that helps us forget for a time, the vexation, trouble and sorrow of daily life is to be welcomed and encouraged.

Probably there is no form of entertainment capable of producing so much innocent fun as a good minstrel show, and certainly there is nothing more popular with all classes.

Negro minstrelsy is comparatively of modern origin. Previous to 1841 there were no organized companies, although performers would occasionally black up and "do a turn"—singing new songs and introducing quaint dances. Many of the songs became vastly popular. Among them were: "Back Side Albany on Lake Champlain," "Jim Crow"—which Rice sang as early as 1830—"Zip Coon," "Clar de Kitchen," "Coal Black Rose," "The Long Tail Blue," "The Blue Tail Fly" and "Roll de Cotton." These old songs were mostly refrains learned from the Southern darkies. The melody was always original and often striking. Many of the songs were forgotten long ago, but some of them like "Zip Coon" and "Jim Crow" seemed destined to live forever.

The first regular minstrel company was organized in 1841 by Dan Bryant, and appeared at the Chatham theater in New York. The company was called the "Virginia Serenaders," and met with immediate success. They played an engagement in Boston, returned to New York for a season and then went to Great Britain where they remained nearly a year. Barney Williams and Cool White were in this company, which had a very successful season in the British Isles.

The famous "Christy Minstrels" were organized at Buffalo in 1842, by E. P. Christy. After traveling about the country for several years they finally located in New York, where they remained from March 22, 1847, until July 13, 1854. During these seven years the company cleared the tidy sum of $161,873. E. P. Christy retired from business in 1854 and died May 21, 1862.

Other companies now sprang up in rapid succession, and negro minstrels became a popular "fad," both at home and abroad. Mr. Lincoln was especially fond of this class of entertainment and "by special command" Queen Victoria had the "Ethiopian Serenaders" appear before her on which occasion history says she actually smiled.

Minstrel entertainments at the outset were very crude, compared with those of to-day. In the olden time, a violin, banjo, the bones and tambourine made up the "orchestra," and the entertainment consisted solely of songs, dances and "gags." To-day the leading companies have the best and highest salaried vocalists, musicians, specialists, "stump speakers" and negro comedians, and the entertainments are models of refined fun.

Amateur minstrel companies can be organized with very little trouble, and are the means of much harmless amusement. In the following chapter will be found complete instructions for organizing, making up, dressing, and in fact everything necessary to arrange an entertainment.

Organizing

With two "end men"—one to play the bones and the other the tambourine—and a dignified "middle man," you have the nucleus of a minstrel company. These three characters should be good singers, and the end men of course, must be able to imitate the negro dialect. To complete the "circle" of the first part, a number of other characters—say six or eight, are necessary. They have nothing to do in the first part beyond answering occasional questions and joining in the chorus. In the second part they can come in for songs and dances, banjo work, stump speeches, and the usual farce.

The middle man generally acts as stage manager, arranges the music and usually takes part in the farce. He should use good English, be grave, dignified and courteous, making as strong a contrast as possible to the loud and noisy end men. His song in the first part should be a ballad, leaving the comic songs to the end men.

The First Part consists of jokes, gags, stories and songs. The performers sit in a half circle, with the bones and tambourine at each end, and the middle man in the center. Black dress coats and pants, white vests and the usual wigs should be worn. The first part closes with a *finalé,* a short, laughable scene, in which the whole company takes part.

End Men should carefully avoid everything approaching vulgarity, and no offensive personalities should be introduced. Avoid slang, and let politics and religion alone.

Stump Speeches are always very popular, if original in thought, and well delivered. This book contains a number of excellent examples. In delivering a stump speech, let your costume be as comical as possible. If you are tall, wear a tight fitting suit, which will make you appear taller yet. On the contrary, if you are short and stout, emphasize it by wearing very loose clothing. Some stump speakers come on in a ragged suit and damaged "plug" hat, carrying an old-fashioned valise and huge umbrella. A negro stump speech, being only a burlesque, admits of any peculiarities you may choose to introduce.

The Song and Dance. A neat song and dance is an attractive part of the programme, but it must be well rendered to be effective. A good voice and graceful movements are necessary, but intricate steps are not required. The costume should be neat and tasteful, but the style may be whatever your fancy dictates. Use very few gestures and dance with as little exertion as possible. Amateurs should not attempt to do a "straight" double song and dance, without the most careful and thorough practice, as the movements must all be in unison—something very difficult to accomplish. A grotesque double song and dance is easy and laughable—especially if one of the performers wears female costume. The "dance" is merely a series of jumps, kicks and breaks in time to the music—feats which any one can easily master.

Costumes. The regulation dress for the first part has already been described. The end men dress the same as the others, except that very high collars and comical wigs are usually worn. The costumes for the farces, stump speeches, etc., are easily found. Old clothes, ancient hats, venerable carpet bags and umbrellas, linen dusters, big shoes, and odds and ends of all sorts will come into play. In negro minstrels the female characters are always assumed by men, and the costumes should be in keeping with the character. Most of the farces described elsewhere in this book, contain accurate descriptions of the various costumes required; and when no descriptions are given, the ordinary everyday dress is worn.

Properties. The word "properties" in a theatrical sense means the articles required by the performers. For instance, chairs, tables, umbrellas, brooms, carpet bags, etc., are "properties." It is customary to appoint one member of the company "property man" whose duty it is to look after the various articles required, and see that they are on hand the night of the performance. This is a very important matter, and a good property man is one of the most valuable members of the company. Without his watchful care everything is liable to get at sixes and sevens, and the most laughable farce may fall flat if some necessary property is missing. No unusual nor expensive properties are required in a minstrel entertainment, and whatever is needed should be obtained early in the day, so that there will be no delay nor confusion after the curtain rises.

Making up is a term meaning to prepare the face for the stage. Burnt cork, cocoa butter, carmine and wigs are all that negro minstrels require.

You can prepare the burnt cork yourself by obtaining a quantity of corks, placing them in a metal dish, pouring alcohol over them and burning them to a crisp. Powder and mix with enough water to make a rather thick paste. This trouble can be avoided by securing the prepared burnt cork, which may be had from any dealer in theatrical supplies, for a trifle. Carmine is a brilliant red powder which is used on the lips of the end men, to make them appear larger, and cocoa butter is an indispensable article for removing the burnt cork *without using soap or water.* The end men make up as follows: First rub a cake of cocoa butter lightly over the face, ears and neck; then apply a broad streak of carmine to the lips, carrying it well beyond the corners of the mouth; then take a little of the prepared burnt cork, moisten it with water, and rub it carefully on the face, ears, neck and hands, being careful to avoid touching the lips. Put on the wig, wipe the palms of the hands clean, and the make up is completed. The other characters make up in exactly the same way, except that no carmine is used. For elderly negroes, like "Uncle Tom," wrinkles must first be drawn across the forehead and around the eyes, with India ink. The burnt cork is reduced with whiting to make it lighter, and is applied as usual, except that the lower eyelids and lips are covered with the regular shade of black, which will give them the sunken look of old age.

To Remove Burnt Cork. Rub the features lightly with a cake of cocoa butter, and the burnt cork may be wiped off with a dry cloth.

Wigs. All dealers in theatrical supplies furnish negro minstrel wigs at reasonable prices, and it is more economical to buy them than to manufacture them yourself. However, if it is not convenient to purchase your wig, you can make a very fair substitute in the following manner: Secure a tight fitting, black skull cap, made of light but strong cloth, and cover it with curled hair, such as is used for filling mattresses. For an end man's wig, the style may be as fantastic as you wish. A female wig requires large puffs on each side, another at the back. The gray curled hair is used for old negroes, and a large bald spot is left on the crown. A "fright" wig is quite effective at times, but if one is used it should always be purchased from a dealer, as no amateur wig maker can manufacture one properly.

Rehearsals. All the business between the middle man and end men should be carefully rehearsed. All must be "letter-perfect" in their lines, for if the proper questions and answers are not given, the gags will fall flat. The *finalé,* which closes the first part, and the farce or farces in the second part also require careful and thorough rehearsals. Pay particular attention to the business of the piece, and don't hurry things. The funniest point in many negro farces is the intense would-be dignity of some of the characters. Now if the scene is rushed through, all this is lost and the humor is not apparent. Therefore in a scene of this sort, take plenty of time to elaborate the business.

The Performance. There are a number of methods for opening the first part. One is to have the performers all seated in their places and join in the opening chorus at the rise of the curtain. Then the middle man asks after the health of the end men, who return comic replies. A ballad usually follows, after which the end men get off a series of conundrums. Then one of them sings a comic song, after which the other end man gets off his gags. Another ballad, usually by the middle man, follows, and the first end man gives his gags, followed in turn by a comic song by the other end man. Thus each end man has a set of gags and a song. The remaining ballad is now given, after which the middle man announces the *finalé.* The curtain is lowered after the *finalé,* and when it rises again, the second part begins. This includes stump speeches, songs and dances, farces, etc.

As every enterprise depends largely on proper advertising, I would suggest that your programme be printed in full on your circulars to be distributed around town. People are more disposed to attend a show when they know just what they will get. Many companies fail in this particular. *Judicious* advertising always pays. If you have a few large posters with "scare" heads, placed in advance, give only general outlines on them and refer to "small bills." This will cause people to read the small bills when distributed.

The Hop of Fashion (c. 1856)

Charles T. White

CHARACTERS.

CAPTAIN SLIM *(a Millionaire)* CLAUDE MELNOTT MOSE *(one of the B'hoys)*	Mr. C. White.
ANTHONY *(Captain Slim's Servant)*	Mr. Fox.
CITIZEN	Mr. Neil.
LADY MACBETH	Mr. Donnelly.
MACBETH	Mr. Carroll.
PAULINE	Mr. Vincent.
POPS *(a stage-struck youth)*	Mr. Neil.
IRISHMAN	Mr. Carroll.
RICHARD III	Mr. Wise.
LIZE *(one of the Sykesy crowd)*	Mr. Vincent.

(CHARACTERS WHICH DOUBLE.—Captain Slim, Claude and Mose. Citizen and Pops. Macbeth and Irishman. Lize and Pauline.

THE ORDER OF ENTERING.—Captain Slim. Anthony. Citizen. Lady Macbeth. Macbeth. Claude and Pauline. Pops. Irishman. Richard III. Mose and Lize.)

PROPERTIES.

Chandelier for ball-room—small bell on table—a table-cover—ink-stand, pens, paper and envelopes—salver, cup and saucer—chair—ticket-box—stuffed club—two long swords or foils—a basket horse—a very large pasteboard ticket—small tin sign, lettered "ticket office"—gong and red fire—a bell outside to strike the hour of nine—candle and candlestick.

COSTUMES.

CAPTAIN SLIM.—A very nice dandy make-up, smoking cap and morning gown.

ANTHONY.—Servant style, apron, jacket or short-tail soldier's coat.

CITIZEN.—Dress like one of the band in first part.

LADY MACBETH.—Long veil over the head, band round the forehead.

MACBETH.—Breastplate, Scotch tunic, cap and sword.

PAULINE.—Plain, almost any style.

POPS.—A Roman shirt, belt and tabbs.

IRISHMAN.—Irish suit, extravagant, stuffed stick and pipe.

RICHARD III.—Cloak-piece and crown.

LIZE.—Rather gallus, hat and vizette.

MOSE.—Turned up trousers, red fireshirt, black silk hat with crape on it.

Time of Performance—Thirty Minutes.

SCENE FIRST.—*Chamber in Captain Slim's house. Covered table, having on it candle, small bell, pens, ink, and paper. Covered chair.*

SLIM (*discovered seated at table, smoking a cigar*) Well now, who would ever have thought that old Peter Slim would live to get up in such high style. Thanks to de lottery business for dis lucky accident. I intend to give a grand fancy dress ball at my mansion dis evening, and eberyting goes off smooth, I'm sure we'll hab a merry time, and one dat will do credit to de honour ob my guests and my house. (*calling*) Here, Anthony! (*takes letter up from the table and reads*):—"Major Jones,—Your company am most 'specfully s'licited to 'tend de fust grand annual sore-eye dis ebenin' at de house ob your ole friend and whitewasher.—Captain Slim." (*rings the bell on table, and calls*) Anthony!

ANTHONY (*answers from outside*, L.) Yes, sar, yes, sar, I'm coming.

SLIM I'll bet a dollar he's in de closet eating pies.

Enter ANTHONY, *with his hat on, wiping his mouth,* L.

SLIM Well, sar, hab you got here?

ANTHONY Yes, sar, here I am.

SLIM Anthony, take your hat off when you come in de parlour. Now, sar, did you deliber dem circulars to de people I told you to?

ANTHONY Yes, sar.

SLIM Are you sure dat you hav'n't made no mistake?

ANTHONY Oh, yes, sar, quite sure.

SLIM Anthony, you know dat to-night I give a grand ball for de 'commodation ob my frens, and I want you to 'tend de door, and be very careful dat you don't let anybody in widout a ticket. Now, understand, no matter who dey is, get a ticket from eberybody. If dey don't give one, fight!—get a black eye, if you 'ave a mind to. Well, take this note—it's for Major Jones, a partic'lar fren' ob mine whom I forgot, and be sure dat he gets it.

ANTHONY Oh, yes, yes, I'll be berry sure.

SLIM While you are out, go round the corner, an' get me a penny'sworth ob dem good cigars. I'll go to my room and prepare for de ball. (*Exits, with a strut*, R.

ANTHONY Ah, he's a nice man! yes, indeed—Slim Jim—I mean Captain Slim. He's de gayest feller I eber worked for, 'case he gibs me so many nice clothes. Well, I must go to work, 'case I've got to be de ticket-office. Well, I thought so, and had a sign painted a-purpose for it. (*clock strikes nine*) I golly! who'd a-thought it was so late? I won't have time to go wid dis letter, for de fokes will be coming afore I get back, I guess I'll open shop right away. (*arranges table, gets his sign and ticket-box, and takes his seat. Noise heard outside*) Hullo, here comes some one one now.

Enter CITIZEN, L.

CITIZEN I believe dis is de place. Say, fellow, come here. Do you belong to dese premises?

ANTHONY Yes, sar, yes, sar.

CITIZEN Well, whar is de ball to take place?

ANTHONY In de large parlour on de next floor. (CITIZEN *makes an effort to enter*) Excuse me, sar, but I'll trouble you for a ticket.

CITIZEN Oh, you are de ticket-taker, am you?

ANTHONY Yes, sar, I'm de ticket-office.

CITIZEN Well, sar, you shall be accommodated. (*takes ticket from under his coat and gives it,* ANTHONY *looks at the ticket with astonishment*) Why, sar, what are you looking at? Is dere anyt'ing so mysterious about dat ticket?

ANTHONY No, it's de biggest ticket I eber did see.

CITIZEN Well, you see it's a bery large ball.

ANTHONY Well, I guess dat accounts for it.

CITIZEN I s'pose it's all right. Can I pass?

ANTHONY Oh, yes.

CITIZEN Good night, sar. (*passes in*, C.)

ANTHONY I don't know wedder dat ticket is right or not; it's most as as big de "Times."

Enter LADY MACBETH, L.

LADY M Go wash your hands. Put on your nightgown. Look not so pale. I tell you dat Banquo's buried. He cannot rise from his grave. Come, dere's a knocking at de gate. Come, come, come, to bed, to bed, to bed! (*exit*, C.)

ANTHONY Well, dat is de most singular thing in de world; dar, she's gone in de ball-room widout a ticket. De old man said dat if he didn't get a ticket from ebery one, he'd discharge me. Well, I think dis ticket is most too large. (*he tears the ticket in two pieces*) Now, I think, dat ticket is large enough for any reasonable ball.

Enter MACBETH, L.

MACBETH Can such things be, an' o'ercome us without our special wonder; and now I do behold you keep the natural ruby of your cheek, while mine is blanched with fear. Approach thou like the rugged Russian bear, Hurean tiger, or the armed rhinoceros—take any other shape but dat.

ANTHONY I neber took a sheep in my life.

MACBETH And my firm nerves shall never tremble. Or be alive again, and dare me to the combat wid thy weapon. If trembling Janipathy protest me de baby of de girl. Avaunt, and quit my sight! thy bones are marrowless. Thou hast no speculation in those eyes, with which thou dost glare on me. Thus, hence hence unreal mockery, hence! (*exit* C.)

ANTHONY Well, I guess if they keep coming in in dat way, old Captain Slim will soon have enough to buy a brick house. Well, I kind a-think boff ob dese tickets am too large. (*he tears one of them in two.*)

Enter CLAUDE *and* PAULINE, L.

CLAUDE Ah, there's the door keeper. How to get by him?

PAULINE Whither would you lead me, dear Claude?

CLAUDE I'd take thee to a deep wale shut out by old pine tresses,
Near de big pond whar floats de ducks and geeses.
Persimmons sweet and sweet potatoes grows,
And de perfume of de sunflower salutes de nose.
In a little log hut made out ob pine,

All kibered ober wid de mornin' glory's vine,
Dar, lub, we'd sit and often wonder
If anyting could tear asunder
Two loving hearts like ours.
We'd know no darks 'cept dem dat had de dollars,
And dem dat wore fine clothes wid de largest kind ob big shirt-collars;
Read de police reports and den we'd see
How many coloured men dere be
Sent by his honour for thirty days
At public expense to mend dere ways
And then de telegraph reports we'd read ob darkies killed in showers,
And laugh to think what a happy fate was ours
While lard oil lamps from Cincinnati straight
Should help to keep us wide awake;
And ebery wind dat passed de stillhouse on de green,
Should come loaded wid whiskey made ob de best fourth-proof camphene,
Breathe signs of love, stars and moon,
While eating supper off of roasted coon;
To such a home I'd take you, love, if thou would'st like
My picture finished. How likest thou de story?
(*They proceed to enter when* ANTHONY *touches him.*)

ANTHONY I'll take your ticket, if you please.

CLAUDE Ah, yes, sah, I've left it in my overcoat pocket in de hat room. I'll go get it and return immediately. (*exit* L.—PAULINE, C.)

ANTHONY Now, dat's a nice man.

Enter POPS, L.

POPS Dey call dis Rome, de empire city, de queen ob cities. Dere is not a palace on dese hills dat has not been bought by de blood ob men—men ob consecrated nations—men who neber harmed Rome, for dey neber saw it. If de base blood ob a Roman ran through their veins, I'd let it out, and cast it to de dogs. (*he speaks to door-keeper*) Young man, let me pass.

ANTHONY You can't pass here, my friend.

POPS Would'st trifle wid me?

ANTHONY Oh, you want to fight! You're de bery man I've been looking for. (*they get swords and fight a dumb combat.*)

POPS (*subdues* ANTHONY) "Down, down, to Dixey's land, and say I sent thee thither." (*rushes off,* C.)

ANTHONY Oh, my gracious! I thought I was dead. I must be stabbed somewhere. (*puts his finger in his mouth*) Oh, yes, dere's a hole; neber mind, I ain't hurt any. Well, I'll hab to hab a ticket for him quick before de ole man comes. (*he tears the other large ticket in two.*)

Enter IRISHMAN L., *singing.*

ANTHONY (*whistling.*)

IRISHMAN 'Pon my soul, I think this is the spot, it looks very much like it, anyhow. Who the devil is that chap sitting there? He must know someting about it; I'll ax him at all events. Say, nigger, do you hear the infernal scoundrel whistling while I'm spaking to him? Do you hear me talking to you? (*he braces up, goes to* ANTHONY *and knocks his hat off*) Come out of that, you blackguard. Didn't you hear me when I was talking to you?

ANTHONY I'll hab to talk loud to him. What did you say, sar?

IRISHMAN I want to ax you some questions, you blackguard!

ANTHONY Proceed, sar.

IRISHMAN Well, sir, do you belong around here?

ANTHONY Yes, sar, I live about here.

IRISHMAN Well, then, may be you can tell me some questions that I'm going to ax you. You see, as I was coming down the road, one Dennis Bull Gutridge told me that the widow Maginis was going to have a raffle for a stove. (ANTHONY *laughs and stoops over.*)

IRISHMAN (*cracks him on the back*) What the devil are you laughing at?

ANTHONY Dere's no ruffle about here, sar.

IRISHMAN Who's talking about a ruffle, you blackguard, you? I said a raffle—a dance, I mean.

ANTHONY Oh, yes; dere's a ball here.

IRISHMAN Which way?

ANTHONY Right down dere, sar.

IRISHMAN Well, I'll take a trot down.

ANTHONY Well, you can't trot dere widout a ticket.

IRISHMAN A ticket, is it?

ANTHONY Yes, sar; a ticket.

IRISHMAN De divil save de ticket 'ave I, but dat. (*pointing stick in* ANTHONY'S *face*)

ANTHONY Dat ticket won't pass me.

IRISHMAN I'll pass it across the bridge of your nose.

ANTHONY Den I'll bust you in de nose.

IRISHMAN You'll do what?

ANTHONY I stubb'd one ob my toes, sir.
IRISHMAN Then I'll stubb the oder one for you.
ANTHONY I guess I'll hab to talk louder to him.
IRISHMAN Now look here; I'll have no more talking with you. I'll go into that ball, or I'll have a box with you.
ANTHONY (*takes up the box—aside*) I golly, he wants de box too. Say, do you want dis box?
IRISHMAN No, I want to give you a box on the nose. Look here, nigger; will you fight?
ANTHONY Yes, sar; I'll fight now. (*aside*) I tole you dere'd be a riot.
IRISHMAN You're the very nigger I've been looking for this last five days. Now, then; I'm going to give you what we call Bally Hooly."
ANTHONY Well, den; I'll give you what we call Hooley Balley. (*they fight*—ANTHONY *down*)
IRISHMAN Take that you blackguard. (*exit*, C.)
ANTHONY (*gets up, looks about*) Well, I guess I must hab knocked him clear out ob sight. Well, dere's one Frenchman gone. I kind o' think dem tickets is too large yet. (*he tears another one in two*)

Enter RICHARD III., L.

RICHARD Now is de winter ob our discontent made glorious summer by de sun ob York, and all de clouds dat lowered upon our house am in de deep bosom ob de ocean buried. Now am our brows bound in victorious wreaths—our bruised arms hung up fer monuments—our stern alarms am changed to merry meetings—our dreadful marches to delightful measures. Grim visage war hath smoothed its wrinkled front, and now, instead ob mounting barbed steeds to fright de souls ob fearful adversaries, he capers nimbly to his lady's chamber, to de lasciviousness pleasings ob a lute. But I dat am not stamped for sportive tricks, nor made to court an amorous-looking lass, curtailed ob man's fair proportions, come in this breathless world scarce half-made up, and dat so lamely and unfashionable, dat de dogs do bark at me as I halt by dem.
ANTHONY Well, say; I'll trouble you for a ticket.
RICHARD Go hence, I'm busy now. A horse! (*a basket horse, with a boy under it, crosses before him*) A horse! my kingdom for a horse! (*exit*, C.)
ANTHONY Well, dere goes a horse in de ball. I'll hab to hab two tickets for dem. I'll tell de ole man dat dem tickets is for one fat woman and her chile.

Enter MOSE *and* LIZE, L.

MOSE Say, daddy, ain't dere going to be a ball somewhere in dis shanty, eh?

ANTHONY Yes, sar; right down dat way.

MOSE What room is it in, ole toppy?

ANTHONY Why, de fust large room you come to on de right. You can't help but miss it.

MOSE Come along, Lize. I know'd we had de place down pretty fine. Can't fool me. (*they go to leave.*)

ANTHONY (*taps him on the shoulder*) Say, sar, I'll take a ticket, if you please.

MOSE What? Go way, ole Indian rubber, or I'll burst your trumpet. What! you want a busting! (*he attempts to go in again.*)

ANTHONY (*demands a ticket*) Hab you got a ticket?

MOSE Now, look here, old Moco. I'll squeeze your melon. Go 'long, what you 'bout? (*squaring off*) Daddy, if you keep fighting round me, I'll hurt you now. Come, Lize. (ANTHONY *asks again,* MOSE *knocks him down.*

LIZE Bully for you, Mose. (*both exit* C.)

ANTHONY (*gets up*) Well, there, I can't stand this any longer. Everybody gets in for nothing, and when de ole man counts up his tickets, I'll get turned away. Now, I won't 'tend door no longer; I'll go tell de ole man he'd better get some one dat understands it. I'll go down in de kitchen, and stay among de victuals. (*exit* C.)

SCENE SECOND. —*Ball room with a chandelier—one chair down by* L. I E.—*all the characters discovered moving to and fro—soft music constantly. Enter* MOSE, C., *looking about for* LIZE. *Discovers her dancing with the* IRISHMAN—*separates them—great confusion ensues.*

MOSE Say, look here, what are you dancing wid my company for widout an invitation?

ALL (*looking on intensely*) What's the row?

IRISHMAN Out of that, you spalpeen. Who are you, eh?

MOSE I'll let you know who I am.

THE CROWD Gentlemen, don't fight.

LADY M Oh, my! what low people!

MOSE Oh, go way; you're a woman.

IRISHMAN Say, sir; will you give us a light?

MOSE Are you a know noffin?

IRISHMAN Yes, I am; every inch of me.

MOSE Then take a light. (*offers his cigar.* IRISHMAN *lights his pipe with it, and returns* MOSE *the pipe instead of the cigar.* MOSE *puts it in his mouth—discovers the mistake—throws the pipe away, and makes for the* IRISHMAN.)

LIZE (*catches hold of him*) Oh, Mose; I feel ill.

MOSE What'd de matter wid yer? Sit down. Won't you have something to eat?

LIZE Yes; I'll take a cup of coffee.

MOSE No, no! Get some pork and beans, or a pig's foot. (*calls*) Say, waiter! waiter!

ANTHONY (*enters* L.) Here I am, sar.

MOSE Hab you got any coffee?

ANTHONY Yes, sar; yes, sar.

MOSE Well, bring me a cup ob coffee and some round hearts. Hurry up your cakes.

ANTHONY Yes, sar. (*exit* L.)

MOSE *stands near 1st entrance talking to* LIZE. ANTHONY *enters with a salver, cup and saucer, and runs against* MOSE. *Salver drops, and the coffee is supposed to have spilt over* LIZE'S *dress. A general run ensues—all kinds are trying to pursue the nigger waiter.* LIZE *makes a rush for him herself;* MOSE *holds her back.*)

IRISHMAN By my soul, the girl is a fighting man too.

LIZE Look there! My dress is completely spoiled.

MOSE Say, old indian rubber; I'll squeeze you for dat by and bye. Come, Lize; let's have a dance, and leave dis foo foo ball. (*they begin to dance a gallop.* POPS *with his company, accidentally bump up against* MOSE, *which annoys him again.*)

MOSE (*to* LIZE) Say, does you see dat Shanghai? Seize him, Lize, let's split him. (MOSE *and* LIZE *catch hold of* POP'S *coat tails, and split it completely up the back. A general row—all fight at random. Going strikes.* LADY MACBETH *flying to and fro all over the stage.*)

CURTAIN.

Speech on Woman's Rights (1879)

From "*Dick's Ethiopian Scenes, Variety Sketches, and Stump Speeches*"

My Hearers,—male and female—squenchin' my native modesty, which is nateral to all uv the weaker vessels, uv whom I am wich, I feel impelled to speak to yoo this evenin' on the subjeck uv woman—her origin, her mission, her destiny—a subjeck, bein' ez I am a woman myself, I hev given much attenshun to.

Man, my hearers, claims to be the sooperior uv woman! Is it so? and ef so, in what, and how much? Wuz he the fust creashun? He wuz, my hearers; but what does that prove? Man wuz made fust, but the experience gained in makin' man wuz applied to the makin' uv a betterer and more finerer bein', uv whom I am a sample. Nacher made man, but saw in a breef space uv time thet he coodent take keer of hisself alone, and so he made a woman to take keer uv him, and thet's why we wuz created, tho' seein' all the trubble we hev, I don't doubt thet it wood hev bin money in our pockets ef we hedn't bin med at all.

Imagine, my antiquated sisters, Adam, afore Eve wuz med! Who sowed on his shirt buttins? Who cooked his beef-steak? Who med his coffee in the mornin' and did his washin'? He wuz mizzable, he wuz—he must hev boarded out, and eat hash! But when Eve cum, the scene changed. Her gentle hand suthed his akin' brow wen he cum in from a hard day's work. She hed his house in order; she hed his slippers and dressin' gown reddy, and after tea he smoked his meershaum in peece.

Men, crooel, hard-hearted men, assert thet Eve wuz the cause uv his expulshun from Eden—thet she plucked the apple and give him half; oh, my sisters, it's troo: it's too troo, but what uv it? It proves, fustly, her goodness. Hed Adam plucked the apple, ef it hed bin a good one, he'd never thought of his wife at home, but wood hev gobbled it all. Eve, angel that we all are, thought uv him, and went havers with him! Secondly, it wuz the meens uv good, anyhow. It interdoost deth inter the wurld, which separated 'em wile they still hed luv fur each uther. I appeal to the sterner sex present to-night, Wood yoo, oh, wood yoo, desire for immortality, onless, indede, you lived in Injeany, where yoo cood git divorces, and change your names wunst in 10 or 15 yeers? S'pos'n all uv yoo hed bin fortoonit enuff to win sich virgin soles ez me, cood yoo endoor charms like mine for a eternity? Methinks not. I know that ef I hed a husband he wood bless Eve for interdoosin' death inter the world.

I progress. Woman, then, is man's ekal, but is she okkepyin' her proper speer? Alas, not! We are deprived uv the ballit, and ain't allowed to make stump-speeches, or take part in politix. Is it right? Troo, we aint as yit learned in these matters, but what uv thet? How many men vote who know what they'r votin' for, and how many stump speakers know what they'r talkin' about? I demand the ballit. I want to be a torchlight procession. I want to sit in Congris, among the other old grannies. I want to demonstrate my fitness for governin' by comin' home elevated on 'leckshun nites. I want to assoom thet speer wich nacher fitted me fur ekally with man, but from wich maskeline jellasy hez thus fur exclooded me. Weak! why I wunst noed a female friend of mine wich hed strength reglarly to carry her husband, who weighed 207 lbs. averdupois, into the house every nite after he wuz lifted off frum a dray onto wich his friends wich cood stand more flooids than he cood, hed deposited him. Many a time I've seed her lift thet barrel uv whiskey, with a man outside of it.

Matrimoney, thus far in the wurld's histery, hez bin our only destiny. I am glad to hed allus strenth uv mind enuff to resist all prepisihuns lookin' to my enslavement. I had too much respeck for myself to make myself the slave of a man. Wunst, indeed, I mite hev done so, but the merest axedent in the world saved me. A yung man, in my yunger dase, wen the bloom wuz on the peach, ere sleepless nites spent in meditatin' the wrongs uv my sex hed worn furroes into these wunst blushin' cheeks, a yung man cum to our house, and conversed sweetly with me. It was my fust beau. And, oh, my sisters, if he thet nite hed asked me to be his'n, I shood hev bin week enuff to hev sed "yes"; and I wood hev bin a washer of dishes, and a mender of stockin's fur life. But fate saved me. He didn't ask me that nite, nor ever afterward.

There hev bin women in the world who hev done suthin'. There wuz the Queen uv Sheba, who was eggselled only by Solomon, and all that surprised her in him wuz that he could support 3,000 women. Bless Solomon's heart, I'd like to see him do it now! With the size pin-backs and the trains yoo wear, where cood he find a house big enuff to hold 'em? He'd hev to put a wing onto each side uv the temple, and put another story on top uv it. And how cood he dress 'em with muslin at 50 cents a yard, stockin's a dollar a pare, and winter bonnits $20 per one? $20,000 per anum for stockin's! $240,000 per anum for bonnits! Ef he hed lived in these times he'd hev to hev Congris pass sevral internal revenue bills, to stand sich expenses. And there was Joan of Arc, who whipped the English, who wuz maid of New Orleans, which wuzn't the same as Noah's Ark, fur that was *made* of gopher wood, besides the latter was pitched without and pitched within. There wuz Queen Elizabeth, who wuz the virgin queen; and Mrs. Swisshelm; there's Lucy Stone, and Anna Dickinson; there's Lucretia Mott, and Mrs. Jinks, all uv whom showed thet women cood seese to be women, and be ez neer men ez nacher allowed them. Thet's what all our sex want—to be ez neer men ez possible.

MUSIC

Early Minstrel Show Music, 1843–1852

Robert B. Winans

The first complete minstrel show was put on in 1843 and was an immediate "hit," spawning many imitations and initiating what was to be the most popular of popular entertainments for the next forty years or more.[1] What was it about, this entertainment, especially in its first, formative decade, 1843–1852, that so captivated a nation? Though many factors might enter into the answer, surely one of the more important ones is the music of the shows. For the minstrel show was primarily a musical event, not really "musical theatre" in the modern sense, but what one might call "theatrical music." Musical performances were what structured the early minstrel show. Printed programs for the shows, which are the primary sources for this essay, look like concert programs. Of course, much more occurred on stage in the actual shows than appears in the programs, which do not indicate all the dialogue and comic "business" that went on in between musical numbers. But the musical pieces on the program structured the evening. And previous scholarship has not dealt very substantially with the music of the early shows, with the partial exception of Hans Nathan's book on Dan Emmett. So my purpose here is to examine some of the features of that music as it was performed on stage between 1843 and 1852.[2]

The starting point for discussing early minstrel show music is instrumentation. Table 1 shows the distribution of instruments in twenty-nine minstrel companies active between 1843 and 1847.[3] Clearly, the banjo and the tambourine were indispensable, followed closely by the bones and the violin.

"Early Minstrel Show Music, 1843–1852" by Robert B. Winans. Originally published in *Musical Theatre in America: Papers and Proceedings of the Conference on Musical Theatre in America*, edited by Glenn Loney. Copyright © 1984 by Greenwood Publishing Group, Inc. Reprinted with permission of Greenwood Publishing Group, Inc., Westport, Conn.

TABLE 1
Minstrel Show Instrumentation, 1843–1847
(29 Troupes)

Instrument	Count
Banjo	29
Tambourine	29
Bones	25
Violin	20
Triangle	11
Second banjo	8
Accordion	7
Jawbone	3
Second violin	2
Drum	2
Flute	1
Tongs	1
Cymbals	1

The banjo of the period was not like a modern banjo. The main differences were a larger diameter body with a deeper but thinner rim and a fretless fingerboard; its *five* strings were gut, tuned, as a whole, either a third or a fourth below modern pitch, depending on the key to be played. These differences are important, because the minstrel banjo was at the heart of the sound of the minstrel ensemble, and it did not sound like a modern banjo. Surviving banjoes from the period have a mellower, fuller, more resonant sound. The style of playing minstrel banjo was, according to contemporary instruction manuals, similar to that folk style called "frailing" or "clawhammer."[4] In the minstrel ensemble the banjo was a melody instrument; it did not provide chordal accompaniment, as might be assumed. The other melody instrument in the core minstrel band was the violin.

The primary rhythm instruments were tambourine and bones. The minstrel tambourine was larger than the common modern one and had fewer rattles. This suggests that, while the modern tambourine is more rattle than drum, the minstrel one was the reverse. The bones were flat, animal rib bones, slightly curved, or hardwood facsimiles. Two pairs were used, one pair in each hand, held between the fingers and played with a rapid wrist action to produce a castanetlike sound capable of great rhythmic complexity. These four instruments, then, banjo, violin, tambourine, and bones, were the core ensemble of minstrel bands of the period, largely because this instrumentation was used by the very first minstrel troupe, the Virginia Minstrels. In addition, evidence from ex-slave narratives shows that these instruments were indeed widely played by slaves on southern plantations at the time.[5]

As noted in Table 1, the other melody instruments that might have been heard in an early minstrel band included a second banjo, an accordion (which the illustrations show to be a kind of button accordion, also called a melodeon, rather than the modern piano accordion), occasionally a second violin, and even more rarely a flute. The accordion, when used, seems always to have been a substitute for the violin, rather than an addition to it.

The most common additional rhythm instrument to be played was the triangle, used in about a third of the groups, supplementing the bones and tambourine. Other rhythm instruments used occasionally included jawbone, drum, fireplace tongs, and cymbals.

The research behind this essay was designed to provide the best possible information for an attempt at recreating the actual sound of the early minstrel band in performance. The results of this effort are being issued by New World Records. I recorded with the core ensemble of banjo, violin, tambourine, and bones, and from this experience have formed some different conclusions about the sound of this combination than those put forward by Nathan. Nathan suggested that such a group would sound "scratchy, tinkling, cackling."[6] I think that the sound was much more solid than that, that the instruments blended surprisingly well, with a more mellow and melodic sound than Nathan suggests.

I entirely disagree with Nathan when he states that the "banjo could not serve as a solid foundation in the ensemble."[7] From various experiments made while recording, when the banjo was purposely silenced in the middle of a piece, my conclusion is that the banjo in fact *is* that very foundation. When it ceases playing, the whole "bottom" drops out of the ensemble sound, and the remaining instruments do come across as Nathan suggested. But the banjo holds it all together and gives it substance.

Some have suggested that the sound of the early minstrel band was much like that of the old-time banjo-fiddle string bands that were recorded in the 1920s. Given that both were built around the banjo-fiddle combination, and that the later string bands had probably evolved from the models provided by minstrel bands, some similarity is to be expected. But the sound is not quite the same, because the banjo had changed by then, and the string bands used no nonstring rhythmic instruments. A continuous line of development which is worth exploring further exists between early minstrel bands, old-time string bands, and modern bluegrass bands.

Both the minstrel band and the minstrel troupe as a whole increased in size over time. In the first five years, the band was the whole company, by and large, with the exception, sometimes, of a manager. The evidence of the programs suggests that in this period troupes ranged in size from four to six members, with the average being five. In the second five years (1848–1852), bands numbered from four to eight, the average being six, and the size of the whole company ranged anywhere from four to fifteen members. Clearly, specialization was developing in these larger troupes, with some in the company being just ballad singers, or just dancers, which had not been true earlier.

In terms of instrumentation, not much new was introduced in the 1848–1852 period. Banjo, violin, tambourine, and bones remained the core, with more of a tendency to double up on instruments, especially the banjo. A few more groups added a flute player, while some use was made of the guitar, the clarinet, and also of the piano, especially by a few groups such as Ordway's Aeolians in Boston.

After 1852 ensembles and companies continued to grow and standard orchestra instruments were increasingly employed, until the original "plantation" quartet was relegated to a specialty act.

Instrumental solos were nearly always a part of the minstrel program in the first decade. Table 2 shows the most common kinds of instrumental solos in terms of the percentage of the programs in which they appeared. Solos became more frequent in the second half of the decade. This difference points to the gradual development of the "olio" section of the minstrel show, where such solos came to be concentrated. But the olio as a separate section of specialty acts was only beginning to take shape at the end of the decade. Although many other writers seem to assume that the olio came into being very early in minstrel history, nothing like it existed before about 1850; before then instrumental solos might appear anywhere in the program.

Clearly, the most common solo was on the banjo. Banjo solos were not often listed in the programs, but among those that were, the most frequent was "Hard Times," written by Tom Briggs, a famous performer who played with many companies and wrote a banjo instruction book in 1855 which included this piece.[8] As a typical banjo solo of the first decade, "Hard Times" illustrates some of the features of banjo pieces

TABLE 2
Principal Instrumental Solos

	Percentage of programs in which solos appeared, by instrument	
	1843–1847	1848–1852
Banjo	30	70
Duet	5	30
Trio	0	30
Violin	20	50
Tambourine	10	18
Accordion	10	23
Bones	0	21

that Nathan discusses, especially the repetition of brief motives with slight variations, the use of triadic figures, and the general emphasis on rhythmic rather than melodic complexity.[9]

Not only did banjo solos, and duets and trios, become increasingly performed during the decade, but the banjo was also frequently used to accompany specialty dances, in addition to its ensemble function. The banjo pieces seem always to have been "plantation" material: that is, more or less in imitation of the dance music of the southern plantation, sometimes played to show virtuosity and sometimes for comedy.

Much less information has been preserved about the nature of minstrel violin solos of the period. I suspect that they were based on "plantation" material toward the beginning of the period; in addition, performers surely burlesqued virtuosos such as Ole Bull, who became enormously popular just as the minstrel era began. Toward the end of the decade, however, the evidence suggests that violin solos were serious music, played seriously, to show virtuosity.

In the early part of the decade, violinists were probably playing as solos such pieces as can be found in the Dan Emmett manuscript tune book of which Nathan makes use. Nathan calls that manuscript a collection of *banjo* tunes. An examination of the original (now at the Ohio Historical Society) shows that it is not labeled as a banjo collection, and I have concluded that although versions of these tunes were undoubtedly played by banjo players, probably even originally played by banjo players, *as written*, they look like fiddle tunes. On the whole, they are more idiomatic to the violin than to the banjo; furthermore, many of the "composer credits" are to well-known minstrel violinists. This does not really alter the importance of these tunes or Nathan's analysis of them.[10]

Tambourine, bones, and other kinds of solos were also presented. One of the earliest tambourine solos is described in a program as imitating railroad trains, cannon, bugle calls, a French drummer, a grist mill, and a cotton mill.[11] Bones solos usually involved imitations of drums and horses. Late in the period, minstrels presented occasional solos on guitar, concertina, mandolin, hammered dulcimer, and such oddball novelties as "solo on kitchen bellows."

Besides solos, various instrumental duets and trios were not uncommon, involving all possible combinations of the available instruments. And instrumental ensemble pieces, played by the full band, were regularly performed. In fact, an introductory instrumental overture very quickly became absolutely standard. In the early years, an instrumental ensemble piece might also end the program, though this shortly gave way to other types of finales.

Throughout the minstrel show's history, however, vocal music was more important than strictly instrumental music; it was mostly minstrel songs that people came to hear. In minstrel songs throughout the first decade, the melodies were simple and folklike (some, in fact, were folk-derived), and the verse/refrain format was the rule for the texts.[12] The most common way of presenting these songs in performance was with solo voice on the verse and a small chorus of voices on the refrain, with instrumental accompaniment, usually the full band, although all possible combinations of voices and instruments were used. On chorus/refrains, the first minstrel troupe, the Virginia Minstrels, apparently sang in unison, but group singing quickly became harmonized, usually in four parts (sometimes three), on the model of the Rainer family and the Hutchinsons. These four-person family singing groups, who were all the rage just as the minstrel era began, had a tremendous impact on the singing style in the shows. At the same time, the minstrel show promptly turned around and mocked the family groups with Rainer and Hutchinson burlesques, an aspect to which I will return. Songs done completely in four-part harmony were also common. This kind of harmonized choral singing is one aspect of the early minstrel show that clearly came from then-current popular entertainment, rather than from a desire to imitate real black folk-musical practice. Black musical traditions of the time did not include this kind of harmonized choral singing.

In the early years, the singers were also the instrumentalists, providing their own accompaniment. The performance of most of the troupes was lively and raucous, in an attempt to portray that "exotic" (to northern audiences) creature, the plantation "darkey," or his cousin, the urban dandy.

The minstrel performers sang in dialect, which as written in the song sheets bears little resemblance to actual black American speech patterns. But they sang that way, of course, because they were whites, only parading for a time in blackface, as some of the programs and sheet music covers were careful to point out, showing the troupe both in and out of blackface.[13] Sometimes the labeling of these contrasted illustrations overtly displayed the insidious social and political caste system of the time. The picture of the troupe in blackface and comic "plantation" costume might be captioned "As Plantation Darkeys," while the caption under the picture of them in street clothes and without makeup reads "As Citizens."

How heavy the dialect was in performance is not clear. It had to be heavy enough to suggest the real thing (some people were actually fooled), with room for comic exaggeration, but not so heavy that the diction was obscured for the primarily white audience, especially in the northern urban centers where the form reached its peak popularity. Some idea of the style can probably be derived from the turn-of-the-century black dialect recordings of such performers as Billy Golden and Arthur Collins, since these are a direct continuation of the minstrel tradition, and must make the same compromise between authenticity, comedy, and clarity.

Table 3 lists the "hit" songs of the first decade of the minstrel stage, based on the percentage of programs on which each song was included. But I do not want to dwell on this list, since the distribution of the programs that provide the data makes it reflect the second half of the decade much more than the first. Focusing separately on the two halves of the decade will be more informative.

Table 4 presents the "hit" minstrel songs of 1843–1847: the songs, according to the playbills, which were actually performed most frequently on the minstrel stage in this period. The blackface songs that prepared the way for minstrelsy and are remembered as being among the most famous minstrel songs are not on this list of early hits. Songs such as "Jim Crow," "Old Zip Coon," "My Long-Tailed Blue," "Clare de Kitchen," and "Coal Black Rose" became popular on their own before 1843,

TABLE 3
Minstrel Show Hits, 1843–1852
(151 Programs)

Song title	Percentage of programs in which song appeared
Miss Lucy Long	34
Virginia Rosebud	20
Railroad Overture	20
Stop Dat Knocking	19
Phantom Chorus	19
Old Dan Tucker	17
Boatman Dance	16
Ole Jaw Bone	15
Camptown Races	15
Let's Be Gay	13
Miss Lucy Neal	12
Old Tar River	11
Old Joe	11
See, Sir, See	11
Dinah's Wedding Day	11
I'm Off for Charleston	10
Old Folks at Home	10
Mary Blane	10
A Life by the Galley Fire	10
Buffalo Gals	10
Lucinda Snow	10
Nelly Was a Lady	10

TABLE 4
Minstrel Show Hits, 1843–1847
(47 programs)

Song title	Percentage of programs in which song appeared
Miss Lucy Long	55
Old Dan Tucker	49
Railroad Overture	47
Boatman Dance	40
Miss Lucy Neal	34
Fine Old Colored Gentleman	26
Old Joe	23
Ole Jaw Bone	23
Buffalo Gals	23
Old Grey Goose	23
I'm Going ober de Mountain	23
Dandy Jim from Caroline	21
A Life by the Galley Fire	19
Old Tar River	19
Ole Bull and Old Dan Tucker	19
Twill Neber Do to Gib It Up So	17
Where Did You Come From	17
Mary Blane	15
Who's Dat Knocking?	15
In de Wild Raccoon Track	15
Cynthia Sue	15
Old Aunt Sally	15
Walk Along John	15

before the existence of the full minstrel show as a vehicle. These songs did not disappear after 1843, but they certainly were not performed as often as the newer hits. Nearly all of the prominent minstrel troupes created much of their own new material, including songs; some of these songs remained identified with only one group, while others became more widely performed.

Although Table 4 and the succeeding tables will be used as a basis for discussing the songs, what they say about the relative popularity of particular songs should be taken with a grain of salt—not because the sample of playbills from which the lists were derived is unrepresentative, but because of the problem of multiple texts and multiple tunes.

Every one of the songs in these tables can be found in several printed editions, with tunes that vary from one another slightly. But some of the songs even have several distinctly different tunes. For instance, I have found two tunes each for "Buffalo Gals" and "Mary Blane," and four for "Miss Lucy Neal," and each of these exists in minor variants.

With texts, not only does one find many slight verbal variants and additional new verses, but also entirely different sets of verses. "Old Joe," "Ole Jaw Bone," "I'm Going Ober de Mountain," "Miss Lucy Neal," and "Old Tar River" all have at least two different texts, while "Old Dan Tucker," "Dandy Jim from Caroline," "Buffalo Gals," and "Mary Blane" have at least four different texts. This is less of a problem in the second half of the decade, but it never quite disappears. Interestingly, this phenomenon of early minstrel show songs makes them analogous, in print and performance, to folk songs in oral tradition, where one of the hallmarks of traditionality is variance of text and tune.

Interesting though it might be, the phenomenon presents a practical problem to the scholar: in looking at the programs, it is hard to know which version was heard for some of these titles. This is not a large problem when the basic meanings or effects of the different texts or tunes of a song are similar, as they usually are. In a few cases, however, one text may be comic while another is sentimental or tragic.

This observation suggests that the most useful way to study these songs is to categorize them according to the type of song, and to see which types were the most frequently performed. Table 5 presents a rough taxonomy of the types of minstrel songs for the early years. Note that the category Parodies really cuts across the other categories, and titles listed there are also listed above. Some other titles are also listed twice because of different versions of the song.

The most obvious thing about the list in Table 5 is that the songs are overwhelmingly comic; only three are not. But rather than merely calling them comic, I would like to put them in a slightly different perspective by calling them "antisentimental." If one looks at the songs published in the 1820s and 1830s, one sees a vast, dreary expanse of sentimental songs, with an occasional "Coal Black Rose." But in 1843 a flood of antisentimental, comic minstrel songs began. There had been comic songs before, of course, but next to the earthy minstrel songs they look pretty effete. And not only the texts were antisentimental. The tunes were based on, or imitated, lively rural dance music, and the performance style was most definitely antisentimental. This, it seems to me, was the main part of the appeal of minstrel songs at first: they were new and different, earthy and "exotic" at the same time, and comic and antisentimental.

This appeal had its negative side, of course. The early minstrel songs, at best, poked gentle fun at blacks, but more often heavy ridicule was involved. The minstrel show and its songs created stereotypes of blacks that have plagued American society ever since. Many of the songs discussed below contain material that ought to make a modern American very uncomfortable or even cringe. But this is no reason not to study minstrel songs seriously. On the other hand, I want to make clear that I do not share or approve of their negative attitudes toward blacks.

TABLE 5
Minstrel Song Types, 1843–1847

Love
- *Comic*
  - Miss Lucy Long
  - Miss Lucy Neal
  - Old Joe
  - Buffalo Gals
  - I'm Going ober de Mountain
- *Sentimental/Tragic*
  - Miss Lucy Neal
  - Mary Blane
  - Cynthia Sue

Other Scenes of "Black" Life
- *Comic*
  - De Boatmen's Dance
  - Old Grey Goose
  - Life by the Galley Fire
  - Old Tar River
  - Ole Bull and Ole Dan Tucker
  - Twill Neber Do to Gib It Up So
  - Old Aunt Sally
- *Nonsense*
  - De Ole Jaw Bone
  - I'm Going ober de Mountain
  - Old Tar River
  - Where Did You Come From
  - Who's Dat Knocking
- *"Character" Songs—Comic*
  - Old Dan Tucker
  - The Fine Old Colored Gentleman
  - Old Joe
  - Dandy Jim from Caroline

Parodies
- *Operatic*
- *Popular Songs*
  - The Fine Old Colored Gentleman
  - A Life by the Galley Fire
  - Railroad Overture

In order to give some idea of the type of song the categories in Table 5 represent, I will present and discuss a typical example from each. First, a comic love song, "Miss Lucy Long," which was unquestionably *the* most popular song of the first minstrel decade. This fact would suggest something about the lack of musical sophistication of minstrel audiences, because the tune is extremely simple and repetitive, though quite lively. (Such lack of sophistication is also suggested by the fact that most playbills include a note requesting that "gentlemen" not stamp their feet in time to the music and not call out for the repetition of pieces.)

Miss Lucy Long

1. I've come again to see you,
I'll sing another song,
Jist listen to my story,
It isn't very long.

Chorus: Oh take your time Miss Lucy,
Take your time Miss Lucy Long.(2×)

2. Miss Lucy, she is handsome,
And Miss Lucy, she is tall;
To see her dance Cachuca,
Is death to Niggers all.

3. Oh! Miss Lucy's teeth is grinning,
Just like an ear ob corn,
And her eyes dey look so winning,
Oh! I would I'd ne'er been born.

4. I axed her for to marry
Myself de toder day,
She said she'd rather tarry,
So I let her hab her way.

5. If she makes a scolding wife,
As sure as she was born,
I'll tote her down to Georgia,
And trade her off for corn.

6. My Mamma's got de tisic,
And my Daddy's got de gout:
Good morning, Mister Physick!
Does your mother know you're out.[14]

This text, which seems to have been the most widespread early version, verges on being a nonsense song but is held together by the focus on Miss Lucy and her lover. The focus, however, is strictly a comic one, playing especially on exaggerated physical characteristics and foolish behavior. Other texts of "Miss Lucy Long" are similar to this in tone and intent, as are the other songs listed in this category.

The next category, Sentimental/Tragic, is one that figures largely in Charles Hamm's chapter on minstrel songs in his recent book *Yesterdays*, wherein he discusses "Mary Blane" and "Miss Lucy Neal" as the earliest examples.[15] The love relationship is treated, on the whole, sentimentally rather than comically; the black characters are portrayed sympathetically, and, while not all songs that might fit into this category end tragically, the three listed in Table 5 do.

Both versions of "Miss Lucy Neal" are about the separation of mates by the slave system, though one of them is also three-quarters a standard comic love song. Below is the text of the more sentimental version, though even this one has a verse or two whose intent is comic. But certainly the end of the song is sympathetic to the slave situation.

Miss Lucy Neal

1. Come listen to my story,
You cant tell how I feel;
Ise gwine to sing de lub I hab
For poor Miss Lucy Neal.

Chorus: O, poor Miss Lucy Neal,
Den O poor Lucy Neal,
Oh! if I had you by my side,
Oh! Den how good I'd feel.

2. She used to go out wid us,
To pick cotton in de field,
And dares where I first fell in love,
Wid my pretty Lucy Neal.

3. When I come to Danville,
I take my horn an blow,
An den you see Miss Lucy Neal,
Cum running to de door.

4. Miss Lucy dress'd in satin,
Its oh, she looked so sweet;
I nebber should hab known her,
I soon cognized her feet.

5. Oh! tell me dearest Sambo,
Where hab you been so long;
Dey say dat you hab lef me,
And cross de sea was gone.

6. I tole her dat it was not so,
An I'd leve her no more,
Oh den poor Lucy kiss me
An fell fainting on de floor.

7. Oh! dars de wite man comin,
To tear you from my side;
Stan back! you white slave dealer
She is my betrothed bride.

8. De poor nigger's fate is hard,
De white man's heart is stone,
Dey part poor nigga from his wife,
An brake up dare happy home.[16]

The case of "Mary Blane" is more complicated. The text that Charles Hamm discusses, probably the earliest, tells of Mary being taken away and sold by the master. In another version she is stolen away by Indians; another is just a sentimental courtship song without tragic ending; and in a fourth variant the whole story takes place in Switzerland and seems to have nothing to do with American slaves. It's almost as though the version Hamm discusses was too sympathetic, leading to the creation of less sympathetic versions. In the third song in the Sentimental/Tragic category, "Cynthia Sue," a man laments that he is the one sold away from his mate.

But, going back to Table 5, most of the really popular minstrel songs in this period were comic. The rest of the categories need only brief commentary. The general designation Other Scenes of "Black" Life is only intended to indicate that these are not love songs; otherwise the subject matter can be most anything, although it is usually something that relates to the supposed domestic or work life of blacks. An example of the type is "De Boatmen's Dance," a lively tune with two refrains, which does not overtly mention blacks at all, although they did indeed function as river boatmen.

De Boatmen's Dance

Chorus: High row, de boatmen row,
Floatin down de river de Ohio.

1. De boatmen dance, de boatmen sing,
De boatmen up to ebry ting,
An when de boatmen gets on shore,
He spends his cash an works for more.

Chorus 2: Den dance de boatmen dance,
O dance de boatmen dance,
O dance all night till broad daylight,
An go home wid de gals in de morning.

2. I went on board de odder day,
To see what de boatmen had to say;
Dar I let my passion loose,
And dey cram me in de callaboose.

3. When de boatmen blow his horn,
Look out old man your hog is gone;
He cotch my sheep, he cotch my shoat,
Den put em in a bag an toat em to de boat.

4. De boatman is a thrifty man,
Dars none can do as de boatman can;
I neber see a putty gal in my life,
But dat she was a boatman's wife.

5. When you go to de boatmen's ball,
Dance wid my wife, or dont dance at all;
Sky blue jacket an tarpaulin hat,
Look out my boys for de nine tail cat.[17]

While some of the verses of this song seem to mock the boatman, others clearly convey a sense of pride in the occupation. Although this song achieved wide popularity through the minstrel shows, it is probably one of those that was at least partially "borrowed" for the shows from preexisting oral tradition. Most of the other songs in this category deal more directly with plantation life.

The next category, Nonsense, comprises songs with a series of unconnected, comic verses, frequently featuring exaggeration or grotesquerie. The fast-paced "De Ole Jaw Bone" is a good example of the type.

De Ole Jaw Bone

1. De Jaw Bone hung on de kitchen wall
Jaw Bone he is berry tall
De Jaw Bone ring Jaw Bone sing
Jaw Bone tell me ebry ting.

Chorus: Walk Jaw Bone wid your turkey too
Neber mind dat buger bu.

2. De lute string blue it will not do
I want a string to tie my shoe
A cotton string it will not do
A cotton string will break into

3. As I was cum from Tennessee
My hoss got mired up to his knee
I whipped him till I saw de blood
Den he hauled me out ob de mud

4. There was a little man he had a little hoss
Went to de riber couldn't get across
I fed my hors in de poplar troff
Ole cow died ob de hooppin coff

5. De niggers at de south dont dress berry well
Day walk about and try for to cut a swell
In de night day meet for to play
Dance all night until de next day

6. Jay Bird pon a swinging limb
Winked at me I winked at him
Cotched up a stone hit him on de shin
And dats de way we sucked him in.[18]

The other songs in this category make no more sense than this one.

"Character" songs build their comic verses around the oddities of some particular character, "Old Dan Tucker" being the most famous of those listed in Table 5. But since he is famous, look instead at the text of "The Fine Old Colored Gentleman" as representative of the type. This has the advantage of also presenting a typical parody song of the period, this one being Dan Emmett's parody of the then popular song "Fine Old English Gentleman." This song works particularly well as an unaccompanied glee for four male voices throughout, at a stately pace.

The Fine Old Colored Gentleman

1. In Tennessee, as I've heard say, dere once did use to dwell
A fine old color'd gemman, and dis Nigger knowed him well;
Dey used to call him Sambo, or somefing near de same;
And de reason why dey call'd him so was because it was his name.

Chorus: For Sambo was a gemmen, One of de oldest kind.

2. His temper was very mild when he was let alone,
But when you get him dander up, he spunk to de back bone,
He whale de sugar off ye by double rule of three
And whip his wate in wildcats, when he got on a spree.

3. He had a good old banjo so well he kept it strung,
He used to sing the good old song, of "go it while you're young";
He sung so long and sung so loud, he scared the pigs and goats,
Because he took a pint of yeast to raise the highest notes.

4. When dis nigga stood upright and was'nt slantindicular
He measured about 'leven feet, he was'nt very partic'lar,
For he could jump, and run a race, an do a little hoppin,
And when he got a-goin fast the devil could'nt stop 'im.

5. Old age came on, his teeth drop out, it made no odds to him,
He eat as many taters and he drank as many gin;
He swallowed two small rail roads wid a spoonful of ice cream,
And a locomotive bulgine while dey blowin off de steam.

6. One berry windy morning dis good old nigger died,
De niggers came from oder states and loud for joy dey cried;
He layin down upon a bench as strait as any post,
De 'coons did roar, de 'possums howled when he guv up de ghost.[19]

Obviously, the only difference between this and a straight nonsense song is that these verses all purport to be about one particular character. And as a parody, this song makes fun not only of old black Sambo, but of the English country gentleman who was the subject of the original song.

But a survey of minstrel "character" songs is not complete without one about the black dandy—the proud, flashy dresser usually from the city but sometimes found on the plantation who was mocked as counterpart to his country bumpkin cousin, the plantation darkey, and who became a key stereotype throughout the rest of the century and into ours. Here then is "Dandy Jim from Caroline."

Dandy Jim from Caroline

1. I've often heard it said ob late,
Dat Souf Carolina was de state,
Whar a handsome nigga's bound to shine,
Like Dandy Jim from Caroline.

Chorus: For my ole massa tole me so,
I was de best looking nigga in de country, O,
I look in de glass an found 'twas so,
Just what massa tole me, O.

2. I drest myself from top to toe,
And down to Dinah I did go
Wid pentaloons strapped down behind,
Like Dandy Jim from Caroline.

3. De bull dog cleared me out ob de yard,
I tought I'd better leabe my card,
I tied it fast to a piece ob twine,
Signed "Dandy Jim from Caroline."

4. She got my card and wrote me a letter,
And ebery word she spelt de better,
For ebery word an ebery line,
Was Dandy Jim from Caroline.

5. Oh, beauty is but skin deep,
But wid Miss Dinah none compete,
She changed her name from lubly Dine,
To Mrs. Dandy Jim from Caroline.

6. And ebery little nig she had,
Was the berry image ob de dad,
Dar heels stick out three feet behind,
Like Dandy Jim from Caroline.

7. I took dem all to church one day,
An hab dem christened widout delay,
De preacher christened eight or nine,
Young Dandy Jims from Caroline.[20]

This song has a very attractive, lively tune, but the lyrics, unfortunately, are racist.

Of the parodies of the bottom of Table 5, I have already noted "The Fine Old Colored Gentleman." "A Life by the Galley Fire" is a parody of another popular song, "A Life on the Ocean Wave." And the "Railroad Overture" was an extravaganza instrumental parody of a piece called "The Railroad Galop." It was sometimes used as an opening overture but most commonly appeared as the finale of the shows in the early period. I would dearly love to find a score for this piece, but so far have been unable to. One program described it as an "imitation of the slocomotive bullgine, dat at de fust ob de beginning is very moderate, den as de steam rises, de power of de circumvolution exaggerates itself into a can'tstopimization, and runs clar ob de track" and explodes.[21]

By the second five years of the minstrel era, 1848–1852, the music sketched out above was already beginning to change, in ways that I want to comment on only briefly. Table 6 shows which songs appeared most often on the minstrel programs of this five-year period. The first thing to notice about this list is that, except for "Miss Lucy Long," the songs most frequently performed in this period are different from those in the first half of the decade. ("Old Jaw Bone" also appears on both lists, but the second version is a distinctly different song from the first.) Not only were

TABLE 6
Minstrel Show Hits, 1848–1852
(104 Programs)

Song title	Percentage of programs in which song appeared
Virginia Rosebud	29
Miss Lucy Long	24
Stop Dat Knocking	23
Camptown Races	22
Phantom Chorus	22
Let's Be Gay	18
See, Sir, See	16
Dinah's Wedding Day	16
Old Folks at Home	15
I'm Off for Charleston	15
Nelly Was a Lady	14
Lucinda Snow	14
Katy Dean	13
Nelly Bly	13
Old Jaw Bone	11
Commence Ye Darkies All	11
Gal from the South	10
Julius' Bride	10
Old Uncle Ned	10
Picayune Butler	10
Silver Shining Moon	10
Hard Times	9
Jenny Lane	9

TABLE 7
Minstrel Song Types, 1848–1852

Love
- *Comic*
  - Miss Lucy Long
  - Stop Dat Knocking
  - Dinah's Wedding Day
  - I'm Off for Charleston
  - Lucinda Snow
  - Julius' Bride
- *Sentimental/Tragic*
  - Virginia Rosebud
  - See, Sir, See
  - Old Folks at Home
  - Nelly Was a Lady
  - Katy Dean
  - Nelly Bly
  - Old Jaw Bone
  - Silver Shining Moon
  - Jenny Lane

Other Scenes of "Black" Life
- *Comic*
  - Camptown Races
  - Phantom Chorus
  - Let's Be Gay
  - Commence Ye Darkies All
  - Picayune Butler
- *Nonsense*
- *"Character" songs*
  - Gal from the South (Comic)
  - Old Uncle Ned (Sentimental)

Parodies
- *Operatic*
  - The Virginia Rosebud
  - Stop Dat Knocking
  - Phantom Chorus
  - Let's Be Gay
  - See, Sir, See
  - Dinah's Wedding Day
  - *Popular Songs*

the individual songs different, which is to be expected in a popular entertainment medium, but the distribution of song types also changes somewhat, as a comparison of Table 7 with Table 5 will show.

Starting at the bottom of Table 7, notice the number of songs that are operatic parodies (a category that again cuts across the others). "Virginia Rosebud" is parodied from *The Bronze Horse*; "Stop Dat Knocking" is a general parody of operatic style; "Phantom Chorus" is from *Somnambula,* as is "See, Sir, See." "Let's Be Gay" comes from *Massaniello*, and "Dinah's Wedding Day" is from *Leonora*.

The other main way in which Table 7 differs from Table 5 is in the increased number of sentimental and tragic love songs and the concomitant decrease in comic songs of all types; there are no real nonsense songs. New comic songs continued to be popular, especially some of the operatic parodies, but the sentimental mode is reestablishing itself.

In songs in the Sentimental/Tragic category, the idea of love now includes love of children and of home as well as "romantic" love. For instance, "The Virginia Rosebud," the most popular minstrel song of this period, is a tragic story of a black child being stolen away, done in dialect and in full-blown burlesque Italian opera style. Charles Hamm quite rightly says of it, "The whole thing is totally bizarre and totally American."[22]

But the most common story in these songs is of a black man grieving at the death of his mate, with the black characters, especially the women, given sympathetic treatment. In his discussion Hamm goes on to suggest that this kind of minstrel song was so popular that it was widely imitated outside of minstrelsy. He gives a whole list of songs about dead and dying ladies, and comes to the conclusion that "there is not a black face in this collection of lovely and beloved ladies, but their tales and tunes would have been unimaginable without the plantation song of the minstrel stage."[23]

I disagree. I think the dying ladies were inevitable, with or without the minstrel show, given the basically sentimental tenor of the times. The minstrel show in its early years provided a brief respite from that sentimentality. But by the late 1840s sentimentality was already reasserting itself in the *songs* in the shows, and by the late 1850s it had just about regained all its lost territory, although other aspects of the shows remained comic.

Other changes were taking place as well. Musically, Hamm points out that minstrel songs were becoming more sophisticated by the late 1840s. "Their melodies . . . clearly imply more sophisticated harmonic, tonal chord progressions. . . . Phrases, periods, and larger sections are regular, symmetrical, and balanced in melody and harmony."[24]

These changes were also structural. Illustrations on the programs and sheet music covers suggest that early minstrel troupes used two basic costume types: formal, connoting northern dandies; and informal, representing southern plantation blacks. Fairly early in the first decade it became common for companies to portray dandies in the first half of the show and plantation darkies in the second. In the first five years there was, despite the costume change, little difference in the material performed in the two parts. In the second half of the decade, the musical material in the northern dandy half of the show became more refined, sophisticated, and sentimental, as noted above. This tendency became even more intensified as more companies in the 1850s opened their shows with a whiteface part.

Clayton Henderson, in his article on minstrelsy in the *New Grove Dictionary*, sums up the trend by stating that in the early 1850s "the inclusion of genteel-tradition music and of the olio began a movement away from the primitive quality of early minstrelsy towards a more sophisticated and standardized variety show."[25] "Primitive" is a rather pejorative word to apply to early minstrelsy, and what was moved away from in the 1850s is, to me, most of what made the minstrel show a really fascinating phenomenon.

One aspect of the early minstrel show and its music has been undervalued, if not ignored, by all writers on the subject, with the exception of Gary Engle.[26] The subject probably deserves an entirely separate paper, but I will introduce it here because I consider it essential to a cultural understanding of early minstrelsy.

Yes, the minstrel show cruelly mocked and denigrated black Americans in a way that had long-term social consequences. But the sword of humor cut the other direction as well. And the *real* essence of minstrelsy was *burlesque*, not just in the playlets that Engle collects in his book, but in every aspect of the show. The very presence of those comic, pseudoblack performers on stage was a burlesque of all serious theatrical and concert performances. Beyond this general principle, all sorts of specific burlesques were staged. Burlesque lectures ("stump speeches") on topics of the day were regularly presented. In the dance, ballet was burlesqued in innumerable "Ethiopian Pas de Deux." When the polka craze finally came to America in 1844, it was immediately parodied in the minstrel shows and became a standard act. Individual celebrity dancers, such as Fanny Ellsler, also were parodied.

Turning to vocal music, first and foremost, over and over, the big minstrel companies put on operatic burlesques. They burlesqued individual songs, scenes from famous operas, and some companies put on complete blackface burlesque operas, or pastiches of material from several operas, as in the following program excerpt.

The audience are supposed not to understand the language of the Opera, as they cannot understand that of the original.

To conclude with a Scene from the Italian Opera, Introducing Scenes from Norma, Somnambula, Fra Diavolo, Lucy-Did-Lam-Her-More, Lucretia Borgia, Bohemian Girl, Massaniello, Marble Bride, &c.

Leader and Conductor, (Bel-lin-nee,) .... Sig. Bird-etti.
Prima Donna of the Troupe, (a la Lind,) .... Madame Lukeo Westeo.
Primo Buffo .... Mons. Clarketti.

Primo Tenor .... Mons. Cambelletti.
Dealers-Hooff .... Mons. Lukeo Westeo.[27]

The minstrel shows were performing these operatic burlesques very successfully at a time when real opera was not a success in America. In addition, individual popular songs, popular song types, popular singing groups—especially the Rainers and the Hutchinsons—and individual celebrities such as Jenny Lind all were regularly burlesqued.

In instrumental music, touring foreign bands, such as the Germania Band, were parodied. When touring Swiss bell ringers became a hit they were burlesqued in acts called "The Cowbellogians." The most frequent instrumental burlesque of all was Louis Antoine Jullien's "Monster Concerts." Jullien, the famous European bandmaster, did not arrive in this country for his successful tour until 1853, but American minstrel shows began putting on burlesques of him and his concerts as early as 1849. One hard to classify burlesque is that of the Black Shakers, which was devised in 1850 and spread like wildfire among the minstrel companies.

Overall, the most frequent burlesques were musical: Italian opera, Rainer Tyrolese singers, and Jullien concerts. The minstrel show in this period was taking much of the mid-century musical world in America, especially anything highbrow (with the apparent exception of religious music), and, so to speak, turning it on its ear.

Notes

1. For discussions of the pre-1843 evolution of the show and evidence of how wide-spread, long-lived, and influential minstrelsy was, see Carl F. Wittke, *Tambo and Bones: A History of the American Minstrel Stage* (Durham, N.C.: Duke University Press, 1930); Hans Nathan, *Dan Emmett and the Rise of Early Negro Minstrelsy* (Norman, Okla.: University of Oklahoma Press, 1962); and Robert C. Toll, *Blacking Up: The Minstrel Show in Nineteenth-Century America* (New York: Oxford University Press, 1974).

2. As presented at the conference, this paper made use of 120 slides, 8 musical examples on tape, and a live performance of a banjo solo to give a sense of the sound of minstrel music of the 1840s in actual performance. Unfortunately, this goal cannot be achieved on the printed page.

3. The data for all the tables in this essay come from actual minstrel show programs, or playbills, 151 of them from the 1843–1853 period, representing a total of 56 different companies. These playbills are located in the Harvard Theater Collection, the New York Public Library Theater Collection, and the American Antiquarian Society.

4. For a full discussion of this issue, see Robert B. Winans, "The Folk, the Stage, and the Five-String Banjo in the Nineteenth Century," *Journal of American Folklore* 89 (1976): 407–37.

5. Robert B. Winans, "Black Instrumental Music Traditions in the WPA Ex-Slave Narratives," *Black Music Research Newsletter.*

6. Nathan, *Dan Emmett*, p. 128.
7. Ibid.
8. Tom Briggs, *Briggs' Banjo Instructor* (Boston: Ditson [1855]); "Hard Times" can be heard on the New World Records album noted above.
9. Nathan, *Dan Emmett*, pp. 191–208, who also discusses other features of early banjo tunes.
10. On the New World Records recording, "Dr. Hekok's Jig," from Emmett's manuscript, is played as an early violin solo. This is one of the tunes that Nathan finds especially interesting. One good reason for performing it as a violin solo is the fact that, as written, it is impossible to play on the banjo in the minstrel style.
11. Playbill, "Ethiopian Minstrels" [1845]; in Harvard Theater Collection.
12. Charles Hamm describes them as having "simple diatonic melodies sometimes suggesting pentatonic scales," and "simple statement of melodic sections with no trace of sequence or development of melodic material" (*Yesterdays: Popular Music in America* [New York: W. W. Norton, 1979], p. 138).
13. See, for instance, the sheet music cover of "Songs of the Virginia Serenaders" (Boston, 1844), most accessible in Toll, *Blacking Up*, p. 39.
14. "Miss Lucy Long," composed by Billy Whitlock, of the Virginia Minstrels (New York: James Hewitt, 1842); reprinted in S. Foster Damon's *Series of Old American Songs* (Providence: Brown University Library, 1936).
15. Hamm, *Yesterdays*, pp. 136–37.
16. "Lucy Neal," words and music by J. P. Carter, of the Virginia Serenaders (Boston: C. H. Keith, 1844); not the version reprinted in Damon, *Old American Songs*, which is the main other variant.
17. "De Boatmen's Dance," by Dan Emmett, of the Virginia Minstrels (Boston: C. H. Keith, 1843); reprinted in Damon, *Old American Songs*; and Nathan, *Dan Emmett*, pp. 320–23.
18. "De Ole Jaw Bone," perhaps by Joel Walker Sweeney (Boston: Henry Prentiss, 1840); reprinted in Nathan, *Dan Emmett*, pp. 464–65.
19. "The Fine Old Colored Gentleman," words by Dan Emmett, in Gumbo Chaff [Elias Howe], *Ethiopian Glee Book* (Boston: Ditson, 1848), 1: 70–71; originally published in 1843. I have omitted several verses to save space.
20. "Dandy Jim from Caroline," probably by Dan Emmett (Philadelphia: A. Fiot, 1844); this seems to have been the most popular version. The earliest published version (1843) is slightly different and is reprinted in Damon, *Old American Songs*. See Nathan, *Dan Emmett*, p. 291, for a discussion of Emmett's probable authorship; Nathan reprints a London (c. 1844) version, pp. 324–27.
21. Playbill, "Georgia Champions," 18 June [1845]; at Harvard Theater Collection.
22. Hamm, *Yesterdays*, p. 135.
23. Ibid., p. 139.
24. Ibid., pp. 138–39.
25. *New Grove Dictionary of Music and Musicians* (London: Macmillan, 1979).
26. Gary Engle touches on the subject in a few paragraphs at the end of his introduction to *This Grotesque Essence: Plays from the American Minstrel Stage* (Baton Rouge: Louisiana State University Press, 1978), pp. xxvii–xxviii.
27. Playbill, "West & Peel's Original Campbell Minstrels," 25 June 1851; at American Antiquarian Society.

The Georgia Minstrels: The Early Years

Eileen Southern

In his landmark publication, *Music and Some Highly Musical People*, James Monroe Trotter devoted his attention to black composers and concert artists, bypassing entertainers who catered to the common man, except in one instance—that of the Georgia Minstrels, a troupe acclaimed the world over for its excellent showmanship and the high quality of the musical performance.[1] Despite his aversion to Ethiopian minstrelsy, Trotter felt it his responsibility to "trace the footsteps of the remarkable colored musician wherever they might lead," and consequently he "forced himself . . . to witness the performances of the Georgia Minstrels." To his surprise, he found that the minstrels had "not only fine natural talent, but much of high musical culture," and he gave over several pages to discussing the troupe and quoting from the favorable press notices they received.

Despite the popularity of the Georgia Minstrels in the last quarter of the nineteenth century, and the important contributions they made to black-American culture, they have attracted little attention in modern times.[2] To be sure, primary materials for the troupe are limited, particularly for its early years: the New York *Clipper* is perhaps the only source that contains more than scattered data—at least until the 1880s when black newspapers and periodicals began to appear.

Although Trotter has earned the gratitude and respect of American music historians for his efforts to document the history of black-American music, his account of the Georgia Minstrels is less than impressive, despite his having been on the scene. Obviously, he took little time to research the subject and, for one reason or another, neglected to interview the minstrels or their associates; his discussion seems to be based solely on the one performance he attended and the "many press notices, regarding their performances, in [his] possession."

Trotter nevertheless provides somewhat of a basis for discussion of these "educated musicians and performers of high merit": he is correct, for example, in stating that a minstrel troupe called the Georgia Minstrels was "organized about twelve years ago, [was] composed of men some of whom had been slaves, [and] began their career under the leadership of Mr. George B. Hicks"—except that the leader's first name was Charles, not George, and he was better known as "Barney" Hicks. But there is much more to the story than Trotter reveals. With a view to fleshing out Trotter's account, the present paper offers an overview of the activities of "Hicks's" Georgia Minstrels during its early years—from 1865, the year of the troupe's origin, to 1878, the year Trotter's book was published.[3]

As is well known, Ethiopian minstrelsy as a full-evening entertainment show originated in New York City in 1843 with the "blackface" Virginia Minstrels, and within a short period had become America's favorite form of stage entertainment. Black minstrel troupes appeared on the scene as early as the 1850s, but, understandably, it was not until after the Civil War that minstrel managers made serious attempts to exploit the talents of black entertainers by putting them on the commercial stage.

Among the first of the black troupes to excite public interest was a group of fifteen ex-slaves, originally of Macon, Georgia, called the Georgia Slave Troupe Minstrels.[4] Organized in April 1865 by a white man, W. H. Lee, they toured widely during the 1865–1866 season, eventually coming under the management and proprietorship of Sam Hague, a white ministrel, who changed the troupe's name to Sam Hague's Slave Troupe of Georgia Minstrels. In June 1866 Hague took his troupe to England, where he settled permanently. At first, Hague used both black and white minstrels, but over the next two years, he gradually replaced his ex-slaves with whites in blackface.

At the same time that Hague's group was attracting public attention, other groups calling themselves Georgia Minstrels were touring in the East, one of them under the management of black-American Charles B. Hicks (c. 1840–1902). In distinguishing this troupe from others of the same name, the *Clipper* commonly referred to it as "Hicks' party" or the Famous Original Georgia Minstrels, with Hicks as director—this undoubtedly under Hicks's instructions. In later years Hicks reported to the *Freeman,* a black newspaper, that he had organized his group in 1865 at Indianapolis, Indiana.[5] By the time the general public had become aware of the fact that there were more than one Georgia Minstrels, Hicks's Georgia Minstrels already had achieved considerable celebrity. It was this group that was the genesis of the world-renowned Georgia Minstrels, the troupe that was to make history.

The *Clipper* regularly carried news about the activities of Hicks's minstrels: they toured continuously, on tight schedules, in New England, the middle-Atlantic states, and lower Canada, generally playing to "good business." On November 7, 1868, a *Clipper* advertisement, which gave notice that the "original and only" Georgia Minstrels was on its Fourth Annual Tour, included some informative details about troupe personnel. The stars of the troupe were identified as Lou Johnson, comedian and bones player; George Danworth (= Danforth), bones soloist; George Skillings, leader of the orchestra; John Wilson, leader of the fifteen-piece brass band; and Hicks, himself, as interlocutor and director.

In other press notices of the 1868–1869 season, acts singled out for praise included the dancing of Alfred Smith, the double trapeze act of the Torres brothers, the banjo solos of Dick Little, and the ballad singing of Henry B. Johnson. During that season the troupe also included comedians Bob Height and Charles Sticks. The press continuously praised the troupe's ensemble singing, and liked the burlesque skits, particularly "Mr. Jinks," starring Barney Hicks, and "The Grand Duchesse."[6]

Again and again the press commented on the "crowded" and "overflowing" houses for performances of Hicks's Georgia Minstrels. Such was the power of the troupe that, when playing in Washington, D.C., in July 1869, the managers were able to demand that "colored persons [be] admitted to all parts of the house," which, the press observed, was "something of a novelty for Washington."[7]

By the beginning of the 1869–1870 season, Hicks, perhaps emboldened by his success in the United States, was ready to try his wings in Europe, and in January 1870 he left with a small group of his minstrels to tour abroad, among them Bob Height and possibly Aaron Banks. It is not clear how he made the necessary contacts; we know, however, from the press that he toured first in Germany, then in England, concluding his tour in Swansea, South Wales. At Hamburg, Hicks introduced the Germans to a plantation song then wildly popular in the States, "Shoo Fly!" In June 1870 he joined forces with Sam Hague's Great American Slave Troupe to perform in Ireland, and later in other parts of Great Britain.[8]

Hicks was in Europe for more than a year, performing some of the time with Sam Hague's troupe and, at other times, apparently only with his own small group. When he closed an engagement on May 6, 1871, in Liverpool, such had been his success that the management presented him with a medal and gifts. After a short tour of the provinces, Hicks left for the States on July 4, 1871.

All had not been sweetness and light, however, between Hicks and Sam Hague. The latter resented Hicks's "illegally assuming the title" of Georgia Minstrels and misrepresenting his group as the "original" Georgia Slave Troupe. Moreover, Hague asserted through his manager, W. H. Lee, that Hicks's touring in Europe had been a failure. Hicks's response was to deny that his performances had met with ill success and to publish press notices from English newspapers that supported his claim. All this bickering between Hague and Hicks took the form of an exchange of letters published in the *Clipper.* Significantly, when Hicks left England, he took with him back to the States at least one of Hague's minstrels, Japanese Tommy, if not more.[9]

Ignoring Hague's accusations, Barney Hicks began the 1871–1872 season advertising that the Original and Only Georgia Minstrels Slave Troupe, under the supervision of Charles B. Hicks, had returned from "Their Great European Tour" and was available for engagements. The season began well for the Georgia Minstrels, and business consistently was "reported excellent."

In September 1871 the company consisted of twelve artists, supported by the orchestra under the direction of George Skillings and the brass band directed by John Wilson. During the course of the 1871–1872 season, changes in personnel brought in several talented new members, whose presence in the group greatly increased the attractiveness of its offerings. Foremost among them were comedian Billy Kersands; endmen James Grace and Peter Devonear; and female impersonator T. Drewette (or Drewitte), called the "prima donna" and singled out for his performances in the skit "Princess of Trebizonde."[10]

Other members included Sam Jones, who joined with Louis Pierson to take over most of the singing, with Billy Wilson doing the character songs; Charles Anderson, who, along with Billy Wilson, functioned as chief dancer; Abe Cox, who joined the ranks of banjoists; Dick Weaver and Jake Zabriskie. As for the minstrels who had been with Hicks in Europe, Japanese Tommy apparently left Hicks soon after reaching home; his name does not appear on any Georgia Minstrels list, and within a year he was playing as "the African Dwarf Tommy" with Josh Hart and His Theatre Comique. On the other hand, Aaron Banks and Bob Height both were listed as members for the 1871–1872 season.

Hicks was acutely aware of the importance of maintaining high standards in order to keep the troupe's deservedly excellent reputation. Personnel might come and go, but he did not allow important positions to remain unfilled. On September 16, 1871, for example, he advertised in the *Clipper* for "a tuba player, who plays other brasses," and a "tenor balladist."

Despite the "good business" and the acclaim of the press, however, it seems obvious that Hicks and his minstrels were having problems. Sometime early in the 1871–1872 season, Barney Hicks lost control of his

Georgia Minstrels, the troupe he had organized in 1865 and successfully steered through the shoals and quicksands of the white show-business world for seven years. The wonder is not that Hicks lost his minstrel troupe, but that he managed to hold on to it for seven years in the racist climate of the United States after the emancipation of the slaves.

Black members of the show world were aware of the problems Hicks met in trying to compete with white business managers and advance men; indeed, it appears that Hicks himself sometimes used whites in management roles. Some black showmen felt that the fact of Hicks's looking like a white man was in his favor, and undoubtedly he did pass for white when necessary. But even more important was the fact that Hicks was very aggressive and innovative throughout his career.

In this instance, however, whatever Hicks had been doing was not good enough. Perhaps his sojourn in Europe had weakened his hold on the Georgia Minstrels troupe he had left behind, and when he returned he was not able to regain control. At any rate, a terse press announcement on April 6, 1872, stated that Charles Callender had bought out the interest of his former partner, William Temple, and was now the sole proprietor of the Georgia Minstrels. Barney Hicks remained with the troupe as business manager for a time, then was replaced by a white manager, George W. Siddons.[11]

There were few, if any, immediate changes in the activities of the troupe after Callender's takeover—at least as revealed in the press. True, the new owner paid for bigger ads in the *Clipper,* but the Georgia Minstrels had always advertised extensively. They continued to maintain a tight and profitable schedule, as in the past; they had long ago extended their touring from primarily on the Eastern Seaboard to the Mid-West, South, and even Far West—and that continued as before.

The season of 1872–1873, however, did bring changes. As early as August 1872 it became apparent that Callender was recruiting new personnel, partially because of the loss of some of the old-timers. One ad, for example, stated, "A balladist and alto singer are advertised for." By the beginning of the season of 1873–1874, one change had become obvious: the great increase in size of the troupe. A list of Georgia Minstrels personnel published on September 13, 1873, in the *Clipper* contained twenty names, whereas formerly the count of the troupe had been twelve or thirteen. Of the enlarged troupe, twelve men were old-timers, dating back to the Barney Hicks period.[12]

During the next two or three years the Georgia Minstrels began to evolve as the troupe that would earn laurels as one of the best in the nation. Callender was credited by both white and black contemporaries, including Trotter, for recruiting the most talented black artists he could find to perform with the Minstrels. By the time Trotter began to write his account in May 1877, the troupe included men of wide versatility and enormous gifts as vocalists, instrumentalists, and comedians. Trotter singles out some of their special talents:

> At least four of their number have been in the past accomplished teachers of music; one has played in some of the best orchestras of England; one is a superior performer upon at least four instruments, while he is a fair player of twelve; several are excellent performers on two or three instruments; and three of the troupe arrange and write music.

In another place Trotter refers to "several members of this troupe [who] possess musical and histrionic abilities of an order so high as to fit them to grace stages of a more elevated character than the one upon which they now perform."[13] He notes in particular a singer/actor who left the troupe to join the "Hyers Opera Company," a point to which I shall return. Actually, it was not an opera company in our sense, but a musical comedy company known variously as the Hyers Sisters Combination, Hyers Sisters Opera Buffa Company, Hyers Sisters Comic Opera Troupe, Hyers Sisters Dramatic Company, or Hyers Sisters Concert Company.

Trotter's discussion is tantalizing; although he offers a list of the troupe's personnel as of May 1877, he does not distinguish among them. The reader is left to wonder which ones are the music teachers; which ones, the multi-instrumentalists, the composer-arrangers, the possessors of "histrionic abilities." Were they really ex-slaves? How did they obtain the musical training necessary to produce shows that could compete successfully with those of the nation's leading white minstrel troupes?

By drawing upon a variety of sources, I have collected enough bits of information to make possible a composite picture of the Georgia Minstrels as they were in the late 1870s at the beginning of their climb to stardom.[14]

John Thomas Douglass (1847–1886) can easily be identified as one of Trotter's "four accomplished teachers of music." Concert violinist, director of a string orchestra, and composer, as well as studio teacher, in later years he received wide public attention as an early benefactor of David Mannes, a violinist with the New York Philharmonic and founder of the Mannes School of Music in New York City. Douglass had encountered Mannes as a child under unusual circumstances, and had given the young white boy his first violin lessons. Mannes never forgot his black violin teacher, and in 1912, long after Douglass's death, helped to establish the Music School Settlement for Colored in New York City in memory of Douglass.

There is some confusion about how much musical training Douglass had: Mannes said that he had been sent abroad to study by wealthy white patrons, but the obituary published in the black press stated that he was self-taught. In all likelihood Mannes should be regarded as the more reliable informant, for it is improbable that Douglass could have taught himself to play classical violin as well as the press reported had he not been professionally trained. The white press called Douglass "the only Negro solo violinist," and his black contemporaries regarded him as "one of the greatest musicians of the race." Certainly he was the first black violinist to tour as a concert artist born in the United States.

Douglass wrote a number of compositions and large-form works, including a three-act opera, *Virginia's Ball,* when he was only 21 years old.[15] It was produced in 1868 at the Stuyvesant Institute in New York, with four of the nation's top black artists in the leading roles. In the 1872–1873 season, Douglass appeared a number of times with the Hyers Sisters Concert Company, winning plaudits for his performances.

A second person on Trotter's list who conducted a music studio was the multi-instrumentalist Frederick Elliot Lewis (1846–1877), one of the two black musicians who performed in Patrick S. Gilmore's orchestra for the World Peace Jubilee at Boston in 1872 after successfully passing the auditions for violinists. (The other was Henry F. Williams, whose career also is discussed by Trotter.) Lewis was active as an accompanist, orchestral conductor, composer, and arranger. He belonged to a veritable dynasty of New England black musicians, dating back to the patriarch Primus Lew, an army musician in the French and Indian Wars of the eighteenth century, and his celebrated son Barzillai Lew, fifer in the Revolutionary War and, after the war, leader of a dance orchestra in great demand among the elite.

It is probable that Trotter was counting George A. Skillings, the troupe's Musical Director, among those who had conducted music studios before joining the Georgia Minstrels. Skillings, the leader of the Georgia Minstrels orchestra as early as 1871, if not earlier, was a violinist and undoubtedly a strings teacher.

There is yet one other music teacher on Trotter's list: the multi-instrumentalist James Emidy. Little is known about the Emidy brothers, both of whom played with the Georgia Minstrels, except that James was a band conductor, and they were black Englishmen. In September, 1872, James advertised from England, in the *Clipper*, that he would be available after October 25th "with or without his band." There is no further mention of Emidy in the press; presumably, he settled in the States soon thereafter. The Emidys joined the Georgia Minstrels about 1877.

It is entirely possible that these were the sons—or more likely grandsons—of the ex-slave Emidee (*fl.* late 1800s), violinist, conductor, and composer. As a slave Emidee had been given the opportunity to study violin in Lisbon, Portugal, and after gaining his freedom he settled in Falmouth, England. He attracted wide attention when his story was related in the *Autobiography of James Silk Buckingham* (1855): the English author, in his youth, studied violin with Emidee in Falmouth and played in Emidee's musical groups. Buckingham tried to promote Emidee's career by showing some of his musical manuscripts to members of the London music establishment, but although the music was well received, London was not ready to accept the black composer of the music.

Trotter knew of only four music teachers among the Georgia Minstrels, but there were others in the troupe during the 1870s. A. Hamilton Moore (1834–19——?), for example, a native of Philadelphia and a gifted trumpeter, studied in England with John Thompson Norton, trumpeter to George IV, and also studied music theory. During his stay abroad (1859–1874), he played trumpet in the Royal Lancaster Artillery, and in various Liverpool theater orchestras. Moore taught music for three years in Philadelphia after returning to the United States, then in 1877 joined the Georgia Minstrels. In addition to functioning as the troupe's star cornet soloist, Moore also directed the brass band.

Another music teacher active with the Georgia Minstrels during the 1870s was Alexander Luca (c. 1830–1883), concert tenor and teacher of vocal music, whose special responsibility with the Minstrels was to coach the singing groups. Luca brought a wealth of experience as well as talent to the Georgia Minstrels: a child member of the Luca Family Singers, he was still in his teens when the family troupe began a professional career after a successful debut in 1857 at New York City.

In 1873 Alex and his brother John, a baritone, were engaged by the Hyers Sisters Celebrated Concert Company, and they toured widely and extensively during the 1873–1874 season, a special feature of their concerts being the quartette singing of the Luca brothers and Hyers sisters, Emma and Anna. Alex, however, remained only a short while with the company; by the summer of 1874 he had left, and before the end of that year was touring with the Georgia Minstrels.

The most celebrated of all the Georgia Minstrels in the early years was Sam Lucas (1840–1916), comedian, ballad singer, guitarist, and gifted songwriter. Joining the Minstrels in July 1873 as an endman, he toured with the troupe, off and on, for the next ten or twelve years. Lucas was advertised as the "King of All Colored Comedians" and was immensely popular with both the critics and the public, especially in singing "character songs," most of which he wrote himself. Unlike the minstrels discussed so far, Lucas, the son of poor ex-slaves, was self-taught, but he had had experience performing with, first, a quadrille band, then with minstrel groups before joining the Georgia Minstrels, and he came to the Minstrels a celebrity.

In the spring of 1876 Lucas left the Georgia Minstrels to join the Hyers Sisters Combination as the star of that company's first musical, *Out of Bondage* (originally entitled *Out of the Wilderness*), and toured with them, off and on, for many years. When Lucas was not with the Hyers troupe, he was touring with the Georgia Minstrels, various dramatic companies, or with his own concert company.[16]

"Silver-voiced" Wallace King (c. 1840–1903), advertised as "the greatest colored tenor in the world," joined Callender's Georgia Minstrels in 1879, having previously toured with the Hyers Sisters Combination during the years 1873–1879. King had musical training in addition to a fine voice and was a great asset to the Georgia Minstrels, as well as to the Hyers Sisters. King remained with the concert company through its transformation in 1876 into a musical comedy company, and although he left the Hyers company in 1879, he returned to tour with the troupe intermittently during the next decade.

During its first dozen or so years, the Georgia Minstrels established itself as a national institution. Crisscrossing the nation in its annual tours, playing in hamlets and small towns, in large towns and the great urban centers, it successfully met the post-war public's insatiable hunger for entertainment and developed loyal followings among both black and white. For black entertainers—or "members of the profession," as they called themselves—the troupe functioned in a unique way: it was at once a haven for the established entertainer temporarily "at large" and a training ground for the neophyte, who could serve his apprenticeship with some of the most eminent black artists of the times.

Like the Original Georgia Minstrels, the Hyers Sisters Combination was a national institution for the almost three decades of its existence and, as such, played an essential role in establishing the groundwork for a black musical theater. If black showmen found the Georgia Minstrels to be a sure source of employment with relatively good financial rewards, at the same time they were required to conform to often demeaning stereotypes and frequently were unable to find full outlet for their talents. The Hyers Sisters company may not have been able to compete with the minstrel troupe in the salaries it offered, but it did provide opportunity for the gifted artist to perform materials that affirmed his human dignity and reflected his professional training. It is not surprising, therefore, that several of the Georgia Minstrels' brightest stars toured with the Hyers

Sisters Combination at one time or another in their careers—including, in addition to those named above, Billy Kersands, Willie Lyle, Fred Lyons, and Tom McIntosh.

Like other black minstrel troupes in the 1860s, the Georgia Minstrels inherited from Ethiopian burnt-cork minstrelsy the standard practices that had been established in the 1840s and, along with this, negative stereotypical images of the black man. But there was enough flexibility in the standard procedures to allow for innovation and improvisation; from the beginning the Georgia Minstrels undertook to produce shows which were novel and distinctively "genuine," plantation black-American, and, at the same time, enough in conformity with minstrel traditions to please their interracial audiences and keep them returning for more.[17]

Their shows followed the conventional three-part format, with the opening and closing parts presented by the full company, and the olio featuring specialty acts before the dropped curtain. The novelty came with what materials were used and how they were used. Programs typically opened with an overture, sometimes followed by a rousing choral number, then by a series of songs, and a walk-around to conclude Part 1. In addition to solos (vocal and dance), the olio featured quartettes and other ensembles. The remainder of the program focused heavily on plantation sketches and skits, which allowed for solo singing with the full company joining on choruses.

The choral, ensemble, and solo singing always won laurels from the press, and the dances, special laurels. Like the white troupes, the Georgia Minstrels had its romantic tenor balladeers, particularly in Wallace King; its "stump orators" in Barney Hicks and Hamilton Moore; its interpreters of "character songs" in Dick Little and Sam Lucas, whose performance of such numbers as "Grandfather's Clock" and "Shivering and Shaking" always brought down the house; and its female impersonators, or "prima donnas," in T. Drewitte and Willie Lyle.

Comedian Bob Height frequently was singled out for praise of his "comic shoe dance," and Billy Kersands was credited with having *invented* his speciality, the Old Essence of Virginia (soft-shoe dance). George Danforth's bones solos moved one critic to extravagant praise of him as "one of the best in his line I ever saw":

> While playing his solo he places himself in every conceivable position on the stage, and also on a chair, and dropping a bone from each hand, he continues playing anything but easy music, with but one bone in each hand.[18]

Contrary to widespread belief, the Georgia Minstrels did not draw heavily upon Negro folksong—at least not in its early years, if we are to judge from extant programs. Sam Lucas, the major songwriter of the troupe, specialized in ballads, "character songs," and comic songs. The other songwriters of the troupe, Jim Grace and Peter Devonear, wrote conventional minstrel or "plantation" songs. All three, however, drew upon the slave songs as sources of refrain texts and melodies. Typically, the verse of the minstrel song was newly invented, the chorus drew upon or used a slave-song, and the piece concluded with an eight- or sixteen-measure dance chorus (that is, without text). Devonear's "Run Home, Levi" is representative; here, however, the borrowed material—from the slave song "I don't want to stay here no longer"—is used as a refrain rather than a chorus.

The Georgia Minstrels frequently broke with tradition in regard to the kind of music they performed. Trotter reports, for instance, that its soloists and vocal ensembles, particularly the quartets, were invited to perform in churches and on classical-music programs of professional organizations, and the contemporary press offers further documentation of this. One of the most spectacular of these "breaks" took place on a Sunday evening, March 12, 1876, at the Boston Theatre in Boston. The advertisement placed in local newspapers indicates the nature of the performance:

> *Grand Sacred Jubilee Concert*
>
> All the Great Colored Singers
> in the World
>
> Including the Favorite Hyers Sisters
> Concert Company Singers
>
> Callender's Georgia Minstrels
> Grand Jubilee Singers

On such occasions as these, audiences were entertained with selections from the masters—Haydn, Verdi, Rossini—and with genuine Negro spirituals, such as had been popularized by the Fisk Jubilee Singers and the Hampton Singers.

On June 22, 1878, the *Clipper* announced that J. H. Haverly had become the proprietor of Callender's Georgia Minstrels, and Callender was being retained as manager. A big-time promoter, Haverly used his considerable promotional skills to advance his newly acquired black troupe in the same way as he did his white troupes. Periodically, beginning as early as 1879, he staged "monster" minstrel carnivals, where he gathered together one hundred or more black entertainers, men and women, to produce shows featuring the most celebrated black artists in the nation in such prestigious halls as the Academy of Music in Philadelphia and Beethoven Hall in Boston.

During his tenure as proprietor (1878–1882), Haverly brought in black-minstrelsy's bigwigs: among others, the celebrated songwriter James Bland, later called "the idol of the music halls"; the virtuoso-banjoists James and George Bohee; famed comedian Tom McIntosh; Horace Weston, the "Von Bulow of the Banjo"; and violinist Joseph B. Brindis, the "Cuban musical wonder." In 1880 Haverly brought back into the fold some of the minstrel stars who had strayed, particularly to Sprague's Georgia Minstrels; included were Lucas, King, Kersands, and Alex Luca. He even persuaded the Hyers Sisters to appear as special guest artists for some of his "minstrel carnivals," which became more and more lavish through the years.

In June 1880, for example, a mammoth outdoors production at Boston's Oakland Gardens was fitted with scenery to represent a southern plantation and, among other exotic acts, featured a steamboat race between the *Robert E. Lee* and the *Natchez.*[19] The next year Haverly took his Colored Minstrels to Europe, where his extensive promotion resulted in lavish productions similar to those staged in the United States.

With Haverly's ownership came the dissolution of the small, close-knit Georgia Minstrels troupe that Barney Hicks had organized in the 1860s, that Callender had developed into a world-class company during the 1870s, and about which Trotter had written in 1877. It was the end of an era.

Notes

1. Trotter, *Music and Some Highly Musical People . . . Sketches of the Lives of Remarkable Musicians of the Colored Race, with Portraits and an Appendix Containing Copies of Music Composed by Colored Men* (Boston: Lee and Shepard, 1878; reprint, New York: Johnson Reprint Company, 1969). All quotations from Trotter are drawn from pp. 274–277, 281. See further about Trotter in Robert Stevenson, "America's First Black Music Historian," *Journal of the American Musicological Society* 26 (Fall 1973), 383–404.

2. The definitive discussion of black Ethiopian minstrelsy is found in Robert C. Toll, *Blacking Up: The Minstrel Show in Nineteenth-Century America* (New York: Oxford University Press, 1974). In the present author's recent publications, discussion of black minstrelsy has been updated, based upon new research: Eileen Southern, *Biographical Dictionary of Afro-American and African Musicians* (New York: Greenwood Press, 1982); *The Music of Black Americans: A History*, rev. ed. (New York: W. W. Norton, 1983).

3. The present discussion, drawing solely upon primary materials and focusing on the early years of the troupe, differs in some details from Toll's excellent and provocative survey of black minstrelsy in general.

4. My chief source of information was the New York *Clipper* (hereafter, NYClip), the most important theatrical publication of the nineteenth century.

News items about Ethiopian minstrelsy generally were published in a column headed "Minstrelsy," but also occasionally under "Musical and Dramatic." Also especially useful were several black newspapers: *The Freeman*, of Indianapolis, often called the "Black Clipper" because of its coverage of the black show world; the *New York Globe, New York Freeman*, and *New York Age*. Useful Boston publications include *Folio, a Journal of Music, Art and Literature* (hereafter Folio). No attempt has been made to list every periodical citation used for this study; the most important ones are given at the end of paragraphs where necessary.

See further about Hague's Georgia Slave Troupe Minstrels in NYClip, 14 April–3 November 1866 passim; 21 May–10 December 1879 passim.

5. Re Hicks: NYClip, 1 September–1 December 1866 passim; *Freeman*, 7 September 1889, 6 September 1902, 13 September 1902.

6. NYClip, 3 October–5 December 1868 passim.

7. NYClip, 26 June–2 October 1869 passim. In view of the rigid segregation practices of the time, this feat was impressive; 17 July 1869.

8. Documentation for Hicks's performances in Europe: NYClip, 21 May–30 July 1870 passim; *Folio*, April 1870 (p. 84); NYClip, 28 January 1871, 10 June–5 August 1871 passim.

9. Re Japanese Tommy, see the *Brooklyn Eagle*, 3 February 1873.

10. NYClip, 9 September–30 December 1871 passim.

11. The details of the transaction have eluded my research. As early as January, 1872, the *Clipper* began referring to the troupe as Callender's Georgia Minstrels, but it is not clear whether Callender was manager or owner. NYClip, 6 April–24 August 1872 passim.

12. NYClip, 7–28 September 1872 passim. More than once Callender was forced to "reorganize" his troupe when dissatisfied members broke away to form competing troupes, but eventually most returned to the "original" Georgia Minstrels. See further, NYClip, 14–28 September 1872; 6, 13 September 1873.

13. Trotter, 276, 281.

14. For further biographical details see Southern, *Biographical Dictionary*. See also Southern, "An Early Black Concert Company: The Hyers Sisters Combination" in *A Celebration of American Music: Words and Music in Honor of H. Wiley Hitchcock*, (University of Michigan Press, 1990).

15. Trotter includes examples of compositions by Douglass and Lewis in his Music Supplement.

16. See Southern, "Two Early Black Musicals: *Out of Bondage* and *The Underground Railroad*."

17. A number of black-minstrel programs are extant in special theater collections around the nation. For a published program, see Southern, *Music of Black Americans*, 230.

18. NYClip, 10 July 1869.

19. *Boston Morning Journal*, 5–7 July 1880.

HUMOR

Ethiopian Skits and Sketches: Contents and Contexts of Blackface Minstrelsy, 1840–1890

William J. Mahar

Blackface minstrelsy is a troublesome topic in popular culture studies. Because burnt-cork comedy originated and thrived in a racist society, many scholars and most nonscholars believe that minstrelsy's primary purpose was the creation and perpetuation of demeaning caricatures or untruthful portraits of African-Americans. Most studies published since the early 1960s emphasize the negative effects of blackface comedy or focus on the development of the principal stereotypes (the urban dandy and the shiftless plantation hand) rather than on the interpretive significance of blackface comedy within the broader context of American ethnic humor. While it is essential that minstrelsy's negative characteristics be explored and explained as overt manifestations of the racist attitudes many Americans shared, the narrow focus on race and/or racism as the primary feature of blackface entertainment limits the application of the interdisciplinary methods and interpretive strategies needed to understand the content and context of one of the most popular forms of American comedy. The limitations imposed by restrictive methodologies can be removed, however, if historians reconsider a few of the issues that have been bypassed in most recent studies of American minstrelsy, namely, (1) the nonracial contents of blackface comedy; (2) the treatment of nonblack ethnic groups; (3) the socializing and class-defining functions of minstrel show humor; (4) the importance of minstrel shows as evidence of American ideas about politics, work, gender differences, domestic life, courtship, and marriage; (5) the use of the burnt-cork "mask" as a vehicle for reflexive, self-deprecating humor among various social, ethnic, and economic groups; and (6) the relationships between minstrel shows and other forms of American and English theater.

Those issues have not received much serious attention because most of minstrelsy's many genres—for example, the Ethiopian sketches, mock sermons, comic songs, burlesque operas, humorous dialogues, and parodies of popular plays—have not been analyzed critically. Even though primary sources have often been used in minstrelsy studies, problems with those sources (mainly the lack of adequate guides to repertories and library inventories) and the methodologies used to interpret them have severely limited explorations of minstrelsy's dependence on other forms of popular culture.[1]

This investigation of the nearly two hundred extant Ethiopian sketches is intended to be a preliminary contribution to the broader study of minstrelsy and its significance for American popular culture. But before turning to the sketches themselves, it is necessary to review the current state of minstrelsy studies and establish the contexts future investigators might consider with respect to blackface comedy.

Most studies of American minstrelsy published since the early 1960s—a decade that marked the appearance of the first strongly negative appraisals of blackface comedy—argue that minstrel shows popularized "personifications of a type of humanity not to be taken seriously" and that "the minstrel black was a living adjunct of the proslavery argument."[2] The questions raised by the new critiques of minstrelsy were undoubtedly the result of the increased sensitivity to the deleterious effects of racial stereotyping described so effectively in Ralph Ellison's 1958 *Partisan Review* essay, "Change the Joke and Slip the Yoke." Ellison argued that "in the Anglo-Saxon branch of American folklore and in the entertainment industry . . . the Negro is reduced to a negative sign that usually appears in a comedy of the grotesque and the unacceptable." For Ellison and those who accepted his argument, minstrelsy was a "ritual of exorcism," which grew out of "the white American's Manichean fascination with the symbolism of blackness and whiteness expressed in such contradictions as the conflict between the white American's Judeo-Christian morality, his democratic political ideals and his daily conduct—indeed in his general anti-tragic approach to experience."[3]

Ellison's "ritual of exorcism" argument emphasized conflicting social values as the key features of blackface entertainment and introduced psychoanalytical, anthropological, and behavioral theory into minstrelsy studies. The greatest strength of "Change the Joke" was that it forced scholars to recognize that minstrelsy's real significance as an exemplar of popular culture lay in the realm of symbolic communication. The idea that low comedy could be interpreted as a form of ritual suggested that one method of dealing with minstrelsy might be to study its social function as a form of popular entertainment capable of affecting a kind of catharsis, that is, a "symbolic discharge of aggressive feelings,"[4] in audiences harboring negative or at least ambivalent feelings toward African-Americans. If this aggression-reduction theory could be applied to the analysis of minstrel show humor and audience behavior, it would help explain how audiences, even those of mixed races and classes, might experience a collective "discharge" of energy or feelings after hearing "a humorist give public expression to their private fantasies in a context safe from destruction or retaliation."[5]

Nathan Huggins (*Harlem Renaissance*) suggested a different rationale for the success of blackface entertainment by arguing that the "minstrel 'Negro' . . . [was] a symbolic scapegoat *alter ego* into which whites projected sinful, guilt-provoking wishes otherwise suppressed by puritan consciences."[6] The projection and aggression displacement theories encouraged a much more serious consideration of the theoretical foundations required to understand ethnic humor. Huggins and Ellison, writing as they did during the 1960s, were also attempting to balance the negative aspects of burnt-cork comedy, particularly the damaging effects of racial stereotyping, against their own pride in the rich contents of African-American culture because "the black-faced figure of white fun . . . [had become] for Negroes a symbol of everything they rejected in the white man's thinking about race." Huggins and Ellison rejected the minstrels' claims of being "Negro impersonators" or "true delineators of Negro character" and argued that blackface comedy should be seen as a mask through which a white audience could enjoy its "fascination with blackness" and repress "its moral identification with its own acts and with the human ambiguities pushed behind the mask."[7]

Ellison's powerful indictment of blackface comedy contradicted the generally positive evaluations of minstrelsy published between 1840 and 1960. At the same time, however, Stanley Elkins introduced his controversial theory that some slaves did indeed adopt the happy, docile, and fun-loving "Sambo" behaviors characteristic of the "plantation darkies" used in minstrel comedy. On the surface at least, Elkins seemed to confirm the minstrels' claims that their blackface portraits contained the "kernel of truth" element that some psychologists believe to be embedded in both positive and negative stereotypes.[8]

It was inevitable that all studies of minstrelsy published after Ellison and Elkins would be affected not only by their work, but also by the debates and arguments their work inspired. By the end of the 1960s, when the offensive and pejorative racial contents of nineteenth-century blackface material were finally recognized, it seemed impossible to understand how Americans could still share Carl Wittke's pride (*Tambo and Bones*) in the claim that minstrelsy was "the only purely native form of entertainment and the only distinctively American contribution to the theatre" or Paskman and Spaeth's naive statement that "the most distinctive form of native entertainment should bear a name charged with all the romance and glamour of mediaeval minstrelsy."[9]

Once the assessment of minstrelsy's role in American culture changed from viewing it as a cultural asset to disowning it as another symptom of American racism, it was understandable that the interest in viewing blackface as a complex example of interracial, intercultural entertainment possessing both positive *and* negative characteristics would wane. The majority of popular and scholarly articles about minstrelsy written between the early 1960s to the late 1980s argued that stereotyping was a primary example of the majority culture's desire to maintain political, social, and economic control by transferring false theories of racial inferiority into a form of comic theater designed to demean African-Americans.

Alan Green argued that "the whole minstrel show was a fabrication of white performers, having no roots whatever in the American slave population."[10] Alexander Saxton, who attributed the genre's success to "the persistence of African borrowings (especially in dance movement and sense of rhythm)," believed that in spite of the positive respect inherent in "borrowing" musical materials, burnt-cork comedy "not only conveyed explicit pro-slavery and anti-Abolitionist propaganda [but] was in and of itself a defense of slavery because its main content stemmed from the myth of the benign plantation."[11] Berndt Ostendorf characterized minstrelsy "as a symbolic slave code, a set of self-humiliating rules designed by white racists for the disenfranchisement of the black self."[12] In his comprehensive survey of American songs about African-Americans, Sam Dennison presented an impressive quantity of evidence to support his judgment that "the crude humor of the minstrel performer obliterated any redeeming qualities possessed by the real black."[13] Robert Toll, whose *Blacking Up* is still the most extensive recent study of minstrelsy and whose conclusions could have pointed the way toward a greater appreciation of the complex forces at work in popular entertainment, argued that blackface entertainment "served critically important social and psychological functions," though he failed to explore the interpretive significance of his astute observation. Toll concluded that (1) the "minstrels created and repeatedly portrayed the contrasting caricatures of inept, ludicrous Northern blacks and contented, fulfilled Southern Negroes," and (2) since the minstrel show reinforced racist attitudes while it simultaneously entertained biased audiences, it "was one of the few comforting and reassuring experiences that nineteenth-century white Americans shared."[14]

"Comforting and reassuring" though minstrelsy may have been, its wide acceptance by American audiences depended on more than its "caricatures" and "racist attitudes." The contents of blackface entertainment ranged over a much broader spectrum of nineteenth-century social, economic, and cultural problems. From the first burlesques introduced by Thomas D. Rice in the 1830s to the many sketches created and/or arranged by Charles White (1820–1891), Andrew Leavitt (1822–1891), Frank Dumont (1848–1919), and George Griffin (1829–1879), few of the Ethiopian sketches dealt with typical "Southern Negroes" or plantation life.[15]

Robert Toll characterized the works of White and his colleagues as "slapstick comedies, featuring Negro low comedy types with their malaprop-laden dialect, and nearly always ending in a flurry of inflated bladders, bombardments of cream pies, or fireworks explosions that literally ended the show with a bang."[16] That characterization is an oversimplification suggesting that the sketches are little more than mere nonsense pieces of little cultural significance. Many of those sketches were burlesques of popular English plays, of great Shakespearean masterpieces, or parodies of the popular Italian operas of the period, all of which were traditional offerings by most American theaters before the development of the tripartite organization characteristic of the minstrel show after the 1840s. Thus, blackface burlesque was well established in the oral tradition and in the performance practices of American entertainers long before the surge of sketches published for professional and amateur performing groups of all social classes during the 1860s and 1870s.

The problems with generalizing about the Ethiopian sketches or any of minstrelsy's other comic genres are that the selections chosen for study must reflect the various changes each genre underwent during the turbulent decades of the nineteenth century and that the conclusions resulting from the analyses of the various examples must be correlated with a reasonably comprehensive understanding of minstrelsy's function as a form of popular theater. The blackface venues of the antebellum era cannot be viewed in the same way as those of the 1890s, when white racism was expressed through the oppressive "Jim Crow" laws, nor can the increased sensitivity with which we face such questions today be applied retroactively to a different period in American culture. As Werner Sollors observed,

> Contemporary readers are easily offended at the broad and farcical humor of the mid-nineteenth century [because] they assume that laughing at mock-Indian plays and Ethiopian sketches is in bad taste, perhaps even morally bad. Yet the borderline between the funny and the offensive is difficult to draw. It is subject to historical change and personal taste, as well as dependent upon the context in which the joke is made or by whom and to whom it is told.[17]

It is a mistake then to maintain that once the negative characterizations of African-Americans were created in the 1820s and 1830s, all minstrel entertainments were built exclusively around those unchanging stereotypes or that the social contexts of ethnic humor did not vary from one decade to another. That is a very difficult hypothesis to support when the same device of ethnic stereotyping was applied to Irish, Chinese, German, and Yiddish characters as soon as those immigrant populations became factors in the urban entertainments produced during the 1850s and 1860s.

The complex racial and ethnic elements in minstrelsy require more serious attention to the social function of humor in American life. The burnt-cork disguise offered the immigrant Irish, Jewish, and other disadvantaged power groups, which already knew about blackface clowning in their own cultures, a typically "American" opportunity to exploit established traditions of ethnic humor in order to clarify their own moral and/or cultural attitudes as well as the acculturation problems inherent in their adjustment to American society. Blackface comedy was a species of ethnic humor with specific and unfortunate social consequences for African-Americans yet, because of the often self-disparaging nature of its contents, minstrelsy also served as a mechanism for defining in-group values, a point Joyce Flynn emphasized when she noted that "the Americanization of immigrant groups on the American stage took place through the filter of the negative portrayal in blackface."[18]

Those "negative portrayals" were reflected in the interchangeability of costumes, props, dialects, and settings in many of the sketches, an observation supported by the following stage directions from Charles White's *The Live Injun; or, Jim Crow* (1865): "the parts can be played in White or Black"; "the whole may appear in blackface, or only Mat and Lulu; or those can be in dialect, Irish or Dutch"; and "parties wishing to alter it will find no difficulties whatever, except in changing the talk and properties."[19] The generic nature of the material suggests that racial specificity was not as essential to the overall comic effect as was the use of perceived racial and cultural differences as devices for ridiculing the cruel contradictions between the dreams and realities that lower- or middle-class Americans found in their daily lives.

Grimsted and Stowe suggested that popular-culture historians would have to deal with such questions when they criticized Toll for failing to see that "blackface, cork or real, seemed to audiences a mask which allowed deep expression of emotions of loss and longing, as well as ridicule of social and intellectual platitudes and the discrepancies between American dreams and American realities."[20] George Rehin warned American scholars to avoid a narrow critical vision by recognizing that blackface entertainment's "universal qualities," by which he meant the genre's concern for broadly human attitudes and its relationships with other earlier forms of Western comedy, were more fruitful areas of investigation than the continuous fixation on minstrelsy's "uniquely American character."[21]

Rehin's concept of "universality" does not mean that the more racially "neutral" types of blackface entertainment, namely, those that did not deal with African-Americans or typically "darkey" conventions, have any abiding aesthetic merit distinct from the political, social, or cultural values found in the repetitious plots and humorous stage business. Rehin wanted his American readers to recognize that some of the themes and issues treated in blackface comedy had long been the subjects of popular comedy outside the United States and that the minstrels, instead of focusing their comic routines on racial matters, attempted to deal with economic deprivation, problems related to the lack of social or economic status, discrimination based on gender or religion, skepticism about the effectiveness and value of American institutions, and a general sense of diminished self-worth among disenfranchised groups. The blackface comedians seem to have recognized what recent psychologists and folklorists have confirmed, namely, that stereotypes are essentially ambivalent vehicles that can be used "to promulgate high values through their negation . . . to impute rejected activities to a subordinate group, to maintain social distance and rationalize subservience," and to allow the audiences to "vicariously enjoy the exercise of forbidden motives or pleasures."[22]

This assessment of the problems related to the study of blackface entertainment should help link the investigation of the Ethiopian sketches with some of the principal methodological problems involved in approaching particular repertories. Because everyone agrees that those repertories contain racist materials or present what are obviously misleading interpretations and outright distortions of African-American culture, it is difficult to approach the subject objectively. But it is necessary to make the attempt because the failure to acknowledge bias or recognize the subtleties inherent in popular entertainment can lead to misinterpretation of the significance of what is arguably America's most noteworthy contribution to nineteenth-century theater.

The complex meanings hidden behind the minstrel comic's use of the blackface mask reflect the fundamental ambivalence about race that characterizes American culture. Minstrelsy has a positive as well as a negative side, which relatively few recent writers (those who did not underestimate the significance of Constance Rourke's *American Humor*) have recognized. As Charles Hamm pointed out in his survey of American songs (*Yesterdays*), the sympathetic portrayals of black Americans in the minstrel songs of the 1840s and 1850s "may well have been an important first step toward the widespread support of abolition."[23] And Robert Cantwell (*Bluegrass Breakdown*), writing from a perspective broader than most who consider minstrelsy, noted that "burnt cork was an attempt to resolve complicated cultural questions in the simple binary language of race; it might conceal, reveal, confuse, or falsify the identity of the minstrel who wrote it, might as surely mean 'white' culturally as it meant 'black' theatrically."[24] The conclusions of Cantwell and Hamm show that once the field of vision is expanded beyond the narrow focus on the minstrels' treatment of racial issues, the resulting image shows that not only was there a greater interdependence between African-American culture and American ethnic humor than previously believed, but also that the vigorous denials of those relationships by Dennison, Engle, Toll, and Ostendorf cited earlier can no longer be considered valid.[25]

Cantwell's observation is certainly correct for most of the two hundred sketches dating from the early 1830s to the mid-1890s, many of which were written or arranged by Charles White and a handful of other famous blackface sketchwriters and producers.[26] Most of the extant sketches were performed in New York, Boston, and Philadelphia, and published by a limited number of companies capable of providing sufficient quantities of copies for amateur groups in England and the United States. The sketches contain few plot variations. Many do not have real plots at all, but consist of two to five sometimes unrelated incidents linked together into scenes. Similar limitations apply to the number of character types and the range of subjects treated.[27]

Shakespeare's works provided the richest and most frequently chosen sources for blackface *and* nonblackface parodies during the nineteenth century. Of the nearly 25,000 burlesques of all types published between 1850 and 1900, somewhere between two hundred and five hundred of that number are believed to have been "Ethiopian." That estimate may be too high, however, because, of the nearly two hundred extant blackface sketches I examined in preparing this study, less than one-half are really based on or related to Shakespearean subjects. The numerical discrepancy is apparently one result of the bibliographical confusion surrounding blackface sources in general.

The blackface and whiteface burlesques of Shakespeare's major plays could travel freely among different classes and types of theaters because his work was part of a shared American culture rather than the inaccessible and hoarded property of the "culturally literate." The authors of the sketches found that the themes of Shakespeare's plays were an integral part of nineteenth-century life because "his plays had meaning to a nation that placed the individual at the center of the universe and personalized the large questions of the day."[28] Rather than transforming the principal characters in *Othello, Hamlet*, or *Macbeth* into plantation workers or urban characters living on society's margins, the Ethiopian sketchwriters reduced royalty to common folk and translated the grand tragedies of life into short sketches about courtship, mixed-race marriages, or conventional domestic life; criticized the effects of urban corruption and economic hardship; and faced up to the inconsistencies inherent in Americans' desire for respectability, comfort, and social recognition.[29]

The most frequently parodied Shakespeare plays were *Othello, Hamlet, Macbeth, Julius Caesar, Romeo and Juliet*, and *Richard III*.[30] Most of the adaptations followed the typical nineteenth-century practice of shortening Shakespeare's longer speeches or soliloquies, altering the text by mixing colloquial (both Standard and Nonstandard American dialects) with Elizabethan English, and emphasizing the blackface performer's outlandish rhetorical flourishes and malapropisms by conflating fragments of speeches from various plays into a single comic presentation. The most commonly added elements were the (1) nearly mandatory use of physical comedy or "comic business" (much of it left to the performers' improvisatory abilities) that concluded almost every sketch and (2) the substitution of a man dressed as a woman for Shakespeare's heroines, not only because most minstrel groups were all-male, but also because cross-dressed characters could exaggerate the negative stereotypes of women as harassing shrews, flighty lovers, and sentimental dreamers.

Three representative examples will illustrate how most of the *blackface* Shakespearean burlesques worked. The first is from George Griffin's *Hamlet the Dainty* (ca. 1880), the second from Charles White's *100th Night of Hamlet* (1874), and the third from Griffin's *Othello* (1866). All of the examples were probably performed several years before they were published, and some, *Othello*, for example, had been in the blackface repertory since Thomas Rice introduced his blackface parody in 1833.[31]

Griffin's *Hamlet* borrows only three of the twenty scenes from the original, two from act 1 (scenes 4 and 5), and one from act 5 (scene 2). The first two focus on the comic interplay Griffin found in the two confrontations between Hamlet and his father's ghost that concluded the first act of Shakespeare's tragedy. Griffin's third scene foreshortens the final scene of *Hamlet* in order to emphasize the duel (transformed here into a *boxing* match) between Hamlet and Laertes, satirize the drinking habits attributed to Hamlet's family (King Hamlet dies of an alcohol overdose and his ghost counsels abstinence as a requirement for Hamlet's happiness), and mock the acting styles used in the death scenes of popular tragedies and melodramas.[32]

Hamlet the Dainty is not so much a burlesque of *Hamlet* as it is a comic sketch based on a few of tragedy's most popular scenes. Griffin parodies Shakespeare's language by simplifying the syntactical elements, retaining the inverted word order typical of verse drama while shortening the sentences for better comic timing, and mixing colloquialisms with archaisms, for example, "Prythee!" "blacked up," "what the deuce."

From Shakespeare's *Hamlet*: Act 1, scene 4, lines 39–56.	From Griffin's *Hamlet*: scene 1
Angels and ministers of grace defend us! Be thou a spirit of health or goblin damned,	He's from the South! Oh grace defend us! Prythee! no more such frightful specters send us! Be thou blacked up or goblin damned! Be thou with whiskey puffed, or old cheese cram'd!
Be thy intents wicked or charitable, Thou com'st in such a questionable shape That I will speak to thee.	Be thy intents indifferent, good or bad,
I'll speak to thee, O, answer me! Let me not burst in ignorance, but tell Why thy canonized bones, hearsed in death, Have burst their cerements . . .	I'll speak to thee, thou look'st so like my dad— In a trim box, so snugly was't thou lain. Say! what the deuce e'er brought you out again?[33]

The text also accentuates the unionist view of the "South" as a threat to the political and social order. The appearance of corpses or "frightful specters" was virtually mandatory in burlesque comedy because audiences were so familiar with the use of such special characters and effects in performances of Shakespeare and because such devices allowed the comics to recast their supernatural agents as drunks or gluttons, whose excesses ("whiskey puffed or old cheese cramm'd" or [King Claudius's line] "One afternoon, as was my use, I went to a gin mill to take a snooze") were related to patterns of social drinking well known to the audience.

Such interaction with the audience was an important feature of the Ethiopian sketches. The opening scene of Charles White's *100th Night of Hamlet* (1874) is a good example of how the promise of an evening of Shakespearean entertainment could be linked to a satirical critique of the sometimes incompetent road players who brought their own "arrangements" of Shakespeare to rural Americans and to the cynical views that traveling actors had of the towns (and audiences) they visited during their tours. White's characters use "insult humor" to attack the audience's insecurity about the cultural "opportunities" available in rural America:

JAKE: This is one of them places that don't grow; the people here are too mean to die. You can't see a tombstone within a hundred miles of the place; they ain't got any money to bury themselves, and all eat hay the same as cattle.[34]

Whether they were performed in New York or New Orleans, Charleston or Cincinnati, the minstrel plays, in Gary Engle's words, were "ultimately shaped by the audience" who could "determine an evening's program by calling for and getting their favorite songs and dance numbers, whether scheduled or not."[35] The opening lines quoted from the *100th Night* illustrate one benign form of interplay in a burlesque sketch whose only obvious Shakespearean reference occurs in the final scene during which a hopelessly confused actor combines the two most famous soliloquies from *Macbeth* and *Hamlet*.[36]

Burlesques of *Othello* were common and predictable because most actors played the lead role in blackface, some, such as Edwin Forrest as an "octoroon," and others, Junius Brutus Booth, for example, in darker makeup. *Othello* was commonly viewed as an "antimiscegenation play" because, even though most audiences believed that such marriages were likely to end tragically, they also had an abiding fascination with and deep curiosity about such relationships.[37]

Griffin's burlesque, however, is never neutral about miscegenation. The negative references to "racial amalgamation" or interracial marriage, as it was known prior to the creation of the term miscegenation in 1863, reinforced the audience's aversion to racial mixing and established narrow boundaries within which fictional relationships might be tolerated. Griffin made it very clear that Othello's marriage to Desdemona was legal and that Desdemona entered the union willingly. The focus on a legal union emphasizes the popular notion that the marriage bond, once made, cannot be set aside because of parental or societal displeasure and that, as far as popular culture is concerned, audiences must have been willing to accept the validity of consent relationships, even when such an acceptance doomed one or more of the characters to a tragic (and often melodramatic) end.

The play deals with interracial marriage *after* the fact because the Othello–Desdemona union is simply accepted as a given from Shakespeare's play. Every character in Griffin's *Othello* (1866) *except* the couple considers the romantic relationship wrong, in spite of the fact that Iago, now recast as a blackface Irishman whose "black" heart exemplifies the duplicity most Americans attributed to the immigrant Irish, had once been Desdemona's suitor. Most urban audiences would not accept the idea or practice of racial mixing *before* the fact, and their opposition to both the theoretical political implications and practical consequences of miscegenation underscore the negative references found in Griffin's play. As Bruce McConachie has shown, New York's Farren riot of 1834 as well as a number of antebellum racial disturbances were caused by fears about racial "amalgamation," one of the social consequences even some of the most adamant antislavery advocates could not tolerate.[38]

While Griffin's sketch was not the first blackface burlesque of *Othello* produced in the United States—Rice's company performed his adaptation of Maurice Dowling's *Othello Travestie* (London, 1834) at least as early as 1846—all of the examples written after the 1850s, for example, Frank Dumont's *Othello and Darsdemoney* and *Desdemonun* (author presently unknown), eliminated all of the truly tragic elements of the original plays, a feature they share with White's burlesque of *Hamlet*. The typical scenes used in the blackface Othellos are Iago's declaration of his intention to ruin Othello (*Othello*, 1.1), Brabantio's pleas to the Duke and Senators (1.3), the handkerchief scene (3.4), and the murder of Desdemona (5.2). Griffin also included Iago's report of Cassio's dream (3.3) in order to accelerate Othello's already burning jealousy: "Sweet Desdemona, how could you e'er wed that dirty beast Othello . . . Oh, damn that nagur, don't you wish he'd die?"

All the *Othello* sketches I have examined treat the handkerchief as a comic property rather than a treasured object because of the weight Shakespeare places on its possession as evidence of Desdemona's infidelity. The minstrels saw the handkerchief as one link in a chain of improbable consequences whose misinterpretation by the jealous Othello led to Desdemona's murder. As Iago puts it, "To catch 'em in the act they'll leave small chances—the only proof you'll get is circumstances."

While the serious consequences of the *Othello* tragedy hinged on Desdemona's ability to produce a revered gift upon Othello's demand, the comic business of the parody rested on the inconsequentiality of common objects in the average person's daily life.

Griffin makes Iago's vengeance a central theme of the sketch, but, as the opening scene reveals, his anger is directed at Desdemona because *she* chose Othello for her husband, even though Iago's actions were designed primarily to bring about Othello's destruction.

> IAGO: When first I Desdemona saw, I thought her very fine,
> And by the way she treated me, I thought she'd soon be mine;
> But she's cleared out and left me now, with a nasty, dirty fellar,
> As black as mud—a white-washer—a nagur named Othello,
> But I'll kick up the devil's own spree with her for the way she served me,
> And the way I'll plague her for marrying that nagur, will be something amazin' to see.[39]

Desdemona's father, Brabantio, recast here as a blackface Dutchman (German), is a ragpicker who views his daughter as little more than an exploitable property that Othello has stolen:

> BRA: For nineteen years this has been a going, about mine house, and of all things had share,
> Mit switzer kase [Swiss cheese] and bread, her bags outblowing . . .
> I feed her up, to see if I could make her,
> So fat to see her dat people would pay,
> Just as I tink dat Barnum would take her,
> Dis nigger comes, and mit her runs away.[40]

Having transformed the dramatic elements into comic situations, Griffin replaced Shakespeare's text with the rhyming couplets typical of popular verse and introduced every scene or action with melodies borrowed from contemporary American and Irish songs. Iago's entrance song uses the melody of Samuel Lover's "The Low Back'd Car," while Brabantio sings about his parenting to the tune of Michael Balfe's "Blighted Flowers."[41] The loving couple enters the play singing and dancing the following parody of Emmett's "Dixie":

> OTHELLO: Oh, Desdy, dear, now you're my wife,
> I mean to pass a happy life,—Away, away, &c.
> I'll never more be melancholy.
> But be happy, gay, and jolly—Away, away, &c.

I love my Desdemona, away, away,
And hand in hand we'll take a stand,
To spend Brabantio's money.—Away, away, &c.

DESDEMONA: For you I've run away from pap,
But I don't care a snap for that.—Away, away, &c.
I love you and you love me,
And all our lives we'll merry be.—Away, away, &c.
With you I'll sport my figures, away, away—
I'll love you dearly all my life,
Although you are a nigger.—Away, away, &c.

IAGO: Go in my darlin's—go it while you're young—
Upon my sowl, you'll sing a different song
Before the day is out.[42]

"Dixie" pulls Shakespeare's characters directly into the world of blackface comedy, and the new lyrics summarize the essential ingredients of the afterpiece. Griffin's Desdemona expresses a youthfully naive and idealistic belief that the couple's love will shelter them from criticisms about their interracial marriage, a union both of them view as legal (Othello says, "I've *married* [emphasis added] her—he [Brabantio] must undo that first." Desdemona makes it clear that her choice was free and that, because romantic love was a condition for that choice, her marriage to Othello meant, " 'til death do us part."

The authors of the Othello burlesques recognized that the audience's fear about racial mixing had greater potential for comedy than the more complex dramatic problems inherent in portraying Othello's jealousy and Iago's obsession with vengeance. After all, Shakespeare had dealt with those themes. Since low comedy tends to reduce subtle dramatic motivations to simplistic actions with immediate consequences, Iago's desire for revenge was motivated by his unsuccessful courtship of Desdemona rather than his loss of power. Griffin exploited the comic opportunities in the miscegenation issue by making Iago a disgruntled suitor and emphasizing the sexual rivalry between him and Othello.

Miscegenation was a concern for the new immigrants in the audiences because, given their worries about defining their personal and group roles in American society, they were also anxious to preserve their racial or ethnic identities. Amalgamation as early as the first generation would have destroyed the strong connection with homeland and kin that was still important to those new Americans. Werner Sollors explained the reasons for such concerns when he observed that the "North American cultural maxim . . . [against] racial mixing was that culturally unacceptable consent relations were considered punished [sic] by a natural lack of descendants, an ideological exaggeration of the general fear of losing a generation."[43] Worries about the social status of descendants were important because most Americans linked the descendants of mixed-race marriages or liaisons with the African-American parent. Fears about interracial marriages were quite groundless, however, because the actual number of such unions was very small in the states that did not explicitly prohibit miscegenation. The burnt-cork comics also seem to have exploited the Northern audiences' concerns about the availability of suitably chaste white spouses and the potential sexual rivalry between white and black men generated by the stereotype of the sexually virile African-American male.[44]

The minstrels' fascination with miscegenation was based on a deeper interest in preserving racial separation by protecting ethnic and cultural identity as well as limiting sexual encounters to partners of one's own race. Desdemona could be ridiculed easily because of her unwillingness to comprehend the socially tolerable boundaries within which acceptable consent relations might occur, and because, regardless of the reasons for her choice, her fate ultimately hinged upon such flimsy circumstantial evidence as her failure to produce a handkerchief.

Griffin's sketch also contains a large number of references to other contemporary social themes. The father–daughter relationship (Brabantio and Desdemona) is severed when the young woman escapes her domineering father's plan for her life, even though that escape is into a marriage likely to have an unhappy outcome. The Iago–Othello conflict is treated as one of sexual rivalry—both men loved the same woman—leading to violent or conspiratorial behaviors consistent with contemporary audiences' willingness to accept that the blackface *and* "Irish" Iago belonged to an ethnic group known for its belligerent and unruly behavior. Again the tragic flaws of the principal characters were translated into common male rivalry themes for an urban audience. Finally, the comedians viewed a wife's role as subservient to her husband, something Othello makes clear when he tells Brabantio, "If for my wife—your daughter—you are looking, you'll find her in the kitchen busy cooking."

The fear of miscegenation (and fear was the primary cause of societal racism) could be exaggerated by introducing the even more morally implausible and socially unacceptable consequences of a tryst between two lovers of the same sex because the part of Desdemona was probably played by George Christy, one of the best female impersonators of the era.[45] Griffin's burlesque is built on the premises that no audience would set aside the double societal taboo against racial *and* gender intermarriage especially in a form of popular entertainment that almost always supported the maintenance of the moral and social status quo. Regardless of how the comic conflicts were worked out in the sketches, the end result reinforced the values that contemporary audiences shared.

The burlesques discussed above linked the audience's love for Shakespeare with issues that various groups considered worthy of satire or ridicule. A second group of sketches, which can best be described as "parade" or processional plays, adopted a more direct approach to treating the conflicts between social and economic values as well as the concerns of different racial or ethnic groups. Those plays performed an important educational function for those who saw them because the sketchwriters often incorporated new images of city life, introduced ideas about the increasingly diverse immigrant groups, offered views (usually negative) about scientific inventions and economic theories, and explored contrasting or competing social or political philosophies.

These sketches were usually set in the context of a contemporary social event, typically a masquerade ball, and featured walk-ons by a variety of exotic or eccentric players. Characters from popular melodrama and the most famous Shakespearean dramas joined a motley cast of stock stage types common to American comedy ever since Thomas Rice sang "Jim Crow" or George "Yankee" Hill played "Brother Jonathan" during interludes or entr'actes to plays performed a decade or two earlier.[46] The main differences between the various types of parade plays lie in whether or not they focused on displaying odd characters in satires about social events, such as masquerade balls or parades, or whether they featured ridiculous representations of characters likely to appear in courtrooms, employment offices, or other quasi-official public venues.

Charles White's *The Hop of Fashion; or, The Bon-Ton Soiree* (ca. 1856) features such an unlikely cast: Richard III, Mose (one of Broadway's B'hoys in another genre of popular comedy), a French gentleman, a drunken Irishman, and a stage-struck *youth* (named "Pops"), who speaks of Rome, "the Queen of Cities," where "there is not a palace on those hills that has not been bought by blood." Those characters join Macbeth and Lady Macbeth as guests at Captain Slim's (a newly made lottery ticket millionaire) masquerade ball. The comic premise of the sketch is that characters drawn from Shakespeare's plays, contemporary melodrama, and urban life "parade" before an unsuspecting doorman who must screen their admission to Captain Slim's home. Among the characters White extracted from a period play is one named Claude "Melnot" [sic for Melnotte], a caricature of the principal role in two contemporary plays entitled *Claude Melnotte* (1844) and *Pauline* (1845).

Both of those plays were American adaptations of Edward Bulwer-Lytton's popular *The Lady of Lyons; or, Love and Pride* (nearly four hundred American performances between 1831 and 1851), in which Pauline Deschappelles, the beautiful but spoiled daughter of a wealthy merchant, is courted by Claude Melnotte, a lowborn, but refined, gardener's son.[47]

Two brief quotations will show how the odd combinations in White's sketch worked:

MACBETH: What? can such things be, an' o'ercome us without our special wonder [*Macbeth*, 3.4.111–12], and now I do behold you keep the natural ruby of your cheek, while mine is balanced with fear [*Macbeth*, 3.4.114–16]. Approach thou like the rugged Russian bear, or Hulcan [sic for Hrycan] the armed rhinoceros—take any other shape but that [*Macbeth*, 3.4.100–2].
ANTHONY: I neber took a sheep in my life.

CLAUDE: In a little log hut made out ob pine,
All kibered ober wid de mornin'glory's vine,
Dar, lub, we'd sit and often wonder,
If anything could tear asunder.
Two loving hearts like ours.
We'd know no darks 'cept them dat had de dollars,
And dem dat wore fine clothes wid de largest kind ob
big shirt collars;
Read police reports and then we'd see
How many colored men there be
Sent by his honor for thirty days
At public expense to mend their ways
And then the telegraph reports we'd read of darkies
killed in showers,
And laugh to think what a happy fate was ours.[48]

"Macbeth's" lines are taken from the ghost scene in act 3, but they are as hopelessly mixed up as Hamlet's and Macbeth's speeches were in the White's *100th Night of Hamlet*. Shakespeare's text and Anthony's malapropism ("sheep" for "shape") are both at home in the new environment of blackface farce. Just as the illusion of an Elizabethan or ancient setting was destroyed by the topical references used in White's *100th Night*, so, too, the incongruous juxtaposition of characters and language from tragedy, popular comedy, and blackface minstrelsy in *The Hop of Fashion* satirizes the social rituals of upper- and middle-class life and capitalizes on the audiences' fascination with questions about how "other" people lived and their unbounded curiosity about the customs of other classes and societies.[49]

Griffin's burlesque included Mose (and a Bogus Mose because the contrast between type and stereotype could be made explicit if both characters appeared at the same time), Macbeth, Richard III, an Irish woman, and a character called Previous Difficulties, whose gatekeeper role is similar to Anthony's part in White's play. Both masquerade-ball examples illustrate the differences between plays chosen as vehicles for a particular company to demonstrate some of its specialities, Shakespearean takeoffs or Mose imitations, for example, and those that dealt more broadly with developing patterns of class consciousness. But all of the social burlesques took as their models such popular period comedies as Anna Mowatt's *Fashion; or Life in New York* (1845), Cornelius Mathew's *False Pretenses; or, Both Sides of Good Society* (1856), Henry Preuss's *Fashions and Follies of Washington Life* (1857), and Eugene Raux's *The Road to Fortune* (1846), produced by writers who were more successful when they dealt with "the newly rich and the less respectable social elements . . . than the more settled, established social groups."[50] Those plays featured specific domestic locales, fashions, and behaviors of newly wealthy social climbers who had accumulated the goods representative of their new economic status, but lacked the "class" and "culture" of a true aristocracy. American audiences seemed to recognize that while financial success, preferably a sudden acquisition with an excellent chance for longevity, might allow people to "show off," it did not necessarily bring contentment.

Claude's speech contains statements reflecting a common belief that a greater percentage of African-Americans ran afoul of the civil authorities, a charge attributed to a number of other economically weak ethnic groups as well. Depending on the period in which the particular sketch or burlesque was performed, criminal activity was "treated as a cultural aberration rather than a symptom of class inequality." As Stephen Steinberg (*The Ethnic Myth*) argued, "there has been an ethnic succession in all areas of crime, beginning with the Irish, who were the first identifiable minority to inhabit urban slums." Using an 1860s *Harper's* observation that "the Irish have behaved themselves [so badly] that nearly 75 percent of our criminals are Irish, that fully 75 percent of the crimes of violence committed among us are the work of Irishmen," Steinberg observed that just as later writers were to attribute the crimes African-Americans committed to their ethnic distinctiveness so too the majority culture of the 1860s attributed the Irishmen's tendency toward violence to "the intemperate disposition of the Irish race."[51] Speeches such as Claude's were adaptable to the group the minstrel sketchwriter had decided to attack. At the same time, the American predisposition toward creative individualism can be seen in the portrayal of Claude as possessing a dignity and quality of character that sets him apart from his economic class or ethnic group, those traits being the ones Pauline finds most attractive in a potential spouse.

Claude's reference to a biased explanation of crime statistics demonstrates his respectability. His value system sets him apart, and his speech suggests, just as many of the period's nonblackface plays did, that romantic love and financial security were the true keys to marital happiness and social respectability. By putting the typically romantic values of the original plays into the mouths of a blackface gentleman and his cross-dressed "companion," White satirizes the romantic idealism embodied in *The Lady of Lyons*, Dion Boucicault's *The Poor of New York* (1857), and a host of other lesser offerings of the period. The point is not that the burnt-cork comedians portrayed only black Americans as unrealistic dreamers, but that they used the blackface disguise to reveal how ridiculous the sentimental idealism embodied in contemporary melodramas could actually be.[52]

The parade plays were directly related to the middle-class audiences' pursuit of respectability as well as their desire to exhibit and display the tangible examples of their financial success. The plays also reinforced the need most upwardly mobile people had to achieve some measure of social distinction both from immigrants and from the emerging (and more belligerent) working classes. The blackface burlesques "paraded" examples of all social types for inspection and parodied the widespread interest in fashion, etiquette, and education. Once the sketchwriters recognized the efficiency of the parade format in allowing for an ever-changing cast of walk-on characters, they were content to use a relatively restricted number of social rituals as the settings for their burlesques.

The *Hop of Fashion* contains revelations about the kinds of invited guests and gate-crashers who might attend what the blackface comedians and their audiences thought were typical social events, for example, the masquerade balls popular among the rising economic classes in urban America, but the minstrels also chose more plebian settings for dealing with other social types. This was most evident in the those processional or parade plays modeled on William T. Moncrieff's successful adaptation of Pierce Egan's popular novel entitled *Life in London; or The day and night scenes of Jerry Hawthorn, esq. and his elegant friend Corinthian Tom . . . in their rambles and sprees through the metropolis* (1821).[53]

Moncrieff's Tom and Jerry shows, at least ten of which were performed in London between 1821 and 1843, were copied and parodied in New York and Philadelphia almost immediately. The original plays and their American adaptations satirized the customs and beliefs of different social and economic classes by placing comic representatives in situations where they could "observe" and comment on life. This type of parade play was usually set in courtrooms, employment offices—a new service developed to meet the needs of rural and immigrant peoples flocking to the urban centers in the North—or any situations in which numerous low-comedy types could be "judged" or "interviewed" by surrogate authority figures. Among the most accessible examples are Leavitt's and Eagan's *The Intelligence Office* (ca. 1890), the subject of which is really a bogus employment agency; *High Jack, the Heeler* (1875), which introduces a judge to a variety of comic criminal types; and Coes's *Scenes from a Sanctum* (1895), which takes place in a newspaper editor's office.[54]

Most of the titles mentioned above are based on role reversal or status inversion and contain at least one scene featuring a blackface servant or other low-comedy type who becomes a "judge" or "boss." The device was certainly not unique to American comedy because under its more common name of "inversion ritual" it was an essential feature of European comedy. Freud recognized its significance (he described the effect as "the degradation—Herabsetzung—of the sublime") in his discussion of comedy.[55] The idea of "inversion" is based on a distrust of class and privilege, and, given the democratic biases of most American audiences, it is easy to understand how the blackface comedians could have adapted "inversion rituals" for dealing with the distinctions between race and class that were developing in the United States as the country changed from an agrarian to an industrial economy.

Status-reversal comedy employs various types of ridicule to reduce the professional status and behavioral characteristics of an individual class or group, judges or businessmen, for example, to such a level of absurdity that no one would take those characters seriously. The device is at least as old as the comedies of Plautus where status reversal was part of a genuinely comic inversion "whose sole aim in turning things upside down . . . [was] to make spectators feel better about themselves and their everyday world."[56]

The low-status individuals in blackface sketches assume "power" roles and control their victims' destinies for short periods of time, but they escape (because in reality they could never really possess power) the troubling responsibilities associated with any real exercise of authority. The audience understood the logical implausibility inherent in the idea that low-status types would ever actually "take over" positions of power.

The lawyers, judges, and supervisors who had serious real-life responsibilities were ridiculed by having their tasks transferred to irresponsible clowns and their vocabularies treated as meaningless jargon. The blackface characters were not depicted as slaves who seized power, but as vulgar comedy types whose ability to control events was limited to their brief appearances as power players in farcical situations. Popular burlesques (both whiteface *and* blackface) were able to dissolve distinctions between social and economic classes by bringing everything and everyone down to the comic persona's level and by selecting only the most easily satirized characteristics of the target groups.

The dissolution of class distinction could occur without penalty in the fantasy world of the theater because even though varying social groups or economic classes might be seated differently, the theater was nonetheless viewed as a "safe" ground for caricature and satire. That observation may explain why "better" audiences were entertained by the public revelation of their own faults. Assuming that one audience in-group might consist of judges and lawyers, it is likely that they could view negative portrayals of their professions as a species of self-disparaging humor directed at group members whose behavior was known to be outrageous. The minstrels' mocking attack could then strengthen the self-esteem the in-group had for itself—after all, "our group never did those things"—or force members whose behaviors were questionable to recognize the validity of the comic sketch and consider, if only momentarily, making such behavioral modifications as would encourage greater professionalism. Such an interpretation, if it can be verified in other social comedies of the period, would support Northrop Frye's theory that comedy creates "an individual release which is also a social reconciliation."[57]

The simplest way of mocking a class or professional group was to attack its lexicon and link that assault with adventurous wordplay and rhetorical extravagance as illustrated in the following example from Arthur Leavitt's *Squire for a Day* (1875):

> This is a slashing case. So you asked him to lend you a spit and he wouldn't and you say that he throwed mud all over your papers; this is a tart case. The party of the first part, a leather burnisher, solicits the loan of a saliva from the party of the second part and was refused, whereupon the said party of the first part, with premeditated malice, violently hurls a compound of mother earth at the party of the second part, causing a destruction of valuable property and doing great bodily harm; the party of the second part is a vender [sic] of literature, who received a slashing demonstration of dirty friendship, and with striking terms of reciprocity repaid the party of the first part by giving him a note of hand delivered at sight. That is the case.[58]

The judge's summary, like the many other mock sermons and stump speeches found in the minstrel repertory, borrows legal jargon in order to transform a trivial disagreement into a "major" criminal issue. The passage satirizes the artificiality and formality of a species of technical discourse that common folk did not appreciate because it could be used as a subterfuge permitting devious professionals and clever charlatans to defraud the public. The creative use of language and its combination with "fancy talk" was a significant comic element in this speech and examples like it because verbal wit and persuasiveness were valued in a society that admired public oratory and still depended in large measure on oral forms of communication.

Having completed their comic assaults on their victims, the low-comedy characters' "punishment" (according to the blackface convention) was seldom more than a mock beating with a flour sack or other comic prop *after* the play's dramatic action had dissipated. Recognizing that the revelation of the comic premise was often an insufficient conclusion even for minstrel comedy, most of the sketchwriters ended the scene with physical "business," a short period of free and improvised horseplay involving all kinds of stage properties (clubs, flour bags, fireworks, noisemakers, and brooms, for example) and a "tableau," that is, a picture created when the actors froze their poses and waited for the audience's applause. Because it has the power to transform even the most trivial action into scenes of comic chaos similar to the "misrule" or mayhem of earlier Western comedy, the "stage business" of minstrel show comedy has its own significance as an element of theater. It is contrived and staged violence designed to end the sketch by disrupting the seemingly orderly, but not necessarily logical, action with nonsensical mayhem. The sketches then concluded with the formal tableau bringing the cast together for the formal bow and the restoration of the distinction between the mock but illusory combats and real life.

The parade play was such a successful vehicle because it could accommodate the presentation of different races, social classes, occupations, and a variety of topical issues of considerable interest to contemporary audiences. The variety format inherent in the walk-on style of the parade also served as a blackface counterpart to the popular nineteenth-century museums as institutions catering to an insatiable public curiosity, including those politicians, who, because their tendencies toward corruption were widely publicized, had emerged as a whole new class of comic miscreants.

The parade play format was flexible enough to include such topical elements as political corruption. One of the most popular of such plays was Ryman and White's *Julius the Snoozer* (1875), one of four burlesques of Shakespeare's *Julius Caesar* that appeared simultaneously in New York during that year. *Julius the Snoozer* combines the topical play with a burlesque of Shakespeare and illustrates the strong interrelationships between the different types of minstrel material. The sketch transforms the conspiracy against Caesar into one against William Marcy "Boss" Tweed, who between 1866 and 1871 "plundered the City of New York with such precision that . . . [the Tweed Ring] has received the singular distinction of being labeled the model of civic corruption in American municipal history."[59] Tweed is made the butt of the conspirators' joke because his extravagances exceeded even the average person's grasp of political corruption. As the following dialogue indicates, the stereotypical politician was easily bought off with promises of money, fame or power:

> CASSIUS: Our dirty streets want cleaning; to this you've no objection?
> JULIUS: We'll have them cleaned just before our next election.
> DECIUS: I'd call your attention to our filthy water.
> CASSIUS: Your royal highness, a request I'd make
> To stop fox hunting in Jersey State.
> BRUTUS: A police reform is asked for everywhere,
> And a street car law, "No seat no fare."
> DECIUS: To the canal frauds I'd call your attention.
> CASSIUS: I call for a vote on the Third Term question.
> BRUTUS: A thousand other evils could be named,
> But what's the use when there's nothing to be gained.
> DECIUS: A deaf ear you turn to all our good intents,
> Waiting to be bought for ten or fifteen cents.[60]

The burlesques also reveal some of the ways corrupt politicians could extend their control over whole classes of people by controlling a city's most vital resource, its real estate. When Brutus says, "On bended knee I present this petition new: The law annexing South Fifth Avenue with Murray Hill [the area where New York's 400 resided] is much against the colored people's will," the blackface comedian recognizes that both the power to make such changes and the will to restrict a group's mobility can be manipulated by corrupt politicians. The implausibility "of annexing South Fifth Avenue" would have been apparent to contemporary New York audiences who knew that African-Americans were not allowed to purchase dwellings there.

Even though there are negative references to African-Americans in this play (Julius dreams that "twenty knives stuck into me, while twenty coons, or even more, washed their hands in my royal gore"), they are incidental to the main action, which details the many schemes of Tweed and his gang. The reference also provides evidence that a more malevolent and inherently more negative image of black male urban dwellers as razor-wielding threats to social order was emerging in popular comedy some twenty years before it appeared in the "coon" songs and stage caricatures of the 1890s.

A selected number of historical events also provided excellent material for topical satire. As with the plots and themes noted earlier, the range of material is quite narrow. A typical example is White's *The Draft* (1865), in which a recruiting sergeant hunts draft dodgers—the most ridiculous being a blackface character named Casey. The sketch acknowledges what most Eastern audiences knew: many Irish immigrants did not want to serve their new country because of the class inequities built into the Conscription Act of 1863 and their fears about the increased competition for jobs if free blacks were to migrate to the North. Those fears fueled the New York draft riots of 1863, in which some 105 (eleven of the victims were black) of the mostly Irish participants died and another 1,000 persons were injured, with property losses of several million dollars.[61]

White's blackface draft dodger, Casey (the Applicant in the passage quoted below), had used a number of excuses to escape the draft. When he was finally caught, Casey could only make the following pitiful plea to avoid induction:

SMALL: Doctor, there's a subject for your decision. Will you take a look at him?
DOCTOR: Yes, I've seen him a great many times before. Young man, come here. What's the matter with you? . . . What are your symptoms—what do you most complain of?
APPLICANT: Everything. I ain't got no clothes, no wittals, no home, no friends, nor no money. I ain't had a drink for two days. One of the fellers on the corner says I've got the jim-jams, and if I don't do something for it I'll go in the box.
DOCTOR: Well, sir, I'll do something for you. I'll give you something to eat, a nice suit of blue, and send you in the country, where you will get plenty of pure air, and make your Uncle Sam give you some spending money besides.[62]

Casey's ailments are attributed to his laziness and dependence on alcohol—stereotypical traits of the stage Irishman—but he is also an example for those veterans and inductees who, by the midpoint of the Civil War, had come to doubt the validity of the effort and were willing to express their feelings by "uncivil" disobedience. What makes Casey funny is not the blackface costume, nor even the fact that some members of the audience might have viewed him as a "symbolic" black man. The blackface mask in this context reflects the audience's skepticism about Union service, not its views about the combat capabilities of "colored" Federal soldiers. The Casey character is ridiculous because his plan to avoid service by feigning mental or psychological incompetence deceived no one while his ineffective entreaties and pitiful pleadings entertained all. The Casey character exemplifies the comedy inherent in the treatment "of the born loser with whom we can commiserate while still feeling infinitely superior."[63]

Economic issues also provided the content for a number of sketches written in the decade surrounding the Panic of 1853. The best-known example is White's arrangement of Dan Emmett's successful *Hard Times: A Negro Extravaganza* (1855), which shared the same general theme with Stephen Foster's popular "Hard Times Come No More" (1855), the song referred to in the opening lines of the sketch. Emmett borrowed a familiar plot device from contemporary drama, namely, the sale of a person's soul in exchange for some material goal. Popular wisdom had it that the temporary release from need or desire for fame was not a sufficient reason to risk eternal damnation *unless* the potential victim had a foolproof plan to outwit the devil. Old Dan Tucker had such a plan and was willing to risk his own eternal life to obtain coal, food, and clothing for his family, as he confesses in the sketch's opening lament:

> TUCKER: Hard Times! hard times! an' worse a comin';
> Hard times thro' my old head keeps runnin';
> I'll cotch de nigger make dat song.
> To shake him well would not be rong;
> Ob him dat's rich, I won't be jealous,
> For don't de big book 'spressly tell us—
> And tells us, too, widout much fussin',
> Whedder we're white or color'd pusson—
> "Bressed am dem dat's berry poor,
> Dey'll nothing get, dats berry sure?"
> Take ort from ort an naught remains;
> But "you're a damn fool for your pains."
> My wife an' children are most froze,
> For want ob fire, food an' clothes,
> I'd sell myself, both body an' soul,
> For jist a peck ob fire coal![64]

The sentiments expressed in that excerpt deal with the frustration many white small businessmen shared with poor and lower-class people. Tucker complains that effort goes unrewarded and that hopelessness is the true lot of the poor. The paraphrase of the biblical beatitude ("Blessed are the poor in spirit, for theirs is the kingdom of heaven") is a common device in minstrel speeches and sermons. It contrasts the hope that the poor will receive some reward with the reality that they are doomed to a life of need. The skepticism embodied in the blackface rewrite of the Christian message relects the comedian's view that the economic disparities of American life apply to all poor people regardless of color.

The concentration on the random nature of financial stability emphasized what Bruce McConachie has observed in the popular plays of Dion Boucicault, namely, that the accumulation of wealth by middle-class families in the 1850s was "due as much to chance as to their innate morality." Tucker's pact with the Devil only makes sense when it is seen as the last desperate act of a person who has not profited from good luck or adherence to traditional American moral values. That is why the conversion of a biblical axiom into a cynical aphorism could provide the rhetorical foundation for a comedy about communal economic misery and, at the same time, reinforce the hard-work ethic of middle-class audiences.[65]

Frank Dumont's *What Shall I Take* (1876) linked the "hard times" theme to the effects of a depressed economy on the small businessman. Dumont, whose plays were performed primarily in Philadelphia, based his sketch on the dark humor underlying the blackface proprietor's complaint that "people used to come and buy arsenic and laudanum to poison themselves with, and now times are so hard no one wants to die or buy any medicine or poison."[66] The humor arises from the exaggeration of a particular conceivable action—an individual suicide by ingestion—into a universal (and patently absurd) principle of behavior that everyone who buys laudanum is looking for an easy and painless death. The same principle applies to those whose real or imagined illnesses made them the likely victims of medical frauds. George Griffin dealt with their complaints about "product reliability" in *The Hypochondriac* (ca. 1870), whose protagonist exclaims that

> I have taken the last bottle of this; [the potion is called "The Joy of the Afflicted"] . . . I have exhausted the medical schools; last week I tried Homeopathy, and the week before I tried Allopathy; and the week before that, Hydropathy! I was advised to try a hot bath, so I plunged into boiling water, *but it didn't do me any good.* Then I tried cold water, and passed five days among the frogs at the bottom of a well, *but it didn't do me any good.*[67]

The last two examples illustrate what appears to have been a general distrust of all "experts," regardless of whether they were common pitchmen or legitimate medical vendors working in an unregulated industry. A short list of examples featuring licensed doctors or medical frauds would include White's *Pompey's Patients; or, The Lunatic Asylum* (1872), *The Sham Doctor* (ca. 1870), *The Black Chemist* (1862), *Laughing Gas* (1858), his arrangement of Dumont's *The Lunatic* (1876), as well as John Smith's *The Quack Doctor* (ca. 1850). Leavitt's *No Pay No Cure* (ca. 1882) borrowed the same theme and featured Dr. Ipecac (a product trade name), who "has a theory that excessive terror will cure the deaf and dumb," while George Coes used the incompetent physician for *The Faith Cure* (1895) and *The Old Parson* (1893).[68]

The sheer quantity of sketches about medical charlatans suggests strong public concern about the quality of medical care, though, like many other kinds of popular comedy, any financially successful routine was bound to be copied. Doctors, pharmacists, scientists, salesmen, and any others who hoped to profit by invention of new machines or collusion in common frauds were satirized in blackface sketches, some of which focused on the promoters of particular products or new scientific discoveries, while others ridiculed the products themselves. In White's *Laughing Gas* (1858), for example, a quack professor tries to convince a group of stock characters (a singer, tragedian, etc.) that inhaling his invention would enhance their natural gifts:

> Ladies and gentlemen . . . doubtless you have seen the flaming posters on the walls announcing the exhibition of laughing gas. Perhaps a few of my auditors are aware of the component parts of laughing gas. No doubt you have observed the gas burning in the street lamps as well as in your houses. That's not the gas I purpose giving you tonight. Observe, I hold in my hand a silken bag. The gas contained in this bag is composed of four different ingredients, viz., hydrogen, oxygen, Holland gin and other gin—more of the latter than the other.[69]

Laughing Gas dealt with the delicate balance between the desire of talented or skilled people to achieve public acclaim and the equally dubious means of taking whatever shortcuts were needed to attain that end. Those behaviors were not depicted as bound to racial or ethnic backgrounds. Indeed, fancy-talking representatives for products or services of questionable value were admired for their verbal agility as well as their clever promotional schemes. At the same time, those very traits were considered extravagant and when suitably enhanced with appropriate comic hyperboles were quite successful as comic subjects.

The second largest collection of sketches (ranking just behind Shakespearean burlesques and well ahead of the topical plays just discussed) focused on courtship, marriage, child-rearing, and other domestic issues. The number of plots was limited to the same ones audiences might expect in nonblackface comedies or comic operas of the period. For example, mistaken identity was the principal device in White's *The Black Statue* (ca. 1880), *The Black Chemist* (1862), *The Coopers* (1856), and *The Serenade* (1876) as well as Coes's *Mistaken Identity* (1893) and *Black Blunders* (1893). White's *The Siamese Twins* (1875) recounts the difficulties encountered when a blackface Irishman and his burnt-cork twin court the same woman, thereby linking the plight of two special indolent outcasts whose unproductive lives ran counter to prevailing American attitudes toward work.

The courtship ritual itself was a common subject for ridicule, the most prominent plot device being a suitor's deception of a young woman's father, a theme found in scores of European comedies from Plautus to Molière. As David Grote has observed, "there is no doubt that . . .

comedy has used humor as the bludgeon with which to assault the rigid, authoritarian, and hypocritical aspects of public society, as personified in the characters and events that block the lovers from each other."[70] The most familiar *object* of ridicule in this type of comedy was the young woman's father, who always objected to the suitor and was always outwitted by that suitor or his agent. In White's *The Darkey's Stratagem* (1874), the miserable father (Old Cruncher) is outwitted by his clever servant (Cupid), who succeeds in humiliating his boss *and* helping the young couple pursue their romance. Under the guise of telling Cruncher a story about his former employer, Cupid carries out his clever plan to insure that the two young lovers escape the old man's control:

CUPID: Come, sit down, and I'll tell you about it. (*They sit. . . . Every time "snoozer" is said* CRUNCHER *jumps up.*) Well, you see, this old snoozer I used to work for . . . he had a daughter just like you, and there was a young feller used to come to see her, but the old man didn't like him, and wouldn't let him come in the house; so, one day he (this young man) made a bargain with the servant, just like me, to get the girl out of the house. Then the old man locked the girl in her room and put the key in his pocket. Well, this servant . . . got the old snoozer to sit down to tell him a story. Then the servant went down in the old man's pocket and took out the key of the door. (*He does so.*) Well, the signal agreed upon by the young man and the servant was a whistle, just like this. The young feller came in. The servant put the key over his right shoulder. The lover came and took the key. [More dialogue follows and the young people leave.]
CRUNCHER: What a *d——d* old fool he must have been!
CUPID:: Wasn't he!
CRUNCHER: They couldn't fool *me* that way.[71]

The courtship farces often combined the verbal trickster's techniques shown in the previous examples with the mistaken identity and physical comedy features found in *Sam's Courtship* (1852). Cesar, Sarah's faithful servant, after reconciling himself with Sarah's suitor, turns the tables on Sam Simple by devising a clothes-switch ruse to make sure that Sarah is not deceived by an unworthy suitor.

SARAH: Now, Mr. Simple, if you will wait for a few minutes, I will return with my hat and shawl and fly with the man I adore.
SAM: Durn that nigger, I say. If that physic killed the old mare how on earth did he expect I was going to stand it? [Cesar tried earlier to poison Sam.] What will Eph say when I bring the gal home? What will Lize Britton say? Here she comes.

Enter CESAR, *dressed in female attire, supposed to be* SARAH.

SARAH: Come, come Mr. Simple, take me to your arms, and, ere I leave the roof of my happy home, let this empty room hear the echo of my future husband's kiss, and then farewell.[72]

Minstrel comedy typically chose marital conflict as a subject, but problems with children's behavior and education were also popular topics. White's *Wake-Up William Henry* (1862) links a parent's inability to discipline a child with a satirical attack on Orson Fowler's "science" of phrenology. Young William Henry cannot be motivated to perform better in school or show respect for his parents. The boy's father (Mr. Hemmingway) contracts with a "professor" (Prof. Fowler), who guarantees that phrenological analysis and hypnosis are the most effective remedies for the son's aberrant behavior:

HEMMINGWAY: Professor, what is de reason dat his head am so much harder dan any other head in de family?
PROFESSOR FOWLER: Simply because the valetudinary hypothesis of the cram disorganizes the currency functions of the digestion pad, which causes great moisture and elasticity in the external velocipede, and fills up the rotary antelope with a dusenberry compound of culinary impediments.
HEMMINGWAY: (Astonished.) My gracious! I neber know'd day he had that. What do dey call it?
PROFESSOR FOWLER: Chop-valve-us Bass beer-us—that is the European term. It is an epidemic very prevalent among the higher class of business men.
HEMMINGWAY: Well, I'm glad dat I found out. What would you advise me to do wid him?
PROFESSOR FOWLER: I'll tell you; and if you follow my directions, I think he will get over it in a short time. Now, you take the boy home, send him to school, and see that he goes to bed every night at nine o'clock, and don't feed him on roast turkey, quail, broiled oysters or fancy pastry, and, take my word for it, he will be well in less than thirty days.[73]

Like the other cure-alls and pseudoscientific theories that caught public attention during the nineteenth century, phrenology and hypnotism were popular subjects for satire. Apart from a reference to the possible relationship between the skulls of blacks and those of apes—one of the many references to the now discredited "science" of cranial measurement as an indicator of intelligence, *Wake Up William Henry* does not deal with black families or with child-rearing in black homes. It focuses instead on the gullibility of a parent who out of desperation accepts an irresponsible external agent or miraculous remedy as a treatment for his stereotypical teenager's behavior problems.

The sketches discussed in this study comprise a small sample (10 to 20 percent) of the core repertory of blackface skits, but they are representative of nearly 125 (about 60 percent of the total existing sketches) that I have examined. Looking back at the issues raised at the beginning of the essay, it should be clear that few of the sketches dealt with racial issues, with Southern plantation life, or with the behaviors of African-Americans. Negative references to blacks and racist or ethnic code words—not all of them specific to blacks—are present in some examples to be sure, but they do not seem as prominent as might be expected given the literature on minstrelsy. Those references are neither as strong as the ones

Dennison discovered in his survey of blackface songs and songsters nor as racist as Ellison's analysis led us to believe.

The argument that blackface was directed at or provided "portraits" of African-Americans cannot be accepted at face value (it is certainly not true of the Ethiopian sketches), nor can the centrality of race be considered the primary *subject matter* of all forms of blackface minstrelsy even though it is obvious racism is certainly apparent in the exploitation of the low status of African-Americans as a comic device. Blackface stressed the use of caricatures and stereotypes because they provided the best vehicles for criticizing the differences between what society promised and what it actually delivered. The sketches overemphasized the importance of perceived and real racial differences in order to ridicule the contradictions lower- or middle-class Americans found in their daily lives. At the same time, the minstrel comedians strongly supported the status quo, often rejecting out of hand any innovations, ideas, or theories that threatened conventional American wisdom.

Most of the references to African-Americans in the examples are brief or often incidental, especially when the plays focused on political satire; explorations of cultural differences, that is, demonstrations of what "other" people were like; satirical or irreverent treatments of the public's enthusiasm for fads, cures, and "scientific" theories; and parodies of other theatrical genres, such as Shakespeare or the contemporary comedies of manners. The sketches illustrate how closely minstrelsy was linked to other forms of popular theater and how loose any of its earlier connections with African-American culture had become. Those connections seem to have fluctuated throughout the history of minstrelsy, often depending more on political and economic fears of the moment rather than on longstanding racial antipathies. The interbreeding among theatrical forms also broke down the artificial distinctions between "highbrow" and "lowbrow" made by early twentieth-century critics.

Regardless of whether the sketches appeared before or after the Emancipation Proclamation, they did not deal with slavery. This should not be surprising for, as Kenneth Lynn observed, "the overwhelming majority of the poets and essayists of the day did not even acknowledge the existence of the gravest moral question in the nation's history."[74] Most of the *published* sketches were printed after the Civil War, but there is no reason to believe that any of the sketches performed before 1861 were significantly revised prior to their publication.

The avoidance of slavery as a subject suggests that minstrelsy's various genres must have served more complex social and cultural purposes even during the antebellum period when the slavery debate was a more prominent political and moral issue. The sketchwriters never saw the humorous potential of the slave type created by Plautus as a vehicle for ridiculing Roman society. It is certainly significant that the blackface comedians seldom implied that their audiences lived "like" slaves and that the many role-reversal sketches dealt more with class differences than with ethnic or racial distinctions. Finally, recognizing that popular entertainment was driven more by practical economic considerations, theater managers certainly knew that slavery was much too complex a question to explore with any success in a comic environment and far too explosive for audiences who viewed the abolition of slavery as a threat to their own right to earn a livelihood.

The fact that the sketches avoided the slavery issue also suggests that a more extensive investigation of the contents of blackface comedy might explain why one of the principal examples of American racism, human bondage, was not a more prominent feature in a form of comedy built on widely shared ideas about race. There is no doubt that there were varying degrees of racism in minstrelsy's many repertories. The blackface convention depended in part on the general conviction that African-Americans were considered low-status individuals especially "by lower-class whites who longed for some assurance of their own status, a sense that they were superior to someone, if only by virtue of the color of their skin."[75] The Ethiopian sketches in particular used the blackface convention for purposes other than merely perpetuating the stereotypes typical of the first two phases of minstrelsy's history, namely, the pre-1843 developmental stage and first great era (1843–60) of its popularity.

As far as the treatment of other ethnic groups is concerned, it appears that much blackface material was audience specific and utilized stereotyping as a convention regardless of which group was depicted. This type of comedy was popular because its formulae were transparent and its situations predictable. Repetition was essential to the sketches because it guaranteed that the comic situations would seldom be interpreted as threatening the status quo and that the conventional stage business—the anarchy of physical comedy, the cross-dressed "wench" as lover or wife, and strong emphasis on character types—remained well within the limits of the audience's expectations.

The contents and character treatments of the sketches suggest that behind the masks and the stereotypes lay serious concerns about social, cultural, and economic issues. The Ethiopian sketches certainly show that class rather than race, individual self-worth rather than conformity to a code or system, and an insatiable curiosity about physical or ethnic differences provided a rich selection of subjects for the sketchwriters. What is often surprising (because revisionist studies would not lead readers to expect it) is how often the blackface servant, employee, or dandy outwits his antagonist. The humorous effect of that comic reversal was apparently one of the major reasons for blackface comedy's success. Those characters were successful, however, not because they were seen as African-Americans, but because they were the clever instruments of an egalitarian audience's need to feel some form of superiority with respect to other classes or races.

The core repertory shows that there are differences in the degree to which racist attitudes pervaded blackface entertainment, differences confirming the need for further study of the various genres. Blackface sketches usually avoided the slavery issue because of its controversial nature and because commercially adept managers directed their products toward subjects which, even when they explored important social issues, generally reinforced commonly held and generally popular values.

The sketches also differed greatly from the plantation scenes often associated with minstrel shows. While those scenes may have presented a "happy-go-lucky" and contented view of life because Sambo was "the predominant white southern image of the securely enslaved Negro, at least in the period from 1830 to 1860,"[76] the published sketches dwelt less on race and more on an amalgamation of the other conventions of American entertainment and the blackface genre. That is why a single topical reference in a given sketch was capable of evoking a whole range of attitudes and feelings among a particular social or economic group.

Based on the relationship of the Ethiopian sketches and their contexts to the other genres of blackface comedy, it would appear that minstrelsy's popularity can only be understood if the assumptions underlying investigations of the subject are based on some broader theories of comedy and American cultural development. Such investigations are now possible and promising; possible, because some of the cultural historians cited at the beginning of this essay have given up the idea that just because "racist phenomena are distasteful they are no longer important," and promising, because even "despised texts . . . [can] illuminate the culture that produced and consumed them."[77]

Notes

The author gratefully acknowledges the financial support of the Penn State Harrisburg Research Council; the assistance of the University's Rare Book Curator, Charles Mann, for providing access to and advice about the primary source materials used for this study; and the editorial/research assistance of Sunshine L. Brown.

1. There are no catalogs of primary sources, no annotated guides for early printed sketches, and, consequently, no bibliographical control of the evidence

required for a thorough study of minstrelsy. The following secondary sources are indispensable: Constance Rourke, *American Humor: A Study of the National Character* (1931; rept. New York: Doubleday, 1953); Hans Nathan, *Dan Emmett and the Rise of Early Negro Minstrelsy* (Norman: University of Oklahoma Press, 1961); Robert C. Toll, *Blacking Up: The Minstrel Show in Nineteenth-Century America* (New York: Oxford University Press, 1974); and Robert Winans, "Early Minstrel Music," in *Musical Theatre in America: Papers and Proceedings of the Conference on the Musical Theatre in America*, ed. Glen B. Loney (Westport, Conn.: Greenwood Press, 1984), pp. 71–98. Background studies on the treatment of blacks in theatrical works include Joseph Boskin, *Sambo: The Rise and Demise of an American Jester* (New York: Oxford University Press, 1986); Langston Hughes, "The Negro and American Entertainment," in *The American Negro Reference Book*, ed. John P. Davis (Englewood Cliffs, N.J.: Prentice-Hall, 1966); and Donald Bogle, *Toms, Coons, Mulattoes, Mammies and Bucks* (New York: Viking, 1973).

2. The first quotation is from George F. Rehin, "Review Article: The Darker Image—American Negro Minstrelsy through the Historian's Lens," *Journal of American Studies* 9 (1975): 365–73, 369; and the second is from James H. Dormon, "The Strange Career of Jim Crow Rice," *Journal of Social History* 3 (1969): 108–22, 122.

3. Ralph Ellison, *Shadow and Act* (New York: Random House, 1964), p. 48.

4. Jacob Levine, "Approaches to Humor Appreciation," in *Motivation in Humor*, ed. Jacob Levine (New York: Atherton Press, 1969), p. 13. See also Patricia Keith-Spiegel, "Early Conceptions of Humor: Varieties and Issues," in *The Psychology of Humor: Theoretical Perspectives and Empirical Issues*, ed. Jeffrey H. Goldstein and Paul E. McGhee (New York: Academic Press, 1972), pp. 4–34; and Robert W. Corrigan, "The Psychology of Comedy," *Comedy: Meaning and Form*, 2nd ed. (New York: Harper and Row, 1981), pp. 165–90, for key essays by Freud, Jekels, Grotjahn, and Sartre.

5. David L. Singer, "Aggression Arousal, Hostile Humor, Catharsis," in Levine, *Motivation*, pp. 103–127, 125.

6. Huggins argued further that "the white man who put on the black mask modeled himself after a subjective black man—a black man of lust and passion and natural freedom (license) which white men carried within themselves and harbored with both fascination and dread" (*Harlem Renaissance* [New York: Oxford University Press, 1971], pp. 253–54). Huggins denies that whites could portray real blacks "objectively" because whites simply could not know the subjects of their portraits. If whites portrayed the "subjective" black man who lived only in the white mind, that portrait was not of the "black" man; it was only a reverse image of the white and another example of the masking function of blackface entertainment.

7. Ellison, *Shadow and Act*, p. 49.

8. See Stanley Elkins, *Slavery: A Problem in American Institutional and Intellectual Life* (Chicago: University of Chicago Press, 1959); and Carl Wittke, *Tambo and Bones: A History of the American Minstrel Stage* (Durham, N.C.: Duke University Press, 1940), p. 3. For an appraisal of the controversy Elkins raised, see Ann J. Lane, ed., *The Debate over Slavery: Stanley Elkins and His Critics* (Urbana: University of Illinois Press, 1971). For a more recent summary of the same issues, see George M. Frederickson, "White Images of Black Slaves in the Old South," in *The Arrogance of Race: Historical Perspectives on Slavery, Racism, and Social Inequality* (Middletown, Conn.: Wesleyan University Press,

1988), pp. 207–15. My conclusions about stereotypes are based on John C. Brigham, "Ethnic Stereotypes," *Psychological Bulletin* 76, no. 1 (1971): 15–38; W. Edgar Vinacke, "Stereotypes as Social Concepts," *Journal of Social Psychology* 46 (1957): 229–43; and those cited in note 22 below.

9. The first quote is from Carl Wittke, *Tambo and Bones*, p. 3; and the second is from Dailey Paskman and Sigmund Spaeth, *"Gentlemen: Be Seated!": A Parade of the Old Time Minstrels* (New York: Doubleday, 1928), p. 1.

10. Alan W. C. Green, "'Jim Crow,' 'Zip Coon': The Northern Origins of Negro Minstrelsy," *Massachusetts Review* 11, no. 2 (1970): 385–97, 397.

11. Alexander Saxton, "Blackface Minstrelsy and Jacksonian Ideology," *American Quarterly* 27 (1975): 3–28, 8.

12. Berndt Ostendorf, "Minstrelsy and Early Jazz," *Massachusetts Review* 20 (1979): 574–602, 575.

13. Sam Dennison, *Scandalize My Name: Black Imagery in American Popular Music* (New York: Garland, 1982), p. 154.

14. Toll, *Blacking Up*, p. 272.

15. My choice of authors is based on the number of known works written by or attributed to a particular individual. The principal authors were Charles White (75 as author, 14 as co-author with Leavitt), Frank Dumont (38), George Griffin (26), Andrew Leavitt (28 as co-author with Hubert Egan, 14 co-authored with White), George Coes (21), and Henry Llewellyn Williams, Jr. (16).

16. Toll, *Blacking Up*, pp. 56–57.

17. Werner Sollors, *Beyond Ethnicity: Consent and Descent in American Culture* (New York: Oxford University Press, 1986), p. 131.

18. Joyce Flynn, "Melting Plots: Patterns of Racial and Ethnic Amalgamation in American Drama Before Eugene O'Neill," *American Quarterly* 38, no. 3 (1986): 417–18, 426. A most helpful study of blackface clowning *outside* the theater is Susan G. Davis, "'Making Night Hideous': Christmas Revelry and Public Order in Nineteenth-Century Philadelphia," *American Quarterly* 34 (1982): 185–99. For essays dealing with the varieties of American ethnic theater, see Maxine Schwartz Seller, ed., *Ethnic Theater in the United States* (Westport, Conn.: Greenwood Press, 1983).

19. Charles White, arr., *The Live Injun; or, Jim Crow* (Chicago: Dramatic Publishing Co., ca. 1874), p. 2. The title page indicates that the play was first performed in 1865. Throughout this study, the date given in parentheses after a title will be the date of the first performance if known or the date of the copyright, whichever comes first. The performance date is taken from the title page of the edition, the copyright date from the *National Union Catalog* [NUC] *Pre-1956 Imprints* (London: Mansell, 1971). If neither date can be established, the date given is an estimate based on information found in NUC, publishers trade catalogs, or, whenever possible, from the contemporary sources and performance data cited by George C. D. Odell, *Annals of the New York Stage*, 15 vols. (New York: Columbia University Press, 1927–49).

20. William F. Stowe and David Grimsted, "Review Essay: White-Black Humor," *Journal of Ethnic Studies* 3 (1976): 78–96.

21. George F. Rehin, "Harlequin Jim Crow: Continuity and Convergence in Blackface Clowning," *Journal of Popular Culture* 9, no. 3 (1975): 682–701, 690.

22. Roger D. Abrahams, "The Negro Stereotype: Negro Folklore and the Riots," in *The Urban Experience and Folk Tradition*, ed. Americo Paredes and Ellen J. Steckert (Austin: University of Texas Press, 1971), p. 69. See also John F.

Szwed, "Race and the Embodiment of Culture," *Ethnicity* 2 (1975): 19–33. Some of these ideas were first presented in my "'Backside Albany' and Early Blackface Minstrelsy: A Contextual Study of America's First Blackface Song," *American Music* 6, no. 1 (1988): 1–27.

23. Charles Hamm, *Yesterdays: Popular Song in America* (New York: Norton, 1979), p. 137.

24. Robert Cantwell, *Bluegrass Breakdown: The Making of the Old Southern Sound* (Urbana: University of Illinois Press, 1984), p. 262.

25. See Carl Bryan Holmberg and Gilbert D. Schneider, "Daniel Decatur Emmett's Stump Sermons: Genuine Afro-American Culture, Language, and Rhetoric in the Negro Minstrel Show," *Journal of Popular Culture* 19, no. 4 (Spring 1986): 27–38; and William J. Mahar, "Black English in Early Blackface Minstrelsy: A New Interpretation of the Sources of Minstrel Show Dialect," *American Quarterly* 37, no. 2 (Summer 1985): 260–85, and "'Backside Albany' and Early Blackface Minstrelsy: A Contextual Study of America's First Blackface Song," *American Music* 6, no. 1 (Spring 1988): 1–27.

26. The sample of works was taken from the lists of plays given in the *Publishers Trade List Annual* (PTLA), 1872–88. The series begins with the *Annual American Catalog*, which covers 1869–72, followed by the PTLA from 1873–88 and *The American Catalog* (New York: Peter Smith, 1941) covering the 1876–1920 period. Other useful sources include *Dramatic Compositions 1870–1916* (Washington, DC: Government Printing Office, 1918), *National Union Catalog Pre-1956 Imprints*, and Gary Engle, "The Atkinson Collection of Ethiopian Drama at the University of Chicago," *Resources for American Literary Study* 1, no. 2 (Autumn 1971): 181–99. At least five hundred titles were published between 1855 and 1900 by the following firms: T. S. Denison (Chicago), Dick and Fitzgerald (New York), Samuel T. French (New York), Lee and Walter (New York and Philadelphia), Robert T. De Witt (New York), The Dramatic Publishing Company (New York and Chicago), The Happy Hours Company (New York and Chicago), and the Ames Publishing Company (Clyde, Ohio). For information on Albert D. Ames (1849–87) and his *Series of Standard and Minor Drama*, see Roger E. Stoddard and Hope P. Litchfield, "A. D. Ames, First Dramatic Publisher in the West," *Books at Brown* 21 (1967): 95–141.

27. The collection contains at least four different types of sketches: (1) burlesques of popular scenes from plays by Shakespeare, English comedy, and French or American melodrama; (2) processional or "parade" pieces, which provided opportunities to exhibit Yankee, Dutch, Irish or other "eccentric" or "exotic" characters; (3) topical skits or short plays satirizing contemporary political or social issues; and (4) domestic or courtship sketches usually dealing with a domineering wife or with a young couple's plots to outwit a cantankerous and overprotective father.

28. Lawrence W. Levine, *Highbrow/Lowbrow: The Emergence of Cultural Hierarchy in America* (Cambridge: Harvard University Press, 1988), p. 40.

29. The best studies of Shakespearean burlesques are Ray B. Browne, "Shakespeare in 19th Century Songsters," *Shakespeare Quarterly* 8 (1957): 207–18, and "Shakespeare in American Vaudeville and Negro Minstrelsy," *American Quarterly* 12 (1960): 374–91; Charles Haywood, "Negro Minstrelsy and Shakespearean Burlesque," in *Folklore and Society: Essays in Honor of Benjamin A. Botkin*, ed. Bruce Jackson (Hatboro, Pa.: American Folklore Society, 1966), pp. 77–92; and Charles H. Shattuck, *Shakespeare on the American Stage: From*

the Hallams to Edwin Booth (Washington, D.C.: Folger Shakespeare Library, 1976).

30. In Charleston, South Carolina, for example, the five most popular antebellum plays (by number of performances) were *Richard III* (90), *Hamlet* (82), *Macbeth* (75), *Othello* (63), and *Romeo and Juliet* (63) (see W. Stanley Hoole, "Shakespeare on the Ante-bellum Charleston Stage," *Shakespeare Association Bulletin* 21 [1946]: 37–45). Other useful bibliographical information can be found in Henry E. Jacobs and Claudia Johnson, *An Annotated Bibliography of Shakespearean Burlesques, Parodies, and Travesties* (New York: Garland, 1976).

31. Rice's *Otello: A Burlesque Opera* is virtually identical to Maurice Dowling's *Othello Travestie* (1834), except for the New York references and the American songs. Rice purchased his copy of the burlesque during his trip to England (1836–1837) and played his adaptation throughout the late 1840s. An 1853 manuscript copy by John Bernard Knight is now in the New York Public Library. For Rice's early career, see Odell, *Annals*, vols. 3, 4, and 5, passim; Sol Smith, *Theatrical Management in the West and South for Thirty Years* (1868; rept. New York: Benjamin Blom, 1968); Lawrence Hutton, *Curiosities of the American Stage* (New York: Harper and Row, 1891), pp. 115–19; and Dormon, "The Strange Career," Nathan, *Dan Emmett*, and Molly N. Ramshaw, "'Jump Jim Crow': A Biographical Sketch of Thomas D. Rice," *Theatre Annual* 17 (1960): 36–47.

32. The acting styles of great American and English actors were frequently parodied because of the many excesses and idiosyncracies associated with their conceptions of Shakespeare's characters. For information on actors and acting styles, see Alan S. Downer, "Players and the Painted Stage: Nineteenth-Century Acting," *Publications of the Modern Language Association* 61 (June 1946): 522–76; the "Acting and Actors" section of "A Bibliography on Theatre and Drama," *Speech Monographs* 16, no. 3 (November 1949): 1–112; and Garff B. Wilson, *A History of American Acting* (Bloomington: Indiana University Press, 1966).

33. George W. Griffin, *Hamlet the Dainty, an Ethiopian Burlesque on Shakespeare's Hamlet* (New York: Samuel French, ca. 1875), reprinted in *This Grotesque Essence*, ed. Gary D. Engle (Baton Rouge: Louisiana State University Press, 1978), pp. 85–90, 88. My Shakespeare quotation is taken from the Norton Critical Edition of *Hamlet: An Authoritative Text*, ed. Cyrus Hoy (New York: Norton, 1963), pp. 18–19. After reviewing *Hamlet the Dainty* and John Poole's *Hamlet Travestie* (1810), I have found that Griffin's text is virtually identical with the edition of Poole's play reprinted in Jacob B. Salomon, *Nineteenth-Century Dramatic Burlesques of Shakespeare: A Selection of British Parodies* (Norwood, Pa.: Norwood Editions, 1979), pp. 8–35. See Engle for reprints of Ryman and White's *Julius the Snoozer* (1875), *Uncle Eph's Dream* (1871), and other blackface plays.

34. Charles T. White, *100th Night of Hamlet, a Negro Sketch* (New York: Robert M. De Witt, 1874 [performed at the American Theatre, April 3, 1865]), p. 2. Charles White is known today only as the composer of "De Floating Scow of Ole Virginia," with its famous refrain "Oh! Carry me back to ole Virginia shore" (1847). A brief summary of his life will be found in Edward LeRoy Rice, *Monarchs of Minstrelsy, from Daddy Rice to Date* (New York: Kenny, 1911). White was often billed as the "celebrated black Apollo" because of his appearance in "reproductions of ancient sculpture and paintings, usually by men of athletic mold, who figured in the circus or between play and farce at the minor

theatres" (Odell, *Annals*, vol. 5, pp. 378, 491). White ended his career playing the blackface "wench" part of Mrs. Jackson in Harrigan and Hart's *Reilly and the 400*. See Alvin F. Harlow, *Old Bowery Days: The Chronicles of a Famous Street* (New York: Appleton, 1931), p. 442.

35. Engle, *Grotesque Essence*, p. xxiii. Dormon's excellent discussion of audiences in *Theatre in the Antebellum South* complements Engle's observation (p. 241) that "there is considerable evidence that some incidents involving audience participation resulted from the curious phenomenon of an auditor's becoming so involved in the plot . . . that make believe became reality" (pp. 235–36). Dormon also discussed seating arrangements for audiences, observing that "insofar as they were able, period managers segregated their lower-class patrons from the upper classes, and the Negroes from the whites." Audience studies are fairly rare, but good overviews of the New York scene will be found in Vera Brodsky Lawrence, *Strong on Music: The New York Scene in the Days of George Templeton Strong, 1836–1875* (New York: Oxford University Press, 1988), vol. 1; for New Orleans, see Joseph P. Roppollo, "Local and Topical Plays in New Orleans, 1806–1865," *Tulane Studies in English* 4 (1954): 91–124, and "Audiences in New Orleans Theatres, 1845–1861," *Tulane Studies in English* 2 (1950): 121–35.

36. White, *100th Night*, p. 4. Sam's lines are "To be or not to be? That is the question [*Hamlet*, 3.1.56]. List 'tis now the witching time of night and crows have gone to roost. Now o'er one half the world nature seems dead and wicked dreams dome in your head. . . . I go; the bell invites me; hear it not Smithers; 'tis a knell that summons them to heaven or–[sic]" (*Macbeth*, 2.1.49–64).

37. Dormon notes that *Othello* was "among the most popular of the Shakespearean tragedies in the South as in the North, despite its celebrated inter-racial match" and that the "anomaly" was because "*Othello* was commonly viewed as an anti-miscegenation play" (Dormon, *Theatre*, p. 276). The strongest evidence comes from James Hackett's statement that "the great moral lesson of the tragedy of *Othello* is, that black and white blood cannot be intermingled in marriage without a gross outrage upon the law of Nature" (James Hackett, *Notes, Criticisms and Correspondence on Shakespeare's Plays and Actors* [1863; rept. New York: Benjamin Blom, 1968], p. 224). For a study of Edwin Forrest's conception of the role as revealed in his own promptbooks, see Barbara Allen, "Edwin Forrest's Othello," *Theatre Annual* 14 (1956): 7–18. A few playrights, such as Eugene Raux in *The Road to Fortune* (Philadelphia: G. B. Ziegler, 1846), did not treat racial intermarriage as a serious social problem.

38. Bruce A. McConachie, "'The Theatre of the Mob': Apocalyptic Melodrama and Preindustrial Riots in Antebellum New York," in *Theatre for Working-Class Audiences in the United States, 1830–1890*, ed. Bruce A. McConachie and Daniel Friedman (Westport, Conn.: Greenwood Press, 1985), pp. 17–46, 35.

39. George W. Griffin, *Othello, a Burlesque* (New York: Happy Hours Company, ca. 1880). Quoted from Engle, *Grotesque Essence*, p. 70.

40. Engle, *Grotesque Essence*, pp. 70–71.

41. The most popular version of the comic courtship song known as "The Low-Back'd Car" was Samuel Lover's (1797–1868) setting of a traditional Irish air known in England as "The Jolly Ploughboy." For an arrangement with all the verses, see Burl Ives, *Irish Songs* (New York: Duell, Sloan and Pearce, 1955), pp. 37–39. Lover's "Irish evenings" were very popular in the United States, where he appeared between 1846 and 1848. "Blighted Flowers" was probably written

by Michael Balfe (1808–70), the composer of *The Bohemian Girl* (1843). The song was available in the United States as late as the 1880s because it was listed in Dena Epstein, ed., *Complete Catalogue of Sheet Music and Musical Works, 1870* (New York: De Capo Press, 1973), a reprint of the 1871 catalog published by the Board of Music Trade of the United States of America. The song does not seem to have been as popular as other Balfe favorites. I was unable to locate a copy of the song to compare with the parody used in this sketch.

42. Engle, *Grotesque Essences*, p. 71.

43. Sollors, *Beyond Ethnicity*, p. 226. Language differences played an important role in many American comedies because they were the primary indicators of differences for every ethnic type. According to Irving Allen, "Ethnicity, in fact, may be the largest single social theme in North American slang and popular speech" (Irving Lewis Allen, *The Language of Ethnic Conflict: Social Organization and Lexical Culture* [New York: Columbia University Press, 1983], p. 9).

44. The statistical evidence will be found in James D. Bruce and Hyman Rodman, "Black–White Marriages in the United States: A Review of the Empirical Evidence," in *Interracial Marriages: Expectations and Realities*, ed. Irving R. Stuart and Lawrence E. Abt (New York: Grossman, 1973), pp. 147–60. See also Beth Day Romulo, *Sexual Life between Blacks and Whites* (New York: World, 1977).

45. George N. Christy (1827–68; *recte* Harrington) was in Edward Rice's words "one of the greatest performers that ever graced the minstrel stage." His work can be dated fairly well because his associations with various companies were documented in his autobiography (see Rice, *Monarchs of Minstrelsy*, p. 20). Christy appeared with Griffin between January and September 1867. It would appear likely that the series of plays mentioned here was produced during that association.

46. For the principal stage Yankees, see Francis Hodge, *Yankee Theatre: The Image of America on the Stage, 1825–1850* (Austin: University of Texas Press, 1964); and Richard M. Dorson, *Jonathan Draws the Long Bow* (New York: Rockland Editions, 1939).

47. White's parade play may have been taken from Griffin's *The Ticket Taker; or, The Masquerade Ball*, which is reprinted in Engle, *Grotesque Essence*, pp. 78–84. The only difference between the two is that Macbeth's witches (played by beard-costumed males) and Hamlet suffer from an all-consuming passion for alcohol:

HAMLET: To be or not to be—that's the question. Whether it were better to suffer the slings and juleps to go by discarded, or to take up arms against the outrageous Excise Law [an 1866 New York law regulating liquor distribution], and find myself ten dollars out in the jail; to drink—[sic]

The importance of lotteries and other games of chance for nineteenth-century audiences cannot be underestimated. White's Captain Slim is a stereotype based on popular characters who "struck it rich," but Slim's sudden wealth also illustrates a widely held belief that economic success is merely a matter of chance. For information about lotteries and other confidence games, see Francis Emmitt Williams, *Lotteries, Laws, and Morals* (New York: Vantage, 1958); and John Samuel Ezell, *Fortune's Merry Wheel: The Lottery in America* (Cambridge: Harvard University Press, 1960). How Claude and Pauline got into minstrel shows is somewhat complex because both were originally characters in Edward Bulwer-Lytton's *The Lady of Lyons; or, Love and Pride.* For the play, see Calvin Smith Brown, ed., *The Later English Drama* (New York: A. S. Barnes, 1898), pp. 293–371; for a summary of the *Lady of Lyons* and its sequels, see Dormon, *Theatre*, pp. 266–68. Dormon also notes an 1846 St. Louis burlesque entitled *The Lady of Lions*, which featured Clod Meddlenot, a "Boston gardener" (Dormon, *Theatre*, p. 267). For information about the play's popularity in New York, see Joseph N. Ireland, *Records of the New York Stage from 1750 to 1860*, 2 vols. (1866; rept. New York: Benjamin Blom, 1966), vol. 2, pp. 436–40. For more on Mose, who was introduced to New York audiences in *A Glance at New York* (1848), see Richard M. Dorson, "Mose the Far-Famed and World-Renowned," *American Literature* 15 (1943): 287–300. The Mose plays were also "parade" shows featuring characters "typical" of specific local scenes.

48. Charles T. White, *The Hop of Fashion; or, The Bon Ton Soiree* (New York: F. A. Brady, ca. 1856), pp. 11, 12. White's quotations from *Macbeth* differ in several minor respects from the modern editions of the play. My comparison was based on *The Tragedy of Macbeth* ed. Eugene M. Waith, rev. ed. (New Haven, Conn.: Yale University Press, 1954), p. 56.

49. Glenn Blayney, "City Life in American Drama, 1825–1860," in *Studies in Honor of John Wilcox*, ed. A. Doyle Wallace and Woodburn Ross (1958; rept. Freeport, N.Y.: Books for Libraries, 1972), pp. 99–128, cites a number of such works, the best known of which may be Royall Tyler, *The Contrast* (1787), J. N. Barker, *Tears and Smiles* (1807), A. B. Linsley, *Love and Friendship; or, Yankee Notions* (1807–8), Robert Montgomery Bird, *The City Looking Glass* (1828), and John Brougham, *Life in New York; or, Tom and Jerry on a Visit* (1856).

50. Blayney, "City Life," p. 117. For the plays mentioned in the text, see Anne Cora Mowatt, *Fashion* (1845), in *Best Plays of the American Theatre: From the Beginning to 1916*, ed. John Gassner (New York: Crown, 1967), pp. 97–135; Henry Preuss, *Fashions and Follies of Washington Life* (Washington, D.C.: published by the author, 1857); Cornelius Matthews, *False Pretenses; or, Both Sides of Good Society* (New York: n.p.); and Eugene Raux, *The Road to Fortune* (1846).

51. Stephen Steinberg, *The Ethnic Myth: Race, Ethnicity and Class in America* (New York: Atheneum, 1981), pp. 117–18.

52. Bruce McConachie's essay "Using the Concept of Cultural Hegemony to Write Theatre History" in *Interpreting the Theatrical Past: Essays in the Historiography of Performance*, ed. Thomas Postlewait and Bruce McConachie (Iowa City: University of Iowa Press, 1989), pp. 37–58, was helpful in clarifying some of the social and cultural implications of blackface entertainment.

53. The Tom and Jerry show was one of the models for the American "slice of life" plays. William T. Moncrieff's *Tom and Jerry; or, Life in London* (1823) and *Tom and Jerry's Funeral* (1824) were imitated by *Tom, Jerry and Logic's Visit to Philadelphia* (1844). *Tom and Jerry in America* (1845) provided a vehicle for showing the diversity and oddities associated with the United States. See Gerald Boardman, *American Musical Theatre: A Chronicle* (New York: Oxford University Press, 1978), p. 9.

54. The sketches have generally been viewed as emphasizing that African Americans were incapable of holding "power roles" in American life. Even if some members of the audience accepted such an absurd notion, others could

understand the broader application of the lines to all the powerless classes in American society.

55. See William E. Gruber, *Comic Theatres: Studies in Performance and Audience Response* (Athens: University of Georgia Press, 1986), for a discussion of the various concepts of status reversal, inversion ritual, and misrule. For a reprint of Freud's "Jokes and the Comic," see Corrigan, *Comedy: Meaning and Form*, pp. 167–74.

56. Anthony Caputi, *Buffo: The Genius of Vulgar Comedy* (Detroit: Wayne State University Press, 1978), p. 93. Caputi's discussion of *buffo* suggests that there is a much stronger correlation between the American blackface humor and the "vulgar" or popular traditions of European comedy than has been noted in the literature about minstrelsy.

57. Northrop Frye, "The Argument of Comedy," in *English Institute Essays, 1948*, ed. Eugene Robinson (New York: Columbia University Press, 1949), p. 61. My discussion is also indebted to William H. Martineau, "A Model of the Social Functions of Humor," in Goldstein and McGhee, *Psychology of Humor*, pp. 101–24, especially because the theory of in-group and out-group responses to humor stimuli suggests that minstrel show audiences might be viewed as a collection of in-groups, each of which could develop quite different and not necessarily compatible interpretations of the comic actions taking place on the stage.

58. Andrew J. Leavitt, *Squire for a Day* (New York: De Witt, ca. 1875 [performed at the Theatre Comique. . . . , New York, November 24, 1873]), p. 7.

59. Alexander B. Callow, Jr., *The Tweed Ring* (New York: Oxford University Press, 1966), p. vii. The canal and county courthouse scandals, discussed on pp. 182–206, are especially relevant to the dialogue of *Julius the Snoozer.*

60. Addison Ryman and Charles T. White, arr., *Julius the Snoozer; or, The Conspirators of Thompson Street* (New York: Robert M. De Witt, 1876); and Engle, *Grotesque Essence*, pp. 164–172, 170. Blayney ("City Life," pp. 115–16) cites a number of plays satirizing the actions of "sham commissioners and coroners," law enforcement officers, and politicians of New York, Philadelphia, and Boston.

61. For information on the draft riots, see Philip S. Foner, *History of Black Americans: From the Compromise of 1850 to the End of the Civil War* (Westport, Conn.: Greenwood Press, 1983), pp. 398–402; and James McCague, *The Second Rebellion: The Story of the New York City Draft Riots of 1863* (New York: Dial Press, 1968). James M. McPherson, in *Battle Cry of Freedom: The Civil War Era* (New York: Oxford University Press, 1988), pp. 609–11, reviewed all the recent studies of the riots and concluded that the 1,000 "killed" casualty figure still mentioned in many sources is exaggerated and that the actual death toll did not exceed 105.

62. Charles T. White, *The Draft* (New York: De Witt, 1874 [performed at American Theatre, December 7, 1865]), pp. 4–5.

63. Paul H. Grawe, *Comedy in Space, Time and Imagination* (Chicago: Nelson-Hall, 1983), p. 14. For more on why audiences laugh at the classic fool or incompetent clown, see Benjamin H. Lehman, "Comedy and Laughter," *University of California English Studies* 10 (1954): 84–101.

64. Charles T. White, arr., *Hard Times: A Negro Extravaganza in One Scene by Daniel D. Emmett* (New York: De Witt, 1874 [first performed in New York,

October 12, 1855]), p. 3. *Hard Times* is also reprinted in Nathan, *Emmett*, pp. 415–26.

65. Bruce McConachie, "Using the Concept of Cultural Hegemony to Write Theatre History," in Postlewait and McConachie, *Interpreting the Theatrical Past*, pp. 37–58, 62.

66. Frank Dumont, *What Shall I Take?* (New York: R. M. De Witt, ca. 1876 [performed by Dupres' and Benedict's Minstrels, September, 1874]), p. 3.

67. George Griffin, *The Hypochondriac: An Ethiopian Farce* (New York: Happy Hours Company, ca. 1875), p. 7.

68. Plot summaries are taken from "Denison's Descriptive List" of plays "of approved merit suited to the present day," which was bound into the Townsend's *Negro Minstrels*, pp. 17–18.

69. Charles T. White, *Laughing Gas* (New York: De Witt, ca. 1874 [first performed by Wood's Minstrels, 1858]), p. 3.

70. Grote, *The End of Comedy* (Hamden, Conn.: Archon Books, 1983), p. 31.

71. Charles T. White, arr., *The Darkey's Stratagem* (New York: De Witt, 1874), p. 8. The same kind of comic twist occurs in White's *The Black Chemist.* Pete Grabem, a poor, uneducated black character, outwits a pompous doctor/chemist by impersonating the son of Horace Greeley—a "noted bachelor" according to the script—and stealing the Doctor's prize invention, the Secesh [sic] Soother, which is a storage battery capable of killing 25,000 men. See Charles T. White, *The Black Chemist* (New York: De Witt, ca. 1874 [performed at the American Theatre, June 16, 1862]), p. 3.

72. Charles T. White, *Sam's Courtship* (Chicago: Dramatic Publishing Company, ca. 1874 [performed at White's Opera House, New York, 1852]), p. 7.

73. Charles T. White, *Wake Up William Henry* (New York: De Witt, ca. 1874 [performed at the American Theatre, March 24, 1862]), p. 5. Emphasis is added to distinguish between the stage directions and the text. Russel Nye noted that seventy-two books on phrenology were published between 1825 and 1855 and that, however foolish the idea may appear today, "the concept of the individual that it projected reinforced the individualistic, democratic spirit of the age" (Russel Nye, *Society and Culture in America, 1830–1860* [New York: Harper and Row, 1874], p. 335. As shown in the following introduction, minstrel lecturers saw phrenology and mesmerism as related "sciences": "De subject dat I call upon myseff to spoke to you about on dis 'tickler 'caision am de twin sister to Freenology." For that lecture, see William H. Levison, ed., *Black Diamonds; or, Humor, Satire, and Sentiment Treated Scientifically . . . a Series of Burlesque Lectures* (Upper Saddle Brook, N.J.: Gregg Press, 1969), pp. 144–46; for the one on phrenology, pp. 140–43. This publication is virtually identical to an English collection entitled *Irish Diamonds; or, A Theory of Irish Wit and Blunders* (London: Chapman and Hall, 1847). The easy passage of the same jokes and comic sketches across ethnic and racial boundaries supports Rehin's view (see the note above) about the "universality" of some comic material and suggests another significant research topic for investigations of ethnic humor.

74. Kenneth S. Lynn, "Uncle Tom's Cabin," in *Visions of America: Eleven Literary Historical Essays* (Westport, Conn.: Greenwood Press, 1973), pp. 27–48, 27.

75. Frederickson, "Social Origins of American Racism," *Arrogance of Race*, p. 204.

76. Frederickson, "White Images of Black Slaves in the Old South," p. 210.

77. The first quotation is from James H. Dormon, "Shaping the Popular Image of Post-Reconstruction American Blacks: The 'Coon Song' Phenomenon of the Gilded Age," *American Quarterly* 40, no. 4 (1988): 450–71, 480, and the second is from Michael Denning, *Mechanic Accents: Dime Novels and Working-Class Culture in America* (New York: Verso, 1987), p. 207.

DANCE

Juba and American Minstrelsy

Marian Hannah Winter

The history of Negro dance and its music in North America is fundamentally so integrated with our entire music and dance history that it may seem curious here to isolate or limit its boundless divergences. However, no sequential survey has been made in any general history to date, and episodic treatments can give no concept of the Afro-American contribution in continuity or importance. Hazards are always involved when social and economic problems inexorably impinge on any phase of Negro cultural history, and objectivity becomes an elusive lodestar.

This is in part the saga of William Henry Lane, known as Master Juba. This most influential single performer of nineteenth-century American dance was a prodigy of our entire theatre history. Almost legendary among his contemporary colleagues, the Juba epic dwindled into oblivion. Negro historians, intent on apotheosizing Ira Aldridge, the African Roscius, ignored him. Yet this is equivalent to writing a twentieth century theatrical history of the Negro mentioning only Paul Robeson and omitting Bill Robinson, the great Bojangles. It is more outrageous in that Robinson has embellished an already established form, whereas Juba was actually an initiator and determinant of the form itself. The repertoire of any current tap-dancer contains elements which were established theatrically by him. Herein is the cornerstone of his memorial.

Negroes were first brought to America in the sixteenth century. They came principally from the Gold Coast, Ivory Coast, Congo, Angola, Benin, Gambia, Senegal, Nigeria, Dahomey, and Togoland. Conditioned physiologically and psychologically to elaborate, legalistic tribal ritual and the extrovert, centrifugal community ring-shout, then to the restricted disorder of slave-ship holds, plantation huts, and enforced dissolution of their cultural traditions, with only the slightest elements of Western European tradition to draw upon, they evolved art forms which became indigenous manifestations of American culture.

That Negro music-making survived is miraculous when we consider the Slave Laws of 1740, which remained among the basic regulatory laws for Negroes during the subsequent century and a quarter. These were promulgated after the Stono Insurrection of 1739, in South Carolina. A group of slaves attempted an escape to Florida, got hold of some rum en route, stopped to celebrate with a song and dance bout, and were captured in a bloody charge. They had marched "with colors flying and drums beating." The laws of 1740 stringently prohibited any Negro from "beating drums, blowing horns or the like which might on occasion be used to arouse slaves to insurrectionary activity." Since most states patterned their slave laws after those of South Carolina and Virginia, the effect of these prohibitions would have discouraged any people inherently less musical.

Substitutions for the forbidden drum were accomplished with facility—bone clappers in the manner of castanets, jawbones, scrap iron such as blacksmiths' rasps, handclapping and footbeats. Virtuosity of footwork, with heel beats and toe beats, became a simulacrum of the drum. In modern tap-dancing the "conversation" tapped out by two performers is a survival of African telegraphy by drums. Since African dance had already developed rhythms stamped or beat out by dancers as counterpoint to antiphonal musical accompaniment, and solo dances set against the communal ring-shout, the formal source material surmounted any restrictions. The slave created the *bonja* too, made from a hollow gourd without resonance board, slack strung, which developed into the banjo of minstrelsy and jazz.

The Juba dance (simplified from *giouba*) was an African step-dance which somewhat resembled a jig with elaborate variations, and occurs wherever the Negro settled, whether in the West Indies or South Carolina. One variation—crossing and uncrossing the hands against kneecaps which fanned back and forth—was incorporated in the Charleston of the 1920s. Juba and Jube are recurrent slave names with particular association to dancers and musicians. Juba also occurs as the name of a supernatural being in some American Negro folk-lore, and became the popular name for an expansive weed, the *Juba's bush* or *Juba's brush*.

The Negro dancer on the American stage was originally an exotic, much the same as blackamoors in a Rameau ballet-opera. Blackface "Negroes" appeared in eighteenth century Captain Cook pantomimes and Sheridan's *Robinson Crusoe* (New York, 1785). In 1791 a Negro troupe of comedians and entertainers, under the direction of one Louis Tabary, gave performances in New Orleans. A typical playbill announcement offers *Paul and Virginia*, with music by Mazzinghi and Reeve, and accompaniments by James Hewitt, featuring a "NEGRO DANCE by Monsieur Labottiere and Mrs. Darby" (New York, 1805). By 1810 the singing and dancing "Negro Boy" was established with the traditional clown as a dance-hall and circus character. These blackface impersonators simply performed jigs and clogs of Irish or English origin to popular songs with topical allusions to Negroes in the lyrics.

Blackface minstrel songs, to the accompaniment of a genuine Negro instrument, the banjo, abetted by tambourine and bone clappers, were popular by 1820, but genuine Negro performers continue to appear only in sporadic interludes. The African Company gave a New York version of the London burletta *Tom and Jerry* in 1821, but the comic dance by the characters African Sal and Dusty Bob had long been performed in blackface.

"Daddy" Rice, the famous, original "Jim Crow," was a blackface performer who first definitely used a Negro work-song. Picked up from a livery stable porter, this monotonously cheerful refrain—"spin about and turn about and jump Jim Crow"—with accompanying jig and shuffle, focused attention on the Negro as theatrical source material in 1829. Traditional Anglo-American fiddle break-downs, such as *Turkey in the Straw*, and popular ballads as well, were absorbed into the minstrel amalgam. The minstrel show, as a unit of songs, dances and jokes, crystallized in the eighteen-forties. Although the stock "Negro" was already formed, there was some slight effort initially to approximate Negro music.

Composer-performer Dan Emmett, for example, made a particular effort to keep Negro elements in his work, especially in the "walk-around" finales for which he was noted. These were usually in two parts—the first containing melodies embellished with rhythmic phrases, ejaculations and verbal interjections (in the best Negro tradition), followed by a chorus and dance based on an old-fashioned fiddle tune. These early works are in distinctly different vein from Foster and the later sentimental ballad repertoire. An anonymous scribe for the *New York Herald*, writing at the late date of 1895, was exceptional in realizing this difference.

> One great essential to the proper presentation of Negro character, song-and-dance acts was fitting music of a catchy, swinging, Ethiopian nature. While "Dan" Emmett never figured or posed as a dancer, he is responsible for some of the very best "walk-arounds" ever written. Most of these, if not all, were composed for Bryant's Minstrels in the year 1859. Among the most notable and popular ones may be mentioned "I Ain't Got Time to Tarry," "Billy Patterson," "High, Low, Jack," "Chaw Roast Beef," "Turkey in de Straw," "Loozyanna Low Grounds," (not lowlands, as it is generally sung), "K.Y. Ky. or Whose Foot Am Dat Aburnin'?" which was produced in 1860, and "High Daddy" in 1863.

Unquestionably the Negro qualities of minstrel music dwindled, and even the adapted Negro techniques of performance which had been taken over grew vague and sloppy, save in rare instances. Yet because of the vast influence of one Negro performer, the minstrel show dance retained more integrity as a Negro art form than any other theatrical derivative of Negro culture.

Juba, born William Henry Lane, circa 1825 or later, seems to have sprung full-panoplied from the brow of Terpsichore. Probably a free-born Negro, and from the first records of his appearance at about fifteen, unencumbered by family, he was generally adopted by the entire fraternity of white minstrel players, who unreservedly recognized his genius. He had supposedly learned much of his art from "Uncle" Jim Lowe, a Negro jig and reel dancer of exceptional skill, whose performances were confined to saloons, dance halls, and similar locales outside the regular theatres. By 1845 it was flatly stated by members of the profession that Juba was "beyond question the very greatest of all dancers. He was possessed not only of wonderful and unique execution, but also of unsurpassed grace and endurance." A *New York Herald* feature-writer has left us a description of his early extra-theatrical performances.

At the time when he performed at Pete Williams', in Orange Street, New York, those who passed through the long hallway and entered the dance hall, after paying their shilling to the darky doorkeeper, whose "box-office" was a plain soap box, or a wooden one of that description, saw this phenomenon, "Juba," imitate all the dancers of the day and their special steps. Then Bob Ellingham, the interlocutor and master of ceremonies, would say, "Now, Master Juba, show your own jig." Whereupon he would go through all his own steps and specialities, with never a resemblance in any of them to those he had just imitated.

The best in the profession danced there, as well as Juba. A most amusing feature of the entertainment was the comic "walk-around," given in true darky style, with the lean, the fat, the tall, the short, the hunchbacked and the wooden-legged, all mixed in and hard at it. It was from a one-legged performer there, whose second leg was a wooden one, that Dave Reed learned his celebrated "stiff" leg steps.

(This reminds one of Peg-Leg Bates, whose handicap turned him into an amazing virtuoso performer among our current dancers.) Negro art forms always reached the public, in the popular dance halls, even when the legitimate theatres were closed to them.

Juba's fame was already so legendary that by 1845 he achieved the unprecedented distinction of touring with four white minstrels and received *top billing!* I am quoting their 1845 handbill, from the Harvard Theatre Collection, in full, since it gives an idea of the musical mainstays. Juba, incidentally, was a first-rate singer and tambourine virtuoso.

Great Attraction! Master Juba! The Greatest Dancer in the World! and the Ethiopian Minstrels! Respectfully announce to the Citizens of this place that they will have the pleasure of appearing before them During the Day Under a Pavilion. The Company is composed of Four Skilful Members, and from the immense success which has attended them wherever they have appeared, they are confident in promising their auditors the most irresistible, ludicrous, as well as scientific Entertainment that they have ever listened to.

Master Juba — Mr. J. T. Brown, *The Champion Tamburineur*

Mr. T. Fluter, *The Unrivalled Banjo Player* — Mr. A. L. Thayer

Program—Part I

Song Life by de Galley Fire	Brown and chorus
" Town of Tuscalore	Fluter
" Who dat knocking at de door	Thayer

Part II

Statue Dance	by Juba

Part III

Song I must go to Richmond	Thayer and chorus
" Old Gal come to de garden gate	Brown and chorus
" Juliana Johnson	Juba and chorus
" Forty five miles	Thayer and chorus

Part IV

Solo on the Tambourine	by J. T. Brown

Who will go through his imitative powers on the Tambourine, particularly where the locomotive runs off the track and bursts the Boiler, also the rattling of Cannon in the distance, his Reveillie beating the Troops to quarters, his imitations of a celebrated French Drummer, executing single and double drags in perfect time—his Grist Mill grindings showing the power of steam, (of course) and the rattling of a Cotton mill and machinery. Language cannot convey any idea of his brilliant rapidity of execution on his Tambourine.

Part V

Song Early in de morning	Thayer
" Farewell Ladies	Juba
" Lynchburg Town	Brown

Part VI

Solo on the Banjo	by T. Fluter

The entertainment to conclude with the

Imitation Dance, by Mast. Juba,

in which he will give correct Imitation Dances of all the principal Ethiopian Dancers in the United States. After which he will give an imitation of himself—and then you will see the vast difference between those that have heretofore attempted dancing and this WONDERFUL YOUNG MAN. Names of the Persons Imitated: 1. Mr. Richard Pelham. New York. 2. Mr. Francis Brower. New York. 3. Mr. John Daniels. Buffalo. 4. Mr. John Smith. Albany. 5. Mr. James Sanford. Philadelphia. 6. Mr. Frank Diamond. Troy. 7. Master John Diamond. New York.

The program is an interesting dictionary of the foremost "Ethiopian" dancers at that period. Of these, Pelham, Brower, and most particularly

Master John Diamond, were most important. The latter, somewhat Juba's senior, was his only serious rival, and considered second only to Juba.

Master Diamond (1823–1857) achieved prominence about 1839. He was billed as a performer of the Negro Camptown Hornpipe, Ole Virginny Breakdown, Smoke House Dance and Five Mile Out of Town Dance, in "all of which he will come those Unheard of, Outlandish and Inimitable Licks, what is Death to all de Long Island Darkies, and which secures to him the title of King of Diamonds." (In jazz repertoire today there are at least three *Smokehouse* variations and the *Camptown* is well represented. Those "Inimitable Licks" survived as the "hot licks" of swing. There is a definite continuity of terminology.)

Diamond's style was considered a wonder. "Small of stature, he executed in an extremely neat and slow fashion." An incurable dipsomaniac, his dancing was held to be "considerably better than his temper and disposition." Since the "Masters'" respective merits were continually debated, a series of "Challenge Dances" was initiated to award the indisputable palm. They danced their first match at John Tryon's Amphitheatre in 1844.

These challenge matches demanded the same attention for an artistic matter that our ancestors lavished on their sporting events. There were at least three judges, for time, style, and execution. On occasion an audience had the decisive voice in determining the victor. "The time judge sat on the stage in the first right entrance, the style judge sat in or near the orchestra pit, and the judge of execution sat *under* the stage. There, with pad and pencil, the execution judge checked the missing taps, defective rolls and heel work, the lagging in the breaks. At the conclusion of the contest the judges compared notes and awarded the prize on points." (Douglas Gilbert, *Lost Chords*, N. Y., 1943.)

When Juba next toured with the Georgia Champion Minstrels in the New England states, he was entitled to this billing: "The Wonder of the World Juba, Acknowledged to be the Greatest Dancer in the World. Having danced with John Diamond at the Chatham Theatre for $500, and at the Bowery Theatre for the same amount, and established himself as the King of All Dancers. No conception can be formed of the variety of beautiful and intricate steps exhibited by him with ease. You must see to believe." (The word "beautiful" was almost never used to described minstrel dancing.)

In the summer of 1848 Juba arrived in London, to augment an already famous blackface minstrel troupe—Pell's Ethiopian Serenaders. His press releases had the spirited description from Charles Dickens' *American Notes* (1842), which purportedly represented Juba. For lack of further documentation there is a slight uncertainty here, although the dancer was everywhere billed as "Boz's Juba," and it was flatly stated by such respectable journals as *The London Illustrated News* that he was the youth Dickens had celebrated. Since Boz was an extremely vocal person he would probably have protested any infringement on or misrepresentation of his work. Thus his record of a Negro dance-hall in New York's Five Points district must be included in the Juba saga, at least in part.

> The corpulent black fiddler, and his friend who plays the tambourine, stamp upon the boarding of the small raised orchestra in which they sit, and play a lively measure. Five or six couples come upon the floor, marshalled by a lively young Negro, who is the wit of the assembly, and the greatest dancer known. He never leaves off making queer faces, and is the delight of all the rest, who grin from ear to ear incessantly. Among the dancers are two young mulatto girls, with large, black, drooping eyes, and headgear after the fashion of the hostess, who are as shy, or feign to be, as though they had never danced before, and so look down before the visitors, that their partners can see nothing but the long fringed lashes.
>
> But the dance commences. Every gentleman sets as long as he likes to the opposite lady, and the opposite lady to his, and all are so long about it that the sport begins to languish, when suddenly the lively hero dashes in to the rescue. Instantly the fiddler grins, and goes at it tooth and nail; there is new energy in the tambourine; new laughter in the dancers; new smiles in the landlady; new confidence in the landlord; new brightness in the very candles. Single shuffle, double shuffle, cut and cross-cut; snapping his fingers, rolling his eyes, turning in his knees, presenting the backs of his legs in front, spinning about on his toes and heels like nothing but the man's fingers on the tambourine; dancing with two left legs, two right legs, two wooden legs, two wire legs, two spring legs—all sorts of legs and no legs—what is this to him? And in what walk of life, or dance of life, does man ever get such stimulating applause as thunders about him, when, having danced his partner off her feet, and himself too, he finishes by leaping gloriously on the bar-counter and calling for something to drink, with the chuckle of a million of counterfeit Jim Crows, in one inimitable sound!

The British were completely transported by their American visitor, and wrote of him with an enthusiasm and affection usually reserved for pantomime clown Grimaldi and ballerina Fanny Ellsler. Among the effusions one finds an occasional astute evaluation—an unusual occurrence in either the gushing or pompous "harkback" schools of criticism then prevalent in England and the United States. Regrettably Juba did not appear in France, for Gautier was supremely the critic of that period who could have done a masterly analysis and description of his style.

London rank, fashion, and people all frequented Vauxhall Gardens at one time or another. Instantly Juba appeared there the London journals rightly predicted that he would attract many thousands to the gardens during the season. An anonymous critic wrote:

> There never was such a Juba as the ebony-tinted gentleman who is now drawing all the world and its neighbors to Vauxhall; there never was such a laugh as the

laugh of Juba—there is in it the concentrated laugh of fifty comic pantomimes; it has no relation to the chuckle, and, least of all to the famous horse laugh; not a bit of it—it is a laugh distinct, a laugh apart, a laugh by itself—clear, ringing, echoing, resonant, harmonious, full of rejoicing and mighty mirth, and fervent fun; you may hear it like the continuous humming sound of nature, permeating everywhere; it enters your heart and you laugh sympathetically—it creeps into your ear, and clings to it, and all the subsequent sounds seemed to be endued with the cachinatory quality. . . . "Well, though the laugh of Juba be wondrous, what may be said of Juba's dancing?"

The critic answers himself by saying that there was never such a combination of "mobility of muscles, such flexibility of joints, such boundings, such slidings, such gyrations, such toes and heelings, such backwardings and forwardings, such posturings, such firmness of foot, such elasticity of tendon, such mutation of movement, such vigor, such variety, such natural grace, such powers of endurance, such potency of pastern."

A sardonic sidelight, in relation to the later intensive propaganda to prove that plantation slavery was the beneficent patron of Negro genius, is this critic's recollection of dancing at "Major Bosh Sanderson's, who owned two thousand niggers at the junction of the Wabash and Congaree rivers, in South Car'lina," whose "choreographic manifestations were but poor shufflings compared to the pedal inspirations of Juba"; our good observer seems to have been surprised. Then there is the concluding accolade—"We hear that Juba has been commanded to Buckingham Palace."

The *Illustrated London News* (May 8, 1848), which offered a woodcut of Juba, noted in the text that

. . . the Nigger Dance is a reality. The "Virginny Breakdown," or the "Alabama Kick-up," the "Tennessee Double-shuffle," or the "Louisiana Toe-and-Heel," we know to exist. If they did not, how could Juba enter into their wonderful complications so naturally? How could he tie his legs into such knots, and fling them about so recklessly, or make his feet twinkle until you lose sight of them altogether in his energy. The great Boz immortalized him; and he deserved the glory thus conferred. If our readers doubt this, let them go the very next Monday or other evening that arrives, and see him at Vauxhall Gardens.

Another anonymous clipping of that same season is prophetically headed *Juba The American Dancer.*

Last night a select party was invited to Vauxhall Gardens to witness a private exhibition of the dancing capabilities of Juba, the celebrated American dancer. He is one of a party of six Americans, whom Mr. Wardell, the spirited proprietor of the gardens, has brought to this country. Their performances, vocal and instrumental, were last night of a character which cannot fail to prove a great attraction, but the dancing of Juba exceeded anything ever witnessed in Europe. The style as well as the execution is unlike anything ever seen in this country. The manner in which he beats time with his feet, and the extraordinary command he possesses over them, can only be believed by those who have been present at his exhibition. Scarcely less singular is the rapidity with which he sings one of his favorite songs. The American Juba has for some years drawn immense audiences whenever he has appeared. He is quite young, being only in his seventeenth year. Mr. Dickens, in his "American Notes," gives a graphic description of this extraordinary youth, who, we doubt not, before many weeks have elapsed, will have the honor of displaying his dancing attainments in Buckingham Palace.

The *Theatrical Times* critic in August 1848 gave one supremely important reason for Juba's greatness. "The performances of this young man are far above the common performances of the mountebanks who give imitations of American and Negro character; there is an *ideality* in what he does that makes his efforts at once *grotesque and poetical, without losing sight of the reality of representation.*" (Italics mine.)

In Liverpool Pell's Serenaders continued their triumphal progress, with Juba performing tirelessly. Again, one of the critics notes in passing one of the great characteristics of American tap-dancing, even today, that the dancer is equivalent to a musical instrument. He compares Juba's steps to Pell on the bones and Briggs on the banjo; ". . . this youth is the delight and astonishment of all who witness his extraordinary dancing; to our mind he dances demisemi, semi, and quavers, as well as the slower steps."

Working an almost superhuman schedule, thoroughly enjoying his work, and reacting normally to the excitement of his triumphs, Juba burned up his energies and health. In America a pious commentator and theatre historian, Allston Brown, smugly noted that "Success proved too much for him. He married too late (and a white woman besides) and died early and miserably." Rice is considerably more restrained, noting only that he was considered the greatest dancer in his line and that he died in 1852, in London.

From the age of fourteen Juba seems to have danced for his supper; at that time the standard culinary recompense "on the house" where he danced was a dish of fried eels and ale, which was scarcely a balanced diet. That Juba worked both night and day, consistently, from 1839 to 1850, is record. Small wonder if years of irregular food, irregular sleep, and regular strenuous physical exertion, finally produced a breakdown, which had nothing at all to do with "success proving too much for him." His greatest white contemporary—John Diamond—had a somewhat similar background, was an acute dipsomaniac and melancholic, and also died prematurely—in Philadelphia.

The influence of Master Juba and other minstrel dancers who followed him to England was extensive. There was a curious transference of his characteristics to English clowns. The "Gay Negro Boy" had made his initial entrée in American circuses, and was adopted by the British in that same medium. The minstrel dance changed the clowns' entrée, adding splits, jumps and cabrioles, as well as blackface make-up, to form a new type. Between 1860 and 1865 this character was taken over to France by touring British circuses, and later became a fixture in French and Belgian *cirques et carrousels.* The vogue for Lautrec's famous Negro clown Footit was part of this trend. English clowns, such as the Majiltons and Hanlon-Lees, returned to whiteface, but kept certain characteristics of blackface performers—the manic gaiety, he-who-gets-slapped apprehensions, and dance-acrobatics—evolving thereby a slightly macabre, almost surrealist personage.

The blackface clown persisted in European circuses and fairs; his grotesque mask emerges in the paintings of Ensor, and his influence just touched a new generation of painters and composers considerably before 1900. It supplanted another exotic impetus of the nineteenth century, Orientalism, which had prevailed in such diverse works as Moore's *Lalla Rookh*, Delacroix's *Arabs* and Whistler's *Japonoiserie.* Coincident with the rise of western imperialism in Africa came the influence of Afro-American jazz and Gold Coast sculptures. Orientalisms of the 1900 Paris Exposition eventually ceded to Stravinsky's *Ragtime* and Milhaud's experiments with *le jazz hot.*

In America it was Juba's influence primarily which kept the minstrel show dance, in contrast to the body of minstrel show music, in touch with the integrity of Negro source material. There was almost a "school after Juba." Certain of these white performers maintained his tradition with such integrity, and were such worthy artists, that a brief notice of them is necessary to our history.

Richard M. Carroll (1831–1899?) made his first public appearance at the age of fifteen as "Master Marks"; he was an understudy to the bibulous John Diamond. A contemporary writes:

> Carroll took pattern to a great extent from Juba, and after him, may safely be said to be one of the very first "all-around" dancers this country has ever seen.

Dave Reed (1830–1906) was another blackface performer who went directly to the Negro for his source material. He took a fancy to a fairly indifferent music-hall ballad, *Sally, Come Up*, which did not go too well. He then decided to work in some additions which he had learned from the Negroes when he used to dance on the steamboat *Banjo* on the Mississippi, a "certain comical and characteristic movement of the hands, by placing his elbows near his hips and extending the rest of his arms at right angles to his body, with the palms of his hands down," in addition to some new footwork. The dance caught on like wildfire.

The *Herald* correspondent also gives an interesting version of the origin of the famous *Shoo-Fly* song and dance.

Shoo-Fly is said to have come originally from the Isthmus of Panama, where the Negroes sang "Shoo-Fly" and 'Don't Bodder Me" antiphonally while at their work. A Negro from there, Helon Johnson, took it first to California and taught the song to Billy Birch. Dick Carroll and others also had versions of it which they performed.

The entire dance repertoire finally became synthesized in the so-called "essence" dances, made famous by Billy Newcomb. The music for these drew upon folk fiddle tunes, enhanced by the Negro's rhythmic gift and development of the offbeat which is the syncopation of jazz. Southern mountain songs—*Cotton Eyed Joe, Cripple Creek, Sourwood Mountain* (based on the yodel-song), and popular traditional jigs and hornpipes—*Turkey in the Straw, Old Zip Coon, Arkansas Traveller, Durang's Hornpipe* and *Fishar's Hornpipe*, were incorporated. In turn, many square dances of the South and Southwest used or adapted minstrel songs—*Old Dan Tucker, Buffalo Girls, Jim Along Josey,* and *Hop Light Loo* recur most frequently, and Botkin notes that the *danse aux chansons* of American play-party games had "songs often sung by the non-dancing part of the party to mark the rhythms—much, it might be added, after the fashion of patting out the rhythm in Negro dances." (*American Play-Party Song*, cf. Hudson).

Against this musical mélange was set minstrelsy's most famous dance—*Essence of Old Virginny*—performed initially in the make-up of a decrepit and tatterdemalion darky, but soon turned into a flashy young dude number. Based firmly on Negro source material, this theatrical showpiece was made famous by several excellent blackface performers. W. W. Newcomb is credited as its originator; his style was called "quintessence" and was done in rather fast time. In contradistinction Dan Bryant, its most famous exponent, who made important technical advances in the development of clog dancing, performed his famous *Essence* very slowly. George F. Moore originated the noiseless, soft-shoe *Essence* about 1875, and the last, whirlaway performance was that of Eddie Girard.

At this point, after looking at the blackface masks, it is necessary to evaluate the Negro position. By the eighteen-seventies there was a relentless, and impalpable, pressure to stereotype the stage Negro completely. Although groups such as the Fisk Jubilee Singers toured America and Europe they reached only a small minority of the general audience.

Increasingly the Negro was forced into his caricature. Lack of education had caused the Negro to retain, through word of mouth retelling, innumerable superstitions which had been commonplaces among the white settlers in the seventeenth and eighteenth centuries, ergo superstition and fear were "Negro peculiarities," and an adjunct of Negro "make-up" was the "shock" or "fright" wig, listed in the old theatrical catalogues, which could be made to rise and stand on end. Ignorance, vanity and childlike display of emotions constituted other characteristics which writers of that period continually referred to as "peculiar to the Negro." This last stricture is particularly interesting in view of an analysis by Herskovits (in *Freudian Mechanisms in Negro Psychology*) of the African "insult" song and dance, which are used as "socially institutionalized release." According to West African ritual, repressing emotions such as anger and hate is considered a primary cause of insanity; hypocrisy is a cause of illness, and the person who practices it gradually sickens. Thus there was a traditionally rather sound and healthy basis for emotional display, which was caricatured out of all proportion into a component of the cliché.

The Negro performer found that unless he fitted himself into the mold cast for him as typical he could get no work. This represents one facet of a vast attempt at justification of the slave system long propounded—the cliché that plantation life for the Negro had been a joyous lark, that happy, lazy Negroes spent their days dancing, singing, and indulging in childish pranks, with occasional spells of cotton-picking, and that the Negroes were wistfully lonely to be back at said plantations, which they were convinced constituted the happy land of Dixie. A Negro who had left the plantation or local mill was selected as a butt of ridicule—in the character of the "dandy nigger"—who squandered his earnings on flashy clothes and scorned his own people. Particular emphasis was always placed on class distinctions among the Negroes themselves, which were the basis for countless skits and dialogues.

There were songs such as P. S. Gilmore's *Freedom on the Old Plantation*, and program descriptions such as *Plantation Pastimes, Plantation Revels*, and *Plantation Frolics*, "to show Negro life in the south before the war, introducing solos, duets, choruses, moonlight pastimes, cotton-field frolics, and terminating the scene with the exciting Virginia Reel" . . . "a most realistic sketch." (1884). That same year the Frohmans, now proprietors of Callender's and Haverly's companies, took a troupe to London with a now inevitable *Alabama Pickininnies in Plantation Pastimes*. A book of words to this company's songs was published in London for their tour; it was a complete recapitulation of all current minstrel ditties, with no glimmer of original material.

Another curiosity was the extremely successful attempt to reintroduce the Negro as an exotic, attempted about 1883 by the Callender–Kersands company. The dancers' drill, a nineteenth-century theatrical fashion, which had its inception in classic ballet, was popularized in France, and taken over by England and America for all types of extravaganza. There were drills of Tartars, Amazons, Naiads, Turks, Brigands, Airy Sprites and Skeletons. The Zouaves, with their colorful red and blue costumes and dark complexions, were a "natural" for the Negro dancers.

One Sergeant Simms, "formerly an officer in the 6th Mass. Regiment," organized this "Grand Military Pageant Presenting an Army of Clog Dancers in an entirely New Kaleidoscope Phase; conceived and arranged by Wm. Welch." Holcomb, the famous clog dancer; Anderson and Kersands, the famous "Bones" and "Tambo" team; and Banks the comedian are among the top-notch Negro performers listed as *The Dancing Zouaves*. The program descriptive outline offers: "A. Dress Parade of African Zouaves. B. Grand Drill. C. Lightning Bayonet Exercise. D. Sergt. Simms and Musket. Clog Tournament terminating with the following Battlefield Pictures: 1. Awaiting the Attack. 2. Skirmishing. 3. The Defence. 4. The Rally by Fours. 5. The Charge. 6. The Dying Zouave." There is no clue to the music, but one can imagine the "Military Potpourri" which was pieced together. Sergeant Simms was still prospering more than a decade later, for he played New York with his "original novelty by his twelve little Indian boys from the Bahamas. Life on the Tented Field." This was a new version of his old Zouave drill, and the program states that "this novelty was especially engaged for the World's Fair, and brought from the Bahamas in charge of Sergeant Simms." With or without the Sergeant, the Callender Zouaves became an established feature, and similar drills were incorporated in Callender's blackface minstrel companies as well.

Occasionally a Negro artist would even gain some celebrity outside the minstrel field. Such a notable figure was Horace (or Howard) Weston. He was born a free Yankee Negro in Derby, Connecticut, in 1825. His father was Jube Weston, teacher of music and dancing. It would be interesting to know more of the history of a Negro music and dancing master in a small New England community such as this. In 1855, Horace, who continued his father's métier of music and dancing teacher, took up the banjo, which had become a great popular instrument. His professional career was interrupted by service in the Civil War. He resumed it by appearing in blackface minstrel companies and subsequently went to England with the Georgia Colored Minstrels in 1867. On his return to America he worked for Barnum, then played at Baur's Saloon, Robinson's Hall, and continued teaching. For three seasons, from 1876 to

1878, he played on the showboat *Plymouth Rock* for Jarrett & Palmer; late in 1878 he went to England with their *Uncle Tom* company and scored an enormous hit. He then made what at any time, by any artist, would have been considered an exceptional tour—Berlin, Breslau, Vienna, Hamburg, then a tour of France, and back to America for coast to coast appearances. He also toured with the two important Negro minstrel shows, Haverly's and Callender's. His obituary in the New York *Clipper* for June 7, 1890, presents him as one of the most esteemed performers of his period.

Kersands, Weston, the Hunn brothers, and some few others were actually the only Negroes *on the stage* who had steady employment; even they were more or less compelled to comply with the stereotypes. Their musical repertoire consisted increasingly of the sentimental ballad budget and music-hall jigs typical of all minstrel shows; the Negro element remained primarily in the rhythmic treatment of this material, the "intangibles of performance," and a phenomenal virtuosity in "trick" dances. William Allen's *Pedestal Clog* was danced on a surface fifteen inches square and four feet high; stunt dancing on a peck measure or a square of glass one inch thick was commonplace. Generally, Negro dancers and musicians had a better chance for artistic integrity in the music halls.

Negro iconography is scant in contrast to the vast body of "blackface" material. The pictures have a vitality which inspires and confounds. Possibly it is because those people who achieved the professional stature to warrant such records knew that theirs was an almost unique achievement, a tribute grudgingly accorded by that hostile world, wherein a Negro minstrel company's manager was described in the publicity as "white, *of course.*" Italics mine.

Even as the Negro performer was at the threshold of his first great "period" theatrically, which might be generally characterized as the Williams & Walker era, concerted efforts were made to place every difficulty athwart his path. With historical persistence anti-minority action was used as a mask for unrelated grievances. Thus a clipping from the *Sun*, July 22, 1894, under the title *Some Negro Actors*, offers the following documentary evidence:

> At a rehearsal during the last week of "1492" before it closed for its summer vacation, Herman Perlet, the musical director, threw down his baton and refused to direct the orchestra for a Negro boy whom Manager Rice had engaged to do a dancing speciality.
>
> Mr. Perlet did not draw the color line exactly, but when the darkey walked down to the footlights and said, "Say, cull, you'll have to play dat faster if you wants dis coon to dance," the indignity of "being called down by a nigger" was too much for the leader's pride. He left the director's chair and turned in his notice to Mr. Rice. The manager tried to persuade him to reconsider, but the

leader was obdurate and insisted on his resignation being accepted at the end of the week. Rice himself got into the leader's chair and conducted the remainder of the rehearsal after a fashion. . . .

The action of Musical Director Perlet in refusing to direct for the Negro dancer cannot be regarded entirely as a case of prejudice on his part, because it has been ascertained that he and Rice had been at loggerheads for a long time, owing to the fact Rice would never give him credit on the programme for having written nearly all of the musical numbers for "1492." But in objecting to the Negro dancer he showed that he had hit upon a pretext that would win him popular approval. And it did in the theatrical profession.

It is a familiar pattern. The next item too has many facsimiles.

Last week a mulatto man was singing on a roof garden in this city, billed as "Koo-i-baba, the Hindoo baritone." He did not sing well from a legitimate vocal standpoint, nor did he sing badly. He would have been regarded by an unprejudiced manager as having a good chorus voice. Yet the manager of the roof garden assured the reporter that it would never have done to bill him under the name of Johnson or Jackson. There was such a prejudice, he said, against "niggers" that unless he could be advertised as a Hindoo or some other dusky foreigner it would burst up his show. A notable fact was that the colored man was the only person on the programme who made any serious vocal efforts.

It was a rather sad commentary upon the artistic standard of the roof garden entertainments that the only refined singing permitted was that of the Negro, and whereas the manager was willing to employ his talents, he was unwilling to give him credit for being what he really was—an Afro-American.

What then can be the fate of the aspiring Negro singer, reciter, or actor in the face of such prejudice among people who began fighting thirty-three years ago to set him free and put him upon an equality with the whites of the South? The theatrical manager can with honesty maintain an indifference in regard to the social status of the colored man, because all the manager has to deal with is sure-thing cards, and he knows from former experience that the unadulterated Negro performer drives patrons away from his house. He refuses him upon no other grounds.

It is curious that this last paragraph was written just at the point when the public was shortly to applaud all-Negro shows. It may be that there was the usual fear of sharing the theatrical circuit with additional companies, on the part of the white performers, and so it was expedient to dispense with minority competition, which was unorganized and inarticulate, on the ground that the public didn't want it anyway. Yet a certain public demand must have prompted some venturesome manager to follow in the wake of Callender and Haverly with a Negro company recruited as follows, in a further report by the *Sun* reporter.

That there is no lack of Negro talent was recently demonstrated by a well-known minstrel manager, who intendes [sic] this season to take out a company composed of half Negro and half white minstrels. He advertised in the dramatic weeklies for forty colored persons who could either sing, dance, play the banjo and bones, or tell a funny story. They were to call on Twenty-second street near Broadway at 10 A.M.

At the hour named Twenty-second street was jammed with colored persons waiting to display their various talents to the manager. It was estimated that at least 2,000 had congregated, for many left before the 1,012 first comers had registered their names and addresses with the manager.

Several hotels and barber shops thought that their employees had all gone on strike when they rushed out at 10 o'clock to register their names and addresses with the minstrel manager.

But this manager is shrewd enough to know that he cannot get fifty white men to work with thirty colored men on the stage, so he is to have practically two entirely separate shows. The first show will consist of the real Negroes in "minstrelsy as it was," and the second show upon the same stage the same evening, will have the burnt-cork whites in "minstrelsy as it is." Each show will have its own stage manager, and every effort will be made to keep the colored and white actors separate in hotels and travelling, to avoid trouble that has hitherto attended every attempt to work them together.

In the last minstrel troupe of real darkies which went over the country the end men insisted on corking up as black as possible over their naturally dark skin, because, as they said, the public had gotten used to seeing the Negro minstrel as he is depicted by the whites and when the genuine article came along the public was a little disappointed to find that he was not so black as he was painted.

It was for the same reason that a similar ludicrous event happened at Saratoga several seasons ago. The guests of one of the fashionable hotels had all purchased tickets one evening and were assembled in the large dining rooms awaiting with curiosity a performance to be given by the Negro waiters. When the folding doors were opened they beheld a semi-circle of persons of a uniform blackened visage. The Negroes had all corked up in imitation of their white imitators.

Our anonymous reporter, who certainly had an exceptionally sincere and intelligent interest in the whole problem, went to interview T. Thomas Fortune, Negro editor of the Afro-American organ *New York Age*, who told him hopefully:

I believe that within fifteen years the leading comedians, dancers, and musicians of the day will include many Afro-Americans. The colored man is a natural born humorist, musician, and dancer, and when the prejudice against him which is now moderating shall have been entirely or nearly wiped out, you will find him occupying prominent places upon the amusement stage. The pickaninny band in "Old Kentucky," composed entirely of colored boys, made a hit. Sam T. Jack's creoles have raised the standard one notch higher than the minstrel show.

Mr. Fortune's hopes for Negro employment within the next number of years were to a certain degree fulfilled. But the larger issue of the racial stereotype was far from resolved. Since the opportunity for literal, literary presentation was not afforded, nor any representation of Negro humor save the "unconscious" humor of an outsider having difficulty with an alien tongue (and how many thousands of blackface dialogue "sermons" there were!), it was only in the field of music and dance that the Negro might really leave an impress. An interesting note on the way in which the restrictions of the stereotype finally helped kill off the minstrel show itself was sounded in an interview by Lew Dockstader in 1902, when he told a *Sun* reporter that the Negro had so advanced that the dialects and material for the old-fashioned take-offs were already lacking, and so the "Negro character" was being invalidated, bringing to a close one phase of Negro contribution to the American stage. The clichés and stereotypes persisted of course, to this day, even among Negro performers. Yet during the latter days of the minstrel shows and the transition period of the nineties, when Negro dance and music in the theatre seemed to be losing their identity, the real Negro art kept alive and re-entered through another channel—the social dance—as well as through a medium which we might call a type of highly specialized social entertainment.

We have seen that the Negro as entertainer and musician was long welcome in saloons and dance-halls, even when the theatres were difficult for him to attain. This was equally true of bawdy-houses. And in such milieus, where there was no interest in imposing extraneous artistic standards, the Negro musician was empowered to create and perfect his own art. In dance-halls and barrooms of New Orleans, St. Louis, Chicago and the Barbary Coast small Negro orchestras, now with a full complement of instruments, further developed that music which was to sweep the world. Syncopated off-beats, which had been known to western musicians for centuries, became a particular earmark associated almost exclusively with Afro-American music. The sense of timing and rhythmic "breaks" were equally a part of the dance. A great exhibition dance, the cake-walk, was also developed, with such superb theatrical potentialities that it served as a Negro re-entry permit to the stage. In the declining days of minstrelsy it was incorporated in finale "walk-arounds," an authentic American note at a period when imported operetta and extravaganza were eclipsing most of our indigenous theatrical forms.

Although handled with the bad taste of a super-colossal raree-show, *Black America*, presented in 1894 by Buffalo Bill's impresario, Nate Salsbury, was a first effort to make some presentation of the Negro as a person. Salsbury, a kindly man, who had offered such exotics as Pawnee Indians to the public, felt warranted in presenting the Negro in what was considered his native habitat—a plantation village. Large acreage, such as Ambrose Park in Brooklyn or the Huntington Avenue grounds in Boston, was made the site of a "Negro village," in which cabins and general living quarters were set up, with preacher and meeting house, mules, washtubs and hay-wagons included, so that visitors might have occasion to see "the unconscious humor of darkies" (publicity release). Salsbury had gathered a choir of five hundred untrained voices, belonging, as a Boston newspaper touchingly explained, "to black men, women, and children, who themselves are devoid of culture." According to the *Illustrated American*: "They were recruited among the farm and mill hands of Georgia, Alabama, and Florida, with a view to securing perfect Negro types, rather than theatrical or musical talent. They arrived in New York ten days previous to the opening of the show, when a Negro minstrel stage manager took them in hand, and, building upon a foundation of inborn imitative aptitude, taught each what he or she was expected to do."

The spectacle itself had a brief introduction of "African tribal episodes and war dance," followed by interludes of song and dance, including a grand cake-walk contest. In every review it is immediately apparent that no audience was able to resist the beauty of Negro music. Again and again there is the same amazement at the beauty and technical ability of these untrained singers. Perhaps this admiration wrested from general audiences, in contrast to the select concert public of the Fisk Jubilee Singers, made this venture something of a triumph in spite of all the tawdry antics which were attendant to it.

As the survey of Negro minstrelsy closes it might be well to recapitulate the outstanding companies, which were managed invariably by white impresarios. Charles Callender's troupe, later combined with Haverly's, was variously known as Callender's Georgia Minstrels, Callender's Consolidated Coloured Minstrels, Callender's Consolidated Coloured Spectacular Minstrels and Callender's Monster Minstrel Festival; Haverly's Mastodon Genuine Coloured Minstrels, Hicks & Sawyer's Consolidated Coloured Minstrels, Lew Johnson's Georgia Minstrels, the Great Nonpareil Coloured Troupe, Sprague's Original Minstrels, and Yarber's Coloured Minstrels were among the more active companies. Billy Kersands was the only Negro who at any time seems to have conducted an extensive tour with his own company, although usually he was starred by Callender or Haverly. Among the notable Negro artists were Kersands and his son, an amazing dancer billed as the Infant Kersans, Billy Banks, the Hunn Brothers, the Hyers Sisters, Joseph Holcomb, the pedestal clog dancer, Billy Wilson, William Goss, and many other fine performers, the fraction who represented their people.

In 1897 a brilliant period for Negro entertainment, lasting something more than a brief decade, was inaugurated. It produced musical comedies or extravaganzas which assembled the talents of Will Marion Cook, Ernest Hogan, Will Vedry, Paul Laurence Dunbar, Aida Walker, Jesse

Shipp, Bob Cole and many others. Their bright particular stars were the famous team of Williams and Walker.

The titles of many of these shows—*Senegambian Carnival, A Trip to Coontown, The Sons of Ham, In Dahomey, The Smart Set, In Bandana Land, Abyssinia, Shoofly Regiment, Rufus Rastus*—have a close relationship to the minstrel show stereotype, and the comedians wore the burnt cork and enormous painted mouth which were de rigeur for Negro comics. But the music and dances were unfettered by past conventions, and the raw elements of twentieth-century popular music acquired a style which would supersede the schottisches, waltzes and cotillions of the nineteenth.

The transition did not come at the turn of the century, but with the first World War. It was a Negro composer, Ford Dabney, working with Vernon and Irene Castle, who set a general pattern both for social dance and theatrical forms. In its purest form hot music is essentially for listening. The great soloists of jazz, the improvisations of the jam session, demanded as much concentrated attention as any other piece of chamber music. Dabney, as accompanist, composer and collaborator with the Castles, was initiator and popularizer of a new dance music.

Ford Dabney came to New York in 1900 with James Reese Europe, the noted band-leader, to appear at the Ziegfeld Roof. From 1904–1907 he was official pianist to the President of Haiti. He knew at first hand the unusual rhythms of the *tambours*, and of heel-beats against smooth earth. He listened to and remembered African ceremonial melodies, many of which the Haitians had preserved unchanged. On his return to New York he became one of that talented group of Negro musicians known as the Clef Club. In 1913 he met the Castles and worked with them until Vernon's untimely death. He was the alchemist who fused the divers jazz elements into a popular style.

Master Juba had imposed the Negro tradition on tap-dancing. Ford Dabney, with his musical *Rang Tang*, consolidated Negro traditions theatrically as he had done socially. Negro music and dance, which had a virtuosity supported by native vitality, making them difficult to adapt, were finally integrated in the complete panorama of American music and dance.

IMAGES OF GENDER AND CLASS

Transgressing the Gender Divide: The Female Impersonator in Nineteenth-Century Blackface Minstrelsy

Annemarie Bean

Ralph Ellison insightfully identified nineteenth-century blackface minstrelsy as the first theatrical venue where Americans performed their repressed desires. The minstrel stage, Ellison noted in his essay "Change the Joke and Slip the Yoke," is where "private is public and the public private, where black is white and white black, where the immoral becomes moral, and the moral is anything that makes one feel good" (1972:49–50). Although the practitioners and spectators were mostly northern and urban, the musical performances of early minstrelsy were situated in the South, which had a symbolic significance as it constructed a contained order of the universe, located on the plantation while, conversely, allowing a liberal attitude of "anything goes." Blackface minstrelsy was based in a hypernostalgic state where the plantation culture of the South existed as a performed cultural imaginary of the urban displaced white man. Nationalism was on the rise in 1850s, an age of abolitionist and women's movements, and blackface minstrelsy kept at bay an urban culture that was based in consumption, demanding that men give up their individual identity to the mega-identity of the city.[1] The desired, mythologized Southern lifestyle was perceived as fixed and unmoving—home-based, passive—as can be evidenced by such minstrelsy favorites as "My Old Kentucky Home" and "Old Folks at Home."[2] In contrast, the lifestyle of unstable black families, as a result of purported infidelity or emancipation, was often interpreted, especially in later minstrelsy, as crippled (as in the crippled jump of "Jim Crow"), and ultimately, feminized. It is the portrayal of femininity in its most elaborate form—that of a blackened, cross-dressed white male minstrel portraying an ultrafeminine prima donna female impersonator—that I consider in this chapter.

Developed in the 1830s, blackface minstrelsy's legendary beginning usually is credited to Thomas "Daddy" Rice, who, at a loss for a new routine, imitated the dance of a crippled, black stablehand he had observed earlier in the day (Lott 1993:51–52). Reaching beyond attending a live performance, Y. S. Nathanson's 1855 account tells of the lasting effect of the first minstrel song and dance, entitled "Jumpin' Jim Crow," on its audience:

> [I]t may be proper to remark that "Jim Crow" is what may be called a dramatic song, depending on its success, perhaps more than any play ever written for the stage, upon the action and mimetic powers of the performer. Its success was immediate and marked. *It touched a chord in the American heart which had never before vibrated*, but which now responded to the skilful [sic] fingers of its first expounder, like the music of the Bermoothes to the magic wand of Prospero. (In Jackson 1967:37; emphasis mine)

The song and dance "Jim Crow" empowered the performer with "mimetic powers" and the ability to "touch [. . .] a chord in the American heart which had never been vibrated." For the first truly American mass entertainment of nineteenth-century meaning on the stage was a negotiated code,[3] where the white male audience members relied on performances, such as that of the female impersonator, to be grounded in passivity, eroticism, and femininity to define their anxious time. In an early essay on gender impersonation, Laurence Senelick notes that the word "impersonator" was coined in the 1850s (Senelick 1982:32)—paralleling the rise of blackface minstrelsy. Therefore, gender impersonation and blackface minstrelsy are two uniquely Anglophone forms that combined in performances in the Jacksonian age of America. One reading of this theatrical event is that the primary object of early minstrelsy, the South (as performed by the minstrels), maintained a fixed object for the collective libido of a displaced (by urbanity and its related issues of capitalism and immigration) male audience. Additionally, beyond the practical demand of dramatic necessity, the search for a secured masculine identity required that a fantasy of a living female be performed, and thus came the advent of the role of the prima donna female impersonator as an integral part of the minstrelsy. Through the blackened-up female impersonator, sexuality was saved from disappearance and contained by the white male body at the same time.

It is likely that George Christy was the first female impersonator when he acted the part of Miss Lucy Long in the 1840s. "Lucy Long" (1842) was among the many early blackface minstrelsy songs to be performed by a white male cross-dressed as a mulatta female (Paskman and Spaeth 1928:92):

I've come again to see you,
  I'll sing another song,
Jist listen to my story,
  It isn't very long.

Oh take your time Miss Lucy,
Take your time Miss Lucy Long.

Oh! Miss Lucy's teeth is grinning,
  Just like an ear ob corn,
And her eyes dey look so winning
  Oh! would I'd ne'er been born,

If she makes me a scolding wife,
  As sure as she were born,
I'll tote her down to Georgia,
  And trade her off for corn. (Lott 1993:160)

Not atypical of the genre, the song tells us that Lucy Long's illustrated worth, if she forsakes love by reprimanding her suitor, is less than an edible commodity, corn. Lucy Long and characters like her were women who were assured in their value as sexual objects and they occasionally needed to be reminded that they had the status of property, not personhood. In *Love and Theft,* Eric Lott notes that no one has been able to prove that the early "wench" (the character term of the time) actually sang in the sketches that included her as a character—the Southern mulatta coquette became the "lyric and theatrical object of the song" (160) and of the entire theatre arena in the early minstrel show. Indeed, early minstrelsy was founded in songs that combined both the erotic and the commodification of the sexual being of the characters, usually involving a mulatta wench and two darker skinned men rivaling for her attention, named the "dark triangle" in one minstrelsy book (Paskman and Spaeth 1928:91).

Most major companies had female impersonators by the mid-1850s; they were as integral as the endmen and Interlocutor. Wench players noted in Paskman and Spaeth's 1928 minstrelsy book *Gentlemen, Be Seated!* are George Holland, M. S. Pike, Henry Wood, Charlie Backus, William Henry Rice, Lew Dockstader, and Willis P. Sweatman (93). Given the physiques of some of these minstrels, it can be ascertained that these men either played the "wench" role or the low-comedy "Funny Old Gal" role. The early "Funny Old Gal" recalled the performance tradition of the comic Dame role in burlesque. Deeply rooted in American burlesque was a blatant ridicule for Shakespeare, and from that tradition and general anti-Enlightenment disdain were developed the beginnings of "legitimate burlesque" (Hutton 1891:157), which was often produced in the same houses as white minstrelsy. George Holland, who later perfected a minstrelsy afterpiece featuring "Ms. Araminta Belinda Caudle Toodles" (Paskman and Spaeth 1928:92), began his New York career portraying both the First Grave-Digger and Ophelia in John Poole's send-up of *Hamlet* in 1828 (Hutton 1891:157). The wench role probably emerged from burlesque performance tradition as well. The "male soprano" with an androgynous name reached its apex about the same time that biological women accessed the post-Civil War American popular stage in " 'leg shows,' ballet extravaganzas like *The Black Crook* and English burlesque as introduced by Lydia Thompson and her British Blondes" (Senelick 1993:90). Additionally, Senelick notes that "glamour drag" had performance roots in circus and equestrian transvestite performance in the nineteenth century, as well as in British public school drama and American collegiate theatrical groups such as Harvard's Hasty Pudding Club. Senelick's thesis of origins is notable in that it forefronts the class-transgression that nineteenth-century performance exhibited. White minstrelsy, as the first theatrical offering of the middle-class, reified the white male's position as enabler of his own gender and cultural politics on the popular stage.

Presenting the Prima Donna

> Oh! Ada, do you love me?
> Tell me if you love me.
> She said, I love you;
> Which made me feel so queer,
> As we walked in Brompton Square.
> Here eyes so blue, her feet so small,
> I thought I should die right there.
> She took my arm—oh, yes she did,
> Ada with the golden hair.
>
> —"Ada with the Golden Hair" (1868)

The advent of the female impersonator, however (in the 1860s designated as "the prima donna" [Toll 1974:140]), would provide the minstrelsy spectators with visual pleasure that rivaled the "new" presence of biological women on stage, and would challenge the belief system set up to laud the accomplishments of spectacle. In early minstrelsy, the wench character served as the object of stage desire, and she may have been too active a participant—too passionate—to serve as the still, rigid, almost paralytic feminine being which was needed to insure the formation of a successful masculine identity, an identity that needed to be established and re-established in the sentimental songs of minstrelsy. In the 1850s emerged the role of the cross-dressed featured tenor called, by the role's heyday in the 1880s, the prima donna. Coming out of the darkened shell of the wench, the prima donna required the mulatta to forego her position as the "lyrical and theatrical object" in minstrelsy to a superior position—that of a highly stylized and costumed near-white woman[4] in the "second part" or "afterpiece" of the minstrel show, where songs and dances were featured after the "first part" consisting of jokes and stories.

The star prima donnas were men with singular names—"Eugene," "Ricardo," "Stuart," and "The Only Leon." "Eugene" (D'Ameli, 1836–1907) was a minstrel declaimed for his "delineations of female characters [that] were so finished, so true to life." "Eugene" began with Wood's Minstrels, where he was joined by George Christy in 1853, and ended his career thirty years later with the Leon and Cushman Company in 1883. "Ricardo" was born Foley McKeever in Ireland and worked with several well-known minstrel groups, including Kelly and Leon. "Stuart" was known as the Male Patti, after the Black Patti, and was rescued from a life as a mail clerk by Tom Heath of McIntyre and Heath's Minstrels in 1887 (Rice 1911:344). Other female impersonators of the same era were W. H. Rice, Rollin Howard (who once played Topsy in one of the many minstrelsy-influenced productions of "Uncle Tom's Cabin"), J. T. Huntley, George W. Charles, Lewis J. Donnelly, Fred Dart, Burton Stanley, George Wilkes, Gus Mills, Harry Lansing, James Mack, Harry Constantine, Arthur Doty, Billy Lyons, Fred Malcolm, Charles Heywood, Justin Robinson, Ernest Linden, Lincoln Ellwood, Burt Shepard, Paul Vernon, and Tony Hart (in Rice 1911).

The prima donna female impersonators of the minstrel stage eclipsed the minstrel companies with which they were associated; the emotive responses of their audiences are legendary. As Toll recounts in *Blacking Up*, prima donnas had their wardrobes detailed in newspapers and were interviewed extensively (1974:144). Toll interprets the popularity of the prima donna as an indicator of cultural anxiety: "Men in the audience probably were titillated by the alluring stage characters whom they were momentarily drawn to [;. . . w]omen were probably intrigued by the impeccable grace and femininity of the beautiful illusionists" (144). Eric Lott sees the prima donnas as theatrical achievements of the "sexually variable" (1993:161). According to Lott, the blackfaced minstrel and the white spectator were engaged in a conversion from "sexual defensiveness into same-sex desire" (161–62). Undoubtedly this type of desire was occurring, but I am more inclined toward Laurence Senelick's reading of the prima donna as popular because, in part, "the audience could savor sexually provocative behavior because it had ostensibly been neutralized by the transvestitism" (1993:93). Judith Butler moves in this direction when she discusses the way the performative act reestablishes the system of compulsory heterosexuality [by] reproduc[ing] and conceal[ing . . .] through the cultivation of bodies into discrete sexes with "natural" appearances and "natural" heterosexual dispositions. (1990:275)

This implemented order of the cultural universe began almost at the commencement of minstrelsy with the "dark triangle." Toll sees the prima donna as the feminized version of the "blackface 'fool' who educated audiences while also reassuring them that he was their inferior. Neither man nor woman, the female impersonator threatened no one" (144). Marjorie Garber furthers this reading: " 'Black' (or 'Negro') was as much in quotation and under erasure as 'woman' in the white minstrel show: a black-impersonating female impersonator summed up and disempowered (or emasculated) [several] threatening forces at once" (1992:277). Though masculinity was perceived to be threatened by dark-skinned women, the white male audience members and performers were also titillated and comforted by the mulatta wench and prima donna, as they were, for the American culture at that time, the quintessential mother/whore. In fact, the rejection of the mother who has been desired establishes a filter through which any Other is to be first loved, then hated.[5]

Given the fact that many extant photographs of prima donnas do not appear to exhibit the cross-dress minstrel as blackened, another reading of the prima donna could concern the decision to present near-white "women" and "black" men on the same stage. In this performance, blackface minstrelsy re-staged the perceived tension between the sexually innocent white woman and the carnal black man. An interesting application could be made of Joan Riviere's recounting of the fantasy of her white, Southern woman subject, discussed in her essay "Womanliness as Masquerade" (1929), which reveals that Riviere's subject fantasized as a young girl that "if a negro came to attack her, she planned to defend herself by making him kiss her and make love to her (*ultimately so that she could then deliver him over to justice*)" (Riviere 1991:93; emphasis in original). The pleasure of the white woman is achieved through another's pain; in fact, the white woman is willing to sacrifice the black man to achieve *jouissance*. The white woman can accomplish her fantasy through the laws of whiteness. Therefore, her acting-out of her desire reinforces white supremacy—white "laws of desire" as it were—as based in sadism; the horror is part of the pleasure. By theatrically constructing masked representations of both the near-white "woman" and "black" man, minstrels attempted to protect themselves as Riviere's subject dreamed she could be protected: "by putting masks on [her] face . . . in order to avert disaster" (94).

I would now like to focus on two female impersonators that excelled at the role of prima donna: The Only Leon and Tony Hart. From similar Irish-American backgrounds, Leon's and Hart's performance lives have been considerably well documented, and therefore can serve as testing grounds for my interpretation of their transgressions of race and femininity on the minstrel stage.

The Only Leon

In a fine but pleasing voice he commenced conversation on his art and his wardrobe, which he makes an essential element. With real feminine pride he showed the dress he wore at the performance last evening. It was not of stage material, but, like every article of his wardrobe, was genuine stuff.

— "LEON, THE FEMALE IMPERSONATOR"
NEW YORK CLIPPER
DECEMBER 31, 1881

The article from which this excerpt was taken appeared during the zenith of Francis Leon's career. Born around 1840, Patrick Francis Glassey was gifted with a boy soprano voice that never altered. He began working in white minstrelsy at the age of fourteen with Wood's Minstrels. He studied ballet and voice for eight years, and then formed Kelly and Leon's Minstrels with Edwin Kelly, an Irish immigrant. The Kelly and Leon troupe refitted an old New York City chapel in 1866 and played the space for three years (Wittke 1930:221–22). They then toured England and pleased the Prince of Wales in the audience so much he "evinc[ed] his delight with applause" (*New York Clipper* 1881). Leon flourished beyond the collapse of Kelly and Leon's Minstrels to continue on to Australia (Wittke 1930:222). By 1882, aligned with Haverly's Minstrels, Leon was the profession's highest paid performer. His success spawned so many "impersonators of Leon, The Female Impersonator" that he copyrighted his performance name as "The Only Leon" (Senelick 1993:85).

Robert Toll gives the most detailed compilation of accounts regarding Leon:

Leon is the best male female actor known to the stage. He does it with such dignity, modesty, and refinement that it is truly art.

He is more womanly in his by-play and mannerisms, than the most charming female imaginable.

Heaps of boys in my locality don't believe yet it's a man in spite of my saying it was.

Leon's charms could cause "to make a fool of a man if he wasn't sure." (1974:142)

The 1881 *Clipper* account (subtitled "Leon, The Lovely—The Great Female Impersonator and His Life and Wardrobe") splits its column space between biographical background of Leon and the particularities of his costume. The details of expenditure, no doubt fed to the reporter by proud Leon himself, included all manner of disclosure: "The reporter blushingly asked Leon if he wore underskirts, and in reply the artist produced several of those garments in spotless white, and trimmed with costly embroidery." The evocation of art, purity, authenticity, and illusion all seem to function in the mythical world that surrounded Leon. The male audience members elevated Leon's artistry beyond the public status of women, which Robert Toll and Marjorie Garber indicate bespeaks the "inferior" position in the social hierarchy biological women had on the minstrel stage. Leon played both white and mulatto women (one memorable poster has him costumed as Sarah Bernhardt and creole Rose Michon) throughout his career. His portrayals were seen as highly respectable in their highly charged, but controlled titillation. Eric Lott notes that the game of "gender guessing" (a term quoted from Lillian Schissel) raised the stakes of sexual identity roles in the assumed femininity of the performer Leon and the masculinity of the male audience member (1993:166). The female audience members' accounts are less plentiful than the men's, and I did not find primary-source substantiation of Toll's and others' conclusions that women primarily enjoyed Leon's performances because they could observe, close up, the latest fashions. It appears by all accounts that "Leon's performances can, without any reservation or qualification, be placed under the category of 'truly wonderful'" (*New York Clipper* 1881) in the performance history of American minstrelsy in his ability to accomplish a theatrical body that transcended the limits of his, and his audiences', white maleness.

Tony Hart

Tony Hart, of the famous Harrigan and Hart team, has been described as the finest wench of his day, in either black-face or Irish make-up.

— "The Dark Triangle"
Gentlemen, Be Seated! (1928)

Tony Hart was born in Worcester, Massachusetts, on July 25, 1855, as Anthony J. Cannon. Like Leon, Hart began his career early on, featuring his boy soprano voice in minstrel companies advertised as "Master Antonio, the Boy Soprano." He met Edward Harrigan in 1871 when he was sixteen in Chicago. Irishman Ned Harrigan (b. 1845) had been affiliated with several partners before meeting Hart; at the end of another professional partnership, Harrigan teamed up with Hart for a highly successful thirteen years. From the onset, Hart played the female roles, beginning with the "'The Little Fraud' in which Hart was a fresh-faced Dutch girl with a mellow voice" (*New York Sun* 1891). The "Little Fraud" sketch had previously been performed by Harrigan with his former partner Sam Rickey (with Rickey as the Dutch girl), but "Hart's work did much to make the song famous" (*New York Sun* 1891). Harrigan retrospectively praised Hart as "the best impersonator of women that I ever knew on the stage." Harrigan went on to recall Hart's reluctance to play females, and his "natural" skill in the role:

> I had great trouble at first in persuading him to make the trial of these female characters. In Chicago the spectators would hardly believe it was a boy in the role. "Bill" Pinkerton, the detective, came behind the scenes and studied him at close range in his make-up, and swore he was a woman. (Harrigan n.d.:502–3)

The obituaries of Tony Hart carefully detail the successful acts of Harrigan and Hart, similar to a popular entertainer's obituary today. Hart always played the female roles, though not exclusively; he was Rebecca Allup in their famous Mulligan series and the Widow Nolan: "In all of them Hart appeared either as an unctuously funny negro wench or as a rollicking Irishwoman" (*New York Sun* 1891).

The popular duo built their own minstrel house, the New Theatre Comique, at 728 Broadway in 1881, only to have it burn down in 1884. Harrigan and Hart, strained by the fire (the theatre's staff members were relatives of both men), dissolved their partnership almost immediately. Hart had married Gertie Granville in 1882, and the couple formed their own company after the Harrigan and Hart breakup, often with both spouses playing female roles. Just as the obituaries document the triumphs of Tony Hart's early career, they fastidiously outline his downfall, precipitated by bad material and acute syphilis (known then as paresis). For example, a chapter in a 1955 book on Harrigan and Hart features the title "Poor Tony." The author relives Hart's professional and emotional descent, starting with a headline from the December 15, 1887, edition of the *New York Herald*, which read "That Telltale Lisp" (Kahn 1955:244). The obituaries also mention a benefit that was held in March 1888 at the Academy of Music, which raised $8,000 to pay for Hart's then residence, the Worcester Insane Asylum. Gertie Hart died in 1890, and Hart himself passed away on November 4, 1891, no surprise as the "demented actor had been failing" (*New York Clipper* 1891).

Tony Hart's initial stage work as a boy soprano, as mentioned before, mimicked the theatrical beginnings of Leon. Both of Irish lineage, Leon and Hart became known, defined, by their feminized, unreal voices in their early lives. Their soprano abilities led to casting in ethnic female roles. To progress from merely singing "female" to impersonating females was the logical step for those minstrels as good at gender "fooling" as Leon and Hart. The skills of both men are well noted, but their specificities defy classifying these two female impersonators as similar. Leon was featured and performed prima donna roles only; there are no accounts of him in comic sketches. His performance was based on gender and culture construction *par excellence*. Hart relied more on comic elements fused with believability. The comic base for Hart gave him access to characters of a variety of ethnicity and age, and his accomplishments at achieving a multitude of believable Others made him much loved and much lamented in his passing. There is a sympathetic sense of loss in Hart's obituaries, tempered only by Ned Harrigan's self-aggrandizement. Tony Hart was one of the people's own.

Containing the Performed Black and Feminine

> One day I called on Ada,
> My sweet little Ada,
> Dear little Ada.
> Her Mamma told me she was dying;
> I thought I should drop right there.
> I rushed up-stairs—Ada screamed out,
> "Just come in if you dare."
> "Are you dying, my dear?"—"Why you silly," she said,
> "I'm only *dye*—ing my hair!"
>
> —FROM "ADA WITH THE GOLDEN HAIR" BY G. W. MOORE, *The St. James Hall Veritable and Legitimate Christy Minstrels Christmas Annual* (1868)

But an examination into Leon's career reveals one surprising aspect—there is no report of his death. As Marjorie Garber addresses as typical of highly stylized drag performers, with Leon's death a mystery, and his life one of carefully mediated disclosure, the realm of the unconscious that Leon occupied is masked or veiled, thereby containing its power in literalization (1993:356). What is a mystery, beyond the death of Leon, is if there was an oppositional consciousness functioning with Leon. As the son of Irish immigrants, Leon was certainly aware that his inherited persona, as Irish, was ridiculed by minstrels in their quest to entertain through caricature: Irishmen on the minstrel stage "had brogues, drank whisky, partied, and fought" (Toll 1974:169), and it was during this time of intense Irish immigration that the phrase "Black Irish" came into use. I would like to postulate that by performing as a female, Leon possibly could have been performing subversion. Butler astutely clarifies her somewhat muted point in *Gender Trouble* that "there is no necessary relation between drag and subversion, and that drag may well be used in the service of both the denaturalization and reidealization of hyperbolic heterosexual gender norms" (Butler 1993:125). However, Leon's perfectionism in performing femininity could be seen as a performative response to minstrelsy's manipulation of ethnic "peculiarities" (Toll 1974:169) such as those of his fellow Irishmen. Leon's willful combatting of the theatrical perpetuation of ethnic stereotypes by becoming a skilled gender transgressor intrigues me as it indicates the ambivalent, inherently political nature of drag when the transgression also involves race.

As the abolitionist movement forged ahead in the 1850s, blackface minstrels began to abandon their hope in the nostalgic state of being that was the South, and moved on to infantilizing and demonizing the black body like never before; with the possibility of having autonomous free blacks with rights in American society, blackface minstrels set out to prove they were not worthy of them. A few years later, biological women accessed the post-Civil War American popular stage in "'leg shows,' ballet extravaganzas like *The Black Crook* and English burlesque as introduced by Lydia Thompson and her British Blondes" (Senelick 1993:90). Race and femininity could no longer be contained on the plantation; the audience now needed "live" women to teach them the rules of love, and "bumbling" Stepin' Fetchits to make sure that any potential threat would be emasculated.

In looking back on nineteenth-century blackface minstrelsy, I foreground one of many moments in American history when white men feared the limitlessness of expansion. In his illuminating book on the Jacksonian period, Alexander Saxton accounts for the permissiveness in gender transgression through cross-dressing and lyrics redolent with masturbation and homosexuality as based in "both urban and frontier" anxieties of the white male.[6] Blackface minstrelsy was founded in a decade fraught with anxieties over the California gold rush and a war with Mexico as well increasing abolitionist and women's movements, and it became the mass entertainment for men in Western frontier settlements and overcrowded Lower East Side boarding houses who were the participant-observers in this violent age. And, as blackface minstrelsy was the staging for this era of conquering (Mexicans and Native Americans) and journeying (westward and, for immigrants, across oceans), it is fitting that the practice of minstrelsy—and the coinciding theatrical material based on re-staging the Other, be it black, female, Irish, German, Jewish, or a *combination*—served as an instrument of establishing limits in an age of limitlessness. It is not surprising, therefore, that the legacy that minstrelsy has left theatrically continues to require that the woman onstage—especially the black woman—carry the fantasies of the social order. The popular theatrical woman was established by cross-dressed male minstrels, and it is indeed ironic that the adventuresome transgressions of race and gender of these white men contained limits on performed femininity maintained in popular entertainment ever since.

Notes

I would like to extend my heartfelt thanks to Pamela Brown, Richard Green, James V. Hatch, André Lepecki, Brooks McNamara, and Peggy Phelan for their illuminating conversations and comments during the writing of this chapter.

1. A similar, illustrative discussion on the collusion of nationalism and a need to find a place of refuge is detailed by David Harvey in *The Condition of Postmodernity* (1991), where he notes that the nineteenth-century philosopher

> [Heidegger] was evidently disturbed by the bland universalisms of technology, the collapse of spatial distinctiveness and identity, and the seemingly uncontrolled acceleration of temporal processes. . . . His search for permanence [the philosophy of Being] connects with a place-bound geopolitics and destiny that was both revolutionary [in the sense of forward looking] and intensely nationalistic. (209)

2. Eric Lott discusses the mediation involved in these two Stephen Foster songs in particular in his chapter on Foster, "California Gold and European Revolution: Stephen Foster and the American 1848" in Lott (1993:169–210). He writes of the nostalgic effects of these songs and the emotional outpouring they created as effects that are dependent upon the black mask of minstrelsy to facilitate this playing out of, borrowing from Alexander Saxton, "psychological identity."

3. See Stuart Hall's "Encoding, Decoding" essay in Simon During's *The Cultural Studies Reader* (1993) for a detailed discussion on how the codings of mass-mediated messages are disseminated. A *negotiated* code is one where audiences are clearly versed in what is "dominantly defined and professionally signified" (102).

4. Thereby providing another example of the historical displacement of the mulatta by a society that attempts to reconstitute itself through a nonwhite female body. Vera M. Kutzinski has provided an intriguing historical overview of the role of the mulatta in Cuban nationalism with *Sugar's Secrets: Race and the Erotics of Cuban Nationalism* (University Press of Virginia, 1993). Although Kutzinski's work focuses on the Caribbean and Latin America, her detailed analysis of the continual presence of the mulatta in Cuban literature and visual arts (including cigar ads!) has posited easily applicable conclusions as to the commodification of the mulatta body in the playing out of other nationalist movements.

5. Please see Judith Butler's chapter "Gender is Burning" in *Bodies That Matter* (1993:120–40).

6. See Saxton (1990), particularly his chapter on "Blackface Minstrelsy."

Daddy Blue: The Evolution of the Dark Dandy

Barbara Lewis

One year before Andrew Jackson won the presidential election and two years before he assumed office, the dark dandy made his melodious debut in "Long Tail Blue," a popular song published by Atwills Music Saloon on Broadway in New York in 1827:

> "Long Tail Blue," sung in an ultra-fashionable coat, was the first song of the negro dandy. George Washington Dixon, who was featuring it as early as 1827, claimed the authorship. Though not so successful as "Coal Black Rose," it remained for half a century one of the standard burnt-cork songs.[1]

T. Allston Brown, an agent and stage historian of the period, locates Dixon in New York in 1827, but mentions only the song, "Coal Black Rose." He does, however, identify Dixon as an early crooner of Negro melodies. On July 19, 1827, according to Brown, Dixon first appeared in New York at the Lafayette Theatre, then the largest stage in England or America. Dixon took his bow "as a singer of comic songs. He attained considerable popularity with his 'Coal Black Rose' and other negro ditties before T. D. Rice and his Jim Crow electrified the public."[2] In an essay, "The Origins of Negro Minstrelsy," Brown offers another version of the song's origin: "Barney Burns was known in those days from Quebec to New Orleans, as a job actor. He was connected with the circus and was also low [sic] comedian. He first sang 'The Long Tail Blue'. . . ."[3]

George Odell, author of a fifteen-volume record of the nineteenth-century New York stage, was not impressed by Dixon's debut. Distancing himself by using the royal we, his predictions were less than sanguine that Dixon would keep a steady grip on the audience's attention.[4] As subsequent events and commentators have shown, this did not prove to be the case.[5] In its original form and in later parodic versions, the various permutations of Long Tail Blue's image have outlasted detractors as well as early impersonators. If Dixon, rather than Burns, was the first to present the blue dandy in 1827, Odell's comment does attest to the initial ambivalence the persona elicited.

The representation of a former slave, freed not long ago and already attired with opulence in twin tails of fine fabric, must have caused pandemonic fascination and consternation. How was one to tame this astounding new bird of amazingly altered feather, the public must have asked itself in parlors, taverns, and other sites of collective assembly. Transformed into a strutting dichotomy, this hybrid creature singing about his urban conquests was an upstart in the city, possessing the pluck to layer an Apollonian veneer over a Dionysian spirit. Dangerous, his threatening dual power had to be quelled and controlled.

In the first sentence of the first stanza, Long Tail Blue identifies himself as no longer rural, with city manners to match ("I've come to town to see you all, I ask you how d'ye do?"). Blue has cleaned himself up, and is immensely pleased with his stylish new clothes. Symbolically, he has absolved himself of the past, and is ready and willing to assume a place in step with others in the teeming metropolis, eager to share in the privilege and prosperity of citizenship. From the second stanza, it is clear that, comparatively speaking, he has improved his social and economic circumstances. He certainly has more options and better clothes than his cousins still in bondage.

He also enjoys more romantic and sexual success, not always endogamously pursued, and therein lies the rub. His amorous intentions toward women not of his complexion almost certainly account for his scuffle with the law. In the fourth stanza, Blue is apprehended by a policeman ("watchman" in the terminology of the 1820s) who does damage to Blue's Sunday suit. But a trip to the tailor's shop, reported in the fifth stanza, quickly rights the wrong, and Blue is able to return, posthaste, to his romantic endeavors. The authority of the law is identified as an antagonist rather than supporter, but Blue survives this run-in with no permanent harm done. The second and last stanzas, according to the S. Foster Damon songbook, follow:

> Some Niggers they have but one coat,
> But you see I've got two;
> I wears a jacket all the week,
> And Sunday my long tail blue.
>
> If you want to win the Ladies' hearts
> I'll tell you what to do;
> Go to a tip top Tailor's shop,
> And buy a long tail blue.

A glance at the iconography of Long Tail Blue, as depicted in the lithograph advertising the song, shows an erect, refined, and respectable figure. He strikes the eye as a man of substance and perhaps even property. What's more, he appears the epitome of propriety, with his formal dress and restrained mannerisms.

The pride and elegance of Long Tail Blue emerged in a transitional period. John Quincy Adams was still president, but his tenure was coming to an end, and so was the world he personified. A member of the educated elite, Adams belonged to a family that, in the span of three generations, had gentrified itself, rising to prestige and privilege from the ranks.[6] Eager for the kind of transformation effected by the Adams family, Long Tail Blue desired to pull himself up by his jacket straps and gain entry to a class status higher than the one into which he was born. Blue believed in the American creed that promised unlimited ascent, dependent only on innate capability garnished by luck.

But chance and fortune were not on Blue's side. Neither was custom, which soon denied his humanity and decreed that he was not entitled to the same advantages as other men. Before long, Blue's head and robust shoulders were bowed. The aristocratic paradigm that Adams had embodied gave way to Jackson's egalitarian program, intended only for white males. Under the democratic Jackson, the political constituency was redefined to exclude from the demos free blacks, many of whom had earned their status by loyal service to the nation in its fight for liberty. The new spirit of equality, certainly a euphemistic term, was intent on laundering the immigrant middle, and determined to exclude the darker and higher reaches of the citizenry. Jackson's leveling program was accomplished with significant media assistance from the penny press and the theatre.[7]

Jim Crow, whose popularity whirled through the nation beginning in 1829, provided a welcome answer to the question of what was to be done with Blue's audacity and arrogance. Crow, as one bird to another, dragged down Long Tail Blue's perky feathers. Crow was not in the same class as Blue, who gloried in his plumage; Crow was a much commoner sort of bird, but he was the one to get the job done. By parodying Blue, being crooked instead of straight and rag-tag instead of debonair, Crow threw a crimp into Blue's style, arresting his upward movement. The next stage in the parodic counterattack to the effrontery of Long Tail Blue was reached in 1834, while Jackson was still president. Zip Coon, who also premiered in song and whose misshapen image decorated a cover sheet, finished the job of clipping Blue's wings, insuring that he would never again rise out of the ranks of meniality. If Crow served as the antithesis to Blue, Coon mixed their individual elements into a scoundrel composite, the gangling servant dressed in the master's clothes. Coon combined the original and its reverse into a mockery of the former.

Blue's handsome, dignified image, the epitome of rationality and reserve, reflected the situation for a sizable and growing segment of African

Americans, particularly in New York, in the beginning years of the nineteenth century; Blue emblematically expressed the assurance and achievement of this group. Through a process of gradual abolition begun in 1799,[8] the remaining percentage of the black population still enslaved in the state of New York achieved emancipation in July 1827.[9] Even before that point, psychologically slipping free of the shackles of slavery, many New York City blacks had made considerable and enviable progress socially, educationally, financially, and culturally, devoting their energies to developing and maintaining autonomous institutions, particularly independent churches, to secure their own welfare.

Industrious, and viewing education as a major exit leading out of their collective degradation, many black parents were able to send their children to an exceptional institution, the African Free School, established in what is now Greenwich Village in 1787 by the Manumission Society. In 1820, the school, which had given Ira Aldridge a taste for Shakespeare and the classics, could boast five hundred students.[10] Many of these students later became prominent in city politics, religion, and the abolitionist movement. The faculty included black teachers, although in at least one instance a black instructor was paid less than a white teacher when the skills of the latter clearly did not warrant such discrepant remuneration.[11]

This aggressive cultural nineteenth-century impetus within the African American community manifested itself early in the theatre. By its very nature, theatre is a collective enterprise, and its presence in a community suggests more than a minimum level of cultural cohesion. Approximately a year before the Denmark Vesey uprising in South Carolina, the African Grove Theatre was founded in New York during the 1821–1822 season. In a bower retreat filled with refreshment and culture of native hue, "flirting and chatter were carried on in direct imitation of white dandies and belles in the bigger gardens to which black people were not admitted."[12] In its initial production of an abbreviated *Richard III*, the Grove followed "the Elizabethan custom . . . of casting all the parts to men."[13] But that practice soon changed, and actresses became affiliated with the company. Located on the corner of Mercer and Bleecker Streets, the theatre also produced pantomimes and ballets and one of its stars, James Hewlett, emerged as a luminary. The theatre was closed for the first time in 1822, and the incident was reported in the *Advocate* for January 1822:

> It appears that the sable managers, not satisfied with a small share of profit and a great portion of fame, determined to rival the great Park Theatre . . . and accordingly hired the Hotel next door to the Theatre, where they announced their performances. The audiences were generally of a riotous character, and amused themselves by throwing crackers on the stage, and cracking their jokes with the actors, until danger from fire and civil discord rendered it necessary to break up

the establishment. The ebony colored wags were notified by the Police, that they must announce their last performance; but they, defying the public authority, went on and acted nightly . . . On Monday evening a dozen watchmen made part of the audience. The play was Richard . . . Several immediately ascended the stage and arrested his Majesty . . . and so forthwith Richard, Richmond, Lady Ann, the dead King Henry, Queen Elizabeth, and the two young Princes, were escorted, in their tinselled robes, to the watch-house . . . Finally, they pleaded so hard in black verse, and promised never to act Shakespeare again, that the Police Magistrates released them at a very late hour.[14]

That promise was soon broken. Their business interrupted by a short hiatus, the sable Shakespeareans resumed their commitment to the bard and were romping on the boards in *Othello* before 1822 ended. Surviving the yellow fever panic in the fall of 1822, the company produced *Tom and Jerry* in June 1823; the same show had been done at the Park Theatre several months prior. At the end of June, a two-night benefit was held for Mr. Brown, the theatre manager and a playwright, author of the *Drama of King Shotaway*.[15] Clearly, the company was experiencing questionable financial circumstances underscored by the interrogative contained in the bill:

Mr. Brown . . . for the first time, throws himself on the liberality of a generous public. Mr. Brown trusts that his unrelinquished exertions to please, will be justly considered by the Gentlemen and Ladies of this City, as on them depends his future support, and they can declare whether he is "To be—or not to be—That is the question?"[16]

Thereafter, Odell includes several references to James Hewlett, a prominent member of the African Grove who went solo and appeared in Brooklyn and at a theatre in Spruce Street during the 1825–26 season.[17] Billed as "Shakespeare's Proud Representative," Hewlett advertised himself as "the New York and London Coloured Comedian" who was saying farewell to his New York audiences before returning to London "to fill an engagement at the Cobourg [sic] Theatre."[18] Odell betrays a liking for the persistent Mr. Hewlett and devotes considerable ink and paper to a description:

He is of lighter color than ordinary mulattos. . . . His songs were excellent, and his style, taste, voice and action such as would have done credit to any stage. His imitations of Kean, Matthews, Phillips and others were recognized as correct, and evincing a nice discrimination and tact . . . which ought to recommend him to every lover of pure acting. Hewlett is yet young enough to receive some of the advantages of education, and we should advise him to persevere in the way his genius seems to direct.

Hewlett was back in town on September 16, 1826, when he once again made a farewell bow at the Grove Hotel.[19] Odell makes two more references to Hewlett, first where he appears as part of a variety bill thronged with acts at the New York Museum during the 1830–31 season and finally at a farewell benefit at Columbian Hall in September 1831, the same year as the Nat Turner Rebellion.

It is believed that Ira Aldridge, who became prominent as a Shakespearean actor on European stages from England to Russia, served his apprenticeship at the African Grove Theatre where he performed the role of Rolla in Kotzebue's *Pizzaro*.[20] It is instructive to compare Aldridge and Hewlett. Having made, perhaps, a few forays across the ocean, Hewlett seems to have been committed to making it in America, but his decision to expend his energies in his homeland did not stand him in nearly as good stead as Aldridge, who severed his ties with the land of his birth. Between the lines in the *Annals of the New York Stage*, we can envision the declining fortunes of James Hewlett, whose circumstances become worse and worse until he is packaged as one more oddity or curiosity on a packed bill at the New York Museum. Metaphorically, Hewlett, with all his promising potential, tumbles or is kicked off an ascending ladder and sent sprawling into dishevelment, emerging bruised, "crowed," and tattered. James Hewlett could easily serve as an emblem of the age, a microcosmic or individual example of the fate of aspiring African Americans, reaching, at an inauspicious time, like dandies aggressively desirous of breaking through the racial boundaries imposed on them in their native land.

On a site across the street from where the World Trade Center now juts into the sky, *Freedom's Journal*, the first black newspaper, was founded in New York in 1827. The paper's organizers were resolved to add a new, and as yet unheard, voice to the debate over slavery, particularly since many in the establishment media viewed the free black as anathema. One major offender was the *Enquirer's* Jewish editor, Mordecai M. Noah, who "deplored the thought of freedom for the slave," and was virulent in his journalistic attacks.[21] In addition, the editors of *Freedom's Journal* sought "to hook together by one solid chain, the whole free black population so as to make them think, and feel, and act, as one solid body, devoted to education and improvement."[22] John B. Russwurm, one of the paper's founders and a convert to colonization (a movement to send blacks back to Africa), was the third black college graduate in America,[23] having graduated from Bowdoin College in Maine in 1826. In 1829, Russwurm expatriated to Liberia where he edited the *Liberia Herald*, and Samuel E. Cornish, the other founder, a clergyman, published the newspaper on his own; he changed the name to *The Rights of All*, which reflected his constituency's long-held resolve to be included under the closing umbrella of the democratic promise.[24]

David Walker, a free black businessman who opened a clothing store on Brattle Street in Boston in 1827, became the Boston representative for *Freedom's Journal*. Two years later in 1829, the year Jackson was inaugurated as the seventh president,[25] Walker wrote and paid to publish an incendiary monograph, *Appeal to the Coloured Citizens of the World, but in particular, and very expressly, to those of the United States of America*, which helped to launch the abolition movement and served to reorient the rhetoric of those favoring as well as those opposed to the continuation of slavery.[26]

Previously, slavery had been depicted in political speeches, in the press, and on stage as a regrettable institution, a necessary evil; John Quincy Adams, for example, had wished that he could rid the nation of its stain and blight. But in the aftermath of Walker's written diatribe and Turner's attempted revolt, slavery was portrayed as essentially benevolent; blacks were incapable of self-government and needed the white man as paternal guide. As proof of slavery's inherent humanitarian platform, its adherents insisted that it even contained a liberal policy for the aged. Hence, the frequent later minstrel references to Old Uncle Ned, the beloved slave who lived contentedly to advanced age and was well cared for until the end. Slavery was good for niggers, the party line went, they would be lost without it. Niggers wouldn't be able to organize themselves, attend college, run businesses, write books, teach school, function successfully on other continents (with the exception of Africa, where, or course, they belonged), or establish newspapers if it weren't for slavery. Slavery was a boon for the slave. Slavery made slaves happy. Freedom wasn't good for niggers. They floundered directionlessly without the overseer in ready attendance to keep their toes on the road to responsibility. They were incapable of conducting their own affairs, bereft without the guidance of compassionate masters who knew what was best for them and considered their welfare an absolute priority. Slavery, they argued, was a godsend.

"Liberty has been to them the greatest of calamities, the heaviest of curses," Robert Hayne of South Carolina charged in 1830, the year David Walker was found murdered outside the business he owned. Hayne continued his diatribe:

> there does not exist, on the face of the earth a population so poor, so wretched, so vile, so loathsome, so utterly destitute of all the comforts, conveniences and decencies of life, as the unfortunate blacks of Philadelphia, New York, and Boston.[27]

Hayne was by no means alone in his wholesale denouncement of the free black population who, it was asserted, had done absolutely nothing to acquit themselves in the public eye. On the contrary, they were "notoriously ignorant, degraded and miserable, mentally diseased, brokenspirited, acted upon by no motive to honourable exertions, scarcely reached in their debasement by the heavenly light,"[28] and so to spare everyone in America further discomfort and possible contamination by their unavailing presence, the whole lot of them should be deported en masse to Africa; better to quarantine them there than let them roam, unleashed, around here. That opinion was printed, unapologetically, in the 1825 house journal of the American Colonization Society,[29] founded ten years before the publication of "Long Tail Blue."

The truth of the matter, if that indeed were the goal (and of course only a convenient truth was sought), was at great variance with this unilateral dismissal. In actuality, the free black population in Philadelphia and other northern cities could no longer be viewed as monochromatic or monolithic in either its appearance, social habits, living patterns or achievements.

> [B]lack society had become nearly as stratified as white society, was full of accomplished and aspiring individuals, and had established a wide array of neighborhood institutions. . . . Between a black elite, whose members lived in nearly every section of the city but were concentrated in Cedar Ward, and indigent souls confined in the penitentiary and alms house or huddled in crowded tenements on the city's northern and southern perimeters, black Philadelphians could be found at every point along the social spectrum.[30]

Mobility from within the lower ranks, it seems, was the crux of the problem. A black middle class (in some instances an upper middle class) was asserting itself in the 1820s, and the rapid rate at which too many had been able to organize themselves despite obstacles constituted a threat to be destabilized. Jim Crow emerged and achieved unprecedented popularity at a critical juncture. The growing economic and social potency in the ranks of the former servant class excited absolute fear in the minds of many whites, who felt that their hereditary privileges and prerogatives were being assaulted.

The dandy, symbolizing the unholy aspirations of this emergent group, was the favored target, the effigy of their unauthorized progress. Reprisals had to be taken. Denial, violence, ridicule, and finally exportation, it was decided, were the best weapons with which to retaliate.

> By the late 1820s, the elegant dress and hair styles of middle-class blacks at fancy balls drew the fire of white Philadelphians, who resented the status inversion symbolized by the arrival of black couples in coaches with white drivers and footmen. In 1828 white ruffians gathered on South Street outside a dancing assembly hall, where a black subscription ball was being held, and assaulted women as they stepped from coaches, insulting them, tearing their gowns, and throwing some guests into the gutter.[31]

Not surprisingly, local papers supported the mobocratic tactics, pointing a disapproving finger at the well-dressed blacks who dared to be driven to a social function by white coachmen:

> *Freedom's Journal* . . . widely read in Philadelphia, responded angrily . . . it condemned the behavior of white bullies and accused white Philadelphia editors

of calculated racism in describing the black partygoers as dressed as "Grandees, Princesses, Shepherdesses, and so on."[32]

The very same year, 1828, according to the S. Damon Foster songbook, Thomas Dartmouth Rice sang "Jim Crow." However, the third stanza of "Long Tail Blue," published the year before Rice's debut, begins with a reference to Jim Crow, who is the loser in a contest for the attentions of a "white gall" who goes by the name of Sue.

Unfortunately, I do not have the space to delve into issues of interracial congress and miscegenation between black men and white women in this chapter (suffice it to say that the "tail" in the title does not only refer to the length of one's coat), but Blue's mention of Crow does make it clear that Jim Crow was already a character with some repute in musical circles before 1828. By recognizing Crow as a rival, Blue unequivocally signals that Crow and Blue are alternatives to each other. The nonpareil popularity that Jim Crow engendered, I believe, indicates the degree to which the public was disturbed by Blue's class switching image. Blue and his obvious ambitions made people exceedingly uncomfortable, but Crow presented an effigy of the black male body reassuringly contained within the precinct of poverty and degradation. With Blue, the black body was designated by color, a difference occasioned by an increase of pigment, the result of environment. With Crow, the black body was depicted as essentially part of the animal kingdom, a separation sanctioned by nature, not just nurture.

Like Dandy Jim, Jim Crow dressed distinctively, but Crow wore motley patches and his toes showed through his shoes. Dandy Blue Jim, on the other hand, wore nothing but the best. The brim of his hat was neither too narrow nor too wide, his fashionable shoes gleamed, and the cloth of his coat was of obvious quality and a superior cut. If the white man wore the tattered clothes of a gnarled slave when singing and dancing Jim Crow, the black body took on the mannerisms and appearance of the white body in the persona of the dandy. Dandy Blue Jim emerged from the underclass and inserted himself into the milieu of wealth, aligning himself with the haves rather than the have-nots like Jim Crow. The Blue Dandy was a class outlaw; he affected an appearance that could never belong to him in an America based on his exclusion and subservience. He had to be taught a lesson. He had to be taught how to dress. He had to be taught that there was only one way for him to dress, and that one way was in rags.

An 1867 account, written by Robert P. Neven in the *Atlantic Monthly,* tells how, in Cincinnati, the commandingly tall Thomas Dartmouth Rice chanced on a peculiar singing, dancing, stagecoach-driving darky while he, Rice, was out walking. Engaged at a theatre in Pittsburgh, Rice left Cincinnati, but the memory of the song and dance stayed in his mind. Another darky named Cuff who worked as a porter on the docks and at a nearby Pittsburgh hotel struck Rice as peculiar because of the size of his mouth and the clothes he was wearing. Rice took Cuff with him to the theatre, installed him behind the scenes and later

> ordered Cuff to disrobe, and proceeded to invest himself in the cast-off apparel. When the arrangements were complete, the bell rang, and Rice, habited in an old coat forlornly dilapidated, with a pair of shoes composed equally of patches and places for patches on his feet, and wearing a coarse straw hat in a melancholy condition of rent and collapse over a dense black wig of matted moss, waddled into view. The extraordinary apparition produced an instant effect.[33]

Asserting absolute physical mastery and denying Cuff possession of his own belongings, Rice removed the garments from the back of a black worker in order to wrap himself in the requisite authenticity and also give the spectators a thrill. By denying the real in favor of the simulacrum, the copy that possesses less real value than the original, Rice privileged the simulated body over the actual. In the process, Rice also contributed to the grotesquification of the dandy image. Watching the incongruous gyrations and hearing the nonsense verse of this anomalous darkened body, the audience was sent into paroxysms of delight. Crow established the black male body as entitled to nothing, not even the clothes on his back or the products of his body, his song or his dance. Finally, the audience had an icon of the slavish, impoverished black body that eased their anxieties and satisfied their procrustean demands for the proper, canonical appearance of the impecunious, nonthreatening, grotesque, and peculiar black male body, a truly ridiculous figure. Through Jim Crow, the public triumphed over the class incursions of the Blue Dandy. The correct and necessary equilibrium between the races was re-established as Crow symbolically ripped Blue Dandy's coat, leaving it full of so many holes, no tailor could ever fix it again.

> Now it happened that, Cuff, who meanwhile was crouching in dishabille under concealment of a projecting *flat* behind the performer, by some means received intelligence, at this point, of the near approach of a steamer to the Monongahela Wharf. Between himself and others of his color in the same line of business, and especially as regarded a certain formidable competitor called Ginger, there existed an active rivalry in the baggage-carrying business. For Cuff to allow Ginger the advantage of an undisputed descent upon the luggage of the approaching vessel would be not only to forfeit all "considerations" from the passengers, but, by proving him a laggard in his calling, to cast a damaging blemish upon his reputation.[34]

Rice stripped Cuff of his clothes and his chances as a laboring man; that's exactly the impact of Crow's iconography on the group Cuff symbolized.

Re-establishing the politicized, *de rigueur* appearance of racialized bodies, Jim Crow confirmed a racial stereotype conferring power on the white masses while divesting the black. The denigrated (or should I say "nigrated") image of Jim Crow was transubstantiated into a replacement for reality, rendering those captured within the frame of the fiction visually incapable of disturbing the sanctity of the status quo. All was right with the world again. The nigger was in his place, back in his divinely ordained slot one peg below the bottom. Jim Crow cast the black male body as an image of derision, the butt of laughter rather than a vision of dignity, as Blue had been.

With Crow, the black body was symbolically eviscerated, put on view as a motley hull, transformed into a hollowed-out savage scarecrow with only the appearance and not the substance of the human. Through the very name of Crow, the black body was animalized, defined as a member of a subhuman species. Crow made materially evident, through the ludicrousness of the clothes and dance, the excommunication of the black body outside humanity's gates. By virtue of his grotesque angularity and the simian curl of his fingers, Crow and his racial dominions were trivialized, deported outside the realm of Homo Erectus. They did not stand upright, a fundamental human requirement. Crow iconographically confirmed the chattelization or demotion of the black body, an attitude that would find legal sanction in the 1857 Dred Scott decision that decreed that black bodies were only fractionally human.

But it is in the 1830s that the next chapter in the evolution of the dark dandy occurs. According to T. Allston Brown, George Washington Dixon "sang his prize extravaganza 'Zip Coon'" on the stage of the Arch Street Theatre on June 19, 1834.[35] The S. Foster Damon songbook agrees that "Zip Coon" was first performed and published in 1834, but in that reference (with George Odell indicated as a source), it is Bob Farrell who is credited with introducing the song. The date ascribed to Farrell, however, postdates the recorded time of Dixon's Philadelphia appearance:

> "Zip Coon," judged by longevity, was the most successful of the early burnt-cork songs. It was sung by Bob Farrell "from the Southern Theatres" in the Bowery Theatre, New York on August 11, 1834. . . . Bob Farrell claimed, and is usually credited with, the authorship of this song, although George Washington Dixon, who also featured it, insisted that it was his. Whichever was right, it was probably adapted and developed from some long-lost negro original.[36]

In the first stanza, Zip Coon emphatically announces that he is an erudite scholar, obviously caricaturing the ability of blacks to write books such as the one written by David Walker. Coon sings three times "O ole Zip Coon he is a larned skoler." The extent of his learning is that he can sing "Possum Up a Gum Tree" and other such melodies. His other talent is being able to jump over "dubble trubble." Like Dandy Blue and Jim Crow before him, Old Zip is irresistible to women, or so he believes.

More importantly, Zip possesses an exalted sense of entitlement, which only proves his utter madness, and so he entertains unjustifiably high political aspirations. The lyrics of the fourth, fifth, and sixth verses of the song, as printed in the S. Foster Damon songbook, reveal that Old Zip Coon, the master of merriment, has presidential ambitions. Old Zip feels he can set the country straight with his second in command, Davy Crockett. He's convinced that a coon on top is all the nation needs:

> I tell you what will happin den, now bery soon,
> De Nited States Bank will be blone to de moon;
> Dare General Jackson will him lampoon,
> An de bery nex President will be Zip Coon.
>
> An wen Zip Coon our President shall be
> He makes all de little Coons sing possum up a tree;
> Oh how de little Coons will dance an sing
> Wen he tie dare tails togedder cross de lindey swing.
>
> Now mind wat you arter, your tarnel kritter Crocket,
> You shant go head without Zip, he is de boy to block it
> Zip shall be President, Crockett shall be vice,
> An den dey two togedder, will had de tings nice.

Boasting that he would split in two and eat raw without any salt any man who wasn't for Jackson, Davy Crockett emerged from the hills of Tennessee in 1827, the same year that Long Tail Blue made his first public appearance. Crockett quickly became a national hero, a kind of homegrown Superman, bigger-than-life symbol of the rugged individual who single-handedly roped and harnessed the wild west. In those days, Tennessee was still considered the west. By eliminating the dark savages, pushing them off their lands, Crockett made the territory habitable for decent, law-abiding white folks and their Christian families. Crockett also presided over Coon, and Coon's lyrical attempts to establish his superiority were all the more ridiculous because the audience knew for sure which one was the master and which the slave. Coon's extravagant pretensions were not disturbing in the least, just laughable.

Juxtaposing the minstrel images of Long Tail Blue, Jim Crow, and Zip Coon reveals how the pattern of black grotesquification which Rice popularized continued with "Zip Coon." With Coon, the image of the stately and affluent black male is deformed or "crowed." Long Tail Blue is all straight lines and formality. Irregularity could be Crow's middle name; nothing about him is regular. His angles are askew, contorted. The iconography of Zip Coon is intermediate between Long Tail Blue and Jim

Crow. Coon's clothes are better in quality and style than Crow's, but his stance is almost as irregular. Unlike Long Tail Blue, the complementary clowns Crow and Coon belong to the brutish continuum. The alliterative twins fit into the lower tiers of the bestial topiary. Long Tail Blue's sobriquet connotes more inherent dignity than either Crow or Coon, both considered base animals.

Two months after Dixon's appearance at the Arch Street Theatre, a riot erupted in Philadelphia:

> In August 1834, a mob of white Philadelphians launched a massive three-day attack on a nearby black community. This riot, the first in a series of such anti-black incidents in Philadelphia, was finally quelled by some 300 special constables and militia. However, before peace was restored, one black church had been destroyed, another defaced, and scores of black people had been injured, at least one fatally so.
>
> . . . [O]ne of the targets of the 1834 rioters, in the early stages of the riot when choice of targets appears to have been most selective, was the son of wealthy black Philadelphian James Forten, owner of a country estate and a carriage—and several rental properties occupied by less well-off whites.
>
> . . . An additional indication that the better-off blacks made more appealing targets is to be found in the fact that of the more than three dozen houses destroyed in the second night of this rioting, many were "substantial brick ones," from which fine furniture was thrown into the streets and destroyed, while many more easily destroyed frame houses, owned by blacks in the same streets, were left untouched.
>
> These choices of targets suggest resentment of the "have nots" specifically against the "haves." . . . Similar insight may be drawn from the descriptions of the kinds of people who were assaulted in the 1834 riot. Contemporaries expressed some outrage that the mob attacked "old, confiding, and unoffending" blacks. Yet this outrage is more comprehensible if one substitutes the words "middle-aged, respectable, and hardworking" for the description of these victims, one of whom was reportedly a one-time servant of George Washington. It then begins to appear that individuals, groups, and property which represented economic and social "success" and "respectability" were prime targets for rioters' resentments.[37]

Of course the claim is not being made that chronology equals causality. But the closeness in date between Dixon's portrayal of Zip Coon and the outbreak of mob violence is worth note. The intensity of the riot and the choice of scapegoats toward whom the rioters chose to direct their assaults can be seen as a measure of the animosity white Philadelphians harbored against privileged blacks. This same enmity undergirded the popularity of Zip Coon, who converted the respectability of Long Tail Blue into an outrageous and blasphemous black buffoon.

An ineradicable enmity against well-to-do blacks is expressed in *Old Zip Coon*, "an Ethiopian Eccentricity in One Scene," which appears in Gary Engle's anthology of minstrel sketches, *This Grotesque Essence.* Engle's introduction follows:

The song "Zip Coon" (known today in instrumental form as "Turkey in the Straw") can be thought of as the epitome of nineteenth-century American popular music. Published in 1834, the song quickly became associated with the figure of the minstrel clown and was used innumerable times as a solo, a dance vehicle, and as the musical number around which minstrel finales were built. The following piece cannot be dated with complete accuracy. The playbook form was copyrighted in 1874, but there is neither cast nor production information available which could help to date the first performance of the piece.

Of particular interest in *Old Zip Coon* are the elements associated with Reconstruction attitudes. The sentimentalized plantation setting is typical of post-Civil War nostalgia, and the jokes created by the inversion of the antebellum social hierarchy illustrate the inherent racism of minstrelsy in its most vicious form. The following text is reprinted from the acting edition published by the Happy Hours Company in 1874.[38]

The playlet is a four-character courtship farce. Actually, there are five characters, but Zip's white butler never speaks. Sal, Zip's daughter, studies Italian opera, and is represented as an accomplished woman whose achievements are at best meager. She massacres the Italian she hears, and her assimilated beauty is peculiar. Her face is divided right down the middle, one side white and the other black. Cuff Cudlip, who is dressed in rags, is her suitor but doesn't appear suitable. Evidently short on resources, he enters carrying a bundle on his shoulders. These outlandish blacks are portrayed as supremely ridiculous and out of place. Zip especially yearns for the good old days when he was a slave on the plantation and didn't have to worry about maintaining an aura of dignity. The perception that blacks are inherently lazy and good-for-nothing drunkards is still in evidence. Zip spends his days sipping mint juleps and admonishes Cuff when he asks for a job, "You wouldn't degrade you'self by workin', would you? Well, go out dere among de white trash, den."[39] *Old Zip Coon*, which begins on the verandah of Old Plantation, demonstrates another consanguineous connection between Crow and Coon. Both operate as figments and fixtures of the nostalgic plantation genre. Long Tail Blue's milieu, however, is urban instead of agrarian. The grotesque and ridiculous image of the caricatured black dandy who has an aversion to a respectable job and was much better off in the days of old under slavery took firm hold in the machinations of Crow and Coon, supplanting the more civilized decorum of Long Tail Blue.

Notes

1. Unpaginated commentary in the S. Foster Damon songbook, *Series of Old American Songs* (Providence: Brown University Library, 1936).

2. T. Allston Brown, *A History of the New York Stage From the First Performance in 1732 to 1901* (New York: Dodd, Mead & Co., 1903), Vol. I, 99–100.

3. Charles H. Day, *Fun in Black; or, Sketches of Minstrel Life* (New York: The DeWitt Publishing House, 1874), 6.

4. "[W]e may tire of him before his final departure." George Odell, *Annals of the New York Stage* (New York: AMS Press, 1970 [c. 1927–1949]), Vol. III, 354.

5. In the first chapter of his book on the Jacksonian era, Schlesinger rates Dixon as a minstrel pioneer, calling him "first of the great black-face artists." Schlesinger mentions Dixon, who was appearing at the Amphitheatre in Washington, as one of the major attractions during Jackson's inaugural festivities. Arthur Schlesinger, *The Age of Jackson* (Boston: Little, Brown, 1945), 4.

6. "The family was of upper yeoman background. His father, the first Adams to become president, was also the first to attend Harvard College. College education, bringing within reach an upwardly mobile marriage to Abigail Qunicy, established John Adams as a young lawyer at the start of the great controversy with England." Alexander Saxton, *The Rise and Fall of the White Republic: Class Politics and Mass Culture in Nineteenth-Century America* (London: Verso, 1990), 33.

7. Ibid., 95.

8. "By 1810 only 16.2% of a . . . black population of 8,918 were still enslaved and New York had become the largest center of free blacks in America." Shane White, "A Question of Style: Blacks in and around New York City in the Late 18th Century," *Journal of American Folklore* 102.1 (1989):24.

9. To be exact, the date was July 4, 1827, although the celebratory parades were not held until July 5 because the Fourth fell on a Sunday that year. "Most of the local newspapers made no mention. . . . An upstate paper, the *Albany Argus and City Gazette* alone, on the morning of the Fourth, printed Governor Tompkins' message, carrying out the act and calling for state-wide emancipation." Roi Ottley and William Weatherby, editors, *The Negro in New York: An Informal Social History, 1626–1940* (New York: Praeger, 1969), 74.

10. *The African American Encyclopedia* (New York: Marshall Cavendish, 1993), Vol. I, 22.

11. Ottley, 63–64.

12. Odell, Vol. III, 35.

13. Ibid., 35.

14. Ibid., 36.

15. Ibid., 71.

16. Ibid., 71.

17. Ibid., 224.

18. Ibid., 228.

19. Ibid., 293.

20. *African American Encyclopedia,* Vol. I, 46.

21. Roland E. Wolseley, *The Black Press, U.S.A.* (Ames: Iowa University Press, 1971), 18.

22. Ottley, 89–90.

23. Jessie Carney-Smith, editor, *Black Firsts* (Detroit: Visible Ink Press, 1994), 88.

24. "In 1800 the three most common surnames—Johnson, Williams, and Thomas—accounted for 8.1% of the names of all free blacks. In 1810 the top three—Johnson, Williams, and Smith—accounted for nearly 11% of all the black names listed in the census. In fact, in 1810 4.5%, or about 1 in 22, of all the heads of free black households had the surname Johnson. Such names were also common among the white population, but to nowhere near the same extent. The

use of such surnames probably reflected, in part, the desire for anonymity prevalent among many ex-slaves, a desire that had helped draw rural blacks to the metropolis. In their choice of names most New York blacks indicated, quite realistically, that their hopes and aspirations, and particularly their desire to be free, were conceived within the framework of a white world." White, 29.

25. "Jacksonians showed on the whole even more distaste for the black population than did the . . . colonizationists." George Fredrickson, *The Black Image in the White Mind: The Debate on Afro-American Character and Destiny, 1817–1914* (Middletown, Conn.: Wesleyan University Press, 1987), 26.

26. "Ushering in the critical decade of the antislavery fight, Walker's *Appeal* marked the transition from the gentle persuasion of the Quakers to the militant crusading of Garrison and Weld, the activism of James G. Birney, the martyrdom of Elijah Lovejoy and John Brown, and the ultimate political triumph of Lincoln. In January 1831, Garrison began publication of the *Liberator* (in which he promptly reprinted most of Walker's work, despite his earlier disapprobation). Then in August of that year, came Nat Turner's rebellion in Virginia, which to the now hypersensitive South was directly traceable to Garrison and Walker." Charles M. Wiltse, ed., *David Walker's Appeal to the Coloured Citizens of the World* (New York: Hill and Wang, 1965), xi.

27. Gary B. Nash, *Forging Freedom: The Formation of Philadelphia's Black Community, 1720–1840* (Cambridge: Harvard University Press, 1988), 246.

28. Ibid., 246–47.

29. "The new colonization movement, which began with the founding of the American Colonization Society in 1817, was in many respects typical of the benevolent movements which burgeoned between the War of 1812 and the late 1820s. Like the American Education Society, the Home Missionary Society, the American Bible Society, and the American Temperance Society, it developed as part of a conservative response to a changing social situation, drawing most of its initial inspiration and support from two interrelated groups—the Protestant clergy of the major 'evangelical' denominations and the adherents of the declining Federalist Party." Fredrickson, 6.

30. Nash, 247 and 250.

31. Ibid., 254.

32. Ibid.

33. Robert P. Neven, "Stephen C. Foster and Negro Minstrelsy," *Atlantic Monthly*, XX (1867):609.

34. Ibid.

35. T. Allston Brown, *History of the American Stage Containing Biographical Sketches of Nearly Every Member of the Profession That Has Appeared On the American Stage, from 1733 to 1870* (New York: Burt Franklin, 1969 Reprint), 101.

36. Unpaginated commentary following the lyrics of "Zip Coon" in the S. Foster Damon songbook.

37. Emma Jones Lapsansky, "'Since They Got Those Separate Churches': Afro-Americans and Racism in Jacksonian Philadelphia," *American Quarterly* 37.1 (1980):54, 63, and 64.

38. Gary D. Engle, *This Grotesque Essence: Plays from the American Minstrel Stage* (Baton Rouge: Louisiana State University Press, 1978), 50.

39. Ibid., 52.

CONTINUUM

Ebery Time I Wheel About I Jump Jim Crow: Cycles of Minstrel Transgression from Cool White to Vanilla Ice

W. T. Lhamon, Jr.

The construction of cross-racial selves for fun and profit has a much longer and more involved history in this country than we often stop to realize. Well before the War of Independence, early black insouciants were flaunting their mimicry of white behavior in folk frolics seldom reported by their owners.[1] And white imitators of black culture were blacking up in eighteenth-century traveling circuses and other low-dignity troupes long before Daddy Rice's jumping Jim Crow began to formalize blackface minstrelsy in the early 1830s. What is generally thought of as the formal minstrel show—with interlocutor and endmen, first part, olio, and walkaround—underwent a craze curve of interest that peaked in the decades on both sides of the Civil War. During that heyday, fantasizing the black self became the most popular form of entertainment in this country, from saloon stages to the White House.

Then, as the nineteenth century deliquesced well into the twentieth, minstrelsy's achievements underwent a long seeping into other genres. *Uncle Tom's Cabin* was a sponge of minstrel business, from Sam and Andy to Liza crossing the icy Ohio and Topsy turning somersaults. Contrary to the consensus, Stowe did not bequeath these images to the minstrel stage; rather, she palmed many of her most powerful images from it. Then minstrelsy reclaimed its images once again. Fiction such as Melville's apparently postmodern *The Confidence Man* and Twain's great late novel of the doubled self, *Pudd'nhead Wilson*, in fact lifted many of their most radical elements from minstrelsy when they absorbed its costuming, vernacular, and stock figures. But what Melville and Twain most beneficially learned from minstrelsy was its structural indeterminacy and improvisation, as well as its insistence on a self that was complexly constituted from a mixed gender, class, and racial sourcepool.

Because these elements contributing to cut and crossed consciousness are usually described as diagnostic of experimental practice, contributed to literature from vanguard painting or philosophy, it is important to see that a popular lore worked out in the marketplace made these properties available to the likes of Twain and Melville. They were using strategies of survival that popular lore evolved to please its public. The American Renaissance writers came "territorially late" to the grounds that vernacular performers had long since colonized.[2]

Minstrelsy also instigated several new forms, such as tap dance and the musical theater (*In Dahomey* to *Show Boat* to *Ain't Misbehavin'*). And it was present at the creation of Vesuvian changes in film (*The Jazz Singer*), and jazz (Ma Rainey, Ida Cox, Bessie Smith, even Ornette Coleman all traveled in late minstrel shows). What's more, such twists on pop music as rock 'n' roll and, most recently of all, rap and hiphop are inconceivable without the minstrel paradigm.

Those are quick highlights in the history of white mimicry of black carnivalesque. But let's go back to the beginning of the cycle, again, abstracting its features more closely. Before the Revolution, black slaves were dressing as white, and white colonists were dressing as black, each "putting on" the other's characteristics. These parodies were at the gestural level of folk practice. Why did they grow?

There are good reasons why cross-racial folk mimicry pushed into professional practice at particular moments, beginning in the 1830s. That's when tens of thousands of runaway slaves passed through border and Northern cities and many merchant abolitionists were accused of promoting amalgamation. This perceived aggression in the abolitionist movement upset the liberal–conservative alliance for African colonization and culminated in such violence as the 1834 riot in New York City.

Blackface minstrelsy responded to these anxieties quite distinctly—not by attacking but by *enacting* miscegenation. Minstrels worked out ways to flash white skin beneath a layer of burnt cork, stage the pastiche grammar of a creole dialect, and recast traditional Irish melodies with fantasy images of fieldhand fun shadowed by violence and dislocation. As fear and fascination grew apace in different parts of a newly urban audience, so did the minstrel show, all the while compacting and compounding its motivating images.

By any measure, blackface minstrelsy was a much more complex attempt to understand racial mixing and accommodate audiences to it than was either abolitionist propaganda or its counter riots. Minstrelsy was a popular form that at its outset played to middle-class boys not yet come into property and, more importantly, to the vast and rapidly changing population of working-class youths swarming through the

American cities from the 1830s until well after the Civil War. This heterogeneous swarm from the countryside and from abroad was a major boon for entrepreneurial manufacturers recruiting cheap labor to do their piecework. But controlling these unsocialized workers' off-hours was a new problem calling forth various solutions.

When artisans had taught their trade to apprentices living in the family household, they dispersed social control through the society, and at least in theory transmitted values stably. The rise of factories destroyed the artisan/apprentice bond, however, and "the unparalleled movement of young people, especially young men, to the cities [in the late 1840s and 1850s] . . . to find work" made worried merchants realize they needed new forms of control. Along with their factories, therefore, merchants instituted libraries, the YMCA, and publication of self-help pamphlets as ways to channel youths constructively.[3]

Thus the beginning of the push and pull to control the emerging youth culture coincided with the breakdown of the apprentice tradition, the growth of factories and sweatshops, a transportation revolution that was shifting the most mobile sectors of the rural population to cities, a burgeoning number of runaway slaves, the recession of the early 1830s, the depression at the end of the decade, and the abolitionist critique of the colonization consensus.[4] Youths were of course no more accepting of external control in the early nineteenth century than they are in the late twentieth. As now, youths worried then about how to represent their overwhelming social forces to themselves. The minstrel show was their form countering the channeling merchants imposed.

The minstrel show belonged to this first youth culture in the United States. It was one development they themselves could shape with their patronage, for what youths did not pay to see did not remain in the nightly posted theatre bills. Minstrels kept close tabs on their gate receipts and changed the skits and patter to keep the sales high. In summary, the minstrel show was the first among many later manifestations, nearly always allied with images of black culture, that allowed youths to resist merchant-defined external impostures.

The way this initial youth culture enlisted images of African American culture in its behalf and then bequeathed its strategy to successive waves of youth culture, up through our own time, is an important part of what the standard analysis of American minstrelsy has missed. White youths in the 1830s were shaping the minstrel show as a way of resisting merchant control. Deprecation of blacks was low on their agenda. Rather, their blackface costuming, their songs and dances were a way of abstracting their own victimization. Abstracting themselves as blacks allowed their heterogeneous parts all access to the same identification. Irish, German, and English recent immigrants, as well as American rustics, could all identify with Tambo and Bones together in ways they could not with other forms of American theater hypostatizing upper-class, English, or other specific ethnic figures.

In early blackface minstrelsy, that of the entr'acte dances and the initial narrative skits, white working youths, many of them Irish immigrants like a portion of their audiences, were identifying with blacks as representations of all that the YMCAs and evangelical organizers were working to suppress. That their songs were inaccurate pictures of African American culture is not the point. We can debate how much or little minstrels were trying to copy black culture until the cows come home. But no matter how racist the resultant crude stereotypes became, we must neither miss nor forget the less obvious uses that youths then made of the material. They were flaunting their affection for these signs of akimbo insurrection against the conventions of control. They were on the side of the spontaneous Tambo and Bones rather than that of the interlocutor, whose correct speech and elaborate attire represented mercantile conventions. It was no accident that the interlocutor began every show addressing the endmen with the exasperated dictum: "Gentlemen, be seated!" From beginning to end, the minstrel show was a struggle over the settlement of youth's chaotic energy, in which youth projected themselves as blacks in order at least in part to rouse and engage the hypocrisies of their fundamentalist opponents.

It was not long before the economy of presenting minstrel theatre reversed the engagement, of course. As minstrelsy gathered momentum, gathered stereotypes, and gathered power, it expanded its public beyond the youth culture. That's when entrepreneurial control absorbed and damped the implicit critique youths in blackface were making of mercantile style. A similar process occurred as conservative forces diluted, reflected, and defused radical labor organizations.[5] But there was a difference: labor organizing and its exhortatory spirit depended on institutions and ideas that were concretely present. Sideways progress and indirection did not work in that sphere. Cultural imagery works differently, however, and so does cultural influence. When the minstrel's insurgent identity with the black Other seemed to be contained, it was still present in fact, but encoded and laying low. Apparently controlled and debased, it was nevertheless working autonomously.

What very rapidly evolved, shortly after the first full minstrel shows in the winter of 1842–43, was a profoundly ambiguous "supplementary rite," to use Ralph Ellison's term,[6] in which established Americans tried to seat their upstart youth in fixed positions symbolized by the happy plantations of Old Virginny. And youths impersonating uppity blacks resisted as well as settled into these stereotypes. They sometimes sang how they longed to be back in Dixie or under Ol' Massa's care, but there they were, a long ways away. Every time they mentioned the old *home*, they rhymed it with *roam*, thus displaying how far they had gone.

The minstrel show came into being along with the anti-abolitionist riots and referred to many of the same issues. But the minstrel shows were equatable neither to the riots nor to their abolitionist targets. The argument between abolitionists and their hostile opponents was a mature and middle-class dispute, as others have shown and I will summarize, external to minstrel performers and their public. Minstrels served a class and peer group, largely distinct, and it is no accident that middle-class mothers, like the mother of young Samuel Clemens, quite ineffectually forbade their boys to attend the shows.[7] Minstrels and their youth culture public were aware of the anti-abolitionist violence, of course, as they mediated among the conflicting social forces of the day. But the way blackface minstrels negotiated the pressures, and represented them, conveyed the powerlessness of their public's position. These unmoored youths could not effect liberation any more than they could enforce slavery. But they would have to suffer the consequences of whatever the power brokers decided. They would be the soldiers in the trenches, it turned out, when the argument turned from push to shove at Fort Sumter and after.

That's why the tone of minstrel conundrums and humorous songs is wry, for the most part, distant from fame even while the actions are vital and passionate, the pratfalls violent, the pace headlong. In these skits, young men are working out their take on large forces rushing toward disaster. *They*, if no other public actors until Stowe, Melville, Twain, and Winslow Homer, see the issues from several angles at once. They laugh *and* hurt. The service of the minstrel show was hardly to resolve a simple image of slaves. Rather, it abstracted an image of opposites in compound suspension. And minstrelsy held them there, in dynamic irresolution, adjusting and negotiating the stresses for more than half a century while it possessed the popular stage.

The anti-abolition riots were both instigated and manned by middle-class "lawyers, politicians, merchants, shopkeepers, and bankers,"[8] established men who thought they were defending their property as their daughters. These "gentlemen of property and standing" rioted in city after city—Philadelphia, Canterbury, Connecticut, Cincinnati repeatedly, Utica, and New York, among many others. They lynched blacks, killed abolitionists and ran them out of town. They burned down public buildings. They passed laws gagging abolitionism. They inhibited the influx of free blacks. Their violence and the pressure it documents are a context necessary to remember as one considers the invention of the minstrel show. Under that pressure, the circus clown's bit part impersonating a Negro had first become a gradually formalizing entr'acte. Then it mushroomed into a whole night's entertainment as the "Ethiopian delineators" subdivided their roles. Instead of parenthetically constructing black images between other concerns, that is, not yet empowered American youths began to fill out, as it were, an entire sentence.

Minstrelsy in its early decades was a staging among marginal youth of the social pressures bearing down on them. They were rehearsing forms of their hopes and fears about whites and blacks merging. "Jim Crow is courting a white gall," sang George Washington Dixon and Daddy Rice. Every burnt-cork minstrel who followed them knew the rest of the words: "And yaller folks call her Sue; / I guess she backed a nigger out, / And swung my long tail blue."[9] These two dozen words of a dance tune position the audience as oscillating back and forth across the many social boundaries minstrelsy transgressed. A white performer inhabiting a black role has denigrated a black brother before a white audience; a black man is boasting of his yellow status; an urban dandy is delighting in besting a rube. That the rube, Jim Crow, is called a "nigger," and that Sue is seeing the singer on the sly encourage the white audience to identify with the cross-racial singer. A white/black man has a white woman swinging his blue tail. But his delight is short-lived because, like the youths in his audience, he is soon caught and beaten by the law: "As I was going up Fulton Street, / I holler'd arter Sue, / The watchman came and took me up, / And spoil'd my long tail blue."[10]

In blackface minstrelsy America's first youth culture tried out miscegenation. Although they sang that they were policed and caught in their transgressions, they survived and persisted in their crossings, night after night for over half a century. The song's swamp of racial nuances, of challenges as well as complicities, shows the many meanings of the minstrel rite as youths enacted it. It was not ever any one thing, nor did it ever have any one effect.

Now leap forward a century. Leap over the Civil War, Reconstruction, and the nadir period with its birth of the blues. Leap the Jazz Age and Harlem Renaissance. Skip for a moment Swing and Bop, and the World Wars. Alight on the 1950s, when amalgamation anxiety was again on the land. In mid-decade a clutch of factors caused the Supreme Court to order desegregation of the schools, once again rousing fears of race mixing, and not only in the South. A further key similarity between the years before the Civil War and those after World War II was the resurgence of youths with unaccustomed leisure. Their renewed visibility spurred the consequent struggle to control them once more. With this return of comparable historical conditions, bunches of white boys singing black songs and giving them the black vernacular name of rock 'n' roll went national from their southern nest. Increasingly, then, the whole nation again rehearsed in song and dance an integrated cultural performance that stayed predominantly black at bottom through the next forty years. You had to go back to the heyday of blackface minstrelsy to find black cultural codes so eagerly and so widely celebrated in American song and dance as in the full-scale emulation that rock 'n' roll constituted.

The surfacing of rock 'n' roll in the 1950s was the largest professional (re)turn of the minstrel lore cycle. It required not only the return of solicitous historical conditions, but also maintenance of the lore during lulls between surges in the rhythm. Folklorists call one version of this process "tale maintenance," and I want to apply the concept in a larger sense. *Lore maintenance* names the phase of persistence between the surges that periodically propel cultural patterns onto public stages. The interval between the mid-nineteenth and mid-twentieth centuries is in fact full of this low-level persistence of folk cross-racial play that prepares for professional flare-ups of evident minstrelsy.

At issue in lore maintenance is the phenomenon of cultural transmission. How do the conventions, gestures, tropes, and images early in a lore cycle survive as seeds to ripen in a subsequent stage of its cycle? In the case of the minstrel lore cycle, I would point to the amateur minstrel show as fund raiser for church, school, and clubs; to the retirement of minstrel banter to the realm of the street joke; to the oozing of minstrel songs back into campfire and hearthside festivity. Nor should we forget professional spin-offs from the main tradition. For instance, nearly all vernacular American dance derives from African American gestures that black William Henry Lane, dancing as Master Juba, and other minstrel performers spread all across the land (and took to England). Also, significant professional performance traditions such as tap were at first part of minstrelsy before they circled free into their own category with their own autonomous momentum. When the large professional minstrel show collapsed at the turn of the century, therefore, it did not die, but dispersed its elements.

Whites playing at being black and blacks playing at being white have thus continually redrawn the longest lasting and the most expressive meeting ground of American life. No other figure of American folklore has even come close to the perennial fascination of the Long-Tail'd Blue—as early minstrels tellingly costumed him and Constance Rourke enduringly named him.[11] There have been Jonathan the New England peddler, Mike Fink and his cohort of Mississippi Valley Gamecocks, B'howery B'hoys rioting at Astor Place, Cowboys and their outlaw compadres. Moreover, each new stage of the frontier and of technology generated popular figures—from steamboat roustabouts to private eyes, motorcycle gangs to rocketeers. But all these have come and gone as figures that tweak the tabloid imagination, thrive awhile in lore, then dwindle to cartoon figures for Disney and the Golden Books.

Only the constructed black figure—what Flannery O'Connor termed "The Artificial Nigger"—has remained constantly lively, still menacing beneath all his sculpted grins. He, rarely she, has stayed liminal and transgressive through every attempt to tame him, metamorphosing from his long coat and striped trousers through the calico collars of Mark Twain's memory, to the harem baggies on video rappers today. Today the stylized contortions of Vanilla Ice still try to haul back from beyond the pale some of that fancied black energy that Cool White, one of the earliest minstrel performers, was after over a hundred and fifty years ago.

These phenomenal stages are deeply and rhythmically related. What holds together the many phenomena of minstrelsy is a cycle of perilously licensed transgression that helps the culture negotiate among its many parts. Minstrelsy in its broad sense has proved to be the secular ritual by which the ever-emerging compact of the Atlantic world has imagined and kept intact a querying, dialogic self. At each surge of minstrel behavior—from the 1830s to the 1880s, again in the Jazz Age 1920s, rocking 1950s, rapping 1980s, and hiphopping '90s—there is always an initial period of fascination and affirmation. Only after it has served its several salutary functions does the dominant representation of blacks then predictably degrade into abusive travesty.

For reasons additional to accuracy, there are advantages to assembling for analysis the phases of white mimicry of black culture. Knowing that any given phase is neither forever nor unprecedented, for instance, saves some of the embarrassment of making naive claims about its virtues or failings. Moreover, when the phases are strung together as I have tried to do here, they provide a paradigm that helps predict the general rise and fall of subcycles. Likewise, when there is deviation from the model then the cycle suggests ways to analyze the deviance. With rap, for instance, what has been most remarkable is the way black youths have retained control of the images the form presents. The Beastie Boys and Vanilla Ice, and the few other white rappers, remain exceptions that prove the form's control by black youths. Black youths now play the race roles professionally without blackface but with all the other long-acquired inversive implications, raising the metalore to the fore. Thus, at one recent moment NWA called their top-selling record "Niggaz4Life," printed in mirror inversion, and the group's members called themselves "professional niggers." And perhaps the best example during that moment was Public Enemy's video, "Can't Truss It," with its multiple narratives, with its same actors in varying historical periods swapping foreground and background, proceeding simultaneously through violence and rape, betrayal and complicity, slavery and industrial factory, confrontation and masked evasion. If groups like Public Enemy and television shows like "Yo! MTV Raps" were to continue in high visibility, then we might draw a novel conclusion. Black culture will have persisted, rising within minstrelsy and regaining control of its moot, root images (but not of their broadcasting). Certainly, black youths are now manipulating their own self-definition, and the legacy of minstrelsy as well. They have reclaimed from white control the power of racial definition as both white and black minstrels in blackface took back their vernacular images from Harriet Beecher Stowe and the novel over a century ago.

In other transgressive chapters of American lore, cowboys and European ethnics, for instance, posed their challenges and were absorbed. At the other end of the spectrum, as in the case of the once-indigenous peoples, far worse fates were available. The cycle of minstrel transgression that seemed to extend from Cool White in the 1840s to Vanilla Ice a century and a half later has, however, turned out to be an interlude of white control. That interlude arose from black folk play, which black youths are now reclaiming. The white interlude continually saw to it that the images stayed compacted in dynamic irresolution. This tension not only has ensured the longevity of the minstrel cycle, but also has most importantly provided what passed for unity in the United States. This reclaiming of black tropes and the conventions of their presentation display a precise measure of (the limits of) black cultural enfranchisement in the Atlantic world.

When we in cultural studies still professed transcendence, we used to call it the melting pot. But, as the bumper sticker says, in melting pots the scum rises to the top and those on the bottom get burned. So we don't believe in melting pots these days. Nor need we. The cycle of minstrel transgression suggests that what holds us together is no unified sameness but our lore's continual re-imagining of ways to represent interrogatory relation. The best reason to assemble the elements of the minstrel cycle is to see it periodically screening the country's deepest differences, all the while recomposing how its participants might stay different together.

Notes

1. Hennig Cohen, "A Negro 'Folk Game' in Colonial South Carolina," *Southern Folklore Quarterly* 16 (1952): 183–84.

2. Philip Fisher, *Hard Facts: Setting and Form in the American Novel* (New York: Oxford University Press, 1987), p. 20.

3. Allan Stanley Horlick, *Country Boys and Merchant Princes: The Social Control of Young Men in New York* (Lewisburg, Pa.: Bucknell University Press, 1975), 11.

4. Carroll Smith-Rosenberg, "Bourgeois Discourse and the Age of Jackson: An Introduction," in *Disorderly Conduct: Visions of Gender in Victorian America* (New York: Knopf, 1985), pp. 79–89.

5. Among many others, see Sean Wilentz, *Chants Democratic: New York City & the Rise of the American Working Class, 1788–1850* (New York: Oxford University Press, 1984); Allan Stanley Horlick, *Country Boys and Merchant Princes: The Social Control of Young Men in New York* (Lewisburg: Bucknell University Press, 1975); Bruce Laurie, *Working People of Philadelphia, 1800–1850* (Philadelphia: Temple University Press, 1980); and Susan E. Hirsch, *Roots of the American Working Class: The Industrialization of Crafts in Newark, 1800–1860* (Philadelphia: University of Pennsylvania Press, 1978).

6. Ralph Ellison, "On Initiation Rites and Power," *Going to the Territory* (New York: Random House, 1986), 50.

7. For Twain's account of his mother's interdiction in his minstrel addiction, and the way he later tricked her into attending, see Bernard Devoto, ed., *Mark Twain in Eruption* (New York: Harper, 1940), pp. 110–18.

8. Leonard L. Richards, *"Gentlemen of Property and Standing": Anti-Abolition Mobs in Jacksonian America* (New York: Oxford University Press, 1970), 149.

9. "Long Tail Blue," no. 14, *Series of Old American Songs,* ed. S. Foster Damon (Providence: Brown University Library, 1936). The image here is hardly subtle—it does not depend on the audience's knowing that *penis* derives etymologically from the Latin for "tail"—but that etymology confirms the salacious intent of the song.

10. Is it too much to ask to connect the *spirit* of these lyrics (if not their surface intertextuality) to that creed a century later: "You can do anything you want / But stay off my Blue Suede Shoes"?

11. *American Humor: A Study of American Character*, ed. W. T. Lhamon, Jr. (1931; Tallahassee: Florida State University Press, 1985), pp. 77–104.

SELECTED BIBLIOGRAPHY

Abrahams, Roger D. "The Negro Stereotype: Negro Folklore and the Riots." In *The Urban Experience and Folk Tradition*, ed. Americo Paredes and Ellen J. Steckert. Austin: University of Texas Press, 1971.

Austin, William W. *"Susanna," "Jeanie," and "The Old Folks at Home": The Songs of Stephen C. Foster from His Time to Ours.* New York: Macmillan, 1975.

Babcock-Abrahams, Barbara. "'A Tolerated Margin of Mess': The Trickster and His Tales Reconsidered." *Journal of the Folklore Institute* 11.3 (1975): 147–86.

Baker, Houston A., Jr. *Modernism and the Harlem Renaissance.* Chicago: University of Chicago Press, 1984.

Baker, Jean H. *Affairs of Party: The Political Culture of Northern Democrats in the Mid-Nineteenth Century.* Ithaca: Cornell University Press, 1983.

Barnum, P. T. *Struggles and Triumphs: Or, Forty Years' Recollections of P. T. Barnum.* Hartford: J. B. Burr, 1869.

Baskervil, Charles Read. *The Elizabethan Jig and Related Song Drama.* Chicago: University of Chicago Press, 1929.

Beckham, Susan Bridwell. "By 'N' Bye Hard Times: Eastman Johnson's 'Life of the South' and American Minstrels." *Journal of American Culture* 6.3 (1983): 19–25.

Bell, Bernard. "Twain's 'Nigger' Jim: The Tragic Face Behind the Minstrel Mask." *Mark Twain Journal* 23.1 (1985): 10–17.

Berret, Anthony J. "*Huckleberry Finn* and the Minstrel Show." *American Studies* 27.2 (1986): 37–49.

"The Black Opera." *New York Tribune*, June 30, 1855. Reprinted in *Journal of Music* 13.14 (1858): 107–8.

Blair, John. "Blackface Minstrels in Cross-Cultural Perspective." *American Studies International* 28.2 (1990): 52–65.

Blassingame, John. *The Slave Community: Plantation Life in the Antebellum South.* New York: Oxford University Press, 1983.

Bogle, Donald. *Toms, Coons, Mulattoes, Mammies and Bucks.* New York: Viking, 1973.

Boime, Albert. *The Art of Exclusion: Representing Blacks in the Nineteenth Century.* Washington, D. C.: Smithsonian, 1990.

Boskin, Joseph. *Sambo: The Rise and Demise of an American Jester.* New York: Oxford University Press, 1986.

Briggs, Tom. *Briggs' Banjo Instructor.* Boston: Ditson, 1855.
Brown, Sterling. *The Negro in American Fiction* [1937]. New York: Arno Press, 1969.
Browne, Ray B. "Shakespeare in American Vaudeville and Negro Minstrelsy." *American Quarterly* 12 (1960): 374–91.
Buckley's Book for the Parlor. New York: P. J. Cozans, 1855.
Burtnett, J. G. "National Elements in Stephen Foster's Art." *South Atlantic Quarterly* 21.4 (1922): 322–26.
Butler, Judith. *Bodies That Matter: On the Discursive Limits of "Sex."* New York: Routledge, 1993.
———. "Performative Acts and Gender Constitution." In *Performing Feminisms: Feminist Critical Theory and Theatre*, ed. Sue-Ellen Case. Baltimore: Johns Hopkins University Press, 1990.
Cantwell, Robert. *Bluegrass Breakdown: The Making of the Old Southern Sound.* Urbana: University of Illinois Press, 1984.
Carby, Hazel. *Reconstructing Womanhood: The Emergence of the Afro-American Woman Novelist.* New York: Oxford University Press, 1987.
Cardwell, Guy A. *Twins of Genius.* East Lansing: Michigan State College Press, 1953.
Carney-Smith, Jessie, ed. *Black Firsts.* Detroit: Visible Ink Press, 1994.
Carter, J. P. *Lucy Neal.* Boston: C. H. Keith, c. 1845.
Channing, William Ellery. "Emancipation" [1840]. In *Works*, vol. 6, 5–89. Boston: James Monroe, 1843.
Christy and Wood's New Song Book. Philadelphia: T. B. Peterson and Bros., 1854.
Christy's Minstrels. *Christy's Plantation Melodies No. 4.* Philadelphia: Fisher and Bros., 1854.
Clark, T. J. *The Painting of Modern Life: Paris in the Art of Manet and His Followers.* Princeton: Princeton University Press, 1984.
Cockrell, Dale. "The Early Blackface Minstrel and His World." Unpublished paper.
———. "Of Gospel Hymns, Minstrel Shows, and Jubilee Singers." *American Music* 5.4 (1987): 417–32.
Cohen, Hennig. "A Negro 'Folk Game' in Colonial South Carolina." *Southern Folklore Quarterly* 16 (1952): 183–84.
Cohen, Patricia Cline. "Unregulated Youth: Masculinity and Murder in the 1830s City." *Radical History Review* 52 (1992): 33–52.
Corrigan, Robert W. "The Psychology of Comedy." In *Comedy: Meaning and Form*, ed. R. W. Corrigan, 2nd ed., 165–90. New York: Harper & Row, 1981.
Damon, S. Foster. "The Negro in Early American Songsters." *Papers of the Bibliographical Society of America* 28 (1934): 132–63.
———. *Series of Old American Songs.* Providence: Brown University Library, 1936.
Davidson, Frank C. "The Rise, Development, Decline, and Influence of the American Minstrel Show." Ph.D. dissertation, New York University, 1952.
Davis, Natalie Zemon. *Society and Culture in Early Modern France.* Stanford, Calif.: Stanford University Press, 1975.
Davis, Susan G. "'Making Night Hideous': Christmas Revelry and Public Order in Nineteenth-Century Philadelphia." *American Quarterly* 43.2 (1982): 185–99.
———. *Parades and Power: Street Theater in Nineteenth-Century Philadelphia.* Berkeley: University of California Press, 1986.

Dawidoff, Robert. "Some of Those Days." *Western Humanities Review* 41.3 (1987): 263–86.
Day, Charles H. *Fun in Black; Or, Sketches of Minstrel Life*. New York: DeWitt, 1874.
Denning, Michael. *Mechanic Accents: Dime Novels and Working-Class Culture in America*. London: Verso, 1987.
Dennison, Sam. *Scandalize My Name: Black Imagery in American Popular Music*. New York: Garland Publishing, 1982.
Devoto, Bernard, ed. *Mark Twain in Eruption*. New York: Harper, 1940.
Dorman, James H. "Shaping the Popular Image of Post-Reconstruction American Blacks: The 'Coon Song' Phenomenon of the Gilded Age." *American Quarterly* 40.4 (1988): 450–71.
———. "The Strange Career of Jim Crow Rice." *Journal of Social History* 3 (1969): 108–22.
Douglass, Frederick. "Gavitt's Original Ethiopian Serenaders." *North Star*, June 29, 1849. Reprinted in *The Life and Writings of Frederick Douglass*, ed. Philip S. Foner, Vol. 1, 141–42. New York: International Publishers, 1950–75. 5 vols.
Du Bois, W. E. B. "The Negro in Literature and Art." In *W. E. B. Du Bois: A Reader*, ed. Meyer Weinberg. New York: Harper & Row, 1970.
———. *The Souls of Black Folk* [1903]. In *Three Negro Classics*, ed. John Hope Franklin, 207–389. New York: Avon, 1965.
Duchatre, Pierre Louis. *The Italian Comedy* [1929], trans. Randolph T. Weaver. New York: Dover, 1966.
Elkins, Stanley. *Slavery: A Problem in American Institutional and Intellectual Life*. Chicago: University of Chicago Press, 1959.
Ellison, Ralph. "Change the Joke and Slip the Yoke." In *Shadow and Act*, 45–59. New York: Vintage, 1972.
———. "On Initiation Rites and Power." In *Going to the Territory*. New York: Random House, 1986.
Emmett, Dan. *Dandy Jim from Caroline*. Philadelphia: A. Fiot, c. 1845
———. *De Boatmen's Dance*. Boston: C. H. Keith, c. 1845
———. "The Fine Old Colored Gentleman." In *Ethiopian Glee Book*, Vol. 1, ed. Elias Howe, 70–71. Boston: Ditson, 1848.
Engle, Gary D., ed. *This Grotesque Essence: Plays from the American Minstrel Stage*. Baton Rouge: Louisiana State University Press, 1978.
Fanon, Frantz. *Black Skin, White Masks*, trans. Charles Lam Markmann. New York: Grove Press, 1967.
Fiedler, Leslie A. *What Was Literature? Class Culture and Mass Society*. New York: Simon and Schuster, 1982.
Field, Al G. *Watch Yourself Go By*. Columbus, 1912.
Fisher, Philip. *Hard Facts: Setting and Form in the American Novel*. New York: Oxford University Press, 1987.
Flynn, Joyce. "Melting Plots: Patterns of Racial and Ethnic Amalgamation in American Drama Before Eugene O'Neill." *American Quarterly* 38.3 (1986): 417–18, 426.
Foner, Eric. "Abolitionism and the Labor Movement in Ante-Bellum America." In *Politics and Ideology in the Age of the Civil War*, 57–76. New York: Oxford University Press, 1980.
———. *Politics and Prejudice: The Free Soil Party and the Negro, 1849–1952*. New York: Oxford University Press, 1965.

Foucault, Michel. "Nietzsche, Genealogy, History." In *Language, Counter-Memory, Practice*, ed. Donald Bouchard, 139–64. Ithaca: Cornell University Press, 1977.

Franco, Jean. "What's in a Name?: Popular Culture Theories and Their Limitations." *Studies in Latin American Popular Culture* 1 (1982): 5–14.

Frederickson, George M. *The Black Image in the White Mind: The Debate on Afro-American Character and Destiny, 1817–1914*. New York: Harper & Row, 1971.

———. "White Images of Black Slaves in the Old South." In *The Arrogance of Race: Historical Perspectives on Slavery, Racism, and Social Inequality*, 207–15. Middletown, Conn.: Wesleyan University Press, 1988.

Fuller, Margaret. "Entertainments of the Past Winter." *Dial* 3.1 (1842): 46–72.

Gaines, Francis Pendleton. *The Southern Plantation: A Study in the Development and the Accuracy of a Tradition*. New York: Columbia University Press, 1924.

Garber, Marjorie. *Vested Interests: Cross-Dressing and Cultural Anxiety*. New York: Routledge, 1992.

Gates, Henry Louis, Jr., *Figures in Black: Words, Signs, and the "Racial" Self*. New York: Oxford University Press, 1987.

Gilje, Paul A. *The Road to Mobocracy: Popular Disorder in New York City, 1763–1834*. Chapel Hill: University of North Carolina Press, 1987.

Gilroy, Paul. *"There Ain't No Black in the Union Jack": The Cultural Politics of Race and Nation*. London: Hutchinson, 1987.

Green, Alan W. C. "'Jim Crow,' 'Zip Coon': The Northern Origins of Negro Minstrelsy." *Massachusetts Review* 11.2 (1970): 385–97.

Grimsted, David. *Melodrama Unveiled: American Theater and Culture, 1800–1850*. Chicago: University of Chicago Press, 1968.

Grimsted, David, and William F. Stowe. "White-Black Humor." Review of *Blacking Up* by Robert C. Toll. *Journal of Ethnic Studies* 3.2 (1975): 78–96.

Hall, Stuart. "Encoding, Decoding." In *The Cultural Studies Reader*, ed. Simon During, 90–103. New York: Routledge, 1993.

———. "New Ethnicities." In *Black Film/British Cinema*, ed. Kobena Mercer, 27–31. London: ICA, 1988.

———. "Notes on Deconstructing 'the Popular'." In *People's History and Socialist Theory*, ed. Raphael Samuel, 227–40. London: Routledge and Kegan Paul, 1981.

Hall, Stuart, et al. *Policing the Crisis: Mugging, the State, and Law and Order*. London: Macmillan, 1978.

Hamm, Charles. *Yesterdays: Popular Song in America*. New York: Norton, 1979.

Harlow, Alvin F. *Old Bowery Days: The Chronicles of a Famous Street*. New York: D. Appleton, 1931.

Harrigan, Edward. "Holding the Mirror up to Nature." *Pearson's Magazine* (n.d.): 499–506. Clipping file, Harvard Theatre Collection.

Harvey, David. *The Condition of Postmodernity*. Cambridge, U.K.: Blackwell Publishers, 1991.

Haywood, Charles. "Negro Minstrelsy and Shakespearean Burlesque." In *Folklore and Society*, ed. Bruce Jackson, 77–92. Hatboro, Pa.: Folklore Associates, 1966.

Hebdige, Dick. *Hiding in the Light: On Images and Things*. New York: Routledge, 1988.

Hobsbawm, E. J. *Primitive Rebels: Studies in Archaic Forms of Social Movement in the Nineteenth and Twentieth Centuries*. New York: Norton, 1959.

Hoggart, Richard. *The Uses of Literacy: Changing Patterns in English Mass Culture.* New York: Oxford University Press, 1957.

Holmberg, Carl Bryan, and Gilbert D. Schneider. "Daniel Decatur Emmett's Stump Speeches: Genuine Afro-American Culture, Language, and Rhetoric in the Negro Minstrel Show." *Journal of Popular Culture* 19.4 (1986): 27–38.

Horlick, Allan Stanley. *Country Boys and Merchant Princes: The Social Control of Young Men in New York.* Lewisburg, Pa.: Bucknell University Press, 1975.

Howard, John Tasker. *Stephen Foster, America's Troubadour.* New York: Thomas Y. Crowell, 1934.

Howe, Henry Warren. *Passages from the Life of Henry Warren Howe.* Lowell, Mass.: Courier-Citizen Company, 1899.

Huggins, Nathan Irving. *Harlem Renaissance.* New York: Oxford University Press, 1971.

Hughes, Langston. "The Negro and American Entertainment." In *The American Negro Reference Book*, ed. John P. Davis. Englewood Cliffs, N.J.: Prentice-Hall, 1966.

Hutton, Lawrence. *Curiosities of the American Stage.* New York: Harper & Row, 1891.

Hyman, Stanley Edgar. "American Negro Literature and Folk Tradition" [1958]. In *The Promised End: Essays and Reviews, 1942–1962*, 44–62. Bloomington: University of Indiana Press, 1986.

Jackson, Bruce, ed. *The Negro and His Folklore in Nineteenth-Century Periodicals.* Austin: University Texas Press, 1967.

Jacobs, Harriet [pseud. Linda Brent]. *Incidents in the Life of a Slave Girl* [1861]. In the *Classic Slave Narratives*, ed. Henry Louis Gates, Jr., 333–515. New York: New American Library, 1987.

Jameson, Frederic. *The Political Unconscious: Narrative as a Socially Symbolic Act.* Ithaca: Cornell University Press, 1981.

———. "Reification and Utopia in Mass Culture." *Social Text* 1 (1979): 130–48.

Johnson, Barbara. "Mirror Stages: Jacques Lacan and Frantz Fanon." Lecture, University of Virginia, October 30, 1991.

Johnson, Claudia D. "That Guilty Third Tier: Prostitution in Nineteenth-Century American Theaters." *American Quarterly* 27.5 (1975): 575–84.

Johnson, James Weldon. *Black Manhattan.* New York: Knopf, 1930.

Johnson, Richard. "What Is Cultural Studies Anyway?" *Social Text* 16 (1986–87): 38–80.

Jones, Leroi. *Blues People: Negro Music in White America.* New York: William Morrow, 1963.

Jordan, Winthrop D. *White over Black: American Attitudes Toward the Negro, 1550–1812.* Baltimore: Penguin, 1968.

Kahn, E. J., Jr. *The Merry Partners: The Age and Stage of Harrigan & Hart.* New York: Random House, 1955.

Kovel, Joel. *White Racism: A Psychohistory.* New York: Columbia University Press, 1970.

Lapsansky, Emma Jones. "'Since They Got Those Separate Churches': Afro-Americans and Racism in Jacksonian Philadelphia." *American Quarterly* 37.1 (1980): 54–78.

Laurie, Bruce. *Working People of Philadelphia, 1800–1850.* Philadelphia: Temple University Press, 1980.

"Leon, the Female Impersonator." *The New York Clipper* December 31, 1881.

"Letter from a Teacher at the South." *Journal of Music* 2.21 (1853): 164.

Levine, Jacob. "Approaches to Humor Appreciation." In *Motivation in Humor*, ed. Jacob Levine. New York: Atherton Press, 1969.

Levine, Lawrence W. *Black Culture and Black Consciousness*. New York: Oxford University Press, 1977.

Lhamon, W. T., Jr. "Constance Rourke's Secret Reserve." In Constance Rourke, *American Humor* [1931], xiii–xxi. Tallahassee: Florida State University Press, 1986.

Lhamon, W. T., Jr., ed. *American Humor: A Study of American Character.* Tallahassee: Florida State University Press, 1985.

Logan, Olive. "The Ancestry of Brudder Bones." *Harper's New Monthly Magazine* 58.347 (1879): 687–98.

Lott, Eric. *Love and Theft: Blackface Minstrelsy and the American Working Class*. New York: Oxford University Press, 1993.

Ludlow, N. M. *Dramatic Life as I Found It* [1880]. New York: Benjamin Blom, 1966.

Lynn, Kenneth. *Mark Twain and Southwestern Humor.* Boston: Little, Brown, 1960.

Mahar, William J. "'Backside Albany' and Early Blackface Minstrelsy: A Contextual Study of America's First Blackface Song." *American Music* 6.1 (1988): 1–27.

———. "Black English in Early Blackface Minstrelsy: A New Interpretation of the Sources of Minstrel Show Dialect." *American Quarterly* 37.2 (1985): 260–85.

Mailloux, Steven. *Rhetorical Power.* Ithaca: Cornell University Press, 1989.

Marcus, Stephen. *The Other Victorians: A Study of Sexuality and Pornography in Mid-Nineteenth-Century England*. New York: Norton, 1985.

Martin, Waldo E., Jr. *The Mind of Frederick Douglass*. Chapel Hill: University of North Carolina Press, 1984.

Mathews, Mrs. Anne. *A Continuation of the Memoirs of Charles Mathews.* Philadelphia: Lea and Blanchard, 1839. 2 vols.

Matthews, Brander. "The Rise and Fall of Negro Minstrelsy." *Scribner's Magazine* 57.6 (1915): 754–59.

Mayer, David. *Harlequin in His Element: The English Pantomime, 1806–1836.* Cambridge: Harvard University Press, 1969.

McConachie, Bruce A. "'The Theatre of the Mob': Apocalyptic Melodrama and Preindustrial Riot in Antebellum New York." In *Theatre for Working-Class Audiences in the United States, 1830–1890*, ed. Bruce A. McConachie and Daniel Friedman. Westport, Conn.: Greenwood Press, 1985.

Modleski, Tania. *Feminism Without Women: Culture and Criticism in a "Postfeminist" Age.* New York: Routledge, 1991.

Moreau, Charles C. *Negro Minstrelsy in New York*. Harvard Theatre Collection, 1891. 2 vols.

Moses, Wilson Jeremiah. *The Golden Age of Black Nationalism, 1850–1925* [1978]. New York: Oxford University Press, 1988.

Nash, Gary B. *Forging Freedom: The Formation of Philadelphia's Black Community, 1720–1840*. Cambridge: Harvard University Press, 1988.

Nathan, Hans. *Dan Emmett and the Rise of Early Negro Minstrelsy.* Norman: University of Oklahoma, 1977.

"Negro Minstrelsy—Ancient and Modern." *Putnam's Monthly* 5.25 (1855): 72–79.

Nevin, Robert P. "Stephen C. Foster and Negro Minstrelsy." *Atlantic Monthly* 20.121 (1867): 608–16.
Nicoll, Allardyce. *The World of Harlequin*. Cambridge, U.K.: Cambridge University Press, 1963.
Nye, Russell. *The Unembarassed Muse: The Popular Arts in America*. New York: Dial, 1970.
"Obituary for Tony Hart." *The New York Clipper* November 14, 1891.
Odell, George C. D. *Annals of the New York Stage*. New York: Columbia University Press, 1928–31. 15 vols.
Ostendorf, Berndt. *Black Literature in White America*. Totowa, N.J.: Harvester, 1982.
———. "Minstrelsy and Early Jazz." *Massachusetts Review* 20 (1979): 574–602.
Ottley, Roi, and William J. Weatherby. *The Negro in New York: An Informal Social History*. New York: New York Public Library, 1967.
Paskman, Dailey, and Sigmund Spaeth. *"Gentlemen, Be Seated!": A Parade of the Old-Time Minstrels*. Garden City, N.Y.: Doubleday, Doran, 1928.
Patterson, Cecil Lloyd. "A Different Drum: The Image of the Negro in the Nineteenth-Century Popular Song Books." Ph.D. dissertation, University of Pennsylvania, 1961.
Phelps, H. P. *Players of a Century: A Record of the Albany Stage* [1880]. New York: Benjamin Blom, 1972.
Pieterse, Jan Nederveen. *White On Black: Images of Africa and Blacks in Western Popular Culture*. New Haven, Conn.: Yale University Press, 1992.
Ramshaw, Molly N. "'Jump Jim Crow': A Biographical Sketch of Thomas D. Rice." *Theatre Annual* 17 (1960): 36–47.
Rawick, George P. *From Sundown to Sunup: The Making of the Black Community*. Westport, Conn.: Greenwood Press, 1972.
Rehin, George F. "The Darker Image: American Negro Minstrelsy Through the Historian's Lens." *Journal of American Studies* 9.3 (1975): 682–701.
———. "Harlequin Jim Crow: Continuity and Convergence in Blackface Clowning." *Journal of Popular Culture* 9.3 (1975): 682–701.
Rice, Edward LeRoy. *Monarchs of Minstrelsy from "Daddy" Rice to Date*. New York: Kenny, 1911.
Richards, Leonard L. *"Gentlemen of Property and Standing": Anti-Abolition Mobs in Jacksonian America*. New York: Oxford University Press, 1970.
Riviere, Joan. "Womanliness as Masquerade." In *The Inner World and Joan Riviere: Collected Papers, 1920–1958*, ed. Athol Hughes. London: Karnac Books, 1991.
Robinson, Forrest G. *In Bad Faith: The Dynamics of Deception in Mark Twain's America*. Cambridge: Harvard University Press, 1986.
Roediger, David. "'Labor in White Skin': Race and Working-Class History." In *Reshaping the U.S. Left: Popular Struggles in the 1980s*, ed. Mike Davis and Michael Sprinker, 287–308. London: Verso, 1988.
———. *The Wages of Whiteness: Race and the Making of the American Working Class*. London: Verso, 1991.
Rourke, Constance. *American Humor: A Study of the National Character*. Tallahassee: Florida State University Press, 1986.
Runcie, John. "'Hunting the Nigs' in Philadelphia: The Race Riot of August 1934." *Pennsylvania History* 39.2 (1972): 187–218.

St. James Hall Veritable and Legitimate Christy Minstrels Christmas Annual. London: J. E. Adlard, 1868.
Sánchez-Eppler, Karen. "Bodily Bonds: The Intersecting Rhetorics of Feminism and Abolition." *Representations* 24 (1988): 28–59.
Saxton, Alexander. *The Rise and Fall of the White Republic.* London: Verso, 1990.
Schlesinger, Arthur. *The Age of Jackson.* Boston: Little, Brown, 1945.
Senelick, Laurence. "Boys and Girls Together: Subculture Origins of Glamour Drag and Male Impersonation on the Nineteenth-Century Stage." In *Crossing the Stage: Controversies on Cross-Dressing*, ed. Lesley Ferris, 80–95. New York: Routledge, 1993.
———. "The Evolution of the Male Impersonator on the Nineteenth-Century Popular Stage." *Essays in Theatre* 1.1 (1982): 30–44.
Smith-Rosenberg, Carroll. "Davy Crockett as Trickster: Pornography, Liminality, and Symbolic Inversion in Victorian America." In *Disorderly Conduct: Visions of Gender in Victorian America*, 90–108. New York: Knopf, 1985.
———. "Bourgeois Discourse and the Age of Jackson: An Introduction." In *Disorderly Conduct: Visions of Gender in Victorian America*, 79–89. New York: Knopf, 1985.
Sollors, Werner. *Beyond Ethnicity: Consent and Descent in American Culture.* New York: Oxford University Press, 1986.
"Songs of the Blacks." *Journal of Music* 10.7 (1856): 51–52.
Southern, Eileen. *Biographical Dictionary of Afro-American and African Musicians.* New York: Greenwood Press, 1982.
———. "Black Musicians and Early Ethiopian Minstrelsy." *The Black Perspective in Music* 3 (1989): 77–99.
Stallybrass, Peter, and Allon White. *The Politics and Poetics of Transgression.* London: Methuen, 1986.
Stearns, Marshall, and Jean Stearns. *Jazz Dance: The Story of American Vernacular Dance.* New York: Macmillan, 1968.
Stevenson, Robert, "America's First Black Music Historian." *Journal of the American Musicologist* 26 (1973): 383–404.
Stone, H. D. *Personal Recollections of the Drama* [1873]. New York: Benjamin Blom, 1969.
Stowe, Harriet Beecher. "The Parson's Horse Race." *Atlantic Monthly* 42.252 (1878): 470–74.
———. *Uncle Tom's Cabin; or, Life among the Lowly* [1852], ed. Ann Douglas. New York: Penguin, 1981.
Suthern, Orrin Clayton. "Minstrelsy and Popular Culture." *Journal of Popular Culture* 4.3 (1971): 658–73.
Szwed, John F. "Race and the Embodiment of Culture." *Ethnicity* 2 (1975): 19–33.
Taylor, William R. *Cavalier and Yankee: The Old South and American National Character.* New York: George Braziller, 1961.
Toll, Robert C. *Blacking Up: The Minstrel Show in Nineteenth-Century America.* New York: Oxford University Press, 1974.
Trotter, James Monroe. *Music and Some Highly Musical People.* Boston: Lee and Shepard, 1883.
Turner, Victor. "Frame, Flow, and Reflection: Ritual and Drama as Public Liminality." In *Performance in Postmodern Culture*, ed. Michel Benamou, 33–55. Madison, Wis.: Coda, 1977.

———. "Myth and Symbol." In the *International Encyclopedia of the Social Sciences*, ed. David L. Sills, Vol. 10, 576–82. New York: Macmillan and Free Press, 1968.

Twain, Mark. *The Autobiography of Mark Twain.* New York: Harper and Row, 1959.

Van Deburg, William L. *Slavery and Race in American Popular Culture.* Madison: University of Wisconsin Press, 1984.

Waterhouse, Richard. *From Minstrel Show to Vaudeville: The Australian Popular Stage, 1788–1914.* New South Wales: NSW Press, 1990.

Watkins, Mel. "Black Minstrelsy to Vaudeville . . . Black on Black." In *On the Real Side: Laughing, Lying, and Signifying—The Underground Tradition of African-American Humor That Transformed American Culture, from Slavery to Richard Pryor*, 105–33. New York: Simon & Schuster, 1994.

Welter, Barbara. "The Cult of True Womanhood." *American Quarterly* 18 (1966): 151–75.

West, Cornel. "Marxist Theory and the Specificity of Afro-American Oppression." In *Marxism and the Interpretation of Culture*, ed. Cary Nelson and Lawrence Grossberg, 17–29. Urbana: University of Illinois Press, 1988.

White, Shane. "A Question of Style: Blacks in and around New York City in the Late 18th-Century." *Journal of American Folklore* 102.1 (1989).

White's New Book of Plantation Melodies. Philadelphia: T. B. Peterson & Brothers, 1849.

White's New Illustrated Melodeon Songbook. Philadelphia: T. B. Peterson & Brothers, 1848.

Wilentz, Sean. *Chants Democratic: New York City and the Rise of the American Working Class, 1788–1850.* New York: Oxford University Press, 1984.

Wiltse, Charles M., ed. *David Walker's Appeal to the Coloured Citizens of the World.* New York: Hill and Wang, 1965.

Winans, Robert B. "The Folk, the Stage, and the Five-String Banjo in the Nineteenth Century." *Journal of American Folklore* 89.354 (1976): 407–37.

Wittke, Carl. *Tambo and Bones: A History of the American Minstrel Stage.* Durham, N.C.: Duke University Press, 1930.

Wolfe, Bernard. "Uncle Remus and the Malevolent Rabbit." *Commentary* 8 (1949): 31–41.

Wolseley, Roland E. *The Black Press, U.S.A.* Ames: Iowa University Press, 1971.

Woodard, Fredrick, and Donnarae MacCann. "*Huckleberry Finn* and the Traditions of Blackface Minstrelsy." *Interracial Books for Children Bulletin* 15.1, 2 (1984): 4–13.

Wynter, Sylvia. "Sambo and Minstrels." *Social Text* 1 (1979):149–56.

Yellin, Jean Fagan. *The Intricate Knot: Black Figures in American Literature, 1776–1863.* New York: New York University Press, 1972.

INDEX

University Press of New England
publishes books under its own imprint and is the publisher for Brandeis University Press, Dartmouth College, Middlebury College Press, University of New Hampshire, Tufts University, Wesleyan University Press, and Salzburg Seminar.

About The Editors

Annemarie Bean is a doctoral candidate in the Department of Performance Studies, New York University. Her dissertation will be a continuation of her current work, focusing on images of women in nineteenth-century minstrelsy.

James V. Hatch is Professor of Theatre at the City College of the City University of New York. His publications include a biography *Sorrow Is the Only Faithful One: The Life of Owen Dodson,* winner of the Bernard Hewitt Award for best theatre history book published in 1993. He is cofounder, with his wife, Camille Billops, of the Hatch–Billops Collection, an archive in African-American cultural history.

Brooks McNamara is Professor of Performance Studies at New York University and Director of the Shubert Archive. He has published ten books on theatre, and has been a Fulbright Scholar and a Guggenheim Fellow.

Library of Congress Cataloging-in-Publication Data
Inside the minstrel mask : readings in nineteenth-century blackface minstrelsy / edited by Annemarie Bean, James V. Hatch, and Brooks McNamara.
p. cm.
Includes bibliographical references and index.
ISBN 0–8195–5294–1 (cloth: alk. paper). — ISBN 0–8195–6300–5 (paper: alk. paper)
1. Minstrel shows—United States—History—19th century.
I. Bean, Annemarie. II. Hatch, James Vernon, 1928– .
III. McNamara, Brooks.
PN3195.158 1996
791'.12'097309034—dc20 96–16572